Encyclopedia
of NORSE and GERMANIC FOLKLORE, MYTHOLOGY, and MAGIC

Encyclopedia
of NORSE and
GERMANIC
FOLKLORE,
MYTHOLOGY,
and MAGIC

CLAUDE LECOUTEUX

Translated by Jon E. Graham
Edited by Michael Moynihan

Inner Traditions
Rochester, Vermont • Toronto, Canada

Inner Traditions
One Park Street
Rochester, Vermont 05767
www.InnerTraditions.com

Text stock is SFI certified

Originally published in French under the title *Dictionnaire de mythologie germanique: Odin, Thor, Siegfried & Cie* by Éditions Imago
First U.S. edition published in 2016 by Inner Traditions

Library of Congress Cataloging-in-Publication Data
Names: Lecouteux, Claude, author. | Moynihan, Michael, editor.
Title: Encyclopedia of Norse and Germanic folklore, mythology, and magic /
    Claude Lecouteux ; translated by Jon E. Graham ; edited by Michael Moynihan.
Other titles: Dictionnaire de mythologie germanique. English
Description: Rochester : Inner Traditions, 2016. | Includes bibliographical references.
Identifiers: LCCN 2015039725| ISBN 9781620554807 (hardcover) |
    ISBN 9781620554814 (e-book)
Subjects: LCSH: Mythology, Germanic—Dictionaries. | Mythology,
    Norse—Dictionaries. | Europe, Northern—Religion.
Classification: LCC BL850 .L4313 2016 | DDC 293.03—dc23
LC record available at http://lccn.loc.gov/2015039725

Printed and bound in the United States by Lake Book Manufacturing, Inc.
The text stock is SFI certified. The Sustainable Forestry Initiative® program promotes sustainable forest management.

10 9 8 7 6 5 4 3 2 1

Text design by Virginia Scott Bowman and layout by Debbie Glogover
This book was typeset in Garamond Premier Pro and Gill Sans

Inner Traditions wishes to express its appreciation for assistance given by the government of France through the National Book Office of the Ministère de la Culture in the preparation of this translation.

Nous tenons à exprimer nos plus vifs remerciements au gouvernement de la France et au ministère de la Culture, Centre National du Livre, pour leur concours dans la préparation de la traduction de cet ouvrage.

To Corinne, ut semper,
and to Perrine
for her first birthday

CONTENTS

Encyclopedia of Norse and Germanic Folklore, Mythology, and Magic   19

From Aage to Zwiesauger

ACKNOWLEDGMENTS

I thank my esteemed teachers Régis Boyer and Georges Zink (Sorbonne); my old friend Ronald Grambo (Oslo) for his help; Jon Graham for his ongoing interest in my books and for his translations; and, last but not least, Michael Moynihan for valuable references and suggestions for expanding and updating the information in this volume.

Fig. 1. Picture stone from Lärbro on the island
of Gotland, Sweden, eighth century. Photo by Jürgen Howaldt.

HOW TO USE THIS ENCYCLOPEDIA

Claude Lecouteux's *Encyclopedia of Norse and Germanic Folklore, Mythology, and Magic* offers a stimulating and fascinating overview of its vast subject matter, which is drawn from the ancient and medieval cultures of Europe, England, and Scandinavia. While this is not the only reference handbook available in English that deals with Norse mythological material, it truly distinguishes itself with the veritable wealth of Germanic folkloric and legendary material that appears here—much of it previously inaccessible to English readers.

We have endeavored to faithfully reproduce various original names and terms in keeping with the traditional orthography (spelling) from languages such as Old Norse, Old English, and modern Icelandic. Two letters that may be unfamiliar to some readers are those known as "eth" (Ð/ð) and "thorn" (Þ/þ), which represent the sound that is reproduced as /th/ in modern texts (the character "eth" corresponds to the voiced /th/ sound, as in the English word "that," while "thorn" corresponds to the unvoiced /th/ sound, as in the English word "thin"). Entry names that begin with the letter Þ appear in the T section, alphabetized as if they begin with "Th."

Old Norse—and its descendant, modern Icelandic—is a highly inflected language, and one indication of this is in the nominative final -*r* ending that appears on certain nouns. This includes many proper names such as Freyr and Heimdallr, Asgarðr (Asgard), Miðgarðr (Midgard), and so forth. The original orthography is generally retained throughout the encyclopedia entries, except for the god names—Odin and Thor—which generally appear in their modern, anglicized spellings instead of their Old Norse forms (Óðinn, Þórr).

Occasionally a reference is made to certain names or words for which no literal attestation exists. This may be due to their great age or simply the arbitrary nature of the historical record that has come down to us. These earlier forms, which have been reliably reconstructed by historical linguists, appear preceded by an asterisk. Two examples would be the names of the proto-Germanic deities *Nerthuz (the antecedent of the continental goddess Nerthus and the Norse god Njörðr) and *Tiwaz (the antecedent of the Norse god Týr, the Anglo-Saxon god Tiw, and the continental German god Ziu).

In the presentation of the individual entries, the English edition follows the same basic format as its French predecessor. The keyword appears in bold capital letters, followed by a translation/interpretation of the word—for example, ÁLFHEIMR ("World of the Elves"). When relevant, additional grammatical information may be included, such as sg. (singular) and pl. (plural), as well as the gender of the noun itself: masc. (masculine), fem. (feminine), or neut. (neuter).

Many entries are followed by suggestions for further reading. References to books appear first, concisely cited by the author's last name together with the main title of the book. For the complete information on a given book, the reader should refer to the bibliography at the back of the encyclopedia. Articles or essays are given full citations as they are not included in the bibliography. These references for further reading are not meant to be complete, nor do they provide the history of scholarship on a given topic, which is often vast. They are simply Professor Lecouteux's suggestions of a few useful starting points that a curious reader may wish to investigate further. With regard to Norse entries in particular, more detailed information can be found by consulting John Lindow's *Norse Mythology: A Guide to Gods, Heroes, Rituals, and Beliefs* (New York: Oxford University Press, 2002) or Rudolf Simek's *Dictionary of Northern Mythology* (Woodbridge, U.K.: Boydell, 1993). The latter work in particular provides detailed references on the history of the scholarship that has been done on these topics. Neither of these volumes makes any attempt to systematically deal with Germanic folklore or continental literature, however.

INTRODUCTION

NORSE AND GERMANIC MYTHOLOGY AND FOLKLORE

Traditions of Considerable Influence

Interest in Norse and Germanic mythology has been growing in recent decades, yet it probably remains less well known to the public at large than Celtic—and especially Arthurian—mythology, which has enjoyed a long period of popularity in Western Europe and North America. For many people, the main frame of reference for Germanic and Norse myth is through Wagner's Ring Cycle, which has done as much harm as good to its source material. Furthermore, Germanic mythology still has an unsavory reputation due to its appropriation for some aspects of Nazi ideology, which has led many to view it as a vehicle for pernicious ideas. Fortunately, there is no truth to this as it is a misunderstanding of the modern myth of the blond, "Aryan" German, a notion that was itself based on erroneous interpretations.[1] Another modern myth, that of the Viking, has popularized the image of burly, violent, blood-thirsty brutes swearing oaths in the name of Odin and Thor and drinking mead from the skulls of their victims.[2] This is the stock portrait of Vikings that we often come across in popular movies and books, or in graphic novels such as *Asterix and the Normans*. In this regard it is

1

interesting to note that in Normandy, France, even into the nineteenth century, the prayer *"A furore Normannorum libera nos domine"* (Lord, deliver us from the fury of the Northmen!) continued to be included among the litanies of the church. Distorted by these sorts of misunderstandings, ancient Germanic and Norse civilization tends to repel rather than attract, all the more so as the bulk of serious works on the topic have been restricted to academics. Germanic mythology remains the victim of prejudice.

The influence of the ancient Germanic peoples on the development of European culture has been considerable. It is too often forgotten that the Franks, who gave their name to the nation of France, were a Germanic people, and French civilization is in fact the result of a massive commingling of Celto-Gallic, Roman, and Germanic cultures. The place-names of France still show vestiges of the Germanic invaders who settled in various regions: the Burgundians in the Rhône Valley and Savoy, the Saxons in Boullonnois, the Alemanni in Alsace, the Visigoths in Narbonnais, and the Taifals in Poitou.

We may ask, then, just what does *Germanic* mean? This adjective is descriptive of a number of peoples who originally all spoke the same language. The result of what happens when those who share a common tongue split off into separate groups is, however, well known: the language evolves differently in each group. We have good examples of this with Portuguese and Spanish, American English and British English, Afrikaans and Dutch. The Germanic linguistic branch contains three major families: North Germanic (represented by Norse and other Scandinavian dialects); East Germanic (mainly attested in Gothic, now a dead language, which—as its name indicates—was spoken by the Goths); and the West Germanic (represented by English and the continental High and Low German dialects).[3]

Germanic mythology is the codified, organized expression of these people and their civilization, beliefs, and religion. Dubbed "paganism" by Christianity, it was vigorously attacked on the one hand but also so successfully acculturated in other respects that only scattered fragments remained: here the name of a god, there the description of a cultural practice or epic legends featuring mysterious figures, and elsewhere personal and place-names that derived from those of the gods. While this body of evidence is sufficient to show that all of these peoples shared a common background, it does not allow us to compile an English or a German mythology, even if we include the information provided by Roman and Byzantine authors,[4] as well as that which is provided by epigraphy,[5] rune stones, and the church texts condemning pagan beliefs. Two medieval writers, the Goth Jordanes and the Lombard Paul the Deacon (Paulus Diaconus), also give us some valuable information.

I. THE SOURCES

The oldest accounts of the gods of the Germans were left to us by Caesar and Tacitus, and, despite the Roman interpretation of the data, they corroborate what the more recent texts tell us. In *The Gallic War*, Caesar reports:

> Among the gods, they most worship Mercury [Odin]. There are numerous images of him; they declare him the inventor of all arts, the guide of every road and journey, and they deem him to have the greatest influence for all money-making and traffic. After him they set Apollo [=Baldr?], Mars [=Týr?], Jupiter [=Thor?], and Minerva [=Freyja?]. Of these deities they have almost the same idea as all other nations: Apollo drives away diseases, Minerva supplies the first principles of arts and crafts, Jupiter holds the empire of heaven, Mars controls wars.[6]

Our knowledge of the Germanic goddess Nerthus comes from the Roman historian Tacitus, who writes:

> Collectively [the Germanic tribes] worship Nerthus, or Mother Earth, and believe that she takes part in human affairs and rides among the peoples.[7]

She lives in a sacred grove on an island and has a son named Tuisto (the name means "Double" or "Hermaphrodite"), who corresponds to the giant Ymir, a significant figure in the Norse cosmogony.

Our principal sources are the Eddas: the *Poetic Edda*, consisting of poems collected in the *Codex Regius* (written down around 1270, based on an original that an oral tradition maintains was lost, as well as on even older writings),[8] and the *Prose Edda,* which we shall discuss in greater detail.

Around 1223 the great Icelandic scholar Snorri Sturluson (1197–1241) wrote his *Prose Edda,*[9] also known as the *Snorra Edda* (Snorri's Edda), which consists of the following three parts.

> *Gylfaginning* (The Deluding of Gylfi),[10] a systematic exposition of the mythic material and an exhaustive, rational portrait of the ancient religion.
>
> *Skáldskaparmál* (Treatise on the Skaldic Art), a collection of poetic circumlocutions (*kenningar,* sg. *kenning*) and bynames (*heiti*) designating persons, objects, and concepts accompanied by a brief summary explaining the origin of this or that turn of phrase— why gold is called "Kraki's seed," for example, or even "Fróði's flour."
>
> *Háttatal* (The List of Meters), a treatise on traditional alliterative verse forms.

One manuscript of the *Snorra Edda,* the *Trektarbók,* also includes extremely valuable lists of names under the headings of "giants," "trolls," "dwarves," and so forth. In Old Norse these lists are known as *þulur* (sg.: *þula*).

Taken together, the Eddas form a coherent narrative that is rich with intertextual relationships. They represent a system of thought, a vision and explanation of the world. This system imposes order on a set of preexisting beliefs, with all their attendant innovations, in order to achieve a homogenous result.[11] But the human imagination relies on memory, and it is not always faithful, which results in hodgepodges, overlaps, and obscure passages. Some of the lays from the *Poetic Edda* also include long *þulur* lists of mythical figures (such as dwarves and giants), rivers, and horses, about which we often know nothing further, because we lack any other information about them. Are these catalogs of names an epic amplification, or do they serve some mnemonic purpose? Are the creatures and places cited of great antiquity, or are they of more recent provenance? Such questions are often very hard to answer.

We possess a variety of texts that serve as secondary sources. Foremost among these would have to be the first twenty chapters of the *Ynglinga saga* (Saga of the Ynglings), which is the first part of *Heimskringla* by Snorri Sturluson.[12] The *Heimskringla* is a history of the kings of Norway that begins with the tales of their mythic ancestors. In this text the gods are depicted as deified men.

There is also the *Gesta Danorum* (History of the Danes), which Saxo Grammaticus composed at the beginning of the thirteenth century.[13] In Saxo's work, mythology is transposed into a novel and an epic.

To the above sources we may add the poetry of the skalds[14] and the sagas, which are useful for cross-referencing what is found in the other texts and provide confirmation for certain details. The sagas are also of undeniable value, for in them we find accounts of the worship of gods, beliefs in elves (*álfar*) and local land spirits (*landvættir*), and so on.

Altogether the sources provide us with more than a thousand mythological names. These are not all of equal importance, however, so I have chosen to include only entries for those names that are featured in a complete text or in one that is fragmentary yet still intelligible. I have also included entries for significant figures from Germanic folklore and those that have played an important role in literature and the arts, from the German Romantic era to the novels of Tolkien.

II. THE GERMANIC GODS

As a result of the work of the medieval mythographers who compiled the Norse and Germanic myths, we know that the gods were divided into two major families: that of the Æsir (the plural form of *áss*, "god"), which primarily represented the warrior class but also included female goddesses referred to as the Ásynjur (sg.: Ásynja), and that of the Vanir, which was representative of fertility, magic, and peaceful relationships based on pleasure. Before discussing the gods, however, we need to provide the context for their activities.

Theogony and Cosmogony

At the dawn of time there was only a fathomless void—Ginnungagap—that stretched between Niflheimr, the land of ice and shadows in the north, and Muspellsheimr, the realm of fire in the south. Rivers flowing out of the south toward Niflheimr would come to a halt in vast, icy masses. These masses of frozen water filled the void, where increasingly warmer winds caused them to melt. The drops of water, revitalized by the wind, fused to form the body of the giant Ymir. The cow Auðumla was born in the same way, and her milk fed Ymir. When Ymir started sweating, a man and woman began to grow beneath his left arm, and one of his feet engendered a son from the other foot. By licking the ice, Auðumla caused the emergence of a man named Búri, who was able to reproduce like Ymir. He had a son, Burr (or Borr), who married Bestla, a descendant of Ymir. From their union were born the gods Óðinn (Odin), Vili, and Vé, who killed Ymir and built the world out of his body. Once they had finished they placed a dwarf at each corner of the sky to uphold the celestial vault. According to the *Poetic Edda,* this is how the gods were born and how the Earth was created.

The universe consists of various worlds. These include Miðgarðr, the "Middle Enclosure" and the world of men; Ásgarðr, the "Enclosure of the Æsir" and thus the world of the gods, which is connected to Miðgarðr by a "rainbow" called Bifröst, or Ásbrú (Æsir-Bridge); and Útgarðr, the "Outer Enclosure" which is the land of giants, demons, and all the malevolent beings. Beneath Miðgarðr lies the realm of the dead, which is ruled by the goddess Hel. The vertical stability of the universe is secured by Yggdrasill, the cosmic tree and world axis, which the Saxons called the Irminsûl ("Pillar of the God Irmin"), and its horizontal coherence by the Miðgarðsormr (Midgard Serpent), the huge sea serpent that is coiled around the Earth.

The Æsir

The most important of the Æsir gods are Óðinn and his sons, Þórr (Thor) and Baldr (Balder); Týr; Heimdallr; and Loki. They live in Ásgarðr, which they had a giant build for them. Located here is Valhalla (Valhöll), the hall of warriors slain in combat, where valkyries serve the valiant dead—the single fighters (*einherjar*) who will act as Óðinn's troops for the world's final battle—the meat of the boar Sæhrímnir and the mead that flows from the udder of the goat Heiðrun.

Óðinn (Wuotan in Old High German, Wodan in Old Saxon, and Woden in Old English) is the supreme god and the chieftain of the divine pantheon. He is the master of runes and magic, the knowledge of which he acquired during nine days and nights hanging on the World Tree, Yggdrasill. Óðinn "was able to cause his enemies to be blind or deaf or fearful in battle, and he could cause their swords to cut no better than wands. His own men went to battle without coats of mail and acted like mad dogs or wolves. They bit their shields and were as strong as bears or bulls."[15] These were the wild warriors known as the *berserkir* (berserkers), which literally means "bear-shirts." Óðinn is also the master of poetry.

When the universe was young, the two divine families of the Æsir and the Vanir were at war with one another. Neither side could defeat the other, however, and to seal a peace treaty they spit into a large vessel. From this saliva they created a man named Kvasir, who was profoundly wise. He was slain one day by two dwarves, who poured his blood into a cauldron and mixed it with honey. Whoever drank of this nectar would become a great poet. A giant killed the dwarves, took the beverage, and kept it inside a mountain. Óðinn managed to steal it from the giant by changing himself into a snake.

Óðinn is the guide of souls (psychopomp), and it is he who selects those warriors who will fall on the battlefield and be carried into Valhalla by the valkyries. Cynical and cruel, apt at changing his appearance and his form, Óðinn was interpreted by classical authors as being equivalent to the god Mercury. He was depicted as a one-eyed, graying old man who wears a blue mantle and a broad hat that slopes down and hides his face. He lives exclusively on wine and owns two ravens, Huginn and Muninn ("Thought" and "Memory"), who bring him news of the world because he has endowed them with the power of speech. His attributes include the spear Gungnir, the magic ring Draupnir, and the eight-legged horse Sleipnir, which can be seen depicted on several of the Gotlandic picture stones. Finally, Óðinn was endowed with many bynames that accurately reflect all the aspects of his activity and his many skills: "God of Cargoes," "Most High," "All-father," "Masked One," "Multifarious One," "Terrible One," and so on. One of these names is explained as follows: "at times he would call to life dead men out of the ground, or he would sit down under men that were hanged; on this account he was called Lord of Ghouls or of the Hanged."[16]

Óðinn's wife is Frigg (Langobardic Frea, Old High German Frîja, Old English Frige), who owns a falcon cloak, an allusion to an early ability to shapeshift. Her son is Baldr, nicknamed "the Good." After having several dire dreams, she asked and received the pledge of all the elements, all plants, all metals, all wood, all stones, and all diseases that they would spare her son, but she forgot to ask this of the mistletoe, a branch of which then mortally injures Baldr during a sporting event. Inconsolable, Óðinn charged his son Hermóðr with the task of going to the realm of the dead and coming back with Baldr. The goddess Hel agrees to let Baldr leave, provided that all of creation will weep for him, but the god Loki, responsible for his murder, refuses, and Hel keeps hold of her prey.

Óðinn's second son is Þórr (Thor, literally "Thunder"; Donar in Old High German, Þunor in Old English, Thunær in Old Saxon), born from the coupling of the master of the pantheon with the giantess Jörð (Earth). He is the strongest of the gods and lives in Þrúðvangr. Quick to anger and truculent, he has a red beard and an incredible appetite. He owns the hammer Mjöllnir (with which he smashes the giants), a pair of iron gloves necessary to wield the hammer, a belt that doubles his strength, and two goats that pull his chariot when he travels.

Þórr is famous for his battles against monsters. Once, on a fishing trip, he almost managed to catch the Midgard Serpent. He also rules over thunder and lightning, wind and rain. His wife is Sif, who bore him two sons, Magni ("Strength") and Móði ("Courage"), and a daughter, Þrúðr ("Force").

Týr (Tiw in Old English) is the son of Óðinn or of the giant Hymir. He is a god of justice whose name underlies that of the weekday Tuesday (Old English *tiwesdæg;* Old Norse *týsdagr*). He is the guardian of the world's order and the patron of the legal assemblies of free men. He is one-armed after having placed his hand as a pledge in the mouth of the wolf Fenrir, whom the gods sought to bind because he had grown so large he had become a threat: "all prophecies foretold that it was destined to cause them harm."[17] Their first two attempts at binding the wolf ended in failure, and the gods then asked the dwarves to forge a new fetter. Now suspicious, Fenrir demanded that a god place his hand in his mouth, otherwise he would not submit to being shackled. "Tyr put forward his right hand and put it in the wolf's mouth. And now when the wolf kicked, the band grew harder, and the harder he struggled, the tougher became the band. Then they all laughed except for Tyr. He lost his hand."[18] Týr is undoubtedly the oldest of all the deities, and his name simply means "god" (it is cognate with Latin *deus* and Sanskrit *dyaus*).

Heimdallr, who is referred to as the "white god," is the guardian of the gods. He lives at the end of the sky and keeps watch over the bridge leading to Ásgarðr. The *Prose Edda* informs us about Heimdallr: "He needs less sleep than a bird. He can see, by night just as well as by day, a distance of hundreds of leagues. He can also hear the grass growing on the earth and wool on sheep and everything that sounds louder than that. He has a trumpet called Gjallarhorn and its blast can be heard in all worlds."[19] We may add that he has gold teeth, carries a sword, and his horse is named Gullfaxi ("Golden Mane"). At the end of the world, he and Loki will kill each other.

Loki is an extremely complex god: the embodiment of evil, a troublemaker, and a sower of discord. He is the son of Laufey and the giant Farbauti. His wife is Sigyn, with whom he had a son. The giantess Angrboða bore him three children: the wolf Fenrir and the Midgard Serpent, both of whom play important roles in the eschatological battle, and Hel, the goddess of the dead.

These are the leading members of the Æsir. The Eddas and place-names provide us with many other names, but this information can be as scanty as the mention of a nickname. An example would be Ullr, known as the "bow god," "ski god," or "hunting god," whose ancient significance is, however, apparent from an enigmatic remark by Saxo Grammaticus: Ollerus (Ullr) allegedly ruled over the gods when Othinus (Odin) was exiled.

Some deities were later removed from the pantheon and transformed into simple heroes; the best example is Völundr (Wayland), who was most certainly a smith god, a gold-crafting god closely connected to the elves. All we know about Sól, the sun goddess, is that she was punished for a mismarriage. The gods placed her in the sky where she travels every day in a chariot drawn by two horses, pursued by a wolf that seeks to devour her.

The Vanir

The second family of gods is that of the Vanir, who seem older than the Æsir. It is thought they represent a settled culture (farmers) that was subjugated by a more warlike nomadic culture (hunters, gatherers, fishermen). A great myth tells how they gained a seat among the Æsir in Ásgarðr. The Vanir sent a witch named Gullveig (her name means

"Drunkeness for Gold," which may suggest that the Vanir believed a lust for precious metal would make the Æsir less bellicose) to the Æsir. The Æsir sought to wrest Gullveig's secrets from her, and when she refused to reveal them they tried to burn her—in vain. The Vanir demanded reparation for these violent acts, asking for either a payment of tribute or admittance among the Æsir. The Æsir preferred to settle the matter by weapons. The war was long and hard, and neither side could win. A truce was finally declared and an exchange of hostages took place: the Vanir gave their most distinguished men, Njörðr and his son Freyr, while the Æsir offered Mímir, a man of deep wisdom, and Hœnir. This was how a new family of gods appeared in Ásgarðr.

The Vanir are essentially represented by Njörðr and his children Freyr and Freyja. They are agrarian gods with connections to the land and water; they dispense goods and pleasures, wealth and fertility, love and peace. The main Vanir god is Freyr ("Lord"), who is the son of Njörðr. He commands the rains, sunshine, and plant life, and, according to Adam of Bremen, he was depicted with an enormous phallus in the temple at Uppsala. The pig and the stallion are his preferred animals. He lives in Ásgarðr in a home called Álfheimr ("World of the Elves") and owns a marvelous boat—it can be folded up, it aways has a good wind, and all the Æsir can fit on it—and a boar with gold bristles. His wife is the giantess Gerðr, whom he won at the expense of his sword. One day in the land of the giants he spied a splendid young woman, Gerðr, daughter of the giant Gymir, and fell desperately in love with her. Freyr's friend Skírnir borrowed his sword and horse and set off to retrieve her; after many ups and downs and through the use of magic, Skírnir (Freyr's "messenger") was successful in his undertaking but loses the sword and Freyr will not have it during the Last Battle when he confronts the fire giant Surtr, who will slay him.

At one time Freyr had a connection with the elves inhabiting Álfheimr, a heavenly realm that was his domain. During this earlier stage Freyr and the elves were probably not entirely separate beings. The elves are experts in magic and detest blemishes and impurities. Historically elves were worshipped, and sacrifices were made to them. In more recent folk beliefs they represent the "good dead" (that is, the good ancestors, elevated to the status of guardian spirits).

Freyja ("Lady"), Freyr's sister, is famed for her gaiety, and the worship devoted to her was erotic in nature. She lives in Fólkvangr and travels in a chariot drawn by cats. Her sphere of activity includes life, battle and death (she shares half of the deceased with Óðinn), fertility, and black magic. She adores jewels and adornments, and one text describes how she came into possession of her famous necklace. Four dwarves lived in a cave near to her palace. One day she saw they had a gold necklace, and she burned with the desire to own it. They refused to sell it to her but instead demanded that she sleep with each of them in exchange for it. She accepted their bargain and received the jewelry. But Loki told Óðinn about this, and Óðinn ordered the trickster god to steal the necklace, which he did by shapeshifting into various animals. Freyja eventually got her item back, however.

A word should be said about the dwarves that are linked to the gods in many myths. They were alive at the origin of the world; one tradition states that they were born from the putrefaction of the body of the primordial giant Ymir. They are skilled blacksmiths who craft all the treasures of the gods, as we have seen, as well as baleful weapons. They are thieves and magicians, and they maintain close relations with the dead (so much so that some scholars think they are the mythic transposition of dangerous dead individuals with evil intent). In fact, the dwarves' names often connote the idea of death. They inhabit the stones and mounds, and they will themselves turn to stone if they are caught out in the light of day.

III. RAGNARÖK AND THE RENEWAL OF THE WORLD

The death of the gods comes about during the eschatological battle called Ragnarök, "the final destiny of the gods," a scenario that was popularized by Richard Wagner in modern times as the *Götterdämmerung*, or "Twilight of the Gods." A Dantean apocalypse of a peerless evocative power, Ragnarök is heralded by a series of terrifying events: three dreadful winters during which the sun will not shine, and then three more winters accompanied by huge battles across the entire world and in which fathers and sons will slay one another. Next, the wolf Sköll will eat the sun and the wolf Hati will devour the moon; the Earth will quake; trees will be uprooted; the mountains will collapse; the wolf

Fenrir will break free from his bonds, and the sea will flood over the Earth because the Midgard Serpent has come ashore. Naglfar, the boat made from the toenails and fingernails of the dead, will set sail with a giantess or Loki at the helm. Fenrir will trot along with his mouth gaping wide—the upper jaw touching the heavens and the lower one the earth—ready to swallow up everything, and the Midgard Serpent will spew its venom. The heavens will part, and the giants, the "sons of the Muspell," will come forth, led by Surtr, and advance to the plain where the final battle will be waged. The Æsir and the *einherjar* will don their armor and emerge through the 540 gates of Valhalla, in rows of 800, with Odin at their head.

> Thor will advance at [Odin's] side and be unable to aid him because he will have his hands full fighting the Midgard Serpent. Freyr will fight Surt and there will be a harsh conflict before Freyr falls. . . . Then will also have got free the dog Garm, which is bound in front of Gnipahellir. This is the most evil creature. He will have a battle with Tyr and they will each be the death of the other. Thor will be victorious over the Midgard Serpent and will step away from it nine paces. Then he will fall to the ground dead from the poison which the serpent will spit at him. The wolf will swallow Odin. That will be the cause of his death. And immediately after Vidar will come forward and step with one foot on the lower jaw of the wolf. On this foot he will have a shoe for which the material has been collected throughout all time. . . . With one hand he will grasp the wolf's upper jaw and tear apart its mouth and this will cause the wolf's death. Loki will have a battle with Heimdall and they will cause each other's death. After that Surt will fling fire over the earth and burn the whole world.[20]

But Ragnarök is not the end. It is the herald of a renewal, because two minor gods will survive: Óðinn's sons Víðarr and Váli. They will soon be joined by the sons of Þórr, Móði and Magni, and then by Baldr and Höðr. Furthermore, two human beings will also survive: Líf ("Life") and Lífþrasir ("Striving for Life"), who will feed on the morning dew and repopulate the world that is lit by the daughter of Sól (the sun).

IV. THE SURVIVAL OF THE GODS

The ancient mythological figures that have survived Christianization are rare. After a transitional period during which paganism and the Christian faith were commingled, they were preserved linguistically in place-names and in frozen expressions and metaphors. This is how "Odin" and "troll" later became synonyms for the devil. Some figures were transformed and incorporated into folk legends—the troll became a dwarf in Scandinavia and in the Shetland islands, where it is called *trow*—but an examination of charms and spells reveals their persistent survival. The former minor lunar goddess Bil can be seen in the *Bilwiz*, a figure in medieval folk beliefs. During the eighteenth century Odin became the leader of the Wild Hunt, as the scholar Johann Peter Schmidt, writing in 1742, informs us.

> It is said in particular that this younger Odin was an archmagician and had no peer in the arts of making war. This is why some people have sought to see his name Woden as a derivative of "to rage" (*wüten*). Further, no one is unaware of the senseless belief held by countless folk, especially some hunters, that the time around Christmas and on the eve of Carnival (*Fastel-Abend*) is when the one called Woor or Goor or the Wild Huntsman passes. They say the Devil organizes a hunt with a troop of rapping spirits. If we get to the bottom of this superstition, we see that it emerged from the story of this younger Odin, and that the common man thinks that Odin or Wodan passes. This is why a company of ghosts like this is called the Furious Army, Wodan's Army, Gooden's Army, or the Army of Odin.[21]

The various Germanic countries did not all share the same course of historical development over time, and the folk traditions of Iceland and Norway have conserved a number of ancient mythological elements. It was not until the mid-nineteenth century that scholars and researchers, influenced by the work of Jacob Grimm, were able to shed new light on these gods who had been relegated to the shadows. Richard Wagner, through his operatic Ring Cycle, contributed to an increased awareness of these mythological figures, but in the decades that followed a pernicious ideology took hold of some aspects of the mythology and utilized them toward creating the myth of a great Reich. These developments served to discredit Germanic mythology for decades. However, recent scholarly studies, undertaken in the wake of the work done by the Indo-Europeanist Georges Dumézil, have demonstrated the significance of the Germanic gods in a wider comparative perspective. Thanks to these new directions, the subject is gradually being relieved of the prejudices with which it was formerly burdened. In fact, the gods of the Germanic-Norse pantheon are simply a local form, an ecotype, of a much larger group whose roots are in the Indo-European world, as has been shown by the multiple parallels shared with other cultures.

V. FOLK MYTHOLOGY

In addition to the scholarly mythology that was passed down by the ancient mythographers, there also exists an entire network of constantly evolving representations and folk beliefs. From this, an image emerges of a distinctive world in which elemental and supernatural beings are no longer the denizens of a distant pantheon but live in close proximity to humans—in the forests and mountains, beneath the stones, and so forth. We occasionally encounter the faded figures of high mythology here, but we also find many other elements. The majority of these beings, which are today labeled as fantasy creatures, continue to live on in folktales and legends—two sources that should never be overlooked, for they contain many riches. The work of the Brothers Grimm, for example, provides a fine overview with its wealth of nixies and kobolds, ogres and giants, changelings and dwarves, not to mention major figures like Frau Holle or Holda, Percht, Loyal Eckart, or the Cursed Huntsman.

Following in the footsteps of Johann Gottfried Herder and the Brothers Grimm, many German romantic poets and writers took up these themes, creatures, and folk beliefs, such as we see in Friedrich de la Motte-Fouqué's *Undine,* Adelbert von Chamisso's *Peter Schlemihl,* and in the tales of the Erlking, the Lorelei, and Tannhäuser. A complete list of such borrowings would be long indeed. These themes were, in turn, taken up by musical composers and enjoyed unfailing success throughout the nineteenth century.

The folkloric elements must all be taken into account if one wishes to draw a good panorama of Germanic mythology, and not merely its Scandinavian branch.

VI. MYTHOLOGY, ARTS, AND LITERATURE

Germanic mythology has had significant impact on literature and the arts. I can only present a small overview of this here.*[22] There are artists such as Henry Fuseli (Füssli), who gave us the famous painting *Thor Battering the Midgard Serpent* (1780), or Mårten Eskil Winge (*Thor's Fight with the Giants,* 1872; *Loki and Sigyn,* 1863), Christoffer Wilhelm Eckersberg (*The Death of Balder,* 1817), Nils Blommér (*Loki and Sigyn,* ca. 1850), John Charles Dollman (*Hermod in Hel; Sif; Thor; The Ride of the Valkyries;* ca. 1900), Dorothy Hardy (*The Binding of Fenris; Loki and Thiassi;* ca. 1909), Peter Nicolai Arbo (*The Wild Hunt,* 1872; *Valkyrie,* 1865/1869), and Moritz von Schwind (*The Dance of the Elves,* ca. 1860). Mythological themes have been taken up by sculptors like Hermann Ernst Freund (*Balder,* 1821; *Thor,* 1828–1829; *Idunn,* 1821; *Loki,* statuette in wood, 1822; *Mimir and Balder,* bas-relief, 1822), Dagfin Werenskiold (*Odin and Mimir,* bas-relief, 1938), and Bengt Erland Fogelberg (*Frey,* 1818), to mention just a few examples, and in Stuttgart there is a public fountain, the *Schicksalsbrunnen* (Well of Fate), designed by Karl Donndorf. It is safe to say that all the principal gods of the Germanic pantheon have been well represented in the arts.

References have also been made to the Germanic gods in modern maritime contexts. For example, we may note that Norwegian boats have borne the names *Ægir, Brage,* and *Heimdallr,* and Dutch ships have been named *Freyr* and *Balder.* Icelandic and Swedish ships were named *Thor* and *Ran,* and a German sailing yacht has the name *Freya.*

Literature shows no shortage of Germanic mythological themes either. There are literary works that depend on the reader having some knowledge of Germanic and Norse mythology in order to understand their content. Such is the case with the poem *Der Wein* (The Wine)

---

*[For the reader's convenience, the titles of the foreign paintings listed here are all given in English translation. —Ed.]

by Friedrich von Hagedorn and *Die Irmin-Säule* (Irmin's Pillar) by Gerhard Anton von Halem, as likewise with Adam Oehlenschläger's 1807 tragedy *Baldur hin Gode* (Balder the Good). In an epic ballad Wilhelm Hertz mentions Nanna, Höther, and Gewar; in *Hermann,* a drama written in 1743, Johann Elias Schlegel speaks of a cult of Tuisto; and several odes by Friedrich Gottlieb Klopstock refer to figures from Germanic mythology: *Braga* (1771), *Wingolf* (1747), *Wir und Sie* (Us and Them; 1766), *Skulda* (1766), and *Odin* (a hymn from *Hermanns Schlacht* [Hermann's Battle], 1769). Hermann Lingg completed his heroic poem *Die Walküren* (The Valkyries) in 1864, and Cyrill Kistler

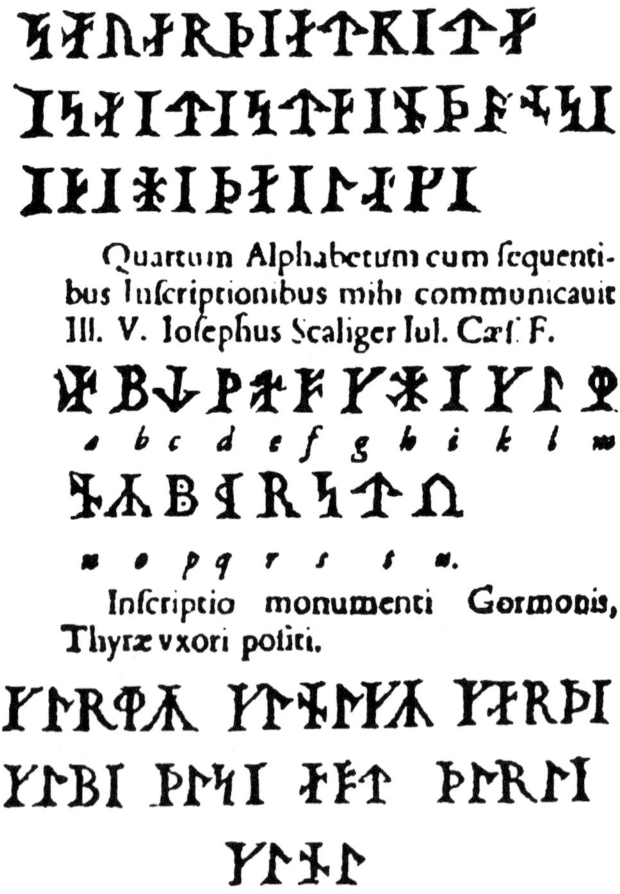

Fig. 2. Runic letters (here called the "Alphabet of the Goths") in Vulcanio Brugensi, *De literis & lingua Getarum, siue, Gothorum*, Leiden: Franciscus Plantiniana, 1597

staged his opera *Baldurs Tod* (The Death of Balder) in 1891. Ernst Toller's comedy *Der entfesselte Wotan* (Wotan Unchained) was first performed in 1893. Heinrich Heine's *Atta Troll* (1848) cannot be deciphered without prior knowledge of the myth of the Wild Hunt, just as Herder's translation of the ballad *Erlkönigs Tochter* (The Erlking's Daughter) will remain mysterious to any reader who is unfamiliar with elves.

Germanic mythology is not confined to the Middle Ages, and therefore I have taken into account the legendary and supernatural beings that appear in what Theodor Vernaleken calls "the mythic and post-mythic legends."

The names cited at the end of certain entries refer the reader to other ones, so as to provide a larger view of the traditions, which are unavoidably divided up in the context of a dictionary. The bibliographical notes make it possible to pursue more extensive research on these topics.

NOTES

1. See Jacques Ridé, *L'Image du Germain dans la pensée et la littérature allemandes, de la redécouverte de Tacite à la fin du XVIe siècle.*
2. Cf. Régis Boyer, *Le Mythe Viking dans les lettres modernes,* and Boyer, *Les Vikings.*
3. For more on this, see Claude Lecouteux, *L'allemand du moyen âge.*
4. These texts can be found in Carl Clemen, *Fontes historiae religionis Germanicae.*
5. Cf. Siegfried Gutenbrunner, *Die germanischen Götternamen der antiken Inschriften.*
6. Caesar, *The Gallic War,* 6, 17. Edwards translation.
7. Tacitus, *Germania,* 40, 1. Rives translation.
8. Original Old Icelandic text in Gustav Neckel, ed., *Edda: Die Lieder des Codex Regius nebst verwandten Denkmälern,* vol. I. English: *The Poetic Edda,* trans. Carolyne Larrington.
9. Original Old Icelandic text in Snorri Sturluson, *Edda: Prologue and Gylfaginning; Skáldskaparmál,* ed. Anthony Faulkes. English: Sturluson, *Edda,* trans. Anthony Faulkes.
10. Gottfried Lorenz, ed. and trans., *Snorri Sturluson: Gylfaginning. Texte, Übersetzung, Kommentar.*

11. Régis Boyer, *Yggdrasill, La religion des anciens Scandinaves.*

12. Snorri Sturluson, *Heimskringla: History of the Kings of Norway,* trans. Lee M. Hollander.

13. English editions: Saxo Grammaticus, *The History of the Danes, Books I–IX,* ed. and trans. Hilda Ellis Davidson and Peter Fisher. Latin text and English translation: Saxo Grammaticus, *Gesta Danorum: The History of the Danes,* ed. Karsten Friis-Jensen, trans. Peter Fisher. Cf. also Georges Dumézil, *From Myth to Fiction: The Saga of Hadingus,* trans. Derek Coltman.

14. Régis Boyer, *La Poésie scaldique.*

15. *Ynglinga saga,* chap. 6, in Sturluson, *Heimskringla,* trans. Hollander, 10.

16. Ibid., chap. 7. Note that "Ghouls" should be understood here as "revenants."

17. *Gylfaginning,* chap. 34, in Sturluson, *Edda,* trans. Faulkes, 27.

18. Ibid., chap. 34, 29.

19. Ibid., chap. 27, 25.

20. Ibid., chap. 51, 54.

21. Johann Peter Schmidt, *Fastel-Abend oder Geschichtmäßige Untersuchung der Fastel-Abends-Gebräuche in Teutschland,* 75–76, n. 49.

22. A large number of references and reproductions can be found in Régis Boyer, *Héros et Dieux du Nord: Guide iconographique.*

Encyclopedia
of Norse and Germanic
Folklore, Mythology, and Magic

∽

From AAGE to ZWIESAUGER

A

AAGE and ELSE: This is the title of a medieval Danish folk ballad centered on the belief in revenants. It relates the following tale. Aage has died, and his fiancée is mourning him when he steps from his grave and scolds her: when she weeps, his grave fills up with blood and his feet are clasped by serpents, but when she is merry, it is filled with roses. When the white rooster crows, followed by the red rooster and then the black rooster, Aage puts his coffin on his back and returns to the cemetery while Else (Elselille) follows him. He tells her that she shall never see him again and commands her to gaze up at the stars. She lifts her eyes toward the sky and he vanishes: "The dead man slipped into the ground." She falls ill and dies of grief. There are five versions of this ballad in Danish and Swedish.

✦ *DRAUGR, LENORE*

📖 Nielsen, ed., *Danske Folkeviser*, vol. II, 52–57 *(Aage og Else)*.

ABDUCTION (Danish *Bjærgtagen*, Norwegian *Bergtaking*): This is a frequent theme in Germanic literature. Supernatural beings (dwarves, giants, nature spirits) abduct children (✦ CHANGELING) or adults. The humans—the Loyal Eckart, Tannhäuser, and so on—are carried off into the mythical Venusberg or Hörselberg Mountain (Thuringia), or some otherworldly paradise. We find Siegfried and Wittich (Witege) in Geroldseck Castle in Wasgau; Frederick Barbarossa sleeps beneath the Untersberg (near Salzburg) or the Kyffhäuser Mountain (Thuringia/Saxony-Anhalt); and Charlemagne and his army wait beneath the Odenberg in Hesse.

It was once hard to comprehend that a sovereign or hero could vanish completely, and, for a long time following his death, people imagined that he continued to live, sleeping inside a mountain, from which he would emerge when the country needed him. This theme had great appeal and served as subject matter for many authors, such as Ludwig

Fig. 3. The king sleeping in the mountain.
Marcus Grønvold, 1874.

Bechstein (1801–1860), Friedrich Rückert (1788–1866), and Clara
Viebig (*Das schlafende Heer*).

📖 Clifton-Everest, *The Tragedy of Knighthood;* Feilberg, *Bjærgtagen,* 55–69;
Grimm, *Deutsche Sagen,* nos. 21, 23, 27, 28; Holbek and Piø, *Fabeldyr og sagnfolk,*
136; Petzold, *Historische Sagen,* vol. II, 15–24 (Untersberg); Ronald Grambo,
"Balladen om Hakje og Bergmannen," *Arv* 28 (1972): 55–81.

ABWASCHL: The "washer" is a rapping spirit (poltergeist) of the
meadows in the Alps where the herds graze in summer. He takes possession of these areas once the herds are brought back into the valleys
for the winter, washing and scraping all the utensils left behind while
making such a racket that all who pass by flee in terror. Sometimes he
shows up to express his irritation when a cowherd goes dancing without
his master's permission.

✦ *POLTERGEIST*

📖 Adrian, ed., *Alte Sagen aus dem Salzburger Land,* 84.

ACCURSED HUNTSMAN: Despite its mutations over time, the legend of the Accursed Huntsman remains an exemplum intended to illustrate the post mortem fate of a sinner. One of the first accounts is by Michael Beheim (1416/21–1474/78). One beautiful day Count Eberhard von Wurttemberg was hunting by himself in the forest. Shortly after entering the woods he hears a great racket and sees an alarming creature appear that is chasing a stag. He dismounts from his horse in fear and hides in a thicket and asks the apparition if he intends him any harm. The stranger responds, "No, I am a man like you. Once I was a lord who had a passion for hunting, and I asked God to allow me to keep hunting until Judgment Day. To my misfortune, my wish was granted, and it is now five hundred years that I have been pursuing this single stag." Eberhard then says to him, "Please show me your face in case I might recognize you." The stranger does so; his face is barely as big as a fist, and it is as dry and wrinkled as a dead leaf. He then rides off in pursuit of the stag.

In other stories the hunter is punished for hunting on Sunday, destroying crops, or killing a deer in a church. His mania for the chase

Fig. 4. Theodoric/Thidrek is carried off to hell while pursuing a stag. Bas-relief in the Basilica of San Zeno in Verona.

is punished, and he is condemned to hunt eternally with no break or respite until the Day of the Last Judgment. This kind of legend was extremely popular, and César Franck wrote a symphonic poem on this theme (1883).

📖 Lecouteux, *Phantom Armies of the Night*.

ÆGIR ("Sea"): Sea giant who possesses all the features of a sea god. His other names are Gymir and Hlér; the latter name can be found in Hlésey, which literally means "Island of Hlér," where he resides. He is the son of Fornjótr, and the sea goddess, Rán is his daughter or wife. He has nine daughters who are identified with the waves. Their names are Himinglæva, Blóðughadda, Hefring, Dúfa, Uðr, Hrönn, Bylgja, Bara, and Kolga.

ÆSIR: One of the two major families of the Germanic pantheon, the other being the Vanir.

The Æsir consists of Óðinn and his sons Þórr and Baldr, as well as the following deities: Njörðr, Freyr, Týr, Heimdallr, Bragi, Víðarr, Váli, Ullr, Hœnir, Forseti, and Loki. The Ásynjur (female Æsir goddesses; sg. Ásynja) are Frigg, Freyja, Gefjon, Iðunn, Gerðr, Sigyn, Fulla, and

Fig. 5. Frigg, Thor, and Freyr. Olaus Magnus, *Historia de gentibus septentrionalibus*, Rome, 1555.

Nanna; sometimes to this list are added Eir, Lofn, Vár, Vör, Sjöfn, Syn, Hlín, Snotra, and Gná. The Æsir live in Ásgarðr, and the more important among them have homes whose names are known to us. In terms of Dumézil's classifications, they are primarily of the martial function (the second function) but spill over into the first function (royalty/priesthood) and the third function (fertility/fecundity).

ALBERICH 1 ("Powerful Elf"): The elf or dwarf who is defeated by Siegfried in the *Nibelungenlied* (Lay of the Nibelungs). Alberich guards the treasure of Schilbung and Nibelung—mythical rulers whose names refer to mist and water—and he owns the cloak of invisibility known as the *Tarnkappe* (*cape folette* in Old French). In the Nordic legends of Sigurðr he corresponds to Andvari. He is adopted into French literature under the name of Aubéron and in English literature as Oberon.

    Lecouteux, *Les Nains et les Elfes au Moyen Âge.*

Fig. 6. The dwarf Alberich. *Das Heldenbuch* (Strasbourg: Johann Prüss, circa 1483).

ALBERICH 2 (Elberich): In the legend of Ortnit, the king of Lombardy, the dwarf Alberich is the father of heroes. He is invisible to everyone except Ortnit, who wears a magic ring that Alberich gave to his mother. This guardian dwarf provides assistance to her son, Ortnit, who is seeking to wed the daughter of the sultan Machorel, who lives at Muntabur (Mount Thabor). He gives the king a full suit of armor and the sword Rosen. During the campaign against the infidels Alberich plays all kinds of tricks on the pagans, breaking their idols and throwing their weapons into the castle moat. He makes fun of Machorel, who is unable to see him. For Ortnit he plays the role of messenger and advisor. Without his aid the king would be unable to kidnap the sultan's daughter. Alberich is more than five hundred years old. He is a skilled smith and an excellent harp player, and, although he is no larger than a four-year-old child, he has the strength of twelve men. He owns a marvelous stone that—when placed in the mouth—makes it possible to understand and speak all languages.

ALBIUN: Queen of Wild Mountain in the romance *Tandareis und Flordibel* by Der Pleier (thirteenth century), she rules over a land inhabited by dwarves and wild men. She is persecuted by the savage Kurion, who has kidnapped one of her handmaidens.

ALCI: Twin gods about whom Tacitus (*Germania,* 43, 3) says: "In the land of the Nahanarvali is displayed a grove long held in awe. A priest in woman's dress presides, but the gods they speak of in Roman translation as Castor and Pollux: that is the essence of this divine power; the actual name is the Alci . . . they are worshipped as young men and brothers" (trans. Rives). It is believed that this sacred spot was in Silesia, in Zobten where Thietmar of Merseburg says an important sanctuary was located. The theme of divine twins is abundantly represented in the Germanic countries, from the pairs of twins in the petroglyphs to the androgynous deities of the Eddas and the quasi-undifferentiated Freyr-Freyja couple. What Tacitus says about the priest wearing feminine garments brings to mind the priestesses (*gyðjar*) that Snorri Sturluson mentions as being in the service of the Vanir.

✦ *IBOR and AIO*

📖 Ward, *The Divine Twins;* Jaan Puhvel, "Aspects of Equine Functionality," in *Myth and Law among the Indo-Europeans,* ed. Puhvel, 159–92.

ALF (masc.): One of the names for the *drac* in East Prussia, the others being *aft* and *rodjäcte* ("Red Jacket"). When a poor person inexplicably and suddenly becomes rich, he was easily suspected of owning an *alf*. *Drac* is used much more rarely in this regard, and the people of Masuria call it *lataniec* and *kaubuk* in their dialect.

The alf stays in houses in the shape of an animal such as a hen, a gray goose, or a bird resembling an owl. It is more rarely described as looking like a large black cat or calf. The alf most often lives in the attic and only his owner has a right to see him, but he can also hang around in the stable, the barn, or near the chimney cap, if not in the chimney itself. He is sometimes said to demand his own room, carpeted in black, into which no one but the master of the household may enter. The alf's owner is responsible for feeding him with milk, prunes, scrambled eggs, or birch-flour porridge.

The alf is also depicted as an igneous phenomenon with no definite shape that travels through the air resembling a broom on fire or a pole. In the stories spread about it, most often it is the flying *alf*, but others focus on the zoomorphic alf, which is either a quadruped or a bird, although these depictions overlap with one another. An allusion is occasionally made to it if someone says, "The hen is flying like a tail of fire." An alf flying through the air in the shape of a pole will change into an animal (a winged creature) in the house, and when it leaves at night it will resume its earlier appearance.

The alf helps people in the house or procures them wealth, or does both things at once. He cooks lunch while the farmwife is in the fields and throws hay down to those who feed the livestock. He also allows the animals to thrive and the butter to turn out perfectly—in short, he makes it possible for all activities to run smoothly. Primarily, he increases the wealth of the household. Some even say that he shits gold. He steals all kinds of valuable property—especially grain—and brings it back to his owner. Because he steals this from silos and grain bins, these storage places often have crosses drawn on them for protection. During the sowing season the alf will even take the seed from one farmer and give it to another, and during the harvesttime he does the same thing with the sheaves. He steals eggs from other people's henhouses for his owner's benefit. When the alf is flying through the air and is red in color, he is bringing money; when he is blue, he is carrying grain. He enters his owner's house through the chimney. If someone sees him traveling through the sky and calls to him, this will force him to drop his cargo. But this individual must find shelter immediately beneath a roof, as the alf will then start raining lice down upon him or her.

In many legends the alf is a creature who needs to live with people. In the form of a hen that is half-dead from the cold, he allows himself to be carried into the house by a merciful individual whom he will then serve faithfully his whole life. If the individual dies, the alf will move into the home of his relatives and continue his service with them. If the alf is angry at his owner, because the latter does not feed him well or is trying to get rid of him, he will cause harm in equal measure to the good he has provided him up to that point. He will take back all the wealth that has been amassed and even set fire to the house (which is something that will always happen if the alf is fed with burning fodder).

📖 Pohl, *Die Volkssagen Ostpreussens*, 182–83.

ÁLFABLÓT ("Sacrifice to the Elves"): This is another name for Jól (Yule), the feast of the winter solstice, the dead, and fertility. A great sacrifice is performed on this occasion "to ensure a fruitful and peaceful year." The sacrifice is a boar or pig.

ÁLFHEIMR ("World of the Elves"): This is one of the dwelling places in Ásgarðr, the world of the gods. It belongs to Freyr, who thus appears as the master of the elves.

ALFÖÐR, ALFAÐIR ("All-father"): This is one of Odin's titles. "He is called this because he is the father of the gods, of all men, and of all that has been created" (Snorri Sturluson). A similar title for Odin is Aldafaðir, "Father of Men."

📖 Falk, *Odensheiti*.

ALFRIGG ("Powerful Elf"): The name of one of the dwarves who forged Brísingamen, the necklace owned by the goddess Freyja.

ALKE: The name of an aquatic demon of Westphalia who would chase anyone who made fun of him. He appears in the shape of a wheel of fire or a dragon. He is said to be the spirit of an innkeeper of the same name who was swallowed up by the earth because of his impious ways. This is also the name of one of the dogs of the Wild Hunt.

📖 Kuhn and Schwartz, *Norddeutsche Sagen, Märchen und Gebräuche,* no. 357, and the footnote to no. 152.

ALMBUTZ: ✦ KASERMAN(N)DL

ALMGEISTER ("Spirits of the Alpine Summer Grazing Lands"): Throughout the Alps, in autumn, after the herds have been brought down from the mountain meadows where they were grazed during the warm months, the alpine cabins are reoccupied by spirits until the return of the flocks in spring. These spirits live in the forests and ravines during the summer. They have a variety of names depending on the region: *Almbütze, Hüttlebutz,* and *Novabutz* in Germany; *Alperer* and *Kaserman(n)dln* in the Tyrol. In Switzerland there is the *Alpmüeterli,* an old humpbacked woman accompanied by theriomorphic kobolds; her appearance is a herald of bad weather. These spirits milk the phantom animals they protect and make butter and cheese. They yodel, whistle, and make knocking sounds. They are friendly as long as they are not provoked.

ALP: A syncretic figure in Germanic folk belief. It was originally an elf, which was then demonized and became conflated with the nightmare (*Mahr, Doggeli, Trud*). The Alp has been variously seen as an incubus, a demon, a dwarf (Switzerland), a ghost (Alsace), the spirit of someone who died prematurely, and the double (alter ego) of a witch or lover. Depending on the region, it has different names. In Frisia it is *Rittmeije* ("The Rider") and *Waldriderske* ("The Staff Rider"); in Franconia, *Trempe* ("The Trampler"); and in Alsace, *Lützelkäppe* ("The One Who Wears His Cap Backward"). The Alp is able to assume the shape of any animal, most often appearing as a furry one with burning eyes. Some people, such as lunatics, are predestined to become an Alp. Someone who is born with teeth, or on a Sunday, or during the "spirits' hour" (between midnight and one in the morning), or beneath an evil star, or three days before the Feast of Saint Gall (October 16) is also at risk of suffering such a fate. If there are seven boys in the same family, one of them will become a werewolf; if there are seven girls, one will be an Alp.

The Alp sits on the chest of the sleeper, crushing, choking, stamping, and otherwise pressing its weight on him or her. The Alp enters through keyholes, through a passageway, a cat door, or any other kind of opening. It can be heard coming because of the noise it makes, which can be a ringing, tinkling, or chewing sound; its breath induces sleep. Sometimes it sucks on the chests of children, which likens it to a vampire. It is blamed for sending illnesses, one of which is called "Alp shot" (*Alpschuß*), and for tangling up the manes of horses, a distinguishing feature of household spirits and dwarves. (✦ ELF-LOCKS) It is said to travel by whirlwind.

In the memorates (oral folklore accounts) it is considered to be the Double of a sleeping person who wants some specific thing. The individual then sends forth his or her alter ego from his or her body in the form of a small animal, and otherwise behaves like a nightmare.

📖 Lecouteux, *Witches, Werewolves, and Fairies;* Meyer-Matheis, *Die Vorstellung eines Alter ego in Volkserzählungen.*

ALSVIÐR ("Most Learned"): This is the name of the giant who knew the secrets of the runes. As the first inhabitants of the Earth, the giants are reputed to possess great knowledge.

ALSVINNR ("Very Swift"): The name of one of the two horses that draw the chariot of the goddess Sól, the sun, which is a feminine noun in Germanic languages. Its companion is Arvakr.

ALÞJÓFR ("Master Thief"): The name of this dwarf reflects one of the personality traits of these creatures.

ALVÍSS ("The One Who Knows All"): This is the dwarf who asked for the hand of Thor's daughter. The god agreed to grant his permission if Alvíss could answer all his questions regarding the names of the Earth, sky, moon, sun, clouds, wind, fire, sea, forests, night, grains, and beer. The conversation lasted until dawn, at which time the first rays of sunlight petrified the dwarf.

ALVITR: ✦ HERVÖR ALVITR

ÄLVKALL ("The Old Man of the River"): An aquatic spirit that can drive humans mad.

ANDHRÍMNIR ("Sooty"): The name of the cook in Valhalla who prepares the boar Sæhrímnir in the cauldron Eldhrímnir. This is the food for the dead warriors who are gathered there.

ANDLANGR ("Endlessly Vast"): The name of the second heaven that lies between the first heaven, which we can see, and the third heaven called Víðbláinn.

ANDVARI ("Breath-keeper"): This dwarf swims in the form of a pike in the pool by a waterfall when he is captured by Loki, who demands that the dwarf give him all the treasure he is guarding. Andvari complies with Loki's demand but keeps one ring. Loki sees it and steals it. The dwarf then curses the treasure so that it will cause the death of all who own it. This treasure eventually finds its way into the hands of Sigurðr/Siegfried.

✦ *OTTR*

Fig. 7. The dwarf Andvari. Carved stone from Altuna in
the Swedish province of Uppland, eleventh century.

ANGANE, ENGUANE, EGUANE (fem.): These are fantasy creatures who are considered wild women, fairies, or witches in Trentino (in the Italian Tyrol). These women live in caves in the middle of forests, in meadows, and in springs. Their primary activity is washing the thread they have spun. Their enemy is the Beatrik, who will tear any of them it meets to pieces. They can be seen at dawn and dusk. They are kind, especially to young men, but whoever vexes them will be struck immediately by their curse. When they give humans a gift, it is often a ball of yarn that has no end.

📖 Schneller, *Märchen und Sagen aus Wälschtirol,* 215–18.

ANGEYJA: One of the nine giant mothers of the god Heimdallr.

ANGRBOÐA ("She Who Stirs Up Trouble"): The giantess who engendered with Loki the wolf Fenrir, the Midgard Serpent, and Hel, the goddess of the underworld.

ANGZRERWEIBL ("The Little Woman of the Meadows"): A dwarf from the Salzburg region in Austria. At night she draws travelers to a bridge where she makes them so scared that the hair stands up on their heads. At the arrival of daybreak, however, she suddenly vanishes with a sharp cry.

📖 Adrian, ed., *Alte Sagen aus dem Salzburger Land,* 83–84.

ANNAR ("The Other One"): Second husband of Nótt, the personification of night, and father of Jörð, the Earth.

ANSES: Ancient form of a word that is cognate with Old Norse *Æsir* and which appears in the Gothic history of the sixth-century writer Jordanes. According to him, the *anses* are the founders of the Amal clan, the most famous representatives of which are Ermanaric and Theodoric the Great. The word appears on the Balingen round brooch from Swabia in the form *ansuz.* It can also be seen carved on the Kragehul spear shaft from the island of Funen in Denmark and on the Myklebostad stone in Romsdal, Norway. An even older votive inscription found in Tongeren (Belgium) mentions a female deity, Vihansa, whose name contains the element *ansa.* Numerous Germanic personal names (Ansgar, Ansba, and so on) offer evidence that what we have here is a tenacious belief shared by all the Germanic peoples.

📖 Edgar Polomé, "L'étymologie du terme germanique *ansuz, 'dieu souverain,'" *Études Germaniques* 8 (1953): 36–44.

ANTELOYE, ANTILOIE, ANTILOIS: King of the dwarves who plays an important role in a short story titled "Alexander and Antiloye," for which texts exist in several different languages of medieval western Europe. He demands reparations from Alexander the Great, who has killed some of his game. He offers his friendship to the Macedonian leader and invites him to visit his kingdom. A short time later Antiloye visits Alexander in his camp where, invisible, he plays numerous tricks on the whole retinue. He customarily rides a small horse and measures four-and-one-half spans.

In Ulrich von Etzenbach's *Alexander* (thirteenth century), Anteloye wears a crown and holds a scepter, is well formed, and has light skin and eyes. He is the size of a two-year-old child.

ANTRISCHE (pl.): This is a collective term in the Tyrol for the dwarves who are believed to be the children that Eve concealed from God when he visited. God said, "What is hidden from me shall forever remain so!" They are also called *Hollenleut*.

📖 Heyl, *Volkssagen, Meinungen und Bräuche aus Tirol*, 564, 608–10; Zingerle, *Sagen aus Tirol*, 46–47.

ARIE: Name of a fairy similar to Holda and Berchta/Perchta in the Franche-Comté region of France; in the Bernese Jura region of Switzerland, this female entity is called Tante Arie ("Aunt Arie"). The figure can probably be traced back to a Germanic or Burgundian goddess or demon.

📖 Grimm, *Teutonic Mythology*, vol. I, 412 (footnote 1).

ARNHÖFÐI ("Eagle Head"): This is one of Odin's bynames. It most likely refers to the myth of the wondrous mead (✦ KVASIR) that was hidden by the giant Suttungr. Odin steals the mead and flees in the form of an eagle.

📖 Falk, *Odensheiti*.

ARVAKR ("Early Riser"): One of the two horses that draws the chariot of the sun goddess Sól.

✦ *ALVINNR*

ÁSABRAGR ("Prince of the Æsir"): One of the titles of the god Thor.

ÁSA-ÞÓRR ("Thor of the Æsir" or "Æsir-god Thor"): One of the titles of the god Thor.

ÁSAHEIMR ("World of the Æsir"): In Snorri Sturluson's euhemeristic interpretation, the Æsir dwell in a country located in Asia Minor.

ÁSBRÚ ("Bridge of the Æsir"): One of the two names for the bridge that connects the Earth to the domain of the gods.

✦ *BILRÖST* or *BIFRÖST*

ASGAARDSREIA: A fantasy hunt that takes place during the Twelve Nights.

✦ *OSKOREIA, WILD HUNT*

ÁSGARÐR ("Enclosure of the Gods"): The place where the Æsir live in the center of Midgarðr, which is surrounded by Útgarðr, the land of giants, demons, harmful creatures, and monsters. This is the home of the great hall called Valhöll ("Hall of the Warriors Fallen in Battle"), which is called Walhall in German and Valhalla in English. Ásgarðr was built by a giant who asked to receive Freyja, the sun, and the moon as his payment. On the advice of Loki, the Æsir accepted the deal. With the help of his horse Svaðilfari, the giant got to work and the construction proceeded rapidly. The gods deliberated on how they could get out of their arrangement. They forced Loki to make up for the poor advice he had given them. Loki transformed into a mare in heat. The giant's horse set off in pursuit, abandoning its work. When the giant saw that he would not be able to meet the agreed upon deadline, he became violently angry, and the Æsir, in terror, called Thor, who smashed the giant's skull with his hammer. The mare gave birth to a gray foal with eight legs, Sleipnir, who became Odin's steed.

📖 Régis Boyer, "Sur la construction d'Ásgarðr," *Perspectives on Indo-European Language, Culture and Religion: Studies in Honor of Edgar C. Polomé* (Washington, D.C.: Journal of Indo-European Studies, 1992), vol. II, 406–26.

ASH: This tree has certainly played a major role in Germanic antiquity. It enjoyed considerable reverence and was called "Thor's savior," because when the god fell into the Vimur River he was able to save himself by grabbing hold of an ash branch. In the anthropogony, the first man's name was Askr ("Ash"), and the cosmic tree, Yggdrasill, is also an ash tree.

ASKR ("Ash"): Name of the first man. One day the gods Odin, Vili, and Vé found two tree trunks on the shore. They used them to make a man, Askr, and a woman, Embla. Odin gave them breath and life, Vili gave them intelligence and movement, and Vé gave them form, speech, hearing, and sight. According to another tradition, Odin was accompanied by Lóðurr and Hœnir. In the *Atharva Veda* the Skambha, "the cosmic pillar" that corresponds to Yggdrasill, would be the first man. Ancient Indian mythology displays a remarkable kinship with Germanic traditions.

ASPRIAN: A giant who first appears in the epic *König Rother* (ca. 1150). He was the leader of twelve giants and so large that no horse could carry him. He had the skills of a juggler and a mantle given him as a gift by the people known as the Flatfeet. He accompanied King Rother on his quest for a bride, the daughter of Emperor Constantine of Constantinople.

Fig. 8. The giant Asprian. *Das Heldenbuch* (Strasbourg: Johann Prüss, circa 1483).

When Asprian is angry he stamps so hard that his feet become buried in the ground. In the legend of Dietrich von Bern he is armed with two swords and an iron bar for a club.

ATLA ("The Quarrelsome One"): One of the nine giant mothers of the god Heimdallr.

ATLI: Attila, King of the Huns, called Etzel in Middle High German and Aetla in Old English. He holds an important place in Germanic epic legends and is most famous for his role in the *Nibelungenlied*. He marries Kriemhild after the death of Siegfried and the Burgundians are massacred at his court.

ATRIÐR ("Attacker"): One of Odin's titles as a god of war.
   📖 Falk, *Odensheiti*.

AUÐR ("Wealth"): Son of Nótt, "night," and her first husband, Naglfari.

AUÐUMLA: Name of the original cow, born from the melting of the primordial frost. Four rivers of milk flow from her udders. She is the one who fed Ymir, the first giant. By licking the frost that covered the stones she caused a being to emerge: Búri, Odin's grandfather.

Fig. 9. Auðumla.
Illustration by
Ólafur Brynjúlfsson,
Snorra Edda, 1760.

AUFHOCKER, HUCKUP: An entity, sometimes a dead man, that hurls itself on the shoulders of someone walking outside at night and becomes heavier and heavier the longer it is on his victim. This attack occurs in specific places such as bridges, crossroads, springs, woods, on a path through a hollow, or in cemeteries. The traveler cannot free himself until he arrives home. It is thought that this creature might be a materialization of night terrors. There is a monument in Hildesheim, Germany, depicting an apple thief with a Huckup on his back.

These "perching spirits" can be found almost everywhere in Europe. In the Charente-Maritime region of France similar traits are ascribed to the entity known as the *ganipote*.

📖 Gerda Grober-Glück, "Aufhocker und Aufhocken," in *Atlas der deutschen Volkskunde*, 127–223.

AULKE: The name for dwarves in Emsland (Lower Saxony). It comes from the diminutive *alveke,* "little elf."

AURBOÐA ("Gravel"): The giantess who wed Gymir (another name of Ægir). She is the mother of Gerðr, whose hand the god Freyr asked in marriage through his intermediary, Skírnir. Gymir accepts on the condition that Freyr gives him his sword as a gift, and the god does so. He will be without a sword during the final battle at Ragnarök.

AURGELMIR: A giant who is most likely identical to Ymir. He is Bergelmir's grandfather. His name derives from the Old Norse *aurr,* "clay," which refers to his origin.

AURKONUNGR: One of the bynames for the god Hœnir, who still remains shrouded in mystery.

AURVANDILL: This figure is spoken of in a myth that relates the following events. Thor confronted the giant Hrungnir and slew him, but a fragment of this giant's weapon, a flint club, became embedded in Thor's skull. Returning home, the god came across Gróa, a seer and wife of Aurvandill. With her incantations she began to slowly dislodge the stone. Thor was so pleased that, without waiting for her treatment to end, he sought to reward her by giving her news of her husband. He thus tells her that when crossing the Élivágar rivers Aurvandill froze one of his toes, whereupon he—Thor—broke it off and cast it into the heavens where it became the star called Aurvandill's Toe. Gróa's joy was so great upon learning this that she forgot her spells, and the stone remained stuck in Thor's skull.

AUSTRI ("East"): One of the four dwarves that stand at the four cardinal points and hold up the celestial vault formed by Ymir's skull. In skaldic poetry, the sky is called the "dwarves' burden" (*byrði dverganna*) for that reason.

One kenning calls the sky the "burden of the kin of Norðri," and the name of this dwarf appears in the poem *Óláfsdrápa* (strophe 26). In the *Skáldskaparmál* (Treatise on the Skaldic Art), Snorri Sturluson designates the sky by *hjálmr*, "helmet of Vestri and Austri, Suðri and Norðri."

📖 Lecouteux, "Trois hypothèses sur nos voisins invisibles," in Lecouteux and Gouchet, eds., *Hugur: mélanges d'histoire, de littérature et de mythologie offerts à Régis Boyer pour son 65e anniversaire*, 289–92.

✦ *COSMOGONY, NORÐRI, SUÐRI, VESTRI*

BABA: Name of Berchta/Perchta in Carinthia (Austria).

BAFANA: An otherworldly figure who represents the personification of Epiphany. It is believed an ancient psychopomp deity is concealed beneath this name, which is variously spelled as Befana, Bephana, or Befania; in Swiss German the Epiphany is *Buania*.

BALDR ("Lord"): He is the son of Odin and Frigg. He is the best of the Æsir and all give him praise; he is nicknamed "the Good." He married Nanna, and they had one son, Forseti. His home in the heavens is called Breiðablikk. He owns a boat called Hringhorni and the magical ring Draupnir, forged by the dwarves. Baldr has dire dreams that he recounts to the other Æsir. They ask all of creation to spare Baldr. Frigg is given an oath that her son will be spared by water, fire, all metals, earth, wood, stones, animals, and diseases.

When this had been ratified, the Æsir organized a game in which each one could throw whatever they liked at Baldr. This irritated Loki, who took on the guise of an old woman and went to Frigg to ask her if all things had indeed sworn an oath to spare her son. She answered that she had not demanded the oath of a very young mistletoe sprig. Loki tore off this sprig and gave it to Baldr's blind brother, Höðr, and then told him in which direction to throw it. Höðr cast the mistletoe at Baldr, who was pierced through by it and died.

A splendid funeral was held for him. He was burned on his ship once the giantess Hyrrokkin launched it out to sea, and Thor blessed the pyre with his hammer, Mjöllnir. Nanna died of grief and was placed alongside her husband. Attending the ceremony were Odin and his valkyries, Freyr and Freyja, Heimdallr, the frost giants, and the mountain giants. Another son of Odin, Hermóðr, set off for the realm of the dead to convince the goddess Hel to let Baldr return to the Æsir. Thanks to Loki, however, his mission fails.

Fig. 10. The Death of Baldr. Illustration by Ólafur Brynjúlfsson, *Snorra Edda*, 1760.

Baldr corresponds with the archetype of an ideal being whose innocence is intolerable to a world that knows itself to be imperfect and blameworthy. After Ragnarök, Baldr will return to the world of men. The great antiquity of this god seems to be demonstrated by an inscription found in Utrecht dating back to the third or fourth century and dedicated to a deity named Baldruus.

📖 Lindow, *Murder and Vengeance among the Gods*; Ferdinand Detter, "Der Baldrmythus," *Beiträge zur Geschichte der deutschen Sprache und Literatur* 19 (1894): 495–510; Otto Höfler, "Balders Bestattung und die nordischen Felszeichnungen," *Anzeiger der Österreichischen Akademie der Wissenschaften, Phil.-Hist. Klasse 88* (1952): 343–72; Rudolf Much, "Balder," *Zeitschrift für deutsches Altertum* 61 (1924): 93–126.

BALDUNC: The Middle High German poem from the thirteenth or fourteenth century known to us the *Jüngerer Sigenot* (The Younger Version of the *Sigenot* Epic) informs us that during the course of his adventures, Dietrich von Bern frees the dwarf Baldunc from the clutches of a wild man. Baldunc expresses his gratitude by giving Dietrich a root which, when held in the same hand as a sword, makes it possible to pierce the wild man's skin. This dwarf has another root that destroys the properties of the first. Once their adversary is dead, more than a thousand dwarves emerge from the hollow mountain and celebrate. Dietrich informs Baldunc that he is looking for the giant Sigenot, and the dwarf gives him a stone that confers courage and strength on its owner as well as protection from hunger and thirst.

✦ *SIGENOT*

BÁLEYGR ("Eye of Fire"): One of Odin's bynames. In the work of Saxo Grammaticus, it appears as Bolwisus, who is described as the brother of a certain Bilwisus.

📖 Falk, *Odensheiti*.

BARA ("Wave"): One of the daughters of Ægir, the sea giant.

BARRI, BARRE: This is the name of the place where the god Freyr met the giantess Gerðr. It is either a small grove or an island, depending on the tradition.

BEATRIK (masc.): The Beatrik is a giant who appears in Tyrolean legends. He lives in inaccessible caves or in the deepest forests. He is so terrifying that no one has ever looked him in the face. In winter he haunts the summer grazing lands in the Alps, and woe to anyone who stumbles upon him there! He is not wicked and will do nothing to brave men who see him pass by and pretend not to see him. He is accompanied by a pack of puppies that barks constantly and are so furry that their heads, paws, and tails are invisible. He only comes close to settled areas in winter, most particularly at Christmas. It is said that he hunts witches called *Eguane*.

According to a tradition collected in Castelnuovo, near Borgo (Trentino, South Tyrol), the Beatrik owns a bowl of milk that he uses to put to sleep any people who are presumptuous enough to respond to his shout; he then cuts open their bellies and coils their intestines around a large comb that is close at hand!

📖 Schneller, *Märchen und Sagen aus Wälschtirol*, 203–9.

BELI ("Bawler"): The name of the giant who challenges the god Freyr during Ragnarök. Because Freyr had earlier given his sword to Gymir as a bride price for the hand of Gerðr, he fights with a stag's horn. He pierces Beli with it, killing him.

BELT OF POWER: One of the extraordinary objects owned by the god Thor. As indicated by its name (Old Norse *megingjörð*), this belt has the power to increase its owner's strength.

BEOWULF: Eponymous hero of *Beowulf,* the Old English epic that was composed in alliterative verse at some point between the seventh and ninth centuries. Beowulf is the nephew of Hygelac, king of the Geats. He goes to Denmark to help King Hroðgar, whose prestigious hall has been repeatedly visited by a demon named Grendel who has been carrying off his men, one after another. Beowulf meets Grendel in single combat and tears off one of his arms. The monster retreats to his lair, a lake in the middle of the marshes. Grendel's mother then enters the stage. Beowulf is forced to dive into the lake, at the bottom of which he finds a cave. There is a sword hanging on one wall of the cave, and Beowulf takes the weapon and uses it to slay the monstrous creature. Much later Beowulf learns that a dragon is ravaging his lands. Accompanied by the young Wiglaf, he confronts it in battle, kills it, and takes possession of the treasure the gigantic reptile had been guarding. He dies soon afterward, however, having succumbed to the wounds he received in the battle. His body is burned and buried in a mound together with the treasure.

Some of the episodes in this epic have analogs in other mythological lays and sagas, and several of the figures mentioned—such as Wayland the Smith, Attila, and Ermanaric—can also be found elsewhere. Beowulf's battle with Grendel corresponds closely to that of the Icelandic outlaw Grettir against the revenant Glamr; the two tales share a common source, most likely a story of a battle against a destructive dead man. The fight with a dragon is a common motif in tales of the Middle Ages.

📖 Fulk, Bjork, and Niles, eds., *Klaeber's 'Beowulf';* Crépin, ed., *Beowulf;* Willem Helder, "Beowulf and the Plundered Hoard," *Neuphilologische Mitteilungen* 88 (1977): 317–25; Sylvia Huntley Horowitz, "The Ravens in Beowulf," *Journal of English und Germanic Philology* 80 (1981): 502–11; Harald Kleinschmidt,

"Architecture and the Dating of Beowulf," *Poetica* 34 (1991): 39–56; Tomoaki Mizuno, "The Magical Necklace and the Fatal Corslet in Beowulf," *English Studies* 80 (1999): 377–97; Thomas Pettitt, "Beowulf: The Mark of the Beast and the Balance of Frenzy," *Neuphilologische Mitteilungen* 77 (1976): 526–35.

BERGELMIR: Grandson of the primordial giant Ymir and son of Þrúðgelmir. He and his wife survived the flood caused by the flowing of Ymir's blood, which drowned the rest of the giants. All the frost giants (*hrímþursar*) are descendants of Bergelmir.

BERGMÄNNCHEN (*Bergmännlein, Bergmönch, Knappenmanndl, Kobel, Gütel; gruvrå* in Sweden): A spirit of the mines, he is male and anthropomorphic but sometimes appears in animal form (horse, blackbird, fly, hornet). The ancient texts call him *daemon subterraneus* and *daemon metallicus*. Sometimes he is dangerous, sometimes helpful.

There is a story that in the eighteenth century two arquebusiers were sent to visit the mines between Innsbruck and Milo; they emerged twelve days later near Kitzbühl and reported what they had seen: villages, streams, a road. They met a small hunchbacked dwarf with a long

Fig. 11. Bergmännchen

gray beard carrying a staff and a lantern. He told them that they were among an underground people who had nothing in common with those living on the surface. He put them on the path to the exit. A similar legend appears to be connected to a Loiblerberg cave in Carniola (a region of present-day Slovenia).

📖 Agricola, *De re metallica;* Agricola, *De animantibus subterraneis;* G. Heilfurth, *Der Vorstellungskreis vom "Berggeist" bei Georg Agricola und seinen Zeitgenossen;* Grimm, *Deutsche Sagen,* no. 298.

BERGMÖNCH ("Monk of the Mines"): In the Harz Mountains of Saxony, the land of Baden, and the Grisons (Switzerland), this is a spirit of the mines who is giant in size and has white or gray hair. He punishes anybody who whistles or curses.

✦ *BERGMÄNNCHEN*

BERILLE: A wild woman who is the sister of the giant Tressan in the *Wolfdietrich* epic. She seeks to hang Wolfdietrich and attacks him with an iron club with sharpened corners because he killed her brother. She captures the hero, binds him, and goes to hide his weapons in a cave. While she is doing this a dwarf rescues Wolfdietrich from this dangerous predicament. One detail worth noting: her breasts are so large that she hits them with her feet when she runs.

BERLINGR ("Small Beam"): One of the four dwarves who forged Freyja's necklace, Brísingamen.

BERSERKR (pl. *Berserkir;* "Bear-shirt"): A race of Odinic warriors famous for their fury in battle. "[Odin's] men went to battle without coats of mail and acted like mad dogs or wolves. They bit their shields and were as strong as bears or bulls. They killed people, and neither fire nor iron affected them" (*Ynglinga saga,* chap. 6, in Sturluson, *Heimskringla,* trans. Hollander). They are also called *ulfheðnar,* "wolf-coats." A term that appears in the Eddic poem *Hárbarðsljóð* (Lay of Hárbarð) may possibly also represent a female counterpart in the form of "wolf women" (*vargynjur*). The figure of the beserkr frequently appears in the sagas. It was first mentioned in the ninth century.

✦ *HAMR, WEREWOLF*

Fig. 12. Helmet plates found in Torslunda, Sweden, dating from around the year 1000

Fig. 13. Masked warriors. Detail from the Gallehus Horn, early fifth century.

📖 Holbek and Piø, *Fabeldyr og sagnfolk*, 165–66; Güntert, *Über altisländische Berserker-Geschichten;* Samson, *Les Guerriers-fauves dans la Scandinavie ancienne, de l'âge de Vendel aux Vikings (VIe-XIe siècle);* François Delpech, "Hommes-fauves et fureurs animales. Aspects du thème zoomorphe dans le folklore de la péninsule Ibérique," in Jean-Paul Duviols and Annie Molinié-Bertrand, eds., *La Violence en Espagne et en Amérique (XVe–XIXe siècle)* (Paris: P.U.P.S., 1997), 59–82.

BESTLA: A giantess who is the daughter of Bölþorn. She married Borr, son of Búri, with whom she had three children: Odin, Vili, and Vé. Her name probably means "Bark."

BEYLA: Wife of Byggvir, servant or hypostasis of the god Freyr. Her name has been interpreted to mean either "Cow" or "Little Bee."

BIBUNG: In the *Wolfdietrich* epic, version D, this dwarf helps Wolfdietrich against Belmunt, brother of the giant Olfan, by giving him a ring and telling him about a spring whose water will endow whoever drinks it with the strength of fifteen men. He also tells him to stick his sword in sand, which will cause the giant's armor to soften. Bibung does this on account of his gratitude toward the hero's father, Hugdietrich.

BIL: An enigmatic goddess who is closely connected to the moon. According to Snorri Sturluson, she is an Ásynja and the daughter of Viðfinnr. Bil is most likely the personification of one of the moon's phases, the waning phase, which was considered harmful as it halted the growth of things. What we have here is apparently the transposition of a folk belief into the sphere of mythology.

◆ *BILWIZ, MANI*

BILEYGR ("Shifty-eyed" or "Feeble-eyed"): Another of Odin's titles; it alludes to the fact that this god is one-eyed because he offered one eye as a pledge to the giant Mímir to obtain knowledge.

📖 Falk, *Odensheiti.*

Fig. 14. Bileygr

BILLINGR: This was most likely a giant. He is the father of a young woman Odin wished to seduce, but she managed to slip away, leaving a female dog in the bed in her place.

BILLUNC: A kidnapping dwarf who dwells in a castle behind a fountain; it is impossible to get past it unless one has a certain root in the mouth and is clad in a cloak of invisibility. Through deceit Billunc had taken over the lands of the son of Tarnunc, another dwarf. He owns two automatons—one plays music and the other pours water—and has two giants in his service. Billunc abducts the wife of Wolfdietrich. Later, when freeing his wife, Wolfdietrich kills him.

BILRÖST, BIFRÖST ("Trembling Road of the Sky"): The bridge built by the gods connecting Ásgarðr to the Earth. At its end in Ásgarðr is Himinbjörg where the god Heimdallr keeps watch against any potential assault by the giants. This construction is also called the Bridge of the Æsir (Ásbrú), because the Æsir cross it each day when going to the Well of Urðr. Snorri Sturluson describes Bifröst as a rainbow.

📖 Alfred Ebenbauer, "Bilröst," in *Reallexikon der germanischen Altertumkunde*, 2nd ed., vol. III, 1–2.

BILSKÍRNIR: Name of the hall owned by Thor. It is in Þrúðvangr, and, like Valhalla, it has 540 doors.

BILWIZ: A small demon akin to a dwarf that has been the subject of legend since the Middle Ages. It shoots invisible arrows that carry disease. It is a representative of the goddess Bil, who is the personification of the waning moon and has a paralyzing effect on living beings. He was transformed into a crop demon at the end of the fifteenth century, and the last sheaf of the harvest was called "the Bilwiz cut" (*Bilwisschnitt*) and set aside for him.

📖 Lecouteux, "Der Bilwiz: Überlegungen zu seiner Entstehungs- und Entwicklungsgeschichte," *Euphorion* 82 (1988): 238–50.

BLAUHÜTL ("Blue Hat"): The name of the Wild Huntsman in Saxon Lusatia. According to one legend his actual identity was the Lord of Biberstein, whose obsession for hunting led to his being condemned to an afterlife in which he eternally indulges his passion for hunting.

📖 Haupt, *Sagenbuch der Lausitz*, 122.

BLAUMANTEL ("Blue Mantle"): One of the names of the devil.

BJÖRN ("Bear"): One of Odin's titles that surely relates to his role as the leader of the berserkers.

   📖 Falk, *Odensheiti.*

BLÁINN: Another name for Ymir, the primordial giant.

   ✦ *COSMOGONY*

BLÅKULLA: The name of the Sabbat location for Swedish witches. It is an immense plain that has a large house at its center. It is said that a church is there with a demon the size of a twelve-year-old child on the altar; this is where the ceremony takes place.

BLIKJANDABÖL ("Pale Misfortune"): The name of the bed curtains in the dwelling of Hel, the goddess of the dead.

   ✦ *HEL*

BLINDI ("Blind"): One of Odin's titles; it alludes to the fact that the god has only one eye.

   📖 Falk, *Odensheiti.*

BLOCKSBERG: The former name for Brocken (Harz, Germany). Since the fourteenth century this mountain has been considered to be the site for the nocturnal gatherings of spirits and witches who travel there on Saint John's Day, All Souls' Day, May Day, the third Thursday in Lent, and Saint Michael's Day.

BLÓÐUGHADDA ("The One with the Blood-stained Hair"): One of the daughters of Ægir and Rán, the goddess of the sea.

BLOOD EAGLE: This is a torture that consists of making vertical incisions in the victim's back on each side of the spine, through which the lungs are then pulled out from the rib cage and splayed on the back like wings. This bears a strong resemblance to a ritual procedure; perhaps the victims were dedicated to Odin this way.

BLOÞÖRN: ✦ BLOOD EAGLE

BLOTKELDA: ✦ SACRIFICIAL BOG

BOÐN ("Vessel"): One of the two vessels in which the blood of Kvasir was kept; the other was called Són. With this blood the dwarves Fjalarr and Galarr brewed a wondrous mead that transforms every man who drinks of it into a poet.

✦ *KVASIR*

BOGEYMAN: There are hundreds of these kinds of creatures in the Germanic regions. Besides the characters that are fabricated in an impromptu fashion to scare children so they will not behave foolishly, there are a number of these beings in folk mythology. Among them are the Bogeyman of the Woods (Mecklenburg), a wild huntsman; the Night Hunter (*Nachtjäger,* Silesia); the *Alp* (Transylvania), an incarnation of the elf; the Rye Wolf (*Roggenwolf*) and the *Tittenwîf* (Mecklenburg); the *Erftenmöin* (Altmark region, Germany); the *Huri* or *Nachthuri* (Four Canton region, Switzerland), who throws children into a large sack, which brings to mind the *Klaubauf* of Bavaria and Austria, an individual who accompanies Saint Nicholas and carries disobedient and lazy children away in his sack (✦ KNECHT RUPRECHT); and *Hanselina* who cuts off the hands of children who steal grapes (Switzerland). In Schleswig-Holstein the *Büsemann* lives in the stable, but he is also a merman. On the German island of Föhr in the North Sea we have Jug the Blind (*der blinde Jug*), and in Dithmarschen, the *Pulterklaas.*

BÖLÞORN ("Thorn of Woe"): Father of the giantess Bestla, the mother of Odin and his brothers.

BÖLVERKR ("Evil-doer"): This is the name that Odin uses for himself in the following tale. One day Odin encounters the mowers of the giant Baugi and provokes a quarrel between them over a whetstone, causing them all to kill each other. Odin takes their place in Baugi's service and is promised a sip of the wondrous mead owned by his brother Suttungr as compensation. Odin does not receive this payment.

✦ *KVASIR*

📖 Falk, *Odensheiti.*

BÖXENWOLF ("Wolf in Short Pants"): This is the name for were-wolf in northern Germany. It designates an individual who has made a pact with the devil in return for a belt that allows him to change into a powerful wolf. He sometimes behaves like a perching spirit, hurling himself on people's backs and forcing them to carry him a great distance.

✦ *AUFHOCKER*

📖 Kuhn and Schwartz, *Norddeutsche Sagen, Märchen und Gebräuche,* 245.

BRACTEATE: A type of embossed single-sided medallion. Most of the Germanic bracteates date from the first to fourth centuries CE. A man's head or a horseman is often depicted on them with solar symbols, swastikas, and triskeles.

Fig. 15. Two examples of Germanic bracteates with mythological and runic motifs; first to fourth century CE

BRAGARFULL: Name of the toast that accompanies solemn oaths. It is primarily made on two specific occasions: the winter solstice Jól feast and during the funeral libation. Snorri writes the word as *bragafull,* meaning "toast of the god Bragi."

BRAGI: God of poetry. He is an Æsir god famous for his wisdom and eloquence. He married Iðunn, the goddess who possessed the apples of eternal youth. It is thought that this god could be simply a deification of the great ninth-century skald Bragi Boddason the Old, but it would be more reasonable to assume that this historical figure was assimilated into an older god bearing the same name. Kennings for Bragi call him Son of Odin, Long-bearded God, and First Maker of Poetry.

 📖 Heinz Klingenberg, "Bragi," *Reallexikon der germanischen Altertumskunde,* 2nd ed., vol. III, 334–37.

BREIÐABLIK ("Far Shining"): Name of the dwelling of Baldr, the son of Odin and Frigg.

BREITHUT, LANGHUT ("Broad Hat," "Long Hat"): This is a spirit that sometimes takes on the appearance of a perching entity, a ghostly tree, or a chopping block, forms often assumed by the Night Huntsman. In Norse mythology one of Odin's bynames, Síðhöttr, has the same meaning. In Germany, Breithut is a demon dressed in the style of the seventeenth and eighteenth centuries. In the Alemannic domain the leader of the Wild Hunt is called *der Muet (Muot) mit dem Breit huot,* "The *Muot* with the wide-brimmed hat," with *Muot* being a corruption of "Wod, Wodan."

 📖 Meyer, *Germanische Mythologie,* 231.

BRIDGI: A kind of monstrous shark found in the waters off the Shetland Islands that can approach boats unnoticed, because its dorsal fin resembles a sail. It either breaks boats apart or drags them to the sea bottom by seizing them between its dorsal and ventral fins. Sailors always bring an ax aboard ship in case they need to defend themselves against this beast. An amber pearl dropped into the sea from time to time is often enough to send it fleeing.

 📖 Jean Renaud, "Le peuple surnaturel des Shetland," *Artus* 21–22 (1986): 28–32.

BRIMIR: Hall where the gods make their libations.

BRÍSINGAMEN ("Necklace of Brisings"): This necklace was forged by the dwarves Alfrigg, Dvalinn, Berlingr, and Grerr. To obtain it, Freyja had to sleep with each of them. Loki found this out and repeated it to Odin, who ordered him to bring the necklace to him. Odin returned it to Freyja on condition she provoke an eternal battle between two kings, and the goddess complied with his command.

✦ *HJAÐNINGAVÍG*

BROCKEN: ✦ BLOCKSBERG

BROKKR ("Smith"): A dwarf who was brother and companion to Sindri. These two dwarves forged the treasures of the gods: Draupnir, the ring of Baldr; Gullinborsti, Freyr's boar; and Mjöllnir, Thor's hammer.

BROONIE: The name of a household spirit of the Shetland Islands, to whom modest offerings are made on various occasions, such as when brewing beer, making butter, or milling flour. On the western part of the archipelago it is also considered to be a guardian of the grain stores on the farm.

📖 Jean Renaud, "Le peuple surnaturel des Shetland," *Artus* 21–22 (1986): 28–32.

BROWNIE: Dwarf and domestic spirit found in England and Ireland. It is helpful and intrepid. If compensated for its labors by giving it a green garment, it will vanish. Once upon a time it was said that a brownie was part of every good family.

BRÚNI ("Brown"): One of Odin's names. It is also the name of a dwarf, and it so happens that in England small supernatural creatures are called brownies.

📖 Falk, *Odensheiti*.

BRYNHILDR ("Hildr with the Breastplate"): A valkyrie who disobeyed Odin by giving the victory to Agnarr. Odin punished her by pricking her with the thorn of sleep as she lay behind a rampart of shields and a wall of fire on Hindarfjall Mountain. Sigurðr made his way there, removed her breastplate, and awakened her. She told him of her life and taught him wisdom and learned arts. Supplanted by Guðrún in Sigurðr's heart, she commits suicide after he is murdered. In the *Nibelungenlied*, Brünhild retains some traits indicative of the mythic origin: she has extraordinary strength, but this is tied to her virginity. She is deceived by Siegfried on two occasions and disappears from the story once the hero has died.

Fig. 16. Primary scenes from the legend of Sigurðr/Siegfried on a wooden portal of Hylestad Church (Norway), circa 1200

A: Death of Reginn
B: Burning of Sigurðr
C: The nuthatches' prediction
D: The treasure carried by Grani,
   Sigurðr's steed

The engraved runes in the border state: "Si(g)rid, mother of Alfrik, daughter of Orm, made this bridge for the spirit of Holmger, her husband, the father of Sigröd."

Fig. 17. Carved stone of Ramsund in Södermanland (Sweden)

BUKOW, BOODIE: The name of a household spirit in the Shetland Islands and Scotland; he wears bells on his clothes.

BURGUNDIANS: A Germanic people who most likely originated on the island of Bornholm, once called Borgundarholm, in the Baltic Sea south of Sweden, or they may have possibly originated from Bordung in Norway. They traveled south in the fifth century, capturing Mainz, and settled along the Rhine. Defeated by the Hun auxiliaries of the Roman Patrician Aetius, the Burgundians moved on into Savoy and Provence. Their king, Gundobad (ca. 473–516), ordered the *Lex Burgundorum* (Burgundian Legal Code) to be set down in writing. The preface to the laws provides a list of kings, many of whose names appear in Germanic heroic poetry and in the *Nibelungenlied;* for example, Gibica, Gudomar, Gislahar (= Giselher), and Gundaharius (= Gunther). The Burgundian kings were famous for the treasure they owned, which entered into legend as the gold of the *Nibelungenlied.* In the latter poem the Burgundian noblemen are named Gunther, Gernot, and Giselher; they live in Worms, and their sister is Kriemhild, who marries Siegfried. After his murder she marries Etzel (Attila) and lures her brothers to Etzelburg to avenge the murder of her husband, and they are all massacred.

✦ *ALBERICH, ANDVARI*

BÚRI ("Begetter"): The ancestor of all the gods. They emerged thanks to Auðumla the cow licking the ice that covered the world. Búri was capable of self-reproduction, and he had a son named Burr (or Borr), who married Bestla; she gave birth to Odin, Vili, and Vé.

BURR or BORR ("Son"): The son of Búri, he wed the giantess Bestla, daughter of Bölþorn, and she bore him three children: Odin, Vili, and Vé.

BUTZ (German *Putz, Box, Butzenmann;* Danish *busemand, boesman, böög*): A generic word used to designate demons, ghosts, dwarves, kobolds, and household spirits. It sometimes assumes the form of an old peasant or a soldier. It is thought to take its name from an old verb meaning "to make noise," or else the term reflects an aspect of its personality, with Butz then meaning "little chopping block."

 📖 Lindig, *Hausgeister,* 55 et passim.

BUTZEGRAALE (neut.): The name of a bogeyman of Württemberg.

BYGGVIR ("Barley"): Servant or hypostasis of the god Freyr. He boasts of knowing the art of brewing good beer. Byggvir was most likely originally a grain spirit.

BYLEISTR: One of the two brothers of the god Loki.

BYLGJA ("Wave"): One of the nine daughters of the sea giant Ægir.

CHANGELING (German *Wechselbalg, Wechselbutte*): Supernatural beings, especially dwarves, commonly substitute their own children for those of humans. The German designations for the changeling or substituted child are *Wechselbalg* and *Wechselbutte;* in Old Norse, the changeling is called *skiptingr* and *vixling;* in Latin, it is *cambio.*

Changelings can be recognized by the following characteristics. They are slow to grow and remain puny; they do not speak, and their hunger is never satisfied. There is a whole series of procedures for causing them to speak and thus reveal their true nature. A person can also beat them: their mother will immediately come running, bringing back the human child whom she has treated well.

📖 Doulet, *Quand les démons enlevaient les enfants*; Grambo, *Svart katt over veien*, 29; Grimm, *Deutsche Sagen*, nos. 81–82; Ilmar Arens and Bengt af Klintberg, "Bortbytingssägner i en gotländsk dombok frå 1690," *Rig* 62:3 (1979): 89–97.

Fig. 18. Changeling. Illustration by Eyvind Nielson, 1921.

CHARM: A very ancient form of verse used for the conjuration of gods and spirits. They are especially common in Old High German and in Old English. The most famous are the Old High German *Merseburg Charms* in which the gods Wodan (Odin), Frîja, Volla, Sinthgunt, and Phol are named. In England the charms fall under the heading of folk mythology and are intended to provide protection from dwarves and the shot they fire, as well as from the Æsir, nightmares, and witches. The best-known examples are *The Nine Herbs Charm, For a Sudden Stitch,* and *Against a Dwarf.* The value of the charms collected from the British Isles is that they reveal the deities in a decayed state. This is how the Æsir have been conflated with evil demons and accorded the same status as nightmares and witches. Furthermore, these charms show us that the preferred method for a supernatural being to take action is by shooting an arrow. In German lumbago was once called *Alpschuß,* "elf shot." In all the Germanic countries, the names of diseases are often derived from the names of supernatural entities reduced to the status of demons.

✦ *MERSEBURG CHARMS*

📖 Lecouteux, *Charmes, Conjurations et Bénédictions,* Lecouteux, *Dictionary of Ancient Magic Words and Spells;* Lecouteux, *The Book of Grimoires*; Jean-Paul Allard, "Du second Charme de Mersebourg au Viatique de Weingarten," *Études Indo-Européennes* 14 (1985): 33–53, with an additional note by Jean Haudry at 54–59.

CHIMMEKE, CHIM, JIMMEKEN ("Little Joachim"): The name of a *drac* and rapping spirit that haunts a castle in Pomerania. He is said to have cut a kitchen boy into little pieces for drinking the milk that had been left out for him.

📖 Grimm, *Deutsche Sagen,* no. 273; Linhart, *Hausgeister in Franken,* 52–53 et passim.

CHLUNGERI: The name of a female demon associated with spinning in Alemannic Switzerland. She has the appearance of a humpbacked woman from the front with long nails and crooked nose, and she lives in a cave. The *Chlungeri* travel about during the Twelve Days to verify if spinners have spun their yarn properly; they make balls from the work of those who have been lazy.

📖 Vernaleken, *Alpensagen,* 37–38.

COSMIC TREE: ✦ YGGDRASILL

COSMOGONY: In the beginning there was chaos, Ginnungagap, a bottomless abyss that extended between Niflheimr (the land of ice, shadow, and mist) in the north and Muspellsheimr (the land of fire) in the south. Rivers flowing out of the south toward Niflheimr became frost-covered and subsided in the vast, frozen waste. Gradually these masses of frozen water filled the abyss, and the southern winds, which were growing warmer and warmer, began melting the ice. Water drops enlivened by the wind combined to form the body of the giant Ymir, who was soon able to feed from the cow Auðumla, born the same way. Ymir began sweating, and a man and woman grew beneath his left arm, while one of his feet engendered a son with his other foot. By licking the ice Auðumla caused the emergence of a man named Búri who was capable of reproduction like Ymir. He had a son, Burr (or Borr), who married one of Ymir's descendants, Bestla. From their union were born the gods Odin, Vili, and Vé. They murdered Ymir and created the world using his body parts. From his bones they made the mountains and from his skull, the sky; they used his blood to create the sea. Once they had finished, the gods placed a dwarf at each of the four cardinal points to hold up the celestial vault.

COSMOLOGY: Roughly speaking, the world consists of Miðgarðr, the world of men; Ásgarðr, the realm of the gods; and Útgarðr, the realm of the giants, demons, and all harmful beings. The realm of the dead, presided over by the goddess Hel, lies beneath Miðgarðr. Jötunheimr, which is inhabited by the giants, lies to the east. The vertical axis of these worlds is the cosmic tree, Yggdrasill, and its horizontal consistency is ensured by the Miðgarðsormr, the great sea serpent that encircles the world. Ásgarðr is in the center of Miðgarðr, to which it is connected by a bridge—Bifröst, or Ásbrú. The world of men is separated from Jötunheimr by rivers that never freeze as well as by the Iron Forest (Járnviðr), where giants that have the shape of wolves dwell.

D

DACHSTEINWEIBL: The "Woman of the Dachstein Massif" (the *Drei-Länder-Berg*, the "Mountain of Three States") is a witch who is small in size, wrinkled, and covered with warts. Her appearance is a portent of bad weather or a catastrophe. It is said she was once a haughty, evil cowherd who was transformed into a hideous woman and condemned to wander until the Final Judgment.

 📖 Adrian, ed., *Alte Sagen aus dem Salzburger Land*, 89–90.

DAGR ("Day"): The son of Nótt ("Night") and Dellingr, he is the personification of day. He is the ancient founder of the line of Döglingar, which includes Helgi, murderer of King Hundingr. Dagr rides the horse Drasill.

DÁINN ("Death"): 1. Dwarf who, with Nabbi, crafted the boar Hildisvíni, on which Freyja rides. 2. One of the four stags that graze among the branches of Yggdrasill.

DARK ELVES: ✦ DÖKKÁLFAR

DESTINY: Although English has only five words (the other four are fate, fortune, lot, and luck) to express this concept, ancient Scandinavian had at least fifteen terms to express the notion of fate. This range of expressions testifies to the importance of the concept and its many subtleties: destiny can be neutral, objective, subjective, active or passive, beneficial or harmful, collective or individual, personified, symbolic, and so forth. It is therefore no surprise to find its echo in the mythology. It is embodied by the *Dísir* (Dises) or *Nornir* (Norns), the latter group being often depicted as spinners.

 ✦ *URÐR, WURD*

 📖 Régis Boyer, "Herfjötur(r)," in *Visages du destin dans les mythologies: Mélanges*

Jacqueline Duchemin, ed. François Jouan (Paris: Les Belles Lettres, 1983), 153–68; Boyer, "Fate as a 'Deus Otiosus' in the *Íslendingasögur: A* Romantic View?" in *Sagnaskemmtun: Studies in Honour of Hermann Pálsson,* ed. Rudolf Simek, et al. (Vienna and Cologne: Böhlau, 1986), 61–67.

DIABOLICAL HUNTSMAN: It was during the thirteenth century, thanks to the writing of the Cistercian monk Caesarius von Heisterbach (*Dialogus miraculorum atque magnum visionum,* XII, 20), that we find mention of a diabolical huntsman in the following story. A priest's concubine on her deathbed urgently requested that a new pair of sturdy shoes with heels be made for her and placed on her feet, which was done. The following night, a good while before dawn and when the moon was still shining, a knight was riding with his squire. They heard the cries of a woman in distress and were wondering who it could be when a woman began running toward them at top speed, screaming, "Help me, help me!" The knight immediately dismounted, drew a circle around himself with his sword, and set the woman, whom he knew well, inside it. She was wearing only a shirt and the shoes described above. Then, all at once, they heard a far-off noise that resembled that of a huntsman blowing his horn in the most horrible way, and the howls of his hunting dogs preceding him. When the woman heard these noises, she began trembling from head to foot, but the knight, having learned the cause, entrusted his horse to his squire, wrapped the locks of the woman's hair around his left hand, and brandished his sword with his right. When the infernal huntsman drew near, the woman began screaming at the knight, "Let me go! Let me go! Look: he is coming!" He continued holding on to her with all his might. But the woman continued struggling until her hair tore loose, and she fled. Racing in pursuit, the demon caught her and threw her across his horse so that her arms and head hung down over one side and her legs down over the other. A short time later the knight saw the demon carrying off his prey. The knight returned to the village in the morning, told people of what he had seen, and showed them the clump of hair. As no one wished to believe him, they opened the grave and all could see that the woman inside no longer had any hair.

📖 Lecouteux, *Phantom Armies of the Night,* 56–64.

DIALA (pl. Dialen): The *Diala* is a wild woman in Swiss folk traditions. They are incredibly beautiful, kind, and helpful, and they live in caves where they sleep on beds of moss. Unfortunately, they also have goat feet. They are also called *Waldfänken*.

📖 Vernaleken, *Alpensagen*, 63–65, 129, W. Lynge, "Dialen, Unifrauen und Vilen: Motivgeschichtliches zu den weiblichen Sagengestalten mit tierfüßen im Alpen- und Karstbereich," *Österreichische Zeitschrift für Volkskunde* 60 (1957): 194–218.

DÍAR ("Gods"): This is the name given by Snorri Sturluson to the group of twelve priests in Ásgarðr who serve Odin. "They were to have charge of sacrifices and to judge between men. . . . All the people were to serve them and show them reverence" (*Ynglinga Saga*, chap. 2, in Sturluson, *Heimskringla,* trans. Hollander).

DIDKEN (sg. Didko): These are elementary spirits of the region of Galicia in eastern Europe; their name makes them akin to the Slovak and Russian *Dedusko* and the *Diblik* (imp) in Bohemia. They appear in the form of a dandy with a magpie's tail, tight pants, and a top hat. They are able to transform into dogs, cats, mice, and so forth. Their lives can only be cut short by lightning or by a rapid right-to-left movement of the hand of a human being. They can be recognized by their shining green eyes. There are two different kinds of these creatures: one type lives in a house; the other is wild and makes contracts with the master of the household. The *Didken* will accept old clothes, a corner in which to sleep, and food that does not contain any salt. If the contract is respected, they make sure the house is run properly and watch over the animals. When the master of the house dies, they will enter the service of his heirs without a contract, but if they are turned down or are not acknowledged, they will cause such a racket in the house that the inhabitants will be forced to leave. The *Didken* will then depart to live in the swamps, where they will become wild and wicked. They will nonetheless still continue to offer their services. Whoever wishes to take them up on their offer must cook nine round loaves without salt on the eve of Saint George's Day, go to the crossroads at night, and, speaking certain spells, invite the *Didken* to come eat the bread.

This kind of creature can also be obtained from an egg that should be buried beneath the threshold to the yard; a *Didko* will hatch from it nine years later.

📖 Vernaleken, *Mythen und Bräuche des Volkes in Österreich*, 238–40.

DÍSABLÓT ("Sacrifice to the Dises"): Offerings made to the *Dísir* (Dises) at the start of winter, mid-October in Norway, and in February in Sweden. Little is known about this expression of domestic worship, except that it featured a banquet. Most likely the purpose was to gain the favor of the Dises, understood here as fertility deities. The origin of these minor gods is certainly Indo-European, and the Germanic Dises have their counterpart in the Vedic *dhisanās*.

✦ *DISES*

DISAPPEARANCE: ✦ ABDUCTION

DÍSARSALR ("Hall of the Dise"): The name of a temple in Uppsala (Sweden) consecrated to the Dises. The use of the singular here is strange and unusual as we generally see the plural form, *Dísir*, used as the Dises are an undifferentiated entity.

DISES (Old Norse *dís*, pl. *dísir*): Female deities who may be identical to the *Idisi* cited in the *First Merseburg Charm* and whose name can also be found in the work of Tacitus, in Idisiaviso, the name of a plain where Germanicus met Arminius (Hermann) in battle. The tradition is quite muddled, because the Dises are much like the valkyries and the Norns (the Germanic Fates) and play the role of guardian spirits as well, which makes them akin to the *fylgjur*. It is said they rush up when children are born, which likens them to Roman fairies. The Dises were also regarded as local land spirits that governed fertility, as testified by the *landdísasteinar* (stones of the Dises of the land) in the Ísafjörður region of northwestern Iceland. Several place-names also attest to the reality of the worship they received. The Dises are probably best interpreted in the context of the mother goddesses. It should be noted that the goddess Freyja is called *vanadís*, the "Dise of the Vanir," and the giantess Skaði is called *öndurdís*, the "Dise of the Skis."

📖 Boyer, *La Grande Déesse du Nord*, 77–78.

DIVINE TWINS: The Germanic past offers a wide variety of images of divine twins, and there are also many sibling pairs (such as Freyr and Freyja, Hengist and Horsa, Ibor and Aio, etc.). These are primarily twin myths and are not directly connected with the Dioscuri of classical antiquity.

✦ *ALCI, HENGIST and HORSA, IBOR and AIO*

📖 Monfort, *Les Jumeaux dans la littérature et les mythes germaniques;* Ward, *The Divine Twins;* François Delpech, "Les jumeaux exclus: cheminements hispanique d'une mythologie de l'impureté," in *Les problèmes de l'exclusion en Espagne (XVIe–XVIIe siècles),* ed. Augustin Redondo (Paris: Publications de la Sorbonne, 1983), 177–203; Jaan Puhvel, "Aspects of Equine Functionality," in *Myth and Law among the Indo-Europeans,* ed. Puhvel, 159–92; Hellmut Rosenfeld, "Germanischer Zwillingskult und indogermanischer Himmelsgottglaube," in *Märchen, Mythos, Dichtung: Festschrift zum 90. Geburtstag Friedrich von der Leyens am 19. August 1963,* eds. Hugo Kuhn and Kurt Schier (Munich: Beck, 1963), 269–86.

DODAMANDERL (neut.): This is the personification of death in the form of a thin, ugly man with a long nose and a hunchback. The *Dodamanderl* is the subject of many songs, some of which claim he is the son of the *Dodamon.*

📖 Vernaleken, *Mythen und Bräuche des Volkes in Österreich,* 71–75.

DODAMON (masc.): The personification of death, the *Dodamon* appears fleetingly on a golden horse at certain times, often with a scythe or a long white nightcap. It is said that whoever sees him on his horse shall be blessed with happiness, but if seen with his scythe or nightcap, the individual will have no more than three years left to live.

📖 Vernaleken, *Mythen und Bräuche des Volkes in Österreich,* 280–82.

DOFRI: A giant that lives in the mountain bearing his name, the Dofrafjall. His name appears in the *þulur* lists and in *Haralds þáttr hárfagra* (The Tale of Harald Fairhair).

DOG: This animal is the first thing one meets at the gate to Hel (✦ GARMR), and his chest is covered in blood. He bears strong resemblance to the Greek Cerberus. Mention is also made in the mythology of the dogs Gífr and Geri, who guard the home of Menglöð, a hypostasis of the goddess Freyja. In more recent Scandinavian Yule customs, a figure wearing a dog mask appears in holiday processions. It should finally be noted that the remains of dogs have been discovered in the funeral mounds. The hero Helgi is famous for slaying King Hundingr—a name that literally means "the descendant of the dog," being composed of *hund,* "dog," plus the suffix *-ingr/-ungr,* which indicates genetic descent. (Incidentally, the same type of construction can be seen in the name of the Merovingians, the "descendants of Meroveus.") A name like Hundingr carries totemic associations, for which there is much supporting evidence.

In folk belief the dog is often the form assumed by the soul in torment, as in the story related in by the fifteenth-century Rhenish peasant Arndt Buschmann.

📖 Lecouteux, ed. and trans., *Dialogue avec un revenant (XVe siècle).*

DÖKKÁLFAR ("Dark Elves"): These beings are only ever mentioned in the *Snorra Edda.* They are almost certainly dwarves and not elves. They are blacker than pitch and live in the world that bears their name, Svartálfheimr. They are mortal enemies of the *ljósálfar,* the Light Elves. They are also the smiths who forge the treasures of the gods.

DÓMALDI: A mythical Swedish king from the major family of the Ynglings (the Ynglingar, the descendants of Yngvi-Freyr). Following three years of famine, he was slain by his subjects, the Svear. Snorri Sturluson reports: "The chieftains held a council, and they agreed that the famine probably was due to Dómaldi, their king, and that they should sacrifice him for better seasons" (*Ynglinga saga,* chap. 15, in Sturluson, *Heimskringla,* trans. Hollander).

DONANADL: This is the name of a Tyrolean dwarf. He is generally regarded as being very good-hearted. He is old and seems of great age and is also always clad in rags. He most often appears by himself but is sometimes accompanied by others like him.

If a *Donanadl* appears at any time in the high pastures where the flock is grazing for the summer, then one can be sure that the livestock will be protected from all accidents, and their milk production will be greater than is the case in other meadows that do not enjoy the protection of such a kind and beneficial spirit. If snow falls at any time during the summer they will guide the livestock away from the steep and slippery

Fig. 19. Meeting the Donanadl

slopes, where they are at risk of falling, to safer pastures. The Donanadl often visit the chalets where they eat with the shepherds, cowherds, and milkers when offered food. They often vanish suddenly and without a trace from the company of those with whom they are feasting. During the winter they live in the mangers of the stables. If the cowherd is late getting to the barn he can be certain to find the spirits already taking care of the animals and giving them large quantities of fodder. Although they are quite prodigal, they are never lacking for anything.

📖 Adrian, ed., *Alte Sagen aus dem Salzburger Land*, 90–92.

DONAR ("Thunder"): Name for Thor among the southern Germans. In Old English the name is Þunor. In the Germano-Roman continental inscriptions, Donar is frequently conflated with Hercules, in conformance with the *interpretatio romana* of the Germanic gods. His name can be found in the vernacular names for Thursday, such as Old English *Þunresdæg* and Old High German *Donarestâc*. In 725, Saint Boniface destroyed his sacred oak in Geismar (Hesse, Germany). An Old Saxon baptismal vow for rejecting paganism says: "I renounce Thunær, Uuôden, and Saxnôt, and all the demons that are their companions."

✦ *THOR*

DOPPELSAUGER: ✦ ZWIESAUGER

DÓRI: The name of a dwarf mentioned in strophe 15 of *Völuspá* in the *Poetic Edda*. Dóri appears as one of the thirteen dwarves in J. R. R. Tolkien's *The Hobbit* (1937). The name has been variously interpreted as meaning "The Harmer," "The Fool," or "The Peg."

📖 Lotte Motz, "New Thoughts on Dwarf-Names in Old Icelandic," *Frühmittelalterliche Studien* 7 (1973): 100–117.

DRAC, DRACHE: The *drac* (cf. German *Drache,* "drake, dragon") is connected with money and brings fortune to the house where he has chosen to live. *Drac* is a generic term that is applied in the Germanic regions to an igneous phenomenon that is often ascribed with demonic qualities—hence its name of "devil" (*Teufel*)—or is attributed to elves, for it is often simultaneously called an *alf* or a kobold. Depending on the country and region, it basically has the meaning of "spirit" and is then given a connection to certain fruits of the earth.

When the *drac* flies through the air and enters the house through the chimney or through a hole in the roof he has the appearance of a long, fiery pole, but he is also described as a little man wearing a red coat—hence his name of *Rödjackte* in Pomerania. His igneous nature emerges clearly from many names found in Lower Saxony such as "Burning Tail" (*Gluhschwanz, Glûswanz*), which suggests a trail of fire, and "Red Iron" (*Glûbolt*). In Westphalia the names that are based on the word *Brand,* "fire," refer to the same notions. Sometimes the *drac* looks like a simple ball of fire or a flaming star. This connection with flames explains why he is attributed in some places with the same form as the devil or a sorcerer, and his preferred abode is regularly assumed to be the chimney or behind the stove—a location that in Germany bears the significant name of "Hell" (*Hölle*).

Regionally his other aspects are those of the common household spirits. The *drac* often assumes the form of an animal—such as a rooster, a hen, or a lizard—and a variety of colors, both depending on the load he is carrying back to his master. If he is sparkling, then he is carrying silver; if he is dark or gray, he is transporting vermin; when he is golden, he is loaded down with gold or wheat; and so on. Most of the time he is acquired by concluding a pact with the devil, but it is also said that the *drac* is born from a yolkless egg. He begins life by causing problems in the barns and stables before flying away to lead his life as a drac. When an egg like this is found it must be thrown over the house so it breaks. In Latvia it is believed to be the outer soul, meaning the double (alter ego) of an evil man, a sorcerer, or a magician. The *drac's* nature is ambiguous, because he enriches his owner at the expense of his neighbors, whose property he steals and brings back. A *drac* is therefore feared by people at the same time as they wish to own one. This ambiguity is linked, of course, to his being conflated with the devil and his retinue, to sorcerers and other magicians.

The *drac* must be given offerings—such as cakes, bits of meat, milk, and millet gruel—that are placed in the hearth or on the stove. These are regarded as his wages for his activity. If one forgets to "pay" him, his vengeance is terrible and reflective of his nature: he sets fire to the house! But if his services are unsatisfactory, it is possible to punish him.

📖 Lecouteux, *The Tradition of Household Spirits,* 56, 143, 153–55, 162–63, 185–86.

DRACHENKOPP: This is a corruption of a Greek word *dracontopodes,* "dragon-footed," used to describe the feet of the giants in ancient mythology and, later, a serpent with a human head. This is part of a scholarly tradition, passed on by the *Physiologus,* the most famous of all the bestiaries, and by the thirteenth-century encyclopedists.

📖 Lecouteux, "Drachenkopp," *Euphorion* 72 (1978): 339–43.

DRAGON: The most dreadful monster of all is the dragon, the largest of all reptiles. "When it comes out of its lair," says Isidore of Seville, "he does it so roughly that it makes the air glow as if it were on fire; he has a large head, a crest, a narrow mouth from which its breath and tongue emerge; its strength is in its tail and not its teeth, and it kills by the blows it makes rather than its bite." This description is that of naturalists and scholars, who do not attribute wings or feet to the beast. Logically examining the dragon's anatomy, Albertus Magnus showed that it could not have feet, "because with such length, it could not move forward with a small number of feet." This is probably why more than one author claimed the beast had six, twelve, and even twenty-four paws. Discussing wings, Albertus admits it could have them, but that they needed to be

Fig. 20. Types of dragons.
Konrad Gessner, *Schlangenbuch*,
Zurich, 1589.

immense and membraneous, he adds; otherwise the wings would be unable to carry it. Some scholars believed that dragons had a kind of mane, but only Bartholomeus Anglicus thought it had teeth.

The image of the dragon in entertainment literature hardly coincided with these minimal descriptions. At the beginning of the thirteenth century Wirnt von Grafenberg provided the best description of the monster.

> Its head was enormous, black, and shaggy; its beak was bare, a fathom long and a yard wide, pointed in front and sharp as a newly whetted spear; in its jaw were teeth like the tusks of a boar. Broad horny scales covered it, and a sharp spine—the sort with which a crocodile cuts ships in two—went from head to tail.
>
> The dragon had a long tail—as dragons do. . . . The dragon had a comb like a rooster's, but huge; its belly was green, its eyes red, its sides yellow; its body was round as a candle, and the sharp spine was pale yellow; its two ears were like those of a mule. The dragon's breath was foul and stank worse than carrion that has lain for a long time in the hot sun. Its griffin-like feet were ugly and as hairy as a

Fig. 21. Combat of a valiant knight (Harald) against a dragon. Olaus Magnus, *Historia de gentibus septentrionalibus,* Rome, 1555.

bear's. It had two beautiful wings with feathers like those of a peacock. Its neck was bent down low to the ground, and its throat was as knotted as a mountain goat's horn (*Wigalois,* 5038–74).

According to the *Legenda Aurea* (Golden Legend) by Jacobus de Voragine, the dragon infects the air, poisons wells, and casts its seed into fountains to incite the lust of men; it is a scourge to humankind and to animals. The bestiaries present it as the enemy of the panther, elephant, and lion. This is the result of a symbolic interpretation that was common among Christian writers: these three animals are said to represent Adam and Eve, God, and Jesus, whereas the dragon is naturally the embodiment of the image of the devil.

✦ *FÁFNIR*

📖 Sansonetti, *Chevaliers et Dragons,* 57–90; Lecouteux, "Der Drache," *Zeitschrift für deutsches Altertum* 108 (1979): 13–31; Lecouteux, "Seyfrid, Kuperan et le dragon," *Études Germaniques* 49 (1994): 257–66; Tomoaki Mizuno, "The Conquest of a Dragon by the Stranger in Holy Combat: Focusing on the Mighty Hero Beowulf and Thor," *Studies in Humanities, Culture and Communications* 36 (2002): 39–66; Lutz Röhrich, "Drache, Drachenkampf, Drachentöter," in *Enzyklopädie des Märchens,* vol. III, col. 787–820; Paul Beekman Taylor, "The Dragon's Treasure in Beowulf," *Neuphilologische Mitteilungen* 98 (1997): 229–40.

DRAKOKKA: Name of a familiar Norwegian spirit. It possesses magical powers and brings wealth. Since the early Middle Ages it was said to work in the service of sorcerers and other magicians.

📖 Bø, Grambo & Hodne, *Norske Segner,* no. 5; Edvardsen, *Gammelt nytt i våre tidligste ukeblader,* 67.

DRAUGR ("Revenant"): According to ancient belief, the Double of a dead man—his physical alter ego—continues to live in the tomb and will leave it if he has any reason to be upset with his fate. This ill-intentioned dead person can cause the death of people and livestock. To get rid of a *draugr,* it is necessary to burn its body completely and even sometimes immerse its ashes in the sea or running water. There is ample evidence for the fear of revenants in all of the Norse and Germanic countries. Archaeology has revealed that this is an extremely ancient belief: mutilated cadavers have been discovered in graves—a decapitated corpse with the head placed at its feet, for example—and others have been bound so they could not return to trouble the living. The Germanic revenant possesses the unique feature of being entirely corporeal with the power to melt away into the ground and vanish as if by enchantment; but if he has been wounded, the marks of those wounds will be found on his body if it is exhumed. Contrary to mistaken opinion, the "living dead" do not exist: what comes back is only the physical Double.

Fig. 22. Revenants of drowning victims appear during shipwrecks. Illustration from Ronald Grambo's book *Gjester fra Graven.*

In northern Germany revenants are called *Gongers* (sg.: *der Gonger,* "he who goes") and are the dead who cannot rest in peace, either because they are missing a certain object or because they have not atoned for a misdeed committed while they were still alive (such as moving a boundary marker, committing suicide, etc.). Their hand should not be shaken as it will then burn up and come off the arm. Drowning victims are also Gongers; they do not appear to their relatives but rather to their immediate descendants.

Revenants have long been a staple in literature, whether in Gottfried August Bürger's 1774 ballad, *Lenore,* or the medieval Danish ballad of *Aage and Else,* or works such as Theodor Storm's 1888 novella *Der Schimmelreiter* (The Rider on the White Horse).

Fig. 23. Illustration from the *Dit des trois morts at des trois vifs, Heures à l'usage de Rome,* Paris, circa 1487

◆ *AAGE and ELSE, LENORE, NACHZEHRER, SCHIMMELREITER*

📖 Boyer, *La Mort chez les anciens Scandinaves;* Lecouteux, ed. and trans., *Dialogue avec un revenant (XVe siècle);* Lecouteux, *Phantom Armies of the Night;* Lecouteux, *The Return of the Dead;* Lecouteux, *Witches, Werewolves, and Fairies;* Lecouteux and Marcq, *Les Esprits et les Morts;* Grambo, *Gjester fra graven;* Müllenhoff, *Sagen, Märchen und Lieder der Herzogthümer Schleswig, Holstein und Lauenburg,* no. 251; Nielsen, ed., *Danske Folkeviser,* vol. II, 51–71 (Danish ballads); Nilssen, *Draugr;* Walter, ed., *Le Mythe de la Chasse sauvage dans l'Europe medieval;* Van den Berg, *De volkssage in de provincie Antwerpen in de 19de en 20ste eeuw,* 1854–1867. C. N. Gould, "They Who Await the Second Death," *Scandinavian Studies and Notes* 9 (1926/1927): 167–201 (on the connection between revenants and dwarves); Lecouteux, "Gespenster und Wiedergänger: Bemerkungen zu einem vernachlässigten Forschungsfeld der Altgermanistik," *Euphorion* 80 (1986): 219–31; Lecouteux, "Typologie de quelques morts malfaisants," *Cahiers slaves* 3 (2001): 227–44; Lecouteux, "Wiedergänger," in *Lexikon des Mittelalters,* vol. IX, col. 79–80; Eugen Mogk, "Altgermanische Spukgeschichten," *Illbergs neue Jahrbücher für das klass. Altertum* 43 (1919): 103–17; Ingeborg Müller, and Lutz Röhrich, "Der Tod und die Toten," *Deutsches Jahrbuch für Volkskunde* 13 (1967): 346–97 (catalogue of the themes); Günter Wiegelmann, "Der lebende Leichnam im Volksbrauch," *Zeitschrift für Volkskunde* 62 (1966): 161–83.

DRAUPNIR ("Dripper"): Ring or arm ring owned by Odin. It is called "Dripper" because on every ninth night eight more rings that are equal to it in weight "drip" from it, thus increasing wealth. It was crafted by the dwarves Brokkr and Sindri. Odin placed it on Baldr's funeral pyre.

Draupnir is also the name of a dwarf mentioned in the Eddic poem *Völuspá* (The Prophecy of the Seeress).

DRÍFA ("Snowdrift"): This name, which is probably that of a giantess, appears among the ancestors of the mythical king Fornjótr in the text *Hversu Nóreg byggðisk* (part of the fourteenth-century Icelandic manuscript *Flateyjarbók*) and is a personification of winter.

DRUDE, TRUTE (fem.): One of the names for "nightmare" in the Austrian-Bavarian region. In Lower Austria the *Drude* is an otherwise nondescript woman who is obliged to go out at night and sit with all her weight on a person, crushing the victim without mercy. Once this has been done, the Drude changes appearance and becomes old and ugly; she is pale and thin, although of increased weight. Her feet have three large toes, one of which points backward. She can enter anywhere, through the window or through a keyhole, and no holy object can hinder her. She can even transform into a feather. According to some, she does not speak or make any noise, while others claim that she is immediately identifiable by the slight slide of her footsteps. Generally she comes to sit on the chest of a sleeper around midnight. According to one legend the Drude is an ancient princess who has been unable to find rest for a thousand years and squeezes sleeping men.

Women whose fate it is to become a Drude know this but never reveal it to anyone. When they leave to crush someone their body remains in place, and it is only their spirit that departs; therefore, they do not know who it is they have attacked. To get rid of Druden it is necessary to throw a pillow at their feet, which paralyzes them, or else to say, if possible, "Come tomorrow for salt!" while one is being crushed, and the attacker will soon be identified, for she will return the next day to the site of her attack. It is also possible to draw a pentacle over all the openings of the house or to bind the latches with a string.

📖 Alpenburg, *Mythen und Sagen Tirols,* 30; Heyl, *Volkssagen, Meinungen und Bräuche aus Tirol,* 288–89, 430–31; Vernaleken, *Mythen und Bräuche des Volkes in Österreich,* 268–72; Zingerle, *Sagen aus Tirol,* 112, 481.

DURANT (masc.): The name of a plant that, when attached to infants, prevents demons from substituting their progeny for that of the humans.

◆ *CHANGELING*

DUTTEN: A people that is said to have lived in the forest of Minden, Westphalia. They were pagans and made pilgrimages to a pond between Minden and Todtenhausen. They offered sacrifices to their gods in this sacred place and bathed in its blessed waters.

📖 Weddingen and Hartmann, *Sagenschatz Westfalens,* 12.

DWARF NAMES: The most common name for dwarves is *Zwerg,* which means "twisted" in a physical sense, but consequently in a "moral" one as well. The form of the word varies according to region: in northern Germany we have *Twarg;* in southern Germany, *Zwargi;* in Westphalia, *Twiärke;* Thuringia, *Tweärken; Querlich* and *Querge* in the Harz; and *Querchlinge* in Hesse, among others. A somewhat less common term is *Wicht* ("thing," "being"), which is used to form many compound words like *Wichtelmännchen.* Dutch speakers use *alvermannekens* (from *alv,* "elf"), *kabouter* (masc.), and *kaboutervrouwtjes* (fem.), *heihessen,* and *hussen.*

The next group of names consists of compound words using *erd-,* "earth," indicative of the chthonic nature of dwarves. *Erdmantje* in eastern Frisia designates a gray dwarf, who is spectral and wicked. *Erdmünken* are household spirits in the former duchy of Oldenburg; their queen was named Fehmöhme. Then there are the *Eirdmannekes, Aardmannetjes,* and *Sgönaunken* in Westphalia, while the *Fegmännchen* ("the sweeper") in Bernese Oberland is a land spirit that lives in the mountains. The large family of underground dwellers in northern Germany bears the names *Odderbaantjes, Odderbaanki, Unnerseke, Onnerbänkissen, Unnervæstöi, Önnereske, Unnerborstöi, Uellerken,* and *Unnerreizkas* (Pomerania); there are also the amical musicians the *Ellieken* (in the Mark, the boundary lands of Germany northeast of Berlin).

The names of dwarves and household spirits can be coined from first names: *Heinzelmännchen* (from Heinrich), *Johannes* (John), *Petermännlein* (Peter), *Ludi* (little Louis), *Wolterken* (from Walter), *Niss/Nisepuk* (little Nicholas), *Chimeke/Chimgen/Schimmeke* ("little Joachim"), who was famous for killing, dismembering, and cooking an insolent kitchen lad of Mecklenburg Castle. Their names can also be drawn from the places they reside (*Kellermännchen,* "little man of the cellar"; *Pfarrmännel,* "wee man of the rectory"; *Ofenmänchen,* "little man of the oven"), the times when they are active (*Nachtmännlein,* "little night-man"), or else from their activity (*Futtermännchen/Fueterknechtli,* from *Fütter,* "fodder"; or *Käsmandel,* from "cheese" or "chalet" because *Kaser/Käser* can mean both of these things, who is described as a gray little man with a pale wrinkled face; *Kistenmännchen* ("wee man of the treasure"), or, lastly, from the color of their clothes (*Graumännchen/Gro mann,* "little gray man"; *Rotjäksch,* "red jacket"). In the fifteenth century the Silesian *stetewaldiu* was "he who governs the premises," a household spirit.

Their size is expressed in the names *Däumling* ("little thumbling") and *Fingerling* (Prussian for "finger"). Their appearance is reflected in names like *Dickkopf* ("fathead"), *Kröppel* ("goitrous"), *Boyaba* ("small boy"), and *lütje lüe* ("wee folk").

There are a plethora of names in the Scandinavian countries, and there is not always a distinction made between dwarves and local land spirits. In Denmark the names include *dværg, Lille Liels, Nis Puge, Puge,* and *Gaardbo* (*Gaardbonisse, Gaardbuk*); in Iceland we have *dvergr, álfr,* and the collective *huldufólk,* the "hidden folk"; in Norway, *Tuss(e), Tomte (Tomtegubbe), Gardsvord (gardsbonde), Tunkall, Tunvord,* and *huldrefolk*; in Sweden, *Gårdsrå, Tomte (Tomtebise, Tomtegubbe),* and *Nisse (Goa Nisse, Nisse-godrång).*

Others names found in the German-speaking countries of Switzerland, Germany, and Austria include *Bergmännlein, Donanadl, Gotwerg, Gotvährinne, Käsmandel, Nebelmännlein, Nörglein/Norgen* ("grumpy"), *Querre, Schrattel/Schrätteli, Spielmännli, Twirgi, Venediger,* and *Zwerg.*

All of these names have multiple dialectal variations that are too numerous to list.

📖 Lecouteux, *Les Nains et les Elfes au Moyen Âge;* Lindig, *Hausgeister;* Linhart, *Hausgeister in Franken.*

DWARVES (Old Norse *dvergr;* Old High German *twerc;* Old English *dveorg*): Contrary to the preconceived notions passed on by folklore, dwarves are not necessarily little: they can assume any size at will. "Dwarf" is a generic term like "god" or "giant" and designates a race of malevolent beings, the opposite of elves. Etymologically speaking, their name means "twisted" both in body and mind.

According to the *Poetic Edda,* two dwarves, Móðsognir and Durinn, existed in the beginning, and they created a race in their image. When the gods created the world, they placed four dwarves at each of the four cardinal points to hold up the sky. According to Snorri Sturluson, dwarves were born from the decomposition of the giant Ymir's corpse, then the gods gave these larvae a human face and intelligence.

Dwarves are skilled artisans and excellent smiths. They crafted the attributes of the gods: Thor's hammer (✦ MJÖLLNIR), Odin's spear (✦ GUNGNIR), Freyr's boat (✦ SKÍÐBLAÐNIR), Freyja's necklace (✦ BRÍSINGAMEN), Sif's hair, the ring Draupnir, and a boar with golden bristles. All these objects were endowed with wonderful powers. When the dwarves forged weapons for humans, the weapons were extremely destructive, like the famous swords Dáinsleif ("Dáinn's Legacy," Dáinn being a dwarf whose name means "death") and Tyrfingr.

Dwarves are also magicians and enjoy such close relations with the dead that it is thought they may be the mythical transposition of evil dead men. There are many with names that are quite revealing in this regard: "Black," "Deceased," "Torpid," "Death," "Corpse," "Cold," "Buried beneath the Cairn," and so forth. They are obviously chthonian—the light of day petrifies them—and bound to the lithic world. They all live in or beneath the stones, mounds, and mountains, which are all places regarded as havens for the dead of their empire, an opinion found in the story of King Herla. Like many chthonian beings, they are the keepers of great wealth and poetry (✦ KVASIR), which is metaphorically termed "dwarves' drink."

Dwarves also have a connection with water (✦ ANDVARI), which makes them akin to their Celtic cousins, the leprechauns and the *Afang*.

Contrary to elves, which have associations with Freyr and the Æsir, dwarves have no connection to anyone, although they are suggestive of the same Dumézilian function as the Vanir (the third function, that of fertility/fecundity) but seem to embody its negative aspects. There is no clear dividing line between dwarves and giants: both are experts in magic and possess great knowledge (✦ ALVISS) and are connected to the dead. The patron of the dwarves could be Loki, whose nature fluctuates between that of a dwarf and that of a giant.

Dwarves are also thieves (✦ ALÞJÓFR). An odd charm in Old English depicts a dwarf perceived as an unidentified misfortune that arrives in the form of a spider.

In the epics and romances of Germany and England, dwarves retain their wicked character, manual dexterity, and their knowledge of the secrets of the Earth. They come in the guise of knights, old men white with age (✦ ALBERICH), or children. They dwell in wondrous hollow mountains illuminated by gems and live in hierarchical communities that apparently obey the same laws as men.

In Switzerland dwarves are called *Gottvährinnen* and *Gotwergi* (Valais); *Spielmännli* (Friburg Canton), because they play violin; *Toggeli*,

Doggi, Tocki, Twirgi (Berner Oberland), *Servans* (Vaux Canton), and *Zwerge.*

Three kinds of dwarves—white, brown, and black—are found on the island of Rügen. Both the white and brown dwarves are kindly and cause no ill to anyone, but the white dwarves are the friendliest. The black dwarves are magicians and are worthless; they are deceitful and double-dealing. All of these dwarves particularly like to live in the mountains of the island.

📖 Holbek and Piø, *Fabeldyr og sagnfolk,* 137–38; Lecouteux, *Les Nains et les Elfes au Moyen Âge;* Motz, *The Wise One of the Mountain;* Van den Berg, *De volkssage in de provincie Antwerpen in de 19de en 20ste eeuw,* 1437–52; Vernaleken, *Alpensagen,* 107–11, 118–24, 147–48, 322.

EARENDEL: In Old English this is the name of the morning star.

✦ *AURVANDILL*

ECHO: In Old Norse, echo is called "dwarves speech" (*dvergmál*), which falls under the headings of beliefs such as those of the *Hupeux*, the Howlers, and other *Hemänner*, the calling spirits.

ECKART, THE LOYAL: In the Middle Ages this was the weapons master of the Harlungen (✦ HARLUNGEN), and, later, the figure who preceded the Infernal Hunt while yelling to people to beware. This is the source for a German proverbial expression, "to be a loyal Eckart" (meaning "to be a trusted friend"), which is known to have been in use since 1529. Eckart has appeared in the legend of Tannhäuser since 1453. In 1813, Goethe wrote a ballad of a moralistic nature titled *Der getreue Eckart* (The Loyal Eckart).

📖 Grimm, *Deutsche Sagen,* nos. 7, 313.

ECKEREN: Name of a household spirit said to have existed in the region of Cleves in the sixteenth century. He helped with the housework, fed the horses, and punished lazy or careless servants. Most of the time he was invisible, but sometimes his hand could be seen. This figure bears some similarity to another kobold named Hütchen (Hugen).

📖 Weyer, *De praestigiis daemonum,* Frankfurt, 1586; Grimm, *Deutsche Sagen,* no. 78 (the Grimms' interpretation of *Eckerken* as derived from *Eidechse,* "lizard," is no longer considered correct).

EGGÞÉR ("Sword Guardian"): Giant who guards a giantess in the Iron Forest (Járnviðr) while sitting on a mound playing the harp.

EGILL: While on his way to visit Hymir, Thor stops at the home of a giant with this name. He leaves the goats that pull his chariot there.

EIKIN ("Vehement"): One of the thirty-seven mythical rivers cited in a strophe of the *Grímnismál* (*Poetic Edda*) that are reputed to surround the dwellings of the gods.

◆ *MYTHICAL RIVERS*

EIKÞYRNIR ("Oak-thorny"): This is the stag that stands on the roof of Valhalla (Valhöll), feeding on the leaves of the tree called Læraðr, which is perhaps identical to the cosmic tree, Yggdrasill. Water from its antlers streams into the spring called Hvergelmir, from which all the world's rivers take their course.

EIMNIR ("Burner"): The name of a giant found in the *þulur* lists. Her name may be an allusion to the end of the world when the giants of Surtr ("The Black One") set fire to everything.

EINHERI ("Solitary Warrior"): One of the god Thor's titles.

EINHERJAR ("Single Fighters"): These are Odin's warriors who live in Valhalla (Vahöll) and spend their days fighting together. Regardless of whether they are wounded or slain during these daily battles, they are fully restored to life and vigor each evening to feast joyfully on the flesh of the boar Sæhrímnir and drink the mead that flows from the udders of the goat Heiðrun and which is served by the valkyries. When the time for the final battle arrives, they will march out in rows of 800 at a time through each of the 540 doors of Valhalla, simultaneously, to confront the forces of evil (the wolf Fenrir, the fire giants, and so on). Only the men who have fallen in combat or who are marked by the sign of Odin—a wound made with a spear—are part of the *einherjar*.

EINRIÐI ("Solitary Horseman"): One of the titles of the god Thor. In Snorri's *Edda,* Einriði is described as the son of Lóriði and the father of Vingþor, but these names are also *cognomina* of Thor. The name has been confirmed to exist on the rune stone of Rimsø (Jutland, Denmark, tenth century) and on that of Grinda (Sweden, eleventh century).

EIR ("Peace," "Mercy"): This is an Ásynja reputed to be the best of physicians; she would be the personification of the concept of assistance, succor, and grace. It is also the name of one of Menglöð's servants and also that of a valkyrie.

EISMANNDLE, EISMÄNNLEIN ("Little Man of the Ice"): Name of a type of dwarf that lives on the snow-covered peaks and glaciers of the Tyrolean Alps. They protect the innocent and punish the sacrilegious. In this same region we find the *Gletschmann,* "the man of the glacier," a kind of wild man.

  📖 Alpenburg, *Mythen und Sagen Tirols,* 86–88, 103.

EISTLA: Name of one of the nine mothers of Heimdallr.

ELBST: A spirit that shows itself in a mountain lake near Seelisberg (Switzerland) in the form of a moss-covered log or a drifting island; he lures careless people into the depths. In moonlight he coils around the lake in the form of a serpent. At night he comes ashore in the form of a dragon or reptile with talons and kills livestock. He is also known to take on the form of a black sow. His appearance is a herald of bad weather.

ELDHRÍMNIR ("Covered with Soot from the Fire"): Cauldron in which the boar Sæhrímnir is cooked to serve as food for the warriors of Valhalla (Vahöll). The cook's name is Andhrímnir.

ELDIR ("Fire-starter"): A servant of the sea god Ægir.

ELDR ("Fire"): The brother of Ægir and Vindr, thus a son of Fornjótr.

ELEMENTAL SPIRITS (German *Elementargeister*): Their name comes from Theophrastus Bombastus von Hohenheim, known as Paracelsus (died 1541), who, in *Liber de Nymphis, sylphis, pygmaeis et salamandris et de caeteris spiritibus* (Book of Nymphs, Sylphs, Pygmies, and Salamanders and Other Spirits), organized the beliefs of his day and assigned a specific element to the creatures of folk mythology. Sirens and nymphs live in water; the sylphs live in the air; pygmies (i.e., dwarves and gnomes) live in the earth; and the salamanders (masculine!)—also called *Vulcani,* which should not be confused with the animal that shares their name—live in fire. Paracelsus developed his theory further in describing their bodies, which are more subtle than those of humans. This allows them "to cross through walls, rocks, stones, like spirits," and Paracelsus peppers his presentation with remarks like "water is the air of the fish" to explain how sirens and nymphs can live underwater. These beings have the same needs as we do: they eat and drink, they dress in clothing, and they exist in a hierarchy.

📖 Holbek and Piø, *Fabeldyr og sagnfolk,* 51–54; Lutz Röhrich, "Elementargeister," in *Enzyklopädie des Märchens,* vol. III, col. 1316–26.

ELF-LOCKS: There is a belief found throughout the whole of Europe concerning horse manes: when the inhabitants of a farm discover their horses' manes to be tangled or plaited, they know that their home houses a spirit. The ancient names given to these braids show that their manufacture was attributed to supernatural beings. In Germany they were referred to as a "dwarf or imp plait" (*Wichtelzopf, Weichselzopf*), "elf plait" (*Alpzopf*), or "nightmare plait" (*Drutenzopf, Drudenzopf*); in Low German as "nightmare locks" (*mahrenlocke, mahrklatte*) or "elf plaits" (*elfklatte, alpklatte*). Similar terms include Danish *marelok,* Swedish *martoswa,* and Polish *skrzot.* In England they are referred to as *elflocks* and also *elvihkrots.* During Shakespeare's time (cf. *King Lear,* II, 3), the verb "to elf" meant "to muffle" [as if with felt —*Trans.*]; in Norway the terms *nisseflette* ("*nisse*-plait") or *tusseflette* ("*tusse*-plait") were used, words coined from two names for spirits. In human beings an elflock can in fact be caused by a medical condition called "Polish plait" (*plica polonica* or *coma caesarea*), which causes the hair to become an irreversibly tangled, sticky mass! The oldest account of elflocks comes from William of Auvergne (1180–1249), who lists the deeds and actions of diabolical spirits: "Evil spirits indulge in other mystifications . . . sometimes in the stables as well . . . the manes of the horses are meticulously braided" (*De universo,* II, 3, 24).

📖 Haavio, *Suomalaiset kodinhaltiat,* 400ff; Lecouteux, *The Tradition of Household Spirits,* 139–41; Carl W. von Sydow, "Övernaturliga väsen," *Folketro* 19 (1935): 124.

ÉLIVÁGAR ("Stormy Seas"): This is the name for the eleven rivers that flow out of the spring Hvergelmir into the primordial abyss Ginnungagap. The ice they transport fills this abyss. The eleven rivers that make up this sea are called Svöl ("Chilly"), Gunnþrá ("Arrogant"),

Fjörm ("Fast One"), Fimbulþul ("Great Prophet"), Slíðr ("Perilous"), Hríð ("Gust"), Ylgr ("She-Wolf"), Sylgr ("Gulf"), Víð ("Wide"), Leiptr ("Lightning"), and Gjöll ("Tumult").

ÉLJÚÐNIR ("Rain-dampened"): Name of the hall of the goddess of the dead, Hel.

ELLEFOLK: The name for elves in Denmark who are believed to be a people who live in the hills and mounds. They correspond to the Norwegian *huldrer* and the Icelandic *huldufólk*.

  📖 Holbek and Piø, *Fabeldyr og sagnfolk*, 127–34.

ELLI ("Age"): The wet nurse for the giant Útgarðaloki. When Thor visits Útgarðaloki he has to wrestle Elli, and she bests him. Elli is the personification of the old age that none can resist.

ELLIKEN, ÖLLERKEN: The name of dwarves in the Mark (the boundary lands of Germany northeast of Berlin). They are about a foot high, wear red caps and robes, and live in the forests and under the ground.

  ✦ *DWARVES, UNDERGROUND DWELLERS*

  📖 Lohre, *Märkische Sagen*, no. 68.

ELS: A female spirit that haunts the region northwest of the Taunus mountains (Hesse, Germany).

ELVES (Old Norse sg. *álfr;* German *Elbe, Alp;* Old English *ælf*): These are creatures of great antiquity, so much so that they were almost fossils by the time the mythological texts were set down in writing. The elf is found in all the Germanic countries. The study of human names shows us that elves were revered and feared; in Anglo-Saxon England, for example, we find thirty-five proper names that contain the word *ælf.* Originally elves were benevolent beings, and the word *álfr* can be traced back to an Indo-European root meaning "white, clear, luminous." It probably did not take long before elves became conflated with the malevolent dwarves. In the Scandinavian north, the elves inhabit Álfheimr, one of the heavenly dwellings owned by the god Freyr, and in the tripartite theory of Georges Dumézil they would correspond to the third function (that of fertility and fecundity). Norse triads suggest that at one time they were gods in their own right, just like the Æsir and Vanir.

According to the alliterative charms that have been preserved in Old English, elves possessed the wisdom of magic and enchantment, and the Old High German name of the mandrake plant, *albrûna,* tends to confirm this point. *Albrûna* in fact means "elf-secret," and this name is also that of a priestess mentioned by Tacitus in his Germania. People genuinely believed in elves and offered sacrifices to them (✦ ÁLFABLÓT). Around the year 1018, the skald Sigvatr Þórðarson was refused hospitality in a house owned by a peasant who was performing sacrifices to the elves.

As pure beings elves cannot tolerate vileness, and the Norse expression *ganga álfreka,* "to relieve oneself, to urinate," literally means "to drive away the elves," which can be compared to a fifteenth-century belief in the Picardy region of France that urinating would send the sprites fleeing. Elves are also the good dead elevated to the status of guardian spirits. Olaf Gudrødsson was nicknamed "Olaf Geirstad-Elf" after being buried in Geirstad, and Hálfdan Hvítbeinn was mourned as the "Elf with the Breastplate." In this sense, elves would be the spirits of the dead as opposed to the physical dead represented by dwarves. Less clear is the relationship between Völundr (✦ WAYLAND THE SMITH) and the elves, although he is referred to as the "prince of elves" three times in

Fig. 24. Elves. Olaus Magnus, *Historia de gentibus septentrionalibus*, Rome, 1555.

the *Poetic Edda*. Likewise obscure is the link between Thor and these beings; the evidence for this appears only in proper names like Þórálfr ("Thor's Elf") or with the plant known as "Jupiter's Beard" (*barba Jovis*), whose German folk names include "Elf Rod" (*Alpruthe*), "Thunder Broom" (*Donnerbesen*), and "Thor's Beard" (*Donarbart*).

Once they had been demonized, elves became dwarves (*Zwerge*) and nightmares (*Alp, Mahr, Trude*).

📖 Lecouteux, *Les Nains et les Elfes au Moyen Âge*; Lecouteux, "Trois hypothèses sur nos voisins invisibles," in Lecouteux and Gouchet, eds., *Hugur: mélanges d'histoire, de littérature et de mythologie offerts à Régis Boyer pour son 65e anniversaire*, 289–97; Hermann Moses, "Die deutschen Pflanzennamen in ihrer Bedeutung für die Geschichts- und Altertumskunde," *Mittheilungen aus dem Archive des Voigtländischen Alterthumsforschenden Vereins*, ed. Ferdinand Metzner (Weida: Voigtländischer Alterthumsforschender Verein, 1871): 90–93; Lutz Röhrich, "Eva," in *Enzyklopädie des Märchens*, vol. IV, col. 569–77.

EMBLA: The first woman.

✦ *ASKR*

ENERBANSKE, ONNERBÄNKISSEN: ✦ UNDERGROUND DWELLERS

ENNILANGR ("Broad-browed"): One of Thor's bynames.

EOTEN (pl. *eotenas*): Old English name for a race of giants; it corresponds to the Scandinavian *jötnar*, and in both cases the name derives from a verbal root meaning "to eat, to devour." Tenth-century clerics claimed these giants were the descendants of Cain.

✦ *GIANTS*

ERDMENDLE: Spirits that are among the company of fallen angels whose downfall preceded the sin of Adam. They did not commit serious crimes against the Lord but were cast down to Earth with the other wicked and evil angels. In contrast to the other spirits, they were given solid and unblemished bodies on Earth, and because of this they still hope to receive grace and salvation. This is why they perform good deeds.

📖 Barack, ed., *Zimmerische Chronik*, vol. IV, 228–29.

ERLKING ("Alder King"; German *Erlkönig*): In 1779, J. G. Herder translated the Danish ballad *Hr. Oluf han rider* (Sir Olaf He Rides), which tells the story of Olaf's meeting with the daughter of the elf king. She wants to dance with him and offers him expensive gifts, but he refuses because it is the eve of his wedding. She exacts her vengeance by striking such a solid blow to his heart that he keels over dead when he reaches home. His mother and his bride die of grief. The substitution in the name of "elf" with "alder" is due, it seems, to a translation error: in Danish "king of the elves" is *ellerkonge,* but in Low German *eller* means "alder" (*Erle* in High German). In 1781, Goethe was inspired by Herder's work and wrote his own ballad, *Erlkönig,* on this theme.

📖 Nielsen, ed., *Danske Folkeviser,* vol. II, 140–45 (Danish ballad).

Fig. 25. The Alder King

ERMANARIC: King of the Ostrogoths, of the Amal dynasty, who founded a powerful empire in southern Russia in the fourth century. It collapsed in 376 under the incursions of the Huns. Ermanaric became a figure of legend quite quickly and holds a prominent place in Germanic epics. These tell us his wife was named Suanhilda, but he had her drawn and quartered for misconduct. Suanhilda's two brothers, Amnius and

Sarus, avenged her death. Jordanes was the first to tell this story, which can also be found in the *Hamðismál* (*Poetic Edda*); there are texts in Old English that also allude to it. In the German Middle Ages, Ermanaric was depicted as the sworn enemy of Dietrich von Bern, Ermanaric's nephew, who was portrayed in the thirteenth century as a model of German virtues. Ermanaric is famous for slaying the Harlungen, two other of his nephews, Hamðir and Sörli, the brothers of Svanhildr.

📖 Zink, *Les Légendes héroïques de Dietrich et d'Ermrich dans les littératures germaniques.*

ESCHATOLOGICAL BATTLE: ✦ RAGNARÖK

ESCHATOLOGY: ✦ RAGNARÖK

ETERNAL BATTLE: ✦ HJAÐNINGAVÍG

EUGEL: A helpful dwarf who appears in *Das Lied vom hürnen Seyfrid* (The Lay of Horn-skinned Siegfried). He is the son of King Nyblinc and, together with his two brothers, possesses his father's treasure. After many hesitations, he grants his aid to Seyfrid (Siegfried) who has set off in search of Kriemhild after she is abducted by a man transformed into a flying dragon.

Fig. 26. The abduction of Kriemhild

Eugel rides a horse that is black as coal, dresses in furs accented with gold, and wears a crown. He reveals to Seyfrid his origins and predicts his murder. When the hero is wounded by the giant Kuperan, Eugel covers him with his cloak of invisibility (*Tarnkappe*) and hides him from the monster until he regains his senses.

EUHEMERISM: In the third century BCE the Greek writer Euhemerus created a skilled synthesis of religion and history and claimed that the gods of mythology were originally humans who had been deified following their deaths, in recognition of the great services they had provided humanity. The pantheon is reduced to a simple human expression, and mythology is relegated to the prosaic realities of history. In the mythological chapters of *Heimskringla,* Snorri Sturluson applies a euhemeristic interpretation to the gods of the Germanic-Scandinavian pantheon, and Saxo Grammaticus does the same in his *History of the Danes.*

EYRGJAFA: One of Heimdallr's nine mothers. The names of the other eight are Gjálp, Greip, Eistla, Ulfrún, Angeyja, Imð, Atla, and Járnsaxa.

F

FÁFNIR: The name of the dragon slain by Sigurðr (Siegfried). In the *Völsunga saga* (Saga of the Volsungs), Fáfnir is one of the sons of Hreiðmar and the brother of Reginn the smith. He stole the gold of the dwarf Andvari, given to him by the Æsir as compensation for the unintentional murder of his other brother, Ótr. Then he transformed into a dragon and went to sleep on the gold. He also owned a helmet of terror. Before dying at the hands of Sigurðr, he predicted to the hero that the gold would bring about his death.

✦ *ANDVARI, DRAGON, ÓTR*

📖 Régis Boyer, "Le sang de Fáfnir," *Bulletin C.R.L.C.,* issue 1 (1982): 19–38.

FAKSAR: ✦ HERNOSS, HOUSEHOLD/PLACE SPIRITS

FALHÓFNIR ("The One with the Hair-covered Hooves"): This is one of the ten horses the Æsir ride when they go to pronounce their verdicts beneath the ash tree Yggdrasill. The others, according to *Grímnismál* 30, are Glaðr ("Brilliant"), Gyllir ("Gold Yellow"), Glær ("Light"), Skeiðbrimir ("Fast Racer"), Silfrintoppr ("Silver Mane"), Sinir ("Sinewy"), Gísl ("Bright"), Gulltoppr ("Golden Mane"), and Léttfeti ("Light Feet"). It will be noted that almost all these names refer to the notion of light and brightness.

FALLANDA-FORAÐ ("Stumbling Block"): The name of the threshold of the house of Hel, goddess of the underworld also called Hel.

FÄNGGEN (pl., also *Fangga*; sg. *Fangga* or *Fanggin*): Woodland demons of large size, clad in animal hides or bark, who are closely related to wild men and women. They have long, tangled beards, and black eyes that sometimes glow like cinders and emit lightning flashes; their voices are harsh and blaring. In the Tyrol the *Fangga* is a terrifying, hairy giantess with a mouth that gapes from ear to ear and a harsh, ringing voice. She grabs children whenever she can and reduces them to a powder by scraping them against dead trees, or she devours them. Her secrets can be stolen from her by getting her intoxicated.

In the Swiss canton of Graubünden, the Fänggen are human in size but have long breasts, which they can sling over their shoulders. There are other varieties of this creature that are similar in size to dwarves; they live in caves and crevasses and tame chamois and wolves to serve them as mounts. They also know the properties of herbs.

📖 Alpenburg, *Mythen und Sagen Tirols*, 51–52; Luck, *Rätische Alpensagen*, 13–17.

FARBAUTI ("Dangerous Striker"): Giant regarded as the father of the god Loki.

FARMAGUÐ ("God of Cargoes"): One of Odin's titles, which notably explains why the Romans conflated him with Mercury.

📖 Falk, *Odensheiti.*

FARMATÝR ("God of Cargoes"): One of Odin's titles. In this instance *týr* simply means "god" and is not in any way a reference to the deity of the same name.

✦ *FARMAGUÐ, GÖNDLIR*

📖 Falk, *Odensheiti.*

FASOLT: Giant from the legends of Dietrich von Bern (Theodoric the Great). He is also mentioned in a fifteenth-century German charm intended to conjure bad weather. In the *Eckenlied* (Lay of Ecke), Fasolt appears as a cursed huntsman pursuing a wood maiden. He is the brother of the giant Ecke and of Birkhild, and his mother is Uodelgart. He is huge in size and wears his hair in two long braids that fall down on either side of his horse. He is seeking to avenge the death of Ecke, slain by Dierich von Bern, but dies.

In another text, titled *Dietrichs erste Ausfahrt* (Dietrich's First Adventure), Fasolt is an ogre who demands a tribute from Virginal, the queen of the dwarves: one young maiden must be handed over to him every year.

FENGR ("Booty"): Title of Odin that refers to his function relating to the warrior class.

📖 Falk, *Odensheiti*.

FENJA: One of the giantesses who turned the mythic mill owned by King Fróði of Denmark. This mill, called Grotti, had the ability to grind whatever the miller desired. A thirteenth-century poem in the *Poetic Edda* has preserved this story.

FENRIR ("Fen-dweller"): The wolf Fenrir was born from the coupling of the god Loki with the giantess Angrboða. The Æsir raised Fenrir, but he grew so large that they decided to tie him down. The first two fetters broke, so the dwarves made a third one called Gleipnir. Now suspicious, Fenrir demanded that one of the gods place his hand in his mouth, otherwise the wolf would not let them slip this fetter over him. Tyr agrees to this request. When Fenrir saw that he could not break Gleipnir, he bit off Tyr's hand. The gods then attached this fetter to a chain named Gelgja, which they drove into the boulder Gjöll with the help of a stone, Þviti. Lastly, they kept the wolf's mouth open by placing a sword in it. Fenrir has been howling ever since, and the slobber flowing from his jaws formed the Ván river. During Ragnarök, Fenrir breaks his bonds and "will go with mouth agape and its upper jaw will be against the sky and its lower one against the earth. It would gape wider if there was room. Flames will burn from its eyes and nostrils" (Snorri Sturluson, *Edda*, trans. Faulkes). He swallows up Odin, but in the very next instant, Víðarr steps on the wolf's lower jaw then grabs his upper jaw which he tears off, thus killing Fenrir.

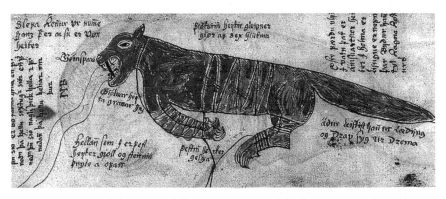

Fig. 27. The wolf Fenrir. Detail from a manuscript of the *Snorra Edda*, circa 1680.

FENRISÚLFR ("Fenris Wolf"): Another name for Fenrir.

FENSALIR ("Fen Halls"): The dwelling of the goddess Frigg.

FIMBULÞULR ("Powerful Speaker"): One of the god Odin's titles.
  📖 Falk, *Odensheiti*.

FIMBULTÝR ("Powerful God"): One of Odin's titles; it reflects his role as the master of the pantheon and father of the gods.
  📖 Falk, *Odensheiti*.

FIMBULVETR ("Great Winter"): The end of the world is announced by a series of natural catastrophes among which is a horrific winter that will last three years in a row and bears this name.

FIMMELFRAU ("The Hemp Woman"): This is the name for a grain spirit in the Untersee region near Thorgau (Harz, Germany) who makes the hemp plants grow heavy and causes harm to the wicked.

FIRE: There are scant traces of fire worship among the Germanic peoples outside of the practice of the "Need-fire" (*niedfyr* or *nodfyr*), which is attested in a Frankish church synod of 742 and by a subsequent Carolingian capitulary collection, the *Indiculus Superstitionem* (Index of Superstitions). The eleventh-century English law code of Cnut the Great also forbids the heathen worship of fire. Fire plays an important role in the mythology, as the world ends in conflagration: spread by the giant Surtr, fire remains as the sole victor of the eschatological battle.

FJALARR: A dwarf and the brother of Galarr; together the two murdered Kvasir and used his blood to make a wondrous mead that transforms everyone who drinks of it into a poet. They also slew the giant Gillingr and his wife, but, when captured by their son, Suttungr, they gave him the mead in return for sparing their lives. The mead was eventually stolen by Odin.
  ✦ *KVASIR*

FJÖLNIR 1 ("Multifarious One"): This byname of Odin refers to the god's ability to change his shape and appearance.

✦ *GÖNDLIR*

📖 Falk, *Odensheiti.*

FJÖLNIR 2: Legendary king of Sweden, son of the god Yngvi-Freyr and the giantess Gerðr. He met his death by drowning in a vat of mead. This story, which is told by Snorri Sturluson and Saxo Grammaticus, dates from before the ninth century. A Celtic counterpart can be found in the story of Muirchertach, who drowns in a cask of wine. This may be a form of ritual death.

FJÖLSVIÐR ("All-knowing"): 1. The "superego" of Odin (✦ GÖNDLIR). 2. Name of the guardian of the maiden Menglöð, whom Svipdagr wishes to wed; he gives the hero a "course" on various mythological points.

📖 Falk, *Odensheiti.*

FJÖLVARR ("Very Cautious"): An individual with whom Odin stayed for five years; unfortunately we know nothing of what he did there, but it can be assumed to have been some sort of initiatory sojourn.

FJÖRGYN ("Life-granter"): This is the goddess Earth, the founding mother, and the poets explain her name as "land, country." She is called mother of Thor, but in the mythology it is Jörð ("Earth") who is regularly regarded as the mother of this god. It is thought that Fjörgyn represents a particular aspect of Jörð as the depiction of the connection between the land and the stormy sky. Relying on the etymology that reveals the kinship of *fjörgyn* with the Baltic Perkunas (the Slavic Perun), we might see in Fjörgyn an oak-covered mountain. The goddess would therefore embody the potent plant-production capabilities of the great telluric goddess, the Terra Mater.

📖 Régis Boyer, "Fjörgyn," in *Mort et fécondité dans les mythologies,* ed. François Jouan (Paris: Les Belles Lettres, 1986), 139–50.

FJÖRGYNN: Father of the goddess Frigg, the wife of Odin, as is the goddess Jörð. It is quite possible that a single entity was divided to give us the feminine Fjörgyn and the male Fjörgynn. In fact, Germanic mythology is not lacking in deities that are alternately viewed as female or male; these goddesses/gods most often belong to the Vanir family and are agrarian deities.

FJÖRM ("Rapid"): One of the rivers that gushes from Hvergelmir.

♦ *ÉLIVÁGAR*

FJÖTURLUNDR ("Fetter Grove"): The place where Dagr (Day) kills Helgi, the murderer of King Hundingr, with the blow of a spear guided by Odin. This place brings to mind the sacred grove of the Semnones, where, according to Tacitus, men were sacrificed and no one could enter unless in fetters.

FLATA: In the romance of *Apollonius von Tyrland* (Apollonius of Tyre) by Heinrich von Neustadt (ca. 1300), Flata is a wild woman and mother to several monsters. She is as large as two men and moves quickly, her face "has the voracious expression of a wild cat," her thighs are "long and dry," and her legs, which are described as "dragon paws," are equally long and end in sharp claws. Her eyebrows are black and long, her breasts hang down over her belly, and she is covered all over with hair. She leaps like a goat. Her rear end is "round like a log." Her nostrils are huge, and the snot that comes out of them "has the length of a sausage." Her eyes sparkle from the bottom of deep sockets, and a pestilential odor wafts from her large mouth. This is one of the finest portraits of the medieval wild woman.

FLYING DUTCHMAN (Dutch *de Vliegende Hollander;* German *der fliegende Holländer*): This is the legend attached to the Dutch captain Willem van der Decken in 1821 and to Barend Fockesz in 1841. This sailor swore an oath that he would round the Cape of Good Hope no matter what the cost, even if it took until the Day of Final Judgment, and he was taken at his word. Seafarers therefore come across this ghost ship that cannot make landfall anywhere and whose sailors give them packets of letters addressed to people who are long since dead. These letters must be nailed to the mainmast or else misfortune will ensue. Heinrich Heine and later Richard Wagner were inspired by this legend.

Other phantom vessels exist in German legend. One was cruising off the port of Emden; the port watchman refused to give the crew assistance, and they drowned. Often the crew is composed of sailors being punished for a crime or transgression—such as blasphemy, perjury, piracy, setting sail on a Friday, the day of Christ's suffering—or

Fig. 28. The ghost ship, nineteenth-century English illustration

else it is made up of murderers and robbers. The *Libera nos!* ("Deliver us!") is one of these ships whose crew will find redemption when living Christian sailors have a Requiem mass said for them.

📖 Gerndt, *Fliegender Holländer und Klabautermann;* Grambo, *Svart katt over veien,* 53; Kalff, *De Sage van den vliegenden Hollander;* Petzold, *Historische Sagen,* vol. II, 28–29.

FÖHRWEIBELE: This is the name of a spirit that looked like a tiny woman who lived for a long time on the lower course of the Inn River (Tyrol). She would make a hellish racket on Christmas night and on Three Kings' Day (Epiphany), which woke the people and animals of that region in terror. A Franciscan managed to rid the land of her presence.

📖 Heyl, *Volkssagen, Meinungen und Bräuche aus Tirol,* 229.

FÓLKVANGR ("Field of the People"): Name of the goddess Freyja's dwelling.

FÖNN ("Snowdrift"): Giantess and daughter of King Snaer ("Snow").
✦ *DRÍFA*

FOREST: The Germanic forest is immense, vast, dense, dark, and impenetrable. It is the refuge of the exiled (Old Norse *skógarmaðr*, "man of the wood") and of outlaws, the site of lairs for terrifying and often monstrous animals, and the dwelling place for brigands and marginal individuals. The forest thereby forms a natural frontier. The Bohemian Forest (or Nemus Boemicum) to the south connects with the Bavarian Forest and the Austrian Nordwald; the forest of Falster separates Denmark from Saxony and has always been a singular place. It was in the Teutoburg Forest that the Roman Legions of Varus were annihilated by the Cherusci leader Arminius in the year 9 CE. Legendary and mythical forests are also plentiful: there is the Myrkviðr of the Norse texts; the Eydaskóg of *Haralds saga ins hárfagra* (Saga of Harald Fairhair), which separates the Värmland (*Wormia* in Latin) from Götaland; and the *Þiðreks saga af Bern* (Saga of Dietrich von Bern) speaks of the Valslöng, the frontier between West Francia and Hunaland and also of Borgar (or Borg), which lies on the edge of Saxony. They sometimes carry descriptive names like the Tröllaskógr, "Trolls' Forest," mentioned in *Njal's saga*. This is the site of crimes and murders. The *Þiðreks saga* tells us that the mother of Sigurðr/Siegfried, betrayed by Duke Artvin and Duke Hermann, was taken into the Swabian forest to be executed. It is in another forest that the smith Reginn finds the hero and then sends him off to be slain by Reginn's brother Fáfnir, who has transformed into a dragon; the plan fails and ends up costing Reginn his life. In the *Nibelungenlied,* Hagen kills Siegfried in the Odenwald, "Odin's Forest." We can understand the laws of Ine, king of the West Saxons (Wessex) in the seventh century, and Wihtred (690–725), king of Kent, which say: "If a man coming from afar or a foreigner is crossing the forest without using the path and without calling out or sounding his horn, he will be considered a brigand and slain."

The forest is also a sanctified location and philologists have long noted that all the words for *temple* in the oldest texts can mean "sacred grove or forest." Many place-names support this conclusion: Wihinloh (attested in 901), Rimslo in Lower Saxony, Heiligenforst (1065) or Sacrum Nemus (eleventh century) near Haguenau, and Heiligenholtz (1180, Baden-Württemberg); Fröslanda, Nördlunda, and Ullunda (Sweden) are coined from the names of the gods Freyr, Njörðr, and Ullr; then we have Torslunda (Denmark), "Thor's Wood." The Old Norse word *lundr* (equivalent to the Old High German *lô* or *lôh*) designates a sacred grove. In the *Poetic Edda* the god Freyr goes to a "peaceful grove" to meet Gerðr, and the *Landnámabók* (Book of the Settlement of Iceland), written down between 1275 and 1280, notes that Þórir snepill Ketilsson, the settler of Hnjóskadalr, made a sacrifice in a *lundr*. Around the year 1220, Oliverus Scholerus indicates that the Pruthenes (ancient Prussians) worshipped forest and river nymphs, and in the middle of the fifteenth century Jerome of Prague stated that they "revered the woods sacred to demons," especially the oldest oak trees. The worship of trees is well confirmed among the Saxons who "consecrated the groves and forests, giving them the names of their gods and attaching an eminent dignity to these places. . . . It was especially the leafy trees and the springs that they found worthy of worship," reports Adam of Bremen in the eleventh century. Tacitus mentions the sacred grove of the Semnones that no one can enter unbound: "At a set time, the peoples who share that name and bloodline send embassies to assemble in a forest hallowed by ancestral auguries and ancient dread . . . . no one enters unless bound by a shackle, as an inferior who makes manifest the might of the divine"— and that of the Naharnavali where an extremely ancient worship is performed, whose master is "a priest in woman's dress" (*Germania,* chap. 39 and 43, trans. Rives). Is it a coincidence that the *Poetic Edda* mentions a Fjöturlundr ("Fetter Grove"), where Odin lends his spear to Dagr, who uses it to impale Helgi? It should come as no surprise to see in chapter 21 of the *Jómsvíkinga saga* (Saga of the Jómsvíkings), written around 1200, that when the jarl Hakon confronted the Jómsborg Vikings and the battle turned against him, he took the following action.

> Thereupon the earl went up on the island of Primsigned, and away into a forest, and fell on his knees and prayed, looking northward. And in his prayer he called upon his patron goddess, Þorgerðr Holgabrúð. . . . He offered her a human sacrifice. (trans. Hollander)

The Eddas mention Myrkviðr, the "Dark Forest," as being located at the borders of the world of the gods, which it separates from the world of the giants. Originally, in a historical sense, this was quite likely the forest separating the Goths and the Huns. In the legend of Wayland the Smith, the swan maidens come from here. Another mythic woodland is mentioned in strophe 40 of the Eddic poem *Völuspá* (The Prophecy of the Seeress) as well as in the tale *Gylfaginning* (The Deluding of Gylfi) by the great Icelandic mythographer Snorri Sturluson (1178–1241): Járnviðr, the "Iron Forest" where giants dwell in the form of wolves and witches, guarded by the giant Eggþér, who sits on a mound playing the harp. We should note in passing that this forest could be an illusion. The giant Útgarðaloki tells the god Thor, whom he has just forced to undergo several ordeals and beneath whose steps he has caused the birth of a forest: "I fooled you by tricking your sight."

The Eddas tell us that two dwellers of this forest are the wolves Sköll and Hati, the first of whom pursues the sun, the second the moon—both will eventually swallow their prey. In his *History of the Danes* (III, 2, 4–3, 3, 6), written between 1210 and 1220, Saxo Grammaticus tells us that Hotherus became lost in a forest and met supernatural women—valkyries—who controlled wars and secretly aided their favorites, for they could grant victory or inflict defeat as they pleased. They give him a coat that makes him invulnerable, and after this their abode vanishes. A short while later Hotherus comes across these same women again while crossing through an uninhabited forest; he discovers a cave in which these "nymphs" dwell, and they share their counsel with him.

The forest is the refuge of the werewolf. The *Völsunga saga* (Saga of the Völsungs; thirteenth century) tells how Sigmund and Sinfjötli found a house in the forest that housed two sleeping men who had been victims of a curse that had transformed them into werewolves, and their "wolf furs" lay alongside them; they had gone into these shapes and were unable to get out of them (chap. 8).

Scandinavia folk belief populates the forests with wood maidens (*skogsnufva, skogsjungfru*), land spirits corresponding to the Roman spirits and to the spirit called *skogsrå* in Sweden and Norway. In Germany we have dwarves, wood maidens (*holzvrowe*), "wood weepers" (*holzmuowe*), spirits called *waltscrate* that have become conflated with dwarves, and giants with wonderful names like Rumedenwalt ("Empty Forest"), Schellenwalt ("Peeling Forest"), and Vellenwalt ("Felling Forest").

The forest is the home of the Wild Huntsman. By means of an exemplum, Caesarius of Heisterbach (ca. 1180–1240) relates an event that would have a long posterity, because it was ceaselessly repeated well into the seventeenth century and became the stuff of legend. One night a knight traveling through the forest spotted a woman fleeing in terror; he questioned her, promised to defend her, drew a circle on the ground with his sword, and heard the sound of a hunting horn and the baying of a pack. Her pursuer appeared—it was a demon. The *Virginal,* a late-thirteenth-century poem centered on the adventures of Dietrich von Bern (Theodoric the Great) and Virginal, the queen of a race of dwarves living in the caverns of the Tyrol, tells how Virginal had to give a young girl as tribute every year to a giant named Orkise (whose name reflects the notion of "ogre"). Once chosen, the victim goes into the forest where she is hunted down by Orkise, who devours her. In the *Eckenlied,* Dietrich von Bern meets a wild maiden named Babehilt in the Tyrolean forests. She possesses a kingdom in the sea. The lord of the forest is pursuing her with his pack. "His name is Fasolt and he rules over the wild lands." Fasolt is a giant who blows a horn, wears armor, and wears his hair braided like a woman. The forest is also where the Accursed Huntsman can be found. Michel Beheim (1416/21–1474/78) relates the following story. One fine day the Count Eberhard of Württemberg set out alone to hunt in the forest. He soon heard a loud racket and saw an alarming creature appear chasing a stag. Frightened, he dismounted from his horse and took refuge in a thicket and asked the apparition if he intended him harm. "No, I am a man like yourself. Once I was a lord who loved hunting passionately, and I asked God one day to let me hunt until Final Judgment. To my misfortune, my wish was granted, and it has already been five hundred years that I have been tracking this single stag."

FORNJÓTR: The founding father of a mythical lineage. His sons are Hlér ("Sea"), Logi ("Fire"), and Kari ("Wind"). Kari is the grandfather of Snaer ("Snow"). This is quite likely a family of frost giants (*hrímþursar*).

FORNÖLVIR: This is one of the titles borne by Odin. It means "Ölvir the Old," or "Ölvir the Pagan."

📖 Falk, *Odensheiti.*

FORSETI ("President"): An Æsir god, the son of Balder and Nanna, who lives in Glitnir. He is most certainly identical to Foseti, a god worshipped by the Frisians on an island located between Frisia and Denmark, according to the eighth-century account of the life of Saint Willibrord. The site was considered to be so sacred by the pagans that no one dared touch anything that they found there, nor drink water from any spring there.

FOSSEGRIM: Local land spirit that lives in waterfalls.

✦ *HOUSEHOLD/PLACE SPIRITS*

FRANANGRSFORS ("Franangr's Falls"): This is the waterfall where Loki hid after transforming himself into a salmon to escape the wrath of the Æsir who, following Baldr's death, could no longer tolerate his evil nature.

FRÁRIÐR ("The Rider"): One of Odin's titles, perhaps an allusion to his steed Sleipnir.

📖 Falk, *Odensheiti.*

FRAU ELSE ("Lady Else"): A perching spirit in Hesse, Germany, who jumps on the rump of the horse to ride behind its horseman.

FREA: According to Paul the Deacon's *History of the Lombards,* she was the wife of Godan (Odin/Wodan). This figure is therefore identical to Frigg.

✦ *LANGBARDR*

FREKI ("Greedy"): One of Odin's two wolves, the other whose name is Geri. It is also another name for Fenrir.

FREYR ("Lord"): Freyr is the primary god of the family of the Vanir, a deity of the Dumézilian third function (fertility, fecundity). He is the son of Njörð and the brother of Freyja. About Freyr, Snorri Sturluson informs us: "He is ruler of rain and sunshine and thus of the produce of the earth, and it is good to pray to him for prosperity and peace. He also rules over the wealth of men" (*Gylfaginning* 23–24, trans. Faulkes). The pig and the stallion are his favorite animals.

He lives in Álfheimr ("World of the Elves"), and owns the wonderful boat called Skíðblaðnir and the boar Gullinborsti (or Slíðrugtanni). His wife is the giantess Gerðr. He obtained her hand from her father Gymir, in exchange for his sword. Because he no longer had this sword during the apocalyptic battle, Surtr, the fire giant, slew him.

Freyr is also called Yngvi and is the ancestor of the Ynglingar. He may therefore be identical to the eponymous founder of the Ingvaeonic people mentioned by Tacitus. In the British Isles he is known as Ing. In the euhemeristic interpretation of the *Ynglinga saga*, Freyr is presented as the king of Sweden living in Uppsala, the husband of Gerðr and father of Fjölnir. Peace and prosperity reigned during his time, which is why he was worshipped after his death.

Freyr (Latinized as Fricco) is also identified with the Danish Frotho and Fróði. In Norway, when making toasts during banquets, the first toast was to Odin, and the others to Njörðr and Freyr. Evidence for the

Fig. 29. Freyr amulet.
Bronze from Rällinge
in Södermanland
(Sweden), sixth century.

worship and popularity of Freyr can be seen in the thirty-seven Swedish, seven Danish, and twenty-six Norwegian place-names that refer to him. There is also the place-name of Fréville in Normandy.

On the functional level, he occupies the same position as the Nāsatya or Ashvins in the Indic tradition and the Roman Quirinus.

FREYJA ("Lady," "Mistress"): She is the primary goddess of the family of the Vanir, daughter of Njörðr and the sister of Freyr. She was married to Óðr, with whom she had a daughter, Hnoss, also called Gersimi. When her husband went away on his travels, she wept gold tears. She lives in Fólkvangr, one of the heavenly dwellings, and her hall is called Sessrumnir. She shares half of the dead with Odin. She is fond of love poetry and is famous for her promiscuity. The worship addressed to her was erotic, which likens her to several Eastern deities, Cybele in particular. Freyja travels in a chariot drawn by cats.

Her field of activity is vast: life (birth) and death, love and battle, fertility and black magic. It is Freyja who taught the Æsir the magic rites most honored by the Vanir (✦ SEIÐR).

She is beautiful and lascivious, which inspired the giants with an urge to wed her (✦ ÞRYMR, HRUNGNIR), and the historiographical texts tell us that she was good to invoke for matters concerning love.

In skaldic poetry she was called Vanadís ("Dise of the Vanir"), Sýr ("Sow"), Gefn ("The Giving One"), Hörn ("Spirit of Flax"?), and Mardöll ("Sea-brightener"). She was quite renowned because of her necklace, Brísingamen. She obtained this piece of jewelry by sleeping with the dwarves who had forged it. The strength of the worship dedicated to Freyja is well attested by Norwegian and Swedish place-names, but the texts remain silent on this point.

📖 Boyer, *La Grande Déesse du Nord*, 120–62; Näsström, *Freyja, the Great Goddess of the North*.

FRICCO: Another name for Freyr, according to the eleventh-century report of Adam of Bremen. In it he describes the temple of Uppsala, which housed statues of Thor, Odin, and Fricco, who was depicted with a huge phallus (*cum ingenti priapo*)—a detail that is also evident on a sixth-century bronze amulet and which is an indication of the Dumézilian third function.

FRIGG/FRÎJA ("Lady"): Principal goddess of the Æsir, wife of Odin, and the mother of Baldr and Fjörgynn. She resides at Fensalir in Ásgarðr and has Fulla and Gná for servants. She owns a falcon cloak, an allusion to an ancient ability to shapeshift. To protect Baldr from the perils of this world, she obtained oaths from each of the plants, minerals, and animals to spare him, but she forgot to demand that oath from the mistletoe plant.

In the Lombard tradition she is called Frea; in the *Second Merseburg Charm,* written in Old High German, the name appears as Frîja; and in Old English it is Frige. She gave her name to the English weekday name "Friday" and German *Freitag.* Place-names in the Scandinavian countries (with the exception of Iceland) attest to her worship.

A telluric and mother goddess who gives life to plants, animals, and men, Frigg is also the divine spinner who initiated mortals into the workings of the spinning wheel and spindle. Her distaff produces a thread that is as soft as silk. She is the patron deity for domestic chores and agriculture.

Originally identical to Freyja, she has retained several of the other goddess's features, such as her notorious conjugal infidelity. She brings prosperity and happiness, aided by Fulla/Folla, the deification of abundance.

📖 Beck, *Die Merseburger Zaubersprüche;* Boyer, *La Grande Déesse du Nord,* 161–83; Jean-Paul Allard, "Du second Charme de Mersebourg au Viatique de Weingarten," *Études Indo-Européennes* 14 (1985): 33–53.

FRÔ ("Lord"): A German god corresponding to Freyr and perhaps identical to Phol whose name is cited in the *Second Merseburg Charm.*

FRØ: The Danish name for Freyr. Sacrifices were made to this god every year or once every nine years (depending on the historical source) at his sanctuary in Uppsala.

FRÓÐI/FROTHO: From an euhemeristic perspective, Freyr becomes the king Fróði of the Skjöldungar lineage. As a figure in heroic Anglo-Saxon poetry, he is named Froda. He is a descendant of Skjöldr, who is himself a descendant of Thor in numerous genealogies.

FROST GIANTS: ✦ HRÍMÞURSAR

FULLA ("Abundance"): A handmaiden and confidante of Frigg. She is a virgin who wears a golden ribbon around her forehead. She is most likely identical to Volla, whose name is cited in the *Second Merseburg Charm*. As the personification of abundance, she is a close relative of the Roman goddess Copia.

FUNCTIONS (the tripartite functions): While undertaking a structural study of the Indo-European gods, Georges Dumézil discovered that they could be divided up according to three functions: (1) sovereignty, (2) war, and (3) fertility. The first function of sovereignty was furthermore of a dual nature, encompassing both royalty and priesthood (the latter of which can be expressed through religion and/or magic). Dumézil's analytical grid does not align all that well in the Germanic sphere, however, because the gods often represent two functions, and there can be several gods per function. For example, we find Odin alternating with Týr in the first function, while Thor falls into both the second and third functions. These difficulties with interpreting the Germanic mythology all stem from the following facts: Each function is represented by an individual or group of individuals, working together or opposing each other, contemporaneously or in succession. A god can concurrently—simultaneously or successively—hold a place in all three functions, as is suggested by the myth of the Scythian royalty related by Herodotus (*Histories*, IV, 5–7). The functions can also be represented by distinct but homonymous figures.

📖 Dumézil, *Gods of the Ancient Northmen*; Dumézil, *Mythe et Épopée I*; Lecouteux, "Die burgundische Königsfamilie im Nibelungenlied und die drei indogermanischen Funktionsebenen: Überlegungen zum Fortleben einer mythologisch-epischen Struktur," *Euphorion* 91 (1997): 279–9; Jean-Marie Maillefer, "Recherche sur l'ancienne royauté suédoise et l'idéologie des trois fonctions," *Études Germaniques* 36 (1981): 377–92.

FYLGJA ("Follower"; pl. *fylgjur*): This is the Old Norse name for one of the three "components" of what the Christians call the "soul." It is simultaneously a guardian deity and the psychic Double of the individual, which leaves the sleeping body while dreaming, and visits friends or foes. The *fylgja* can take the shape of any animal it likes. Depending on how powerful he is, a man can possess several *fylgjur.* The plural term *fylgjur* reflects the notion of destiny. The *fylgja* is undoubtedly an emanation of the *anima mundi* and should be compared to the Greek *daimon,* the Latin *genius,* and the Christian guardian angel, which the Norse called the "follower-angel" (*fylgjuengill*).

✦ *HAMR, SCHLEMIHL*

📖 Blum, *Die Schutzgeister in der altnordischen Literatur.*

GABIAE ("The Giving Ones"): This is the name for a group of goddesses known through a dozen votive inscriptions found on the lower course of the Rhine. Etymologically speaking, these deities are the counterpart of the goddess Gefjon.

GAGNRAÐR/GANGRAÐR ("Contradictor"): Odin called himself this during his verbal contest with the giant Vafþrúðnir.

  📖 Falk, *Odensheiti.*

GALARR ("Howler"): One of the two dwarves that slew Kvasir and prepared the magical mead. He is the brother of Fjalarr.

GALDR (Old High German *galster;* Old English *gealdor*): A generic term meaning "incantation, magic song." The *Eiríks saga rauða* (Saga of Erik the Red) informs us that this singing was used to attract the spirits.

  ✦ *SEIÐR, VARÐLOKUR*

  📖 Lindquist, *Galdrar.*

GALGENMÄNNCHEN: ✦ MANDRAKE

GAMBANTEINN ("Magic Twig"): A magical object that Odin received from the giant Hlébarðr. Freyr's servant or hypostasis Skírnir used it to bewitch the giantess Gerðr, whom his master was lusting after.

GANDÁLFR ("Elf with the Magic Wand"): This dwarf name is evidence of the confusion between elves and dwarves in our remote ancestors' minds. It is also the name of the wizard in *The Hobbit* and *The Lord of the Rings* by Tolkien.

GANDR/GÖNDUL (Latin *gandus*): This is primarily a magic wand used by a sorcerer, but the term can also refer to the evil spell cast on someone by a witch. In the latter case it is viewed as a tiny living being such as a fly. It is also the physical Double of the witch or sorcerer, which leaves the sorcerer's body (which then remains in a temporary cataleptic state) so that it can cast its evil spells. This journey by the witch's Double is called the *gandreið* ("riding the *gandr*"). The Double can assume the shape of an animal, so *gandr* can also mean "wolf." In the Latin historiographical texts, *gandus* means the spirit of the shaman that departs on a mission in the otherworld; for example, to retrieve a soul. A curse spell from 1325, attributed to a certain Ragnhildr Tregagaas and found in Bergen, Norway, says: "I send [you] the spirit of the magic wand (*göndul*), which I ride; may one bite you on the back, may another bite you on the chest, and may the third stir in you hatred and ill-will."

GANGERL (neut.): This is the name of a spirit of the Austrian mountains. It is depicted as a dwarf three feet high with a long white beard and dressed in a gray cap and robe. He wears a gold belt around his waist. He sometimes brings riches to the mountain folk who behave well, and sometimes he causes rockfalls. In the region of Carinthia, Gangerl is one of the names for the devil.

GAPT: Mythical ancestor of the Amali, a dynasty of Gothic kings. It is believed that this could be Odin, one of whose bynames is Gautr ("Goth"). The latter name appears in Old English as Geat.

GARDBO: ✦ HOUSEHOLD/PLACE SPIRITS

GARMANEYS: A sea monster in the service of a demon who kidnapped the fairy Engiselor and the son of Kurie (a counterpart of Cundrie the Witch in *Perceval*), who has come to seek aid from the court of King Arthur. The demon had imprisoned the fairy on a high mountain and had removed all its land so that it was surrounded only by an impassable river or sea, making it so that none could enter or leave that land. Led by Kurie, who knows all the paths, Persibein reaches the mountain, which is defended by Garmaneys. It is necessary to overcome him and force him to place you on the mountain, for there is no other way to reach its summit. Persibein succeeds in freeing Engiselor, who has been enchained by magic spells, and gains possession of some magical stones that provide protection against water and fire (these stones have certain other virtues, too, but unfortunately they are not described). He then leaves to free Kurie's son.

✦ *WAGOLLT*

📖 Füetrer, *Das Buch der Abenteuer;* Lecouteux, *Demons and Spirits of the Land,* 174–76.

GARMR: The dog chained in front of Gnipahellir, the boulder to which the wolf Fenrir has been shackled. In the final battle his foe is Týr, and they kill each other.

GAUTATÝR ("God of the Goths"): One of Odin's titles.

📖 Falk, *Odensheiti.*

GAUTR/GAUTI ("Goth," "Gotlander"): These are names for Odin. They have a counterpart in the name Geat, which appears in the Anglo-Saxon royal genealogies. A Latinized form, Gausus, is also attested.

📖 Falk, *Odensheiti.*

GIANTS: Giants are divided into three families or races: the *jötunar* (Old English *eotenas*), about whom nothing is known; the thurses; and the trolls. They are ugly, sometimes monstrously so, and embody natural forces as revealed by their names, which, in addition to violence and shouting, reflect notions of fire, snow, stone, soil, and water. They are predators who seek to abduct the goddesses Sól (the sun), Iðunn, and Freyja. They are destroyers: the end of the world is orchestrated by the giants Hymir, Surtr, and Loki. They are founders: the world was created from the body of the primordial giant Ymir, and the gods married the daughters of giants. Prestigious lineages resulted from such unions. The boundary between the gods and the giants is considerably fluid because of these multiple marriages. The giants possess magical skills, and they dwell in Útgarðr or Jötunheimr. The god Thor is constantly assailing them with his hammer, Mjöllnir.

In medieval German traditions they are portrayed as dimwittted brutes, barely smarter than animals. They are clad in animal hides and wield tree trunks as weapons. They have roles as guardians, as collectors of gifts or tributes, and as abductors and undesirable suitors. They are often conflated with wild men and no longer retain any mythological character.

According to a fifteenth-century German text, God created the giants after the dwarves so they could protect the latter from the monstrous reptiles that prevented them from tilling the ground; but the giants quickly turned criminal and oppressed the dwarves. For this reason God created heroes so that the giants could be compelled to respect the order he had instituted.

In the Scandinavian lands words for a giant include *risi* (Old Norse), *rysa, jätte* (Swedish), and *jöttul* (Norwegian), while a giantess is a *gýgr* (Old Norse); in the Shetlands the latter are called *guykerl* and *gör*.

📖 Lecouteux, *Les Monstres dans la littérature allemande du Moyen Âge (1150–1350)*; Lecouteux, *Les Monstres dans la pensée médiévale européenne*; Schulz, *Riesen: Von Wissenshütern und Wildnisbewohnern in Edda und Saga*; Van den Berg, *De volkssage in de provincie Antwerpen in de 19de en 20ste eeuw*, 1452ff.

✦ *EOTEN, GRÝLA, JÖTUNN, RISE, THURSE, TROLL*

GEFJON ("Dispenser"): This Ásynja is at the heart of the following myth. King Gylfi was ruling over Svíþjód (the Swedish people). He granted Gefjon as much land as she could circle in the space of one day and one night with a plow drawn by four oxen—a motif that folklorists call a foundation legend and which we likewise find in the *Aeneid* (with the foundation of Carthage), as well as in the *Roman de Mélusine* by Jean d'Arras. Gefjon sought oxen from the giants and began to toil. The plow blade sank so deep that the land was carried off and formed an island called Seland, which is known today as Zealand. According to one tradition, Gefjon took four sons of a giant and gave them the appearance of oxen and it was they who pulled her plow. This was how Lake Lögrinn (present-day Lake Mälar in Sweden) was created. Etymologically, Gefjon is the counterpart of the Gabiae goddesses.

📖 Anne Holtsmark, "Gevjons plog," *Maal og Minne* (1944): 169–79; Tomoaki Mizuno, "The Gefjon Story and Its Magical Significance in *Gylfaginning*," *Bulletin of the Society for Icelandic Studies of Japan* 13 (1993): 22–35; Axel Olrik, "Gefion," *Danske Studier* (1910): 1–31.

GEFN ("Giver"): One of the names of the goddess Freyja.

GEIGGLE (neut.): The name for a Tyrolean spirit who would tear to pieces anyone it overheard speaking curse words. It would cast their skin to one side, their bodies to the other, and cart their heads off somewhere else.

📖 Heyl, *Volkssagen, Meinungen und Bräuche aus Tirol,* 611.

GEIRAHÖD ("Spear-combat"): The name of a valkyrie.

GEIRAVÖR ("Spear Goddess"): The name of a valkyrie.

GEIRDRIFUL ("Spear-caster"): The name of a valkyrie.

GEIRRÖÐARGARÐR ("Geirröðr's Enclosure"): The dwelling of the giant Geirröðr in Jötunheimr where Thor went to free Loki.

GEIRRÖÐR: The giant who captured Loki one day when the latter flew to his home in the shape of a falcon using Frigg's feather cloak. Seeing the falcon, Geirröðr recognized the eyes of a man and sought to make him speak, but Loki kept his silence. The giant imprisoned him inside a chest and starved him. Loki eventually surrendered his name and swore he would make Thor come there without his hammer or his belt of power. While making his way to Geirröðr's dwelling, Thor invited himself into the house of a giantess named Gríðr who loaned him her own belt of power, iron gloves, and her magic wand. Thor next had to cross the Vimur River, which suddenly flooded because Geirröðr's daughter Gjálp urinated into it. When he reached the giant's house Thor was invited to enter a goat stable where there was only one chair. He sat down on it; then felt it lift up and hurl him against the roof beam. He softened the shock with the magic wand and fell back heavily against the chair. A loud racket and howling was heard: Gjálp and Greip had been standing beneath the chair, and Thor had just broken their necks. Geirröðr then called Thor into the great hall and hurled a red-hot block of iron at him, but Thor knocked it back at the giant, who leaped behind an iron pillar to hide. The block crashed through the pillar, through Geirröðr, through the wall behind him, and into the ground. In the version by Saxo Grammaticus, Geirröðr appears under the name Geruthus, and the story is different.

✦ *GERUTHUS*

GEIRSKÖGULL ("Spear-combat"): A valkyrie.

GEIRTÝR ("Spear God"): One of Odin's titles.

📖 Falk, *Odensheiti.*

GEIRVIMULL ("Teeming with Spears"): One of the rivers of Élivágar. It flows close to Hel.

GEITIR: A giant that appears in chapters 5 and 6 of the *Fljótsdæla saga* (Saga of the People of Fljótsdal). Geitir lived in the Shetlands and terrorized the islanders. After being shipwrecked on the Shetland shores, Þorvaldr, a young Icelander, was welcomed by the jarl Björgólfr, whose daughter Droplaug had been captured by the giant. Þorvaldr found his cave, stole the abductor's sword, killed him with it, and freed Droplaug from her horrible prison. The description of Geitir's cave cannot help but bring to mind the lair of Grendel in *Beowulf.*

GELDMÄNNLEINCHEN ("Little Money Man"): As his name clearly indicates, this spirit has one particular specialty. He appears as a little gray man whose eyes are sometimes light. Sometimes he wears a red cap and a green jacket. He can also take the form of certain animals such as a frog, toad, owl, or beetle. He seems to be a projection or direct emanation of the mandrake; this situation determines the majority of the information we can gather on him. The *Geldmännleinchen* can be met at a crossroads by digging beneath a triple clump of hazel at midnight. He can also be purchased. He is most frequently kept in a chest or box placed in a closed room or is attached to the central beam of the common room. When the *Geldmännleinchen* enjoys independence, his preferred dwelling place is in the attic or a dark corner of the house, or even on a pile of manure. His services are rewarded with small loaves of bread fresh from the oven, sometimes sweets, and even a glass of wine. These foodstuffs are placed in the attic. He is cared for in exactly the same manner as a mandrake: He must be bathed in a spoon every day and fed with morsels of food taken from his own plate. He is also given fine clothes. It is almost impossible to get rid of the *Geldmännleinchen*—as a general rule, every attempt to do so will fail, and he can even resist death and fire. The common explanation for this impossibility is that his first two purchasers can sell him, but the third is obliged to keep him and thus irremediably belongs to the devil.

📖 Lecouteux, *The Tradition of Household Spirits*, 155–58.

GELGJA ("Fetter"): The chain the Æsir use to shackle the wolf Fenrir to the boulder called Gjöll.

GEMA, GEMINAS: Earth goddess of the ancient Prussians. One day when Perkunos and Pikollos visited her, she gave Perkunos eternal youth and she rewarded Pikollos with a number of young maidens who performed his nightly duties for him.

📖 Rhesa, *Prutena*, 174.

GERÐR ("Enclosure"?): An Ásynja who is the daughter of the giant Gymir and his wife, Aurboða. She is the wife of the god Freyr and the mother of Fjölnir. To win her hand, Freyr had to surrender his sword to Gymir. Gerðr may be an extremely ancient telluric goddess connected to the Dumézilian third function (fertility, fecundity).

GERI ("Greedy"): One of the hounds of Hel or, according to other traditions, one of Odin's two wolves.

GERSIMI ("Treasure"): One of Freyja's daughters, identical to Hnoss.

GERUTHUS: According to Saxo Grammaticus, he was the king of a legendary land northeast of Scandinavia where Thorkillus led an expedition. They find Geruthus seated in his horrible palace, his body perforated and flanked by three women with broken spines. (In this description we can recognize Geirröðr and his daughters Gjálp and Greip.) Thorkillus advises his company not to touch anything. Three of his men ignore his warning and grab a gold armlet, a horn, and the tusk of a marvelous animal. The armlet becomes a serpent, the horn a dragon, and the tusk a sword; these then slay the three men. When Thorkillus takes possession of a splendid cloak the hall shakes and the visitors are attacked by creatures they had assumed to be lifeless. Only a few of the men survive.

📖 Saxo, *The History of the Danes*, trans. Fisher, bk. VIII, 239–43; Lecouteux, *Mondes parallèles*, 85–100 (French translation of the *Voyage of Thorkillus*).

GESTR ("Guest," "Stranger"): One of the names of Odin. He loved to roam the world incognito, clad in a blue mantle that concealed his features.

📖 Falk, *Odensheiti.*

GESTUMBLINDI ("Blind Guest"): The name Odin used when introducing himself to King Heiðrekr and inviting him to answer his riddles. A very similar situation occurs in the Eddic poem *Vafþrúðnismál,* in which Odin matches wits with the giant Vafþrúðnir.

📖 Falk, *Odensheiti.*

GEVARUS: According to Saxo Grammaticus he was the father of Nanna, Baldr's wife, and the foster father of Høtherus (Höðr), the unintentional murderer of Baldr.

GHOST SHIP: ✦ FLYING DUTCHMAN

GÍFR ("Sorcerer" or "The Dreadful One"): The name of one of the two dogs (the other is Geri) that guard the entrance to Hel and who watch over Menglöð's eleven maidens.

GILLINGR ("Noisy"): A giant, the father of Suttungr. After the dwarves Fjalarr and Galarr killed Kvasir by drowning him in the sea, and after they crushed Gillingr's wife with a millstone, they were captured by Suttungr. He sets them on a sea-swept skerry where, in order to save their own lives, they gave him the wondrous mead.

GIMLÉ ("Shelter from the Flames"): A golden-ceilinged hall where men will live after Ragnarök. It is also the name of one of the heavenly dwellings where good men live after death; it is located in the third heaven, Viðbláinn. It is interesting to note that Gimlé is also the dwelling place of the light elves and thereby illustrates the gradual conflation of the good dead with elves.

GINNUNGAGAP ("Gaping Void"): At the dawn of the world there was only chaos and an unfathomable void. It is filled with ice and frost in the north (this is Niflheimr) and fire to the south (Muspellsheimr). Niflheimr is where the spring Hvergelmir flows, from which all the original rivers—the Élivágar—have their source. Muspell's heat caused the frost to melt, and life sprung forth from it in the form of the giant Ymir, from whom descended the frost giants and then the cow Auðumla.

📖 Jan De Vries, "Ginnungagap," *Acta Philologica Scandinavica* 5 (1930): 41–66; Eugen Mogk, "Ginnungagap," *Beiträge zur Geschichte der deutschen Sprache und Literatur* 8 (1882): 153–60.

GÍSL ("Sunray"): One of the horses of the Æsir. The poem *Grímnismál* in the *Poetic Edda* mentions ten of them.

✦ *FALHÓFNIR*

GIZURR: One of Odin's names. It could mean "He Who Guesses," in which case it would refer to the riddles the god was asked to solve while his identity went unrecognized.

📖 Falk, *Odensheiti.*

GJALLARBRÚ ("Bridge over the Gjöll"): This is a bridge spanning the Gjöll, the river that surrounds the underworld (✦ HEL). It is covered with sparkling gold and guarded by the maiden Móðguðr. The bridge to the underworld is a motif found among all the Indo-European peoples for whom it symbolizes the paradoxical crossing. Christianity recycled this image, and medieval images frequently refer to it.

GJALLARHORN ("Resounding Horn"): This is the horn blown by Heimdallr to warn the gods that the forces of evil have launched an assault on Ásgarðr, the beginning of the eschatological battle.

According to another tradition this is the drinking horn from which Mímir drinks wisdom that gushes up from a well beneath one of the roots of the cosmic ash tree, Yggdrasill.

✦ *RAGNARÖK*

GJÁLP ("Yelping One"): One of the two daughters of the giant Geirröðr. Thor broke her back when he went to Jötunheimr to free Loki. It is also the name of one of the nine mothers of Heimdallr.

GJÖLL 1 ("Tumult"): The river nearest to the underworld of Hel. It is crossed by the bridge called Gjallarbrú.

GJÖLL 2: The name of the rock to which the Æsir fetter the wolf Fenrir.

GLAÐR ("Shining One"): One of the horses ridden by the Æsir to make their way beneath the cosmic tree, Yggdrasill.

✦ *FALHÓFNIR*

GLAPSVIÐR ("Beguiler"): One of Odin's names; it may reflect his amorous adventures with Rindr and Gunnlöð.

✦ *GÖNDLIR*

📖 Falk, *Odensheiti.*

GLASIR ("Sparkling"): A grove whose foliage is made of gold. It is located in Ásgarðr, in front of the gates of Valhalla.

GLAUMARR ("Noisy"): The name of a giant in the *þulur* lists.

GLEIPNIR: The third fetter used by the gods to bind Fenrir. It was made from the noise of a cat's footfalls, the beard of a woman, the roots of a mountain, the sinews of a bear, the breath of a fish, and the spittle of a bird. It was "as smooth and soft as a silk ribbon, but solid and strong" (Snorri).

GLENR ("Sunny Period"): Husband of the goddess Sól, the sun. We know nothing further about him.

GLÆR ("Light"): One of the horses of the Æsir.

✦ *FALHÓFNIR*

GLITNIR ("Glittering"): The name of a dwarf in the *þulur* lists. It reflects the metalsmithing activity of these beings.

GLÓI ("Red Hot"): The name of a dwarf in the *þulur* lists. It reflects the metalsmithing activity of these beings.

GLOSO ("Glowing Sow"): In southern Sweden the glowing sow Gloso appears during the Twelve Days period. She has eyes of fire, sparks fly from her bristles, and she moves like a hungry flame.

Fig. 30. Gloso

To enjoy a good harvest, offerings of gruel and fish were made to her so that she would not cause anyone harm. Once the harvest was in, three sheaves were left in the fields, concerning which people said, "They are for Gloso: one for Christmas, one for New Year, and one for the night of the Kings [Epiphany]." Gloso is sometimes identified as the specter of a murdered child without a Christian burial or as the supernatural guardian of a church (*kirkegrim*). The same creature can be found in Denmark, where it is called Gravsoen; in Zealand it is called Glumsoen.

📖 Hilding Celander, "Gravso och Gloso," *Arv* 8 (1952): 42–76; Eskeröd, *Årets äring: Etnologiska studier i skördens och julens tro och sed*, 115–17 (map of the phenomenon).

GNÁ: This is the fourteenth Ásynja of the pantheon. She seems to work in the service of Frigg, Odin's wife, and travels about on a wondrous horse that races through the air and over the water.

📖 Hans Kuhn, "Gná oder Syr," in *Kleine Schriften*, vol. II, 280–89.

GNIPAHELLIR ("Craggy Cave"): The place where the wolf Garmr (possibly another name for Fenrir) is imprisoned.

GOÐI: In pagan Iceland this was the term for a sacrificing priest, temple warden, and political leader. The clan leader carried out these high duties. After the conversion to Christianity in Iceland, a *goði* held extensive temporal political power.

GODS: ✦ ÆGIR, BALDR, BRAGI, FORSETI, FREYR, FRIGG, FREYJA, HLÍN, HŒNIR, IÐUNN, LOKI, NJÖRÐR, ODIN (WODAN, WODEN), SÁGA, SKAÐI, THOR, TÝR, ULLR

GODS (Dwellings of Gods): ✦ ÁLFHEIMR, ÁSGARÐR, BREIÐABLIK, FÓLKVANGR, GLAÐSHEIMR, GLITNIR, HEL, HIMINBJÖRG, NOATUN, SÖKKVABEKKR, ÞRÚDHEIMR, VALHALLA, ÝDALIR

GÓI: A frost giantess. Her name designates the fifth month of winter, which begins between February 18 and 24.

GÓINN: One of the serpents living beneath—and gnawing at—the roots of the cosmic tree, Yggdrasill. The others are, Móinn ("Swamp Beast"), Grafvitnir ("Burrowing Wolf"), Grábakr ("Grayback"), Grafvölluðr ("The One Who Digs the Plains"), Sváfnir ("Sleep-bringer"), which is also one of Odin's names, and Ófnir ("The Coiling One"). According to the *Snorra Edda,* these snakes live in the Hvergelmir spring.

GOLDEMAR: In the story bearing his name, which forms a part of the legendary material centered on Dietrich von Bern, Goldemar is the king of the dwarves living in Trutmunt, a mountain in Tyrol. He abducted Hertlin, the king of Portugal's daughter. Dietrich frees her and then marries her.

GÖLL ("Din"): One of the thirteen valkyries mentioned in the *Grímnismál* (The Lay of Grímnir).

GÖMUL ("Crone"): One of the forty-one rivers "girding the domain of the gods" whose source is the spring Hvergelmir.

GÖNDLIR: One of the forty-one names of Odin cited in the Eddic poem *Grímnismál* (The Lay of Grímnir). The others are Grímr ("Mask"), Gangleri ("Travel-weary"), Herjann ("Lord of the Armies"), Hjálmberi ("Helm-bearer"), Þekkr ("Beloved"), Þriði ("Third"), Þundr (?), Uðr ("Loved"), Helblindi ("Hel-blinder"), Hárr ("High One"), Saðr ("The True One"), Svipall ("Shapeshifting"), Sanngetall ("Good Guesser/Truth-finder"), Herteitr ("Merry among Warriors"), Hnikarr ("Striker"), Bileygr ("One-eyed"?), Bálegyr ("Flaming Eye"), Bölverkr ("Evil-doer"), Fjölnir ("Multifarious"), Glapsviðr ("Beguiler"), Fjölsviðr ("Very Wise"), Grímnir ("Masked"), Síðhöttr ("Broad Hat"), Alföðr ("All-father"), Valföðr ("Father of the Slain"), Atriðr ("Attacker"), Farmatýr ("God of Cargoes"). Odin also bears the names Hangaguð ("God of the Hanged") and Draugadróttinn ("Lord of Revenants"). Each name refers to an episode of his life or one of his characteristic features.

📖 Falk, *Odensheiti*.

GÖNDUL: A valkyrie. The name refers to *gandr*, which means "charm," mainly in the sense of a spell cast by a "magic wand," and it corresponds nicely with the function of the messenger (of death) sent by Odin.

GORCHO: The god of food and drink for the ancient Prussians. He was worshipped beneath an oak in Heiligenbeil (present-day Mamonovo, Russia). His effigy was destroyed every year, and then, once the crops had been picked, it was remade and worshipped, particularly after the harvest.

📖 Schütz, *Historia rerum Prussicarum*, vol. I, 83.

GRÄGGI: This is the name of a being in Switzerland that shows itself at night in the form of a tree trunk, dog, calf, pig, or a small beast the size of a gourd. It travels by rolling along the side of the road and "cries in a thousand voices." It leads travelers astray and sometimes has a role in the Wild Hunt.

✦ *WILD HUNT*

GRANI: The name of Sigurðr's horse. He is the son of Odin's steed, Sleipnir, and it was Odin who personally gave him as a gift to Sigurðr, appearing to him in the guise of an old man with a long beard. It will be recalled that one of Odin's names is "Graybeard" (Hárbarðr).

GRANT: In thirteenth-century England, the Grant was a demon that resembles a yearling colt rearing up on its hindquarters. It shows up during the warmest part of the day or toward sundown. Each time it appears it announces an imminent fire in the town or village where it shows itself. When danger threatens, it makes the dogs bark.

📖 Liebrecht, ed., *Des Gervasius of Tilbury, Otia imperialia,* III, 62.

GRAUMÄNNCHEN ("Little Gray Man"): A ghost that appears in central and northern Germany; it guards a treasure.

✦ *LITTLE GRAY MAN*

GREIP ("The One Who Grasps"): This is one of Heimdallr's nine mothers or one of the giant Geirröðr's two daughters. Thor broke her spine when he went to Geirröðr's house to free Loki.

GRENDEL: Monster slain by Beowulf in the Old English epic that bears his name. Grendel lived in a swamp, was a cannibal, and belonged to a family of giants (*eotenas*). According to the Christian interpretation, he was a descendant of Cain.

📖 Lars Malmberg, "Grendel and the Devil," *Neuphilologische Mitteilungen* 88 (1977): 241–43; J. R. R. Tolkien, "The Monsters and the Critics, in Tolkien," *The Monsters and the Critics and Other Essays* (Boston: Houghton Mifflin, 1984), 5–48.

GRERR: According to the fourteenth-century text *Sörla þáttr* (The Tale of Sörli), this would be one of the four dwarves that forged Brísingamen, Freyja's necklace.

GRÍÐARVÖLR ("Griðr's Wand"): The magic wand that the giantess Gríðr gave the god Thor when he stayed at her home en route to Geirröðr's house to free Loki.

GRÍÐR ("Vehement"): Giantess with whom Thor stayed while traveling to Geirröðr's home to free Loki. She is the mother of Viðar the Silent and owns a pair of iron gloves, a belt of power, and a magic wand. She lends them to the god and warns him about Geirröðr's ruses.

GRIM: In the cycle of legends concerning Dietrich von Bern, the hero confronts the two giants Grim and Hilde. He meets them one day while traveling with his old armorer, Hildebrand. He decapitates Grim and then splits Hilde in two, but the two halves of his body knit themselves back together. He manages to kill Hilde once and for all by placing himself between the two halves of the body, a motif that can be found in Saxo Grammaticus's *History of the Danes* (VIII, 12). It should be noted that Grim was slain with his own sword, forged by the dwarf Alfrik. Dietrich took possession of this weapon and called it Nagelring. Several thirteenth-century German texts allude to this encounter, such as *Eckenlied* and *Sigenot,* which describes Sigenot as the uncle of Grim.

GRÍMNIR ("Masked One"): One of Odin's bynames. It alludes to his penchant for going about in disguise. It is also a name of a giant found in the *þulur* lists.

📖 Falk, *Odensheiti.*

GRÍMR ("Mask"): One of Odin's names (✦ GRÍMNIR). It is also the name of a dwarf in the *þulur* lists.

📖 Falk, *Odensheiti.*

GRJÓTÚN ("Enclosure of Stones"): Home of the giant Geirröðr; it is a metaphorical reference to the mountains, the place where these beings customarily dwell.

GRJÓTÚNAGARÐAR ("Wall of the Stone Enclosure"): The place where the duel between the god Thor and the giant Hrungnir occurred. This name is certainly a thirteenth-century creation.

GRÓA: She is a seer. According to tradition she is the mother of Svipdagr, who summons her back from the kingdom of the dead to learn the future and gain counsel regarding the quest for a bride that he is about to undertake. She is also the wife of Aurvandill, the morning star. She uses her spells in an attempt to dislodge the stone embedded in Thor's skull during his battle with Hrungnir.

GROTTI: A mythical mill that is turned by the giantesses Fenja and

Menja. It grinds whatever one desires. Fróði owns it. A kenning from skaldic poetry defines *gold* as "Fróði's flour."

GRÝLA: The name of a troll-wife in Icelandic traditions. She has three hundred heads, with six eyes on each one, topped by a tuft of hair. She also has two deathly pale, blue eyes behind each neck. She bears goat horns, and her ears are so long that one end reaches her shoulders and the other meets the end of her three hundred noses. Her teeth resemble burned lava. She wears a sack on each thigh that she uses to carry off disobedient children. Grýla has fifteen tails, each of which holds a hundred leather sacks, each of which can hold twenty children. Originally Grýla is mentioned in the thirteenth century as a troll-wife in the *Sturlunga saga* (Saga of the Sturlungs) and likewise by Snorri Sturluson in the *Háttatal* section of the *Snorra Edda;* in the sixteenth century this troll-wife became a figure of legend, a bogeyman. In the twentieth century she was conflated with the North American figure of Santa Claus: her sack was transformed into a bag of plenty, and Grýla hands out gifts on Christmas Day.

   📖 Hjorleifur Rafn Jonsson, "Trolls, Chiefs and Children: Changing Perspectives on an Icelandic Christmas Myth," *Nord Nytt: Nordisk Tidsskrift for Folkelivsforskning* 41 (1990): 55–63.

GUÐMUNDR, GUTHMUND: A giant that rules over Glæsisvellir, a mythical kingdom located to the northeast of Scandinavia. According to Saxo Grammaticus, Guthmund is the father of Geruthus (Geirröðr), and he gives shelter to Thorkillus and his men when they come to his home. He tries to keep them there by exciting their lust and then helps them to cross the river that separates this world from the underworld. It is presumed that Guðmundr/Guthmund was at one time the master of the realm of the dead.

GUÐRÚN: In the Norse version of the legend of Sigurðr (Siegfried), Guðrún corresponds to Kriemhild in the Middle High German *Nibelungenlied.* She is the daughter of King Gjúki and his wife, Grímhildr, an expert in magic. Guðrún marries Sigurðr, and she bears him a daughter, Svanhildr. Brynhildr conspires to have Sigurðr murdered, and he dies in Guðrún's arms in their bed. Grímhildr concocts a magical potion for Guðrún to drink that makes her forget Sigurðr, and she marries Atli (Attila), who wants to take Sigurðr's treasure. The king of the Huns invites Guðrún's brothers Gunnar and Högni to his court, but Guðrún sees through the treachery and attempts (in vain) to warn them. She survives the final massacre, pretends to reconcile with Atli, prepares a funeral banquet, and then slits the throats of the two sons she has borne to Atli. She has their hearts roasted and given to their father to eat. She makes cups from their skulls, and Atli unwittingly drinks their blood mixed with wine.

Guðrún then reveals to her husband what she has done, and, on the following night, she slays Atli and sets fire to his castle. She tries to commit suicide in the sea, but the waves carry her to the land of King Jónakr, who marries her. She bears him three sons: Hamdir, Sörli, and Erpr.

The *Þiðreks saga af Bern* (Saga of Dietrich von Bern), which is based on continental German sources, differs in several respects from this narrative. In this story Guðrún is named Grímhildr, and she is the sister of Gunnar and Högni. She is responsible for triggering the battle in which the Niflungar (Nibelungen) meet their deaths. She dies at the hands of Þiðrekr (that is to say, Dietrich von Bern, who corresponds to Theodoric the Great).

✦ *NIBELUNGENLIED*

GULLFAXI ("Golden Horse"): The horse of the giant Hrungnir, who challenges Odin to a race. Mounted on Sleipnir, Odin wins the race, but Hrungnir follows him to Ásgarðr, where he is later slain by Thor in single combat. Thor gives Gullfaxi to his three-year-old son, Magni, and Odin reproaches him for it, believing that he should have gotten the horse.

GULLINBORSTI ("Golden Bristles"): The wild boar of the god Freyr. Under the name of Slíðrugtanni ("Dangerous Snout"), he pulls the god's chariot. He runs faster than any horse and can race through the air and over the waters both by day and night by the glow of his golden bristles. This marvelous wild boar was crafted by the dwarf Brokkr. In honor of Freyr, a pig would be sacrificed to the god on Jól (Yule), the pagan precursor to Christmas.

GULLINKAMBI ("Golden Comb"): The rooster whose crowing

announces Ragnarök, the final battle. He lives among the Æsir and has his counterpart in another anonymous rooster whose color is "red as soot" and who lives in the halls of Hel, the goddess of the underworld.

GULLTOPPR ("Golden Mane"): Horse of the god Heimdallr.

GULLVEIG ("Intoxicated with Gold"): A sorceress who is the personification of rapacity. She is also called Heiðr ("Witch"). The Æsir slew her three times and burned her body each time, in vain. The Vanir and Æsir began quarreling about her, which led to the first war in the world. It has been suggested that Gullveig is a hypostasis of Freyja or the goddess herself.

GUNGNIR ("The Swaying One"): The spear that was forged for Odin by dwarves, the sons of Ivaldi. It became a primary attribute of this god, one of whose titles is Geirtýr ("Spear God"). A custom of casting this weapon over the enemy combatants at the onset of a battle shall determine the victors.

GUNNLÖÐ ("Invitation to Battle"): A giantess who guards the magical mead stolen by her father, Suttungr, and kept in the mountain Hnitbjörg. Odin spends three nights with her, and as a reward she allows him to drink a mouthful from each of the three cauldrons of mead (Boðn, Són, and Oðrœrir)—with each mouthful, however, Odin drains the entire cauldron and then flies away in the form of an eagle.

✦ *KVASIR*

GURO RYSSEROVA ("Guro Horsetail"): Norwegian traditions place a woman named Guro Rysserova at the head of the Oskoreia. Sometimes Guro is accompanied by Sigurd Svein ("Young Sigurd," another name for the figure better known as Siegfried). A ballad tells us how Sigurd became a member of the Infernal Hunt: Sigurd Svein had been bullying his playmates, who told him that his time would be better spent searching for his father. His mother sent him to the home of her brother Greip and gave him the horse Grani. Sigurd set off, met an ogre, and allowed him to climb on the horse behind him, but Grani bucked him off. Greip told Sigurd that his father was dead, gave him a chest of gold, and urged him to go back home. Grani took him to the edge of a swamp where he lost a shoe, and the hero dropped the chest. He then met the Infernal Hunt led by Guro Rysserova, who asked him if he would prefer to be the first in her troop or the last in heaven. Sigurd chose to follow her.

✦ *OSKOREIA, WILD HUNT*

📖 Lecouteux, *Phantom Armies of the Night*, 190–92.

GÜTEL, JÜTEL, JÜDEL: A being that, over the course of time, became a household spirit. In the thirteenth century the *Gütel* is an idol; in 1507 it had become a hunchbacked kobold conflated with Swedish trolls and dwarves by Georg Agricola (1499–1555); in sixteenth-century Switzerland the name was seen as a derivative of *guot/gut,* meaning "good." In Saxony the people call it *Güttichen* (a diminutive), and in part two of Goethe's *Faust* (II, 1) he mentions the "pious *Gütchen.*" The *Gütel* is also sometimes the soul of a dead child; occasionally it behaves like a perching spirit.

✦ *AUFHOCKER*

GYLFI: A mythical Swedish king who was probably originally a sea giant. He disguises himself, changes his name to Gangleri, and visits the Æsir to discover wisdom.

GYMIR: One of the names of Ægir, a sea giant, and perhaps even a god of the sea.

H

HABERMANN: A household spirit that wears a multicolored robe with small bells. In the region of Württemberg it watches over children.

HACKELBERG: One of the names for the Wild Huntsman in the Germanic regions. This Master of the Hunt in the region of Brunswick (Braunschweig) was allegedly punished for asking God, while on his deathbed, to let him hunt until Final Judgment in exchange for his place in paradise.

📖 Grimm, *Deutsche Sagen,* no. 219.

HADDINGJAR/HADDINGI: The names of the inseparable brothers in the family of Óttar the Simple. They have ten older brothers and are so close to each other that together they only have the strength of a single man. Georges Dumézil suggests they can be viewed as the heroic and epic version of the mythical twins, the Alci, mentioned by Tacitus.

✦ *ALCI, DIVINE TWINS, HENGIST and HORSA, IBOR and AIO*

HADINGUS: Odinic hero in Saxo Grammaticus's *Gesta Danorum.* According to Georges Dumézil, Hadingus is the euhemeristic transposition of the god Njörðr, his transformation into a Danish king.

📖 Dumézil, *From Myth to Fiction.*

HAGEN (Old Norse *Högni*): In the *Nibelungenlied,* he is the faithful vassal of King Gunther, and he rids his retinue of the burdensome Siegfried, steals his treasure, and casts it into the Rhine. When Etzel (Attila) invites the Burgundians to his court, Hagen realizes that this invitation is a trap. He dies, slain by Kriemhild.

In the *Völsunga saga* (Saga of the Völsungs), Högni is only the half-brother of Gunnar, whose father is Aldrian. Högni was sired by an elf, hence his exceptional vigor and singular appearance: he has very pale features, and his facial expression is terrifying. He and Gunnar are called Niflungar (Nibelungen). Broadly speaking, the outline of the rest of the story corresponds with that of the *Nibelungenlied*.

   📖 Gouchet, *Hagen von Tronje.*

HALDE (Sámi *hal'di*): An anthropomorphic guardian spirit in Lappland (Sámi) belief. It is often a legacy in certain families, but in certain circumstances it can be purchased. The Haldes appear as minuscule individuals resembling infants or elderly persons. They correspond quite closely with the Norse *fylgjur.*

HALLINSKIÐI: A byname of the god Heimdallr.

HAMINGJA: This word designates a tutelary spirit that becomes attached to the head of a clan, generation after generation.

   📖 Lecouteux, "Une singulière conception de l'âme: remarque sur l'arrière-plan de quelques traditions populaires," *Medieval Folklore* 2 (1992): 21–47.

HAMR: This Old Norse word designates the Double (alter ego) of an individual. Some people possess from birth the ability to split themselves in two and are called *hamrammr,* "possessors of a powerful Double," or *eigi einhamr,* "those who do not have only one Double." This Double leaves the body when the individual is sleeping or in a state of trance or lethargy. It is three-dimensional and can act and speak like its owner. This sending of one's Double poses a risk to those who indulge in this activity: if someone moves their sleeping body, the Double will no longer be able to reenter it. The *hamr* can assume a human or an animal shape; the most common forms of the latter are a bear, bull, or wolf.

   ✦ *ALP, FYLGJA, MAHR, SCHLEMIHL, WEREWOLF*

   📖 Lecouteux, "Une singulière conception de l'âme: remarque sur l'arrière-plan de quelques traditions populaires," *Medieval Folklore* 2 (1992): 21–47.

HANGAGUÐ ("God of Hanged Men"): One of Odin's titles. It refers to a ritual hanging—which allows a warrior or the sacrificial victim to reach Valhalla—as well as to the initiatory ordeals through which Odin acquired sacred knowledge. Wounded by the thrust of a spear, Odin hung for nine days and nine nights on a wind-battered tree whose roots were of unknown origin. Several of Odin's other bynames allude to this as well: Hangatýr ("God of the Hanged") and Hangi ("The Hanged One").

📖 Falk, *Odensheiti*.

HANGING: Men sacrificed to Odin were ritually hung, and this deity is the god of hanged men. After being wounded by a spear, Odin hung himself and swayed for nine nights from "the wind-battered tree" in order to gain sacred knowledge. A passage from the *Gautreks saga* tells how when King Vikar's fleet was immobilized for lack of wind, it was learned through divination that Odin demanded the sacrifice of the king. Starkaðr (✦ STARKAÐR) proposes a mock hanging. He ties calves' intestines around Vikar's neck and then attaches these to a tree branch and pretends to stab the king with a reed. But the intestines transform into a solid rope that strangles the king, while the reed changes into a deadly spear.

HAPHLIUS (Old Norse *Hafli*): The giant who, according to Saxo Grammaticus, raised the two sons of Gram: Guthormus and Hadingus.

HAPTAGUÐ ("God of Fetters"): A byname for Odin. As Mircea Eliade recognized, the Indo-European gods are binders (Varuna, Ouranos). Haptaguð alludes to the fact that Odin knows how to paralyze an army.

✦ *HERFJÖTURR*

📖 Falk, *Odensheiti*.

HÁRBARÐR ("Graybeard"): One of Odin's bynames.

📖 Falk, *Odensheiti*.

HARÐVÉURR ("Strong Guardian"): One of Thor's titles.

HARE-MILKER: ✦ MÆLKEHARE

HARKE, FRAU (HERKEN, HACKE, HARFE, HARE, ARCHEN, "Dame Knife"): A female demon of northern Germany who corresponds with the figure of Berchta/Percht found in the southern areas of the country. She roams during the Twelve Days (between Christmas and Epiphany) and punishes lazy servants, especially spinners who have not finished spinning their linen. She lives in the mountain bearing her name, Harkenberg, which lies near Kamern in the Havel region.

HARLUNGEN: One of the representations of the Germanic divine twins in continental heroic legend. The Harlungen are the sons of one of Ermrich's (Ermanaric) brothers; they are persecuted by their uncle and eventually hung. According to many texts the reason for this execution was unfounded. When reasons were supplied, all the sources agree on the role played by the traitor Sibeche, who advised Ermrich to kill his nephews. This figure opposed the efforts of the old servant Eckart (Fritla in the Old Norse version of the legend) to protect the young princes. Depending on the version of the story, the expedition against the Harlungen was inspired by different motives. According to the *Heldenbuch,* Ermrich was seeking to recover the lands of his nephews; whereas in the *Þiðreks saga af Bern* (Saga of Dietrich von Bern), Sifka (the Old Norse version of Sibeche) accuses them of attempting to impugn the honor of the queen. Another important variation is the location of the Harlungen territory: according to the *Heldenbuch* it is in Brisgovia; in the *Þiðreks saga* it is near Trelinburg on the banks of the Rhine. Outside of these two primary sources, the Old English poem *Widsith* relates a list of names that includes the Harlungen, Emerca, and Fridla. The *Annals of Quedlinburg,* dating from the tenth century, present the hanging of the Harlungen by their uncle Ermanaric as a hard fact: "At that time, Ermanaric ruled over all the Goths; he was the most cunning of all in deceit, and the most generous with gifts; after the death of his son, Frederic, whom he had ordered executed, he had his nephews Embrica and Fritla hung from a gibbet."

✦ *DIVINE TWINS, SVANHILDR*

📖 Georges Zink, *Les Légendes héroïques de Dietrich et d'Ermrich dans les littératures germaniques,* 201–11.

HÁRR ("The High One"): A name of Odin reflecting his rank as sovereign god.

📖 Falk, *Odensheiti.*

HARTHGREPA ("Firm Grip"): Daughter of the giant Vagnopthus, the foster father of Hadingus. She was Hadingus's wet nurse and later his mistress, for she could change size at will. She knew necromancy and awoke a dead man so he could predict Hadingus's future for her, but the infernal powers, outraged by this sacrilege, tore her to pieces one night. Harthgrepa plays the role of a guardian spirit for Hadingus.

✦ *HADINGUS*

HATI ("Hate" or "Hateful"): A mythical wolf and the son of Hroðvitnir. He seeks to capture the moon, which he will eventually devour. His companion is Sköll who pursues the sun.

Fig. 31. The wolf Hati trying to swallow the moon.
North portal of the Scots Church of St. James in Regensburg.

HAVMAND, HAVFRUE: ✦ NYKR, WASSERMANN

📖 Keightley, *The World Guide to Gnomes, Fairies, Elves, and Other Little People,* 152–55.

HAYMON: An Italian giant that came to the Inn Valley around 860. He confronted and killed Thyrsus, another giant living in the same valley, and the site of their battle is called Thyrschenbach (present-day Dirschenbach). A short time later he slew a dragon that was preventing the construction of a monastery dedicated to Saint Benedict in Wilten, near Innsbruck. He cut out its tongue and placed it in the monastery, where it remained on view for a long time. This dragon tongue eventually made its way to a museum, and today we can recognize it as the beak of a sawfish.

It should be noted that the name of Haymon's adversary is simply a Latinized version of the Germanic word *thurs,* meaning "giant."

HECKETHALER: An enchanted coin that always returns to its owner's pocket after every purchase. In France it is known as the "flying *pistole* (doubloon)." This belief in a magic penny can be found throughout Europe and even in the countries of the Middle East.

HEFRING ("She Who Rises Up," "Wave"): One of the daughters of the sea deities Ægir and Rán.

HEIÐRÚN: The goat that perches on the roof of Valhalla and feeds on the leaves of Læraðr. From its udder flows the mead that valkyries serve to the warriors called the *einherjar.*

Fig. 32. The goat Heiðrún on the roof of Valhalla. Illustration by Ólafur Brynjúlfsson, *Snorra Edda,* 1760.

HEIMDALLR: A mysterious god of the Æsir family, to which he serves as a guardian. He is the father of all men. He lives in Heaven's Mount (Himinbjörg), at the end of the sky, and keeps watch over the bridge that leads to Ásgarðr (Bifröst, "rainbow"). He can see great distances and can hear the grass growing in the meadows and the wool growing on the backs of sheep, for his hearing is concealed beneath the roots of Yggdrasill, the cosmic tree. He needs no more sleep than a bird. Also referred to as the "white *áss* (Æsir god)," he is the son of nine sisters. His teeth are made of gold. His horse's name is Gulltoppr ("Golden Mane"). He owns a horn called Gjallarhorn ("Resounding Horn"), so named because it can be heard throughout the entire world, and a sword named Höfuð ("Man's Head"). When the world ends at Ragnarök he is killed while slaying Loki.

It is thought that his byname Hallinskiði connects him to the ram, which would then be a counterpart to other divine animals such as Thor's goats, Odin's ravens, and Freyr's boar.

Heimdallr appears in the role of a god-king, and he is linked with the symbolism of the World Tree (Yggdrasill). He is of great antiquity and is in some way a precursor of the cosmic order. He seems to have emerged from the waters of chaos as the son of nine mothers (waves?). However, the information we have at our disposal about him is most fragmentary.

📖 Cöllen, *Heimdallr-der rätselhafte Gott: Eine philologische und religionsgeschichtliche Untersuchung;* Jan De Vries, "Heimdallr, dieu énigmatique," *Études Germaniques* 4 (1955): 257–68.

HEIME (Old English *Hama;* Old Norse *Heimir*): Warrior and inseparable companion of Witege. He first served Ermanaric, then Theodoric, but was forced to flee after stealing the *Brôsinga mene,* "the necklace of the Brisinga," a name that corresponds to that of Freyja's necklace, Brísingamen.

HEITI: A kind of synonym used in skaldic poetry. There are two types: (1) the *heiti* that names in a relatively direct way, without the involvement of extensive knowledge; and (2) the *heiti* that, to the contrary, requires effort to elucidate because it makes use of metonymy. Two designations for Odin may serve as respective examples: the first type of heiti would be Gautr ("Goth") and an example of the second type would be Grímnir ("Masked"). In a religious context a *heiti* suggests that a taboo may exist against uttering the actual name of a god.

HEL ("Concealer"): This is both the name of the goddess Hel and of the realm of the dead over which she presides. Hel is the daughter of Loki and the giantess Angrboða, thus the sister of the wolf Fenrir and the Midgard Serpent. She is half white and half blue and lives in the Niflheimr ("World of Darkness"). Her hall is called Éljúðnir ("Dank"?); her plate is Hungr ("Hunger"); her knife is Sulltr ("Famine"); her serving man, Ganglási ("the Slow One"); her serving maid, Ganglöt ("the Slow One"); the threshold of her home is called Fallanda forað ("Stumbling Block"); her bed, Kör ("Illness"); and her bedcurtains are called Blikjanda böl ("Pale Misfortune"). All men that die in bed or of illness come to her.

The realm of the dead has several names: Niðavellir ("Obscure Plains" or "Fields of Darkness"), Náströnd ("Corpse-shore"), or Násheimr ("Corpse-world"). It seems to consist of nine dwellings, the most terrible of which is Náströnd, in the southern reaches of Hel, where those who broke the moral laws, especially oath breakers, are cast. The dragon Níðhöggr gnaws on their corpses.

Fig. 33. Hermóðr arrives at Hel's Hall to ask for the release of Balder. Illustration by Ólafur Brynjúlfsson, *Snorra Edda*, 1760.

Another conception of the otherworld emerges from the sagas and the historiographical sources: the deceased continue to live in their mounds or rejoin their ancestors in the hollow mountains.

HELBLINDI ("Hel-blinder"): One of Loki's two brothers. Also a byname of Odin.

📕 Falk, *Odensheiti.*

HELGI ("Holy One"): 1. Son of Sigmundr and Borghildr of Bralundr (Denmark). He is remembered for having slain Hundingr, king of Hunaland (Land of the Huns), and for having wed the valkyrie Sigrún, who helps him to slay his enemies and with whom he had children. At Odin's instigation, Sigrún's brother Dagr slew Helgi, who made his way to the home of the dead; later, Helgi emerged from his burial mound to converse with his wife. Sigrún eventually died of grief, but both of them were reincarnated, as is explicitly stated in *Helgakviða Hundingsbana II* (The Second Lay of Helgi).

2. After his reincarnation, Helgi took the family name Haddingjaskati. He married Kara, a valkyrie who was the daughter of Halfdan.

3. There is also a third Helgi, who is the son of Hjörvarðr and Sigrlinn. A large, handsome, taciturn individual, he was not given a name. One day he saw nine valkyries riding by who predicted his future, and one of them, Sváva, daughter of Eylimi, gave him the name of Helgi. She subsequently provided him with protection in battle. Helgi performed many great deeds, went to the home of Eylimi, and gained Sváva's hand in marriage. He was slain in a duel. He too was reincarnated.

HELGRINDR ("Hel's Fence"): A wall that encloses the kingdom of the dead. It is also called Nágrindr ("Corpse-fence") or Valgrindr ("Fence of the Slain").

✦ *HEL*

HELLE: Helle is a giant that appears in the cycle of legends concerning Wolfdietrich. He works in the service of the pagan king Machorel. On the latter's orders Helle transported eggs into Lombardy that hatch into dragons, which later lay waste to the land and cause the death of King Ortnit. Helle was accompanied by the giantess Runze. Ortnit encountered Helle and was overmatched; he took refuge beneath a tree that the giant knocked down and then managed to cut off his two legs before slaying him.

HELVEGR ("Hel's Way"): The road that leads to the realm of the dead. This name can be found in various Germanic lands, where it indicates the road that should be taken to bring the deceased to the cemetery. Similar concepts can be found in Celtic Brittany: there is the *hent ar c'horfou* ("Road of the Body") as well as the *hent an Anaon* ("Road of Departed Souls"). In Old Celtic, however, Anawnn (*Anaon*) is also the name of the otherworld.

✦ *HEL*

HEMANN: This is a *Rufgeist,* a calling or hailing spirit, still called *Hoymann* (Palatinate), *Heitmännchen* (Westphalia), and *Hojemandl* (southern Germany). He terrifies people at night by chasing them and sometimes knocking them down on their backs. One should never respond to his call, for it could have disastrous consequences. It is said that the *Hoymann* is a devil or a soul in torment. He comes in the guise of a large man wearing a wide-brimmed hat, like a giant or hunter. His cry is heard most often during the autumn and during Advent. Along the banks of the river Lech (Austria), the *Hojemandl* is a kobold that lives in abandoned farms and forests. He is a tease and does handstands.

HENGIST and HORSA ("Stallion" and "Horse"): The military leaders of the Angles when they invaded England. Their names may reflect a belief that in ancient times these two men were divine twins who took the form of horses. It should be noted that in the nineteenth century the carved horse heads adorning the farms of Holstein in northern Germany were still called Hengist and Hors. Writing in the sixth century in his *De excidio et conquestu Britanniae,* Gildas only indicates that the Saxons reached Great Britain in three boats, stayed on the Isle of Thanet, and battled Aurelius Ambrosius.

In his *Historia Ecclesiastica Gentis Anglorum,* dating from 731, the Venerable Bede provides more details to Gildas's story. He gives the names of the three Germanic tribes, of the two brothers Hengist and Horsa, and traces the genealogies of the two leaders back to Wodan himself. Bede also states that Horsa was later killed in combat and that a monument to his memory still existed in east Kent. In his *Historia Brittonum,* written around 679, Nennius also mentions the names of Hengist and Horsa and provides a genealogy that goes back from Hengist to Wodan.

✦ *ALCI, DIVINE TWINS, IBOR and AIO*

HERÁSS ("Army God"): A name of Odin found on a seventh-century Norwegian funeral inscription.

📖 Falk, *Odensheiti.*

HERBLINDI ("Army-blinder"): One of Odin's bynames. It is explained by Snorri Sturluson, who tells us that "in combat, Odin had the power to render his enemies deaf and blind."

📖 Falk, *Odensheiti.*

HERCULES: In Germano-Roman epigraphy the name Hercules is most likely a subsitute for Donar/Thor. The name is generally accompanied by an adjective; for example, "powerful," "bearded," and so forth.

HERFJÖTUR ("Army-fetter"): The name of a valkyrie. It refers to a dire scenario: the sudden paralysis that grips warriors when fighting.

✦ *HERFJÖTURR*

HERFJÖTURR: This word designates something that paralyzes an army (in other words, it is a decree of fate). It can take the form of an invisible net or of deadly arrows.

📖 Régis Boyer, "Herfjötur(r)," in *Visages du destin dans les mythologies: Mélanges Jacqueline Duchemin,* ed. François Jouan (Paris: Les Belles Lettres, 1983), 153–68.

HERJA ("Devastating One"): The name of the valkyrie who should be compared to Hariasa, a deity whose existence is confirmed by second-century epigraphy.

HERJANN ("Lord of the Army"): One of Odin's names. It is generally believed to be an allusion to Odin as leader of the "single warriors" (*einherjar*) who live in Valhalla.

📖 Falk, *Odensheiti.*

HERLA: According to twelfth-century English historians, Herla would be a king of the very ancient Britons, although both his name as well as his legend are clearly Germanic. Accepting a dwarf's invitation, Herla follows him into a hollow mountain. Following his host's wedding, Herla and his companions take the road back home, laden with gifts, horses, dogs, and falcons. As the dwarf leads the king out of the mountain he gives him a small bloodhound, forbidding the entire company to dismount and set foot on the ground before the dog jumps down on it. Shortly after parting with the dwarf, Herla meets a shepherd and realizes that during the three days he spent inside the mountain several hundred years have elapsed in the land of mortals. Heedless of the dwarf's order, several of the king's companions get down from their horses and crumble into dust. The dog has never leaped down to the ground, and King Herla has been pursuing his mad rounds in the company of his army ever since. He became the leader of the Wild Hunt, commonly known under the name of *Familia Herlethingi* or *Mesnie Hellquin* (in more recent folklore, the leader of the Wild Hunt is Odin). The legend of Herla tells of a journey into the otherworld and reflects the belief that dwarves are the dead and that the moutains are the realm of shades.

✦ *OSKOREIA, WILD HUNT*

📖 Claude Lecouteux, *Phantom Armies of the Night.*

HERMÓÐR: Brother of Baldr. He borrowed Odin's steed, Sleipnir, to go visit Hel, the goddess of the underworld, to request that she release Baldr, whom Höðr had slain by accident. He rode for nine days and nine nights on Hel's Road (*Helvegr*), crossed the river Gjöll over the Gjallarbrú bridge, leaped over the Hel's Fence, thanks to Sleipnir, and reached the goddess's hall. Hel accepted on condition that all creation, both the living and the dead, mourned for Baldr. Humans, minerals, plants, and animals all mourned except for one giantess, named Þökk. She was none other than Loki in disguise, who refused to shed a single tear, ensuring that Baldr had to stay among the dead.

HERNE THE HUNTER: A famous English ghost who appears in the park of Windsor Castle near a large oak tree. He has the appearance of a hunter clad in a deer's hide and wearing deer's antlers on his head.

He is said to be a forester who committed suicide for fear of the

Fig. 34. Herne the Hunter. Winkfield Inn sign (Berkshire).

punishment he would receive for a murder. Shakespeare mentions him in *The Merry Wives of Windsor* (IV, 4).

> *There is an old tale goes that Herne the hunter,*
> *Sometime a keeper here in Windsor forest,*
> *Doth all the winter-time, at still midnight,*
> *Walk round about an oak, with great ragg'd horns;*
> *And there he blasts the tree and takes the cattle*
> *And makes milch-kine yield blood and shakes a chain*
> *In a most hideous and dreadful manner.*

On the Danish peninsula of Jutland we find a Horns Jaeger who rides a horse in the Aarhus region and attempts to carry off female elves.

📖 Petry, *Herne the Hunter;* Thiele, *Danmarks Folkesagn,* vol. II, 116.

HERNOSS: An idol mounted on a stake with a human head but no arms, which still existed in Sørum and Rike, Norway, in the nineteenth century. Elsewhere people revered the *Faksar,* wooden statuettes depicting a bearded man the size of a twelve-year-old child; these statues are called *vätte* and *tusse.* Food offerings are made to them at Jól. The ancient Norse worshipped posts (*stafr*) as domestic gods and did so despite the ban on this practice written down in *Eidsivathings Kristenrett* in 1152.

 📖 Linhart, *Hausgeister in Franken,* 35; Olav Bø, "Faksar og kyrkjerestar," *By og Bygd* 12 (1969): 43–76; Inger M. Boberg, "Gardvordens seng i dansk tradition," *Maal og Minne* (1956); Reidar T. Christiansen, "Gårdvette og markavette," *Maal og Minne* (1943): 137–60; Lily Weiser, "Germanische Hausgeister und Kobolde," *Niederdeutsche Zeitschrift für Volkskunde* 4 (1926): 1–19.

HERTÝR ("Army-god"): One of Odin's bynames.

 📖 Falk, *Odensheiti.*

HERVÖR, ALVITR: A valkyrie and swan maiden and the daughter of King Hlöðver. She is also called *alvitr* ("all-white" or "all-wise"). Her sisters are Ölrun and Hlaðguðr *svanhvít* ("swan-white"). These three women married Völundr (Wayland) and his two brothers.

 ✦ *HLAÐGUÐR SVANHVÍT, ÖLRUN, SWAN MAIDEN, VALKYRIE, WAYLAND THE SMITH*

HILDE: An aquatic demon of Thuringia. She has blue hair and bewitches people with her song.

HILDÓLFR ("Battle-wolf"): A byname of Odin in the *Hárbarðsljóð* (Lay of Hárbarðr) in which he plays the role of a ferryman who refuses to give Thor transport.

 📖 Falk, *Odensheiti.*

HILDR ("Battle"): Several female figures have this name: 1. A valkyrie. 2. The daughter of Högni. 3. A giantess. 4. A female magician who resuscitates the dead warriors every night in the myth of the Eternal Battle.

 ✦ *HJAÐNINGAVÍG*

HIMINBJÖRG ("Heaven-mount"): The dwelling of Heimdallr. It is located at the end of heaven, where the rainbow that serves as a bridge between Ásgarðr and the rest of the world begins.

✦ *HEIMDALLR*

HIMINHRJÓÐR ("Devastator of Heaven"): A bull belonging to the giant Hymir. The god Thor tears off its head and puts it on a fish-hook to serve as bait for catching the Midgard Serpent. A tenth-century carved stone cross in Gosforth, England, depicts this bull's head, which is clearly recognizable, at the end of Thor's fishing line.

HINZELMANN ("Little Heinz"): The most famous of the German sprites who lived in the castle of Hudemühlen, not far from Lüneburg

Fig. 35. Hinzelmann

(Lower Saxony). He showed his little hand for the first time in 1584 and vanished in 1588. He behaved like a household spirit and was friendly, but he sometimes acted like a rapping spirit and kobold, sowing disorder throughout the castle whenever someone treated him badly. He demanded a bowl full of milk and white breadcrumbs every day. He kept watch over people's behavior, punished careless servants, and helped in the kitchen and stables. He was able to predict the future and avert imminent misfortune. There were attempts to rid the castle of him with exorcisms, but they had no effect.

When asked, he said he was called Hinzelmann but that he was also named Lüring and his wife was named Hille Bingels, that he came from the mountains of Bohemia, and that his mother was a Christian. His voice was that of a child or young girl. The lord of Hudemühlen asked him to show himself. Hinzelmann refused but let him pass his hand across his invisible face. The lord had the impression that he was touching teeth or a skeleton.

A serving maid persuaded Hinzelmann to show himself; when she went down into the cellar she saw a small, naked child lying on the ground with two knives stuck into his heart. It so happens that Martin Luther (1483–1546) tells a similar story in his *Table Talk,* which shows that this theme already existed in the sixteenth century and most likely earlier.

📖 Lindig, *Hausgeister;* Linhart, *Hausgeister in Franken.*

HITT/HUTT, FRAU: Queen of the giants living above Innsbruck. God turned her to stone for squandering bread. According to another tradition she is a giantess dressed in white who can be seen sitting on a stone combing her hair. She would abduct any children who came too close and carry them off to the inside of the mountain, where they would never be seen again.

📖 Alpenburg, *Mythen und Sagen Tirols,* 239; Zingerle, *Sagen aus Tirol,* 127–28.

HJAÐNINGAVÍG ("Battle of the Hjaðningar"): This is the name for the Eternal Battle, a very ancient myth that appears in several texts sharing the same structure. A woman, whose name is Freyja, Hildr, or Göndul, provokes a battle that never ends, because every evening and morning she resurrects the slain to allow them to resume their combat.

One of the adversaries is named Hedinn, which means "the man with the hat" or "the man with the fur mantle," a name referring to the *beserkir,* the wild warriors also called *ulfheðnar* ("wolf-coats"). The word *Hjadningar* refers to "Hedinn's warriors." One interesting detail in the story is that all the dead turn into stones at night.

Responding to the question of why the battle is called "the Hjaðningar weather or storm?" Snorri explains in chapter 61 of his *Skáldskaparmál* (Treatise on the Skaldic Art) that Hedinn carried away on his boat the daughter of King Högni, who instantly set off in pursuit and caught up with his daughter's abductor on a small island. The battle resumes and rages every day because Hogni's daughter Hildr reawakens the dead every night by magic. The battle will go on until Ragnarök.

In Germany the myth can be recognized in the heroic poem *Kudrun,* written circa 1240. Around 1190, Saxo Grammaticus retold a version of the myth in which the protagonists were named Hithinus, Höginus, and Hilda. Hithinus had abducted Höginus's daughter, Hilda. The king pursued the kidnapper and found him near the Orcades (Orkneys). Hilda attempted to reconcile Höginus and Hithinus, but the battle began and continues eternally.

HJÁLMBERI ("Helm-bearer"): One of Odin's names. It corresponds exactly with the depiction of this god on petroglyphs and bronze helmet panels found in Scandinavia. According to Snorri Sturluson, his helmet is made of gold.

📖 Falk, *Odensheiti.*

HJALMÞRIMUL ("Battle-helm"): The name of a valkyrie.

✦ *VALKYRIE*

HJÖRÞRIMUL ("Battle-sword"): The name of a valkyrie.

✦ *VALKYRIE*

HJUKI: Brother of Bil and foster son of Máni (the moon). Hjuki is most likely the personification of the moon's waxing and beneficial phase, whereas his brother is that of the harmful, waning aspect of this astral body.

HLAÐGUÐR, SVANHVÍT ("Hlaðguðr Swan-white"): A valkyrie and swan maiden whose proper name, Hlaðguðr, refers to the notion of "weaving on the loom of battle." She is also called *svanhvít* ("swan-white"). She is the daughter of King Hlöðver and the sister of Hervör and Ölrun. Slagfiðr, one of the brothers of Völundr (Wayland), obliged her to remain with him by stealing her clothes while she bathed.

✦ *HERVÖR ALVITR, ÖLRUN, SWAN MAIDEN, VALKYRIE, WAYLAND THE SMITH*

HLÉR ("Sea"): One of the names of Ægir, the sea giant. This name is evident in that of the Danish island Hléysey (present-day Laessö), "Hler's Island."

HLIÐSKJÁLF ("Guard Tower"): Odin's throne. When he is seated there the god can see the entire world. It is also the name of the hall in which this throne is housed.

HLÍN ("Protectress"): Goddess to whom Odin's wife, Frigg, assigned the duty of protecting mankind. She is most likely simply a hypostasis of Frigg.

HLÓÐYN: Mother of the god Thor. As he is regularly called the son of Jörð ("the Earth"), the deduction has been made that Hlóðyn and Jörð are one and the same. Her great antiquity is proved by five Germano-Roman votive inscriptions found in Frisia and along the lower course of the Rhine, dating from the second and third centuries, which are addressed to the goddess Hludana.

HLÓRA: Thor's foster mother. This figure who plays no role whatsoever appears to be a recent creation extrapolated from Hlóriði, a nickname for this god.

HLÓRIÐI ("The Loud Rider"): Thor's most frequent title.

HNIKARR ("Rapper," "Instigator"): The name Odin uses to introduce himself to Sigurðr when the latter is caught in a storm at sea. Odin calms the waves.

📖 Falk, *Odensheiti.*

HNITBJÖRG ("Clashing Mountain"): The mountain in which Gunnlöð, the guardian of the sacred vessels holding the wondrous mead, lives. It is reminiscent of the Symplegades in Greek mythology.

✦ *KVASIR*

HNOSS ("Jewel"): Daughter of Freyja and Óðr.

HODDMÍMIR ("Treasure-Mímir"): The wood in which the survivors of Ragnarök, Líf and Lifþrasir, hide and live on dew. This wood is nothing other than Yggdrasill, the World Tree, at the foot of which is located the Well of Wisdom, the "treasure" of Mímir.

HÖDR ("Warrior"): One of Odin's sons. He is blind and unintentionally kills Baldr by casting a sprig of mistletoe at him. Váli slays him for this deed. Both Höðr and Baldr return to the reborn world.

HŒNIR: A secondary god about whom little is known. He is mentioned in the Odin-Hœnir-Lóðurr triad with regard to the myth of the creation of mankind. It is Hœnir who endowned human beings with the faculty of reason. In other triads he is cited alongside Odin and Loki. He is one of the Æsir who will survive after Ragnarök in the new world. According to Snorri Sturluson the Æsir gave Hœnir as a hostage to the Vanir along with Mímir, without whom he is incapable of thinking. The Vanir suspect the Æsir of deceiving them and decapitate Mímir.

In skaldic poetry Hœnir is called "the quick god," "long foot," "clay-king," and the "friend of the Raven-God (Odin)."

📖 Willy Krogmann, "Hœnir," *Acta Philologica Scandinavica* 6 (1930–1931): 311–31; Franz Rolf Schröder, "Hœnir, eine mythologische Untersuchung," *Beiträge zur Geschichte der deutschen Sprache und Literatur* 43 (1918): 219–52.

HÖFUÐ ("Man's Head"): Heimdallr's sword. The name may be an allusion to a lost myth, a fragment of which says that the god was killed by a human head.

HÓFVARPNIR ("Hoof-tosser"): Horse of the goddess Gná.

HOLLE, FRAU (HOLDA, HULDA): A syncretic figure whose

features derive from a variety of sources. She is the leader of the female Wild Hunt, which sows abundance along its passage.

In Norway her appearance promises health to the flocks and fertility to women. Frau Holle lives in a spring or lake on the Hörselberg in Thuringia. She corresponds to the Roman fairies Lady Abundia ("Abundance") and Satia ("Satiety"). According to the accounts, Frau Holle can be beautiful or ugly, good or malevolent. She is sometimes depicted as a large woman with black hair who travels the world in a black cart. Her presence is first attested around the year 1000 in the *Decretum* of Burchard of Worms (ca. 960–1025), which conflates her with Herodias. In the thirteenth century it was said that people would set a table for her on Christmas night in their homes so she would treat them kindly.

Frau Holle appears in the *Fairy Tales* of the Brothers Grimm (no. 24) and in the *German Legends* (no. 4) by the same authors. She is said to reside near the Hoher Meißner, and cavities and caves are identified there as being her dwelling. But other traditions place her in various mountains: the Venusberg, the Hörselberg, the Untersberg, or the Kyffhäuser. When it snows, it is said that Frau Holle is shaking out her eiderdown quilt.

📖 Grimm, *Deutsche Sagen,* nos. 4–8; Waschnitius, *Perht, Holda und verwandte Gestalten: Ein Beitrag zur deutschen Religionsgeschichte.*

HOLLEN: Tiny wild men of Westphalia who live in a cave and are inclined to thievery. They abduct children. They take care of horses and only eat wild game.

📖 Weddingen and Hartmann, *Der Sagenschatz Westfalens,* 162.

HÖRN: One of Freyja's names. It can be seen in Swedish place-names such as Härnevi, "Hörn's Sanctuary."

HORSE: This animal played an important role in worship and was often sacrificed during religious ceremonies. Tacitus informs us that the Germans paid attention to the omens and warnings given by horses. In mythology the gods are always transported to the realm of the dead by these animals. The role of the horse as a psychopomp has been confirmed by the discovery of horses in tombs, sacrificed at the sides of their mas-

Fig. 36. Estonian house with horsehead gables

ters. The presence of horse skulls found under the threshold stone of old dwellings testifies that it was the subject of specific worship and played a tutelary role, which can be compared to the building decorations in northern Germany where horse heads were sculpted on farm gables. In folk belief, the horse is the most common form taken by water spirits.

✦ *FALHÓFNIR, NYKR*

📖 Wagner, *Le Cheval dans les croyances*.

HÖRSELBERG (Horsel-, Hursel-, Hosel-, Oselberg): This Thuringian mountain is believed to house hell and purgatory. It is also the residence of Frau Holle (Holda), Venus, and the Loyal Eckart.

Georg Michael Pfefferkorn (1646–1732), a pastor of Freimar and Gräfentonna, said:

> We need now speak of Hörselberg, which stands between Gotha and Eisenach, and about which the old monks have lied and claimed, among other things, that this mountain was part of purgatory, for souls were tortured here. They therefore gave this place the name of "Hear Souls" (*Hör-Seel*), and they also said this: if in the evening you

smooth the ground in front of this mountain's large cave, the next morning you will find the footprints of all manner of men and beasts, as if they had been entering and leaving. They also say the Loyal Eckart, as the peasantry calls him, lives in this mountain, and that he goes before the Furious Army to warn people of the danger. For this reason, it is said that the nearby village of Settelstädt should be called *Satan-Stadt* ("Satanville"). It would appear that the prince of darkness was often up to his old tricks at the time of the superstitious papacy.

📖 Grimm, *Deutsche Sagen,* nos. 5, 7, 170, 173; Lecouteux, *Phantom Armies of the Night.*

HORWENDILLUS: The father of Amlethus (Hamet). Although his name is a Latinized rendering of Aurvandill ("morning star"), there is nothing mythical about him.

HÖTHERUS: This is the name that Saxo Grammaticus gives to the son of the Swedish king Hothbrodus, and he describes him as a rival with Balderus for the affections of the beautiful Nanna. Hötherus married Nanna and killed Balderus before perishing at the hands of Bous. Hötherus is identical to the god Höðr, but Saxo euhemerized him.

HOUSEHOLD/PLACE SPIRITS: In folk beliefs and mythology every dwelling is supposed to be under the protection of a spirit. This could be a land spirit whose good will was earned by inviting it to take up residence, or a dead ancestor since the good dead were once buried inside the house. In more recent Scandinavian traditions, it is said that the first inhabitant of the house will transform into a spirit when he or she dies. We thus find among the Germanic peoples a notion similar to that of the Roman *manes, penates,* and *lares.* These house spirits are called *cofgodas* in Old English, which means "the gods of the house."

A word with a similar sense is the German *Kobold,* which literally means "he who rules over the room"—in other words, "he who rules over the house," since ancient dwellings formerly consisted of only one room. Tenth-century glosses in Old High German have given us the names *ingoumo* and *ingesind* as translations of the Latin *penates* and *lares.* As it happens, *ingesind* can be translated as "servant," which is also

Fig. 37. Household spirits

the designation of a French sprite. We have the valuable testimony of the Cistercian monk Rudolf of Silesia, who was active between 1230 and 1250, which gives us an extremely ancient name: "In the new homes, or in the houses where they have just moved in, they bury pots filled with various things in different corners and sometimes even behind the hearth for the household gods they call *stetewaldiu*."

House spirits have a multitude of names that they also share with place spirits. In Danish we have *Nisse, Lile Niels, Nis, Nis Puge, Puge, gaardbo, gaardbonisse, gaardbuk;* in Norwegian *tuss(e), bokke, tomte, tomtegubbe, tufte* (often as a compound with *-folk, -bonde, -kall*), *tunkall, tunvord, gardvord, gardvord,* and *gardsbonde;* and in Swedish *vätte, gårdsråd, tomte (tomtegubbe, tomtenisse), tomtkall, nisse, goa nisse, nisse-go-dräng.*

These spirits gradually became conflated with dwarves and lost their specific characteristics. Today they survive in the form of garden gnomes and dwarves.

✦ *FAKSAR, HERNOSS*

📖 Bø, Grambo, Hodne, and Hodne, *Norske Segner,* no. 70; Hartlaub, *Der Gartenzwerg und seine Ahnen;* Holbek and Piø, *Fabeldyr og sagnfolk,* 142–55; Lecouteux, *The Tradition of Household Spirits;* Lindig, *Hausgeister;* Linhart, *Hausgeister in Franken;* Joseph Klapper, "Deutscher Volksglaube in Schleisen in ältester Zeit," *Mitteilungen der Schlesischen Gesellschaft für Volkskunde* 17 (1915): 19–57.

HRÆSVELGR ("Corpse-eater"): A gigantic eagle that perches at the end of the world and creates the winds with the beating of its wings. It is also the name of a giant.

📖 Régis Boyer, "Hraesvelgr," in *Foi, Raison, Verbe: Mélanges in honorem Julien Ries,* ed. Charles Marie Ternes (Luxemburg: Centre Universitaire du Luxembourg, 1993), 29–36.

HRAFNAGUÐ ("God of the Ravens"): One of the names for Odin. It refers to his two ravens, Huginn and Muninn, whose names mean "Thought" and "Memory," respectively. The god sends them out at dawn to fly throughout the worlds, and they return to tell him what they have seen. It is possible that these birds were the personification of Odin's double in animal form, for we know that this god could change his shape at will. A skaldic synonym for Hrafnaguð is Hrafnáss ("Raven-god").

📖 Falk, *Odensheiti.*

HRIÐ ("Gust"): One of the mythical rivers that issues from the spring Hvergelmir.

HRÍMFAXI ("Frost-mane"): Horse that "pulls one of the useful gods at evening; he lets the foam fall from his bit each morning from which comes the dew over the valleys," says an Eddic poem. The horse that brings the day is Skinfaxi.

HRÍMGRIMNIR ("Frost-masked"): A giant who dwells near the realm of the dead. Nothing more is known about him.

HRÍMNIR ("Frost-covered"): A giant whose daughter is Heiðr ("Witch") and whose son is Hrossþjófr ("Horse-thief"). He is mentioned in a fourteenth-century poem.

HRÍMÞURS ("Frost Giant"; pl. *hrímþursar*)**:** Original powers whom the gods are continuously fighting. The *hrímthursar* bear descriptive names coined from the words *snow, cold, wintry weather, ice,* and so forth. Their great ancestor is the primordial giant Ymir, born from the melting of the glaciers. They have the power to shapeshift, and they know magic and all the secrets of the world, of which they are the oldest inhabitants.

HRINGHORNI: Name of the ship on which the body of Baldr was cremated. When the gods are unable to launch it out into the waters, they request help from the giantess Hyrrokkin. The corpse is then placed on the ship. When Baldr's wife, Nanna, sees it there, she dies of grief. She is placed next to her husband, and the boat is set on fire after Thor blesses it with his hammer, Mjöllnir. At that very moment a dwarf named Litr ("The Colored One") runs in front of his feet. Thor casts him into the flames.

Evidence for this type of funeral has been provided by the Arab traveler Ibn Fadlan, who attended a similar ceremony in 922. A Swedish chieftain was placed in his boat with a slave, a dog, two horses, two cows, a hen, and a rooster, all of which was then burned and a mound erected on the site. Archaeologists have unearthed numerous ship-burials, notably the famous Oseberg Ship that was excavated in Norway.

✦ *BALDR, MJÖLLNIR*

HROÐVITNIR: Father of Hati, the wolf that seeks to capture the moon.

✦ *HATI*

HRÖNN ("Wave"): One of the mythical rivers originating in the spring Hvergelmir. It is also the name of one of the daughters of Ægir, the giant of the sea.

✦ *HVERGELMIR*

HROPTATÝR ("God of Shouts"): A byname of Odin, who is also quite simply called Hroptr ("Shout"). We have no idea why.

📖 Falk, *Odensheiti.*

HROSSHÁRSGRANI ("Horsehair's Grani"): This nickname for Odin is an allusion to the *Gautreks saga* in which Odin pretends to be Grani, the foster father of Starkaðr. But Grani is also the name of the son of Odin's horse, Sleipnir. In this name for the god we can therefore see an allusion to the importance of the horse in his worship.

📖 Pálsson and Edwards, trans., *Gautrek's Saga and Other Medieval Tales,* 23–55.

HROSSÞJÓF ("Horse-thief"): Giant described as the son of Hrímnir.

HRUNGNIR: Giant that challenges Odin and his horse to a race. Carried away by his enthusiasm, he enters Ásgarðr behind Odin. The gods invite him to drink, but the giant becomes intoxicated and claims he is going to pick up Valhalla and carry it off with him to Jötunheimr and that he will bury Ásgarðr under the ground, kill all the gods, and abduct Freyja and Sif. Exasperated, the gods call Thor, and single combat is organized between him and the giant, who goes home to retrieve his weapons.

In Grjótúnagarðar the giants craft a clay man that is nine leagues long and three leagues wide. They give him a mare's heart and name him Mökkurkálfi. Hrungnir has a heart of stone; his head is also made of stone, as is his shield. Thor goes to the duel accompanied by Þjálfi. He throws his hammer at Hrungnir, splintering his flint club to pieces. One piece falls to the ground and becomes a mountain; another embeds itself in Thor's head. The god then breaks the giant's skull while Þjálfi kills Mökkurkálfi. Thor then goes to the home of Gróa, Aurvandill's wife, so that she can remove the piece of flint stuck in his skull.

A decorative motif found on the carved picture stones of Gotland is called "Hrungnir's heart" (*Hrungnis hjarta*). It is formed of three interlacing triangles; it is also known as the "knot of the slain" (*valknútr*).

HRYMR: Giant that steers the ship Naglfar when the giants launch their assault on the gods during Ragnarök.

HUDEMÜHLEN: The name of a castle in Lüneberg, Saxony, that was haunted by a spirit between 1584 and 1588. This spirit first called attention to itself by tapping, then it began speaking to the servants in the middle of the day, and people became accustomed to its presence. He laughed, performed all kinds of tricks, and sang canticles in a pleasant voice that sounded like that of a young girl. It said it was Christian and had nothing in common with sprites or brownies.

✦ *HINZELMANN*

HUGINN ("Thought"): One of Odin's two ravens.

Odin has been associated with these two birds since the Migration Age (fourth to seventh centuries CE). Evidence for this is provided by archaeological finds, notably that of bracteates.

Fig. 38. Huginn, one of Odin's ravens. This is a piece of a bronze harness found in Vadstena on the island of Gotland in Sweden.

HULDREFOLK: Name of the underground dwellers in Denmark.

📖 Holbek and Piø, *Fabeldyr og sagnfolk,* 136.

HULDRESLATT, HULDRELAAK ("Music, or Play, of the Underground Folk"): These terms designate the music of dwarves or elves, which lures men into their realm.

HULDUFÓLK: A collective name for elves in Iceland.

◆ *ELLEFOLK, ELVES*

HÜTATA: In the Saint-Nabor region of Alsace at the foot of Mont Saint Odile, the Hütata leads the Infernal Hunt, while shouting the cry that gives this entity its name. He is most likely to appear on stormy nights, and woodcutters know the precise boundaries of his domain and take great care not to cross them. They know that if they do, the giant Hütata will loom up at their side wearing a wide-brimmed hat and staring at them with his single eye. If a person is frightened when seeing him, Hütata forms a horn with his hand and roars into his ear, which will leave the individual deaf and ill for several weeks. The description of this man with only one eye and a hat that conceals his features is strongly reminiscent of Odin.

HÜTCHEN ("Little Hat"): This is the name of a sprite that appeared in the court of Bishop Bernard of Hildesheim. He was wearing traditional peasant garb and a small felt hat. He procured an earldom for Bernard and warned him of all kinds of dangers. He promised a traveling merchant of the city who was about to leave on another trip that he would keep an eye on his promiscuous wife, and he threw all the lovers out of bed whom she had invited to share it with her.

📖 Linhart, *Hausgeister in Franken.*

HVEÐRUNGR ("The Foaming One"): One of Loki's bynames.

HVERGELMIR ("Noisy Cauldron"): The spring in the World of Darkness (Niflheimr) that gave birth to the rivers collectively known as the Élivágar. According to other traditions, Hvergelmir gushes forth from beneath the roots of Yggdrasill, the cosmic tree, and is the lair of the dragon Níðhöggr. This spring may be identical to the Well of Urðr (Urðarbrunnr) and the Well of Mímir (Mímisbrunnr), both of which are located close to Yggdrasill.

HYMIR: Giant that gives lodging to Thor when he comes to fish for the Midgard Serpent. They set off together in a boat, but because of Hymir's fearful mistake of cutting the fishing line too soon, Thor is unable to capture the serpent. Furious, he punches Hymir overboard with a single blow of his fist.

According to another tradition, Hymir is the father of the god Týr. He lives east of the Élivágar, at the borders of the sky. Thor and Týr pay him a visit so they can borrow a cauldron large enough for Ægir to brew the beer of the Æsir. They first meet a giantess with nine hundred heads, then the mother of Hymir, and finally his wife. When Hymir returns from the hunt and learns his visitors' identity, his gaze darts to the roof pillar behind which they are standing, and it bursts into pieces. The pillar breaks, and eight cauldrons tumble out, one of which does not break when it strikes the floor. A meal is prepared, and Thor devours two of the three bulls provided by Hymir.

The next day the giant catches two whales while Thor vainly strives to catch the Midgard Serpent. Hymir wants to test the god's strength and asks him to break a cup. Thor throws it against a column, which breaks. Then, heeding the advice of his hostess, he strikes the giant's head with the goblet and passes the test. Thor steals the cauldron and flees with Týr. The giants pursue them, but Thor's hammer causes a massacre. This was how Ægir was able to brew the beer of the Æsir.

HYNDLA ("Puppy"): A giantess that Freyja visits in order to bring her back to Valhalla so she can give Óttarr the Simple the genealogy of his ancestors. Hyndla rides astride her wolf and follows Freyja mounted on her wild boar, Hildsvíni. She fulfills her mission but is greatly irritated when Freyja asks her to serve Óttarr the "beer of remembrance," which will prevent him from forgetting everything he heard. Hyndla scolds the goddess to "scamper off . . . among the he-goats" (*Hyndluljóð* [The Lay of Hyndla], found in the *Flateyjarbók* manuscript but probably part of the original Eddic corpus). In wrath, Freyja threatens the giantess with death by fire, and Hyndla gives in but tries to serve Óttarr poisoned beer. Thanks to a magical spell, Freyja destoys the poison.

HÝR ("Joyous" or "Fire"): A dwelling surrounded by a wall of flames. This was most likely the home of Menglöð, which also has a rampart of fire.

Fig. 39. The giantess or witch Hyrrokkin arrives at Baldr's funeral riding
a wolf. Carved picture stone from Hunnestad (Skåne, Sweden).

HYRROKKIN ("Withered by Fire"): The giantess to whom the
gods turn when trying to launch Balder's ship Hringhorni. She arrives
from Jötunheimr "riding a wolf, with a viper for reins" (Snorri). Odin
summons four berserkers to hold her mount, but they are unsuccessful
until they knock it upside down.

IAROVIT: God of the Rugii whose name might mean "the harsh lord." He was worshipped in Wolgast and Havelberg (Germany). A shield was kept in his temple and brought out to ensure victory in war.

   📖 Kantzow, *Pomerania,* vol. I.

IBOR and AIO: One of several pairs of mythic twins who appear in Germanic traditions. In his *Historia Langobardorum* (History of the Lombards), written in the eighth century, Paul the Deacon mentions two chieftains with these names who were the leaders of a band of exiles. Overpopulation had caused their people, the Winnili, to divide into three camps, and, after drawing lots, the group led by Ibor and Aio was chosen to emigrate and seek out new lands. These two brothers, in the prime of life and superior to all others, bid farewell to their people and left to explore where they might settle. The mother of these two leaders, Gambara, had a wealth of good advice. When they reached a region called Scoringa they encountered the Vandals, who demanded that the Winnili pay tribute or engage in battle. Godan (Odin) decided to grant victory to those he saw first at sunrise. Gambara visited the goddess Frea, who suggested that the Winnili women disguise themselves as men and take up places that would ensure Godan saw them first when rising. They attracted the attention of Godan, who asked his wife, "Who are these long-beards?" Frea responded that he should give victory to those whom he had just named. Godan granted victory to the Winnili.

IĐAVÖLLR ("Shining Plain"): A site belonging to the Æsir that lies near Ásgarðr. This is where the gods will meet again after Ragnarök to recall the great events and the ancient runes. At Iðavöllr wonderful gold tablets are found in the grass; these had belonged to the people of the distant past. This is a legend that is further supported in medieval German literature: all the knowledge of men was carved on tablets or pillars that the Deluge was unable to destroy.

IÐI ("The Industrious One"): A giant who is the son of Ölvaldi and brother of Þjazi and Gangr. Ölvaldi divided his possessions in such a way that each of his sons received a mouthful of gold. This is the reason why skaldic poets call this metal "Iði's (or Þjazi's, or Gangr's) mouthful."

IDISI: Supernatural beings that incarnate fate and are mentioned in the *First Merseburg Charm*. They have been likened to valkyries, who also know how to paralyze an army (✦ HERFJÖTURR). Two corresponding words, Old English *ides* and Old High German *itis,* designate a matron in the old sense of the word (as in Latin *matrona*).

   ✦ *VALKYRIE*

   📖 Beck, *Die Merseburger Zaubersprüche.*

IÐUNN ("Youth"): A minor goddess assumed to be the wife of Bragi, the god of poetry. She is the keeper of the apples that the aging gods eat to restore their youth. As a result of Loki's scheming, she is abducted by the giant Þjazi.

   📖 Sophus Bugge, "Iduns Æbler," *Arkiv för nordisk filologi* 5 (1889): 1–45.

IFING: The river that marks out the terrain and serves as the frontier between the sons of giants and the gods. It will never freeze.

IMÐ ("Scruffy"): One of Heimdallr's nine mothers.

INVISIBILITY: One of the greatest dreams for human beings was to be able to make themselves invisible like certain gods, demons, and fantastic creatures such as fairies, dwarves, and spirits. The invisibility of the dwarves has been attributed to ownership of a cape or cap (*Tarnkappe, Nebelkappe, Helkappe, Helkleit, Verheltniskappe, Wünschhütlein*) made famous by the legend of Siegfried, or even a ring. Beginning in the sixteenth century a variety of other means were promoted as methods for gaining the ability to disappear. It was necessary to get hold of the finger of a child who died unbaptized, or of one who was stillborn. Sometimes it had to be dried and lit like a candle. As long as it was burning, no one could see you. As early as 1580 the records of a witchcraft trial spoke of the use of a candle whose wick was made of threads pulled from a shroud. The same results could be obtained by using a lamp whose flame was fed with the fat of a murder victim. As a general rule, it was enough to procure body parts from a hanged man, a virgin, or someone who died prematurely. In central Franconia the blood from the genitals of an innocent child would suffice. In the Tyrol region the method involved taking a dead man's shirt from his body and replacing it with one of your own.

Among this vast number of "practices," we find one that consisted of taking the fresh and intact tongue of a dead person, having it cooked, and then putting it back in the corpse's mouth. The following spring the head would be buried and three bean seeds planted on top of it, each in the name of the Holy Trinity. By putting one of the beans that then grew in this location in your mouth, you would become invisible. In 1546 a witch from Styria in Austria used the eyes that she had cut out from a crucified Christ figure in this way.

Plants are also used, such as a fern harvested on Saint John's Night or Christmas, or one that has been picked at a crossroads at midnight or on the summer solstice. Wild chicory picked on May 1 could be used the same way.

IRMIN: A god about whom little is known. His name refers to the Herminones (or Irminones), one of the three basic groups that, according to Tacitus (in his *Germania*), together made up the Germanic peoples. The other two groups are the Ingvaeones—a name that reflects that of the god Yngvi-Freyr—and the Istvaeones. Irmin would thus be the major god of the Herminones. Widukind of Corvey mentions the god Hirmin in his chronicle *Res gestae saxonicae* (Deeds of the Saxons), written circa 970, and conflates him with Mars or Hermes, saying that the Germans had a custom of erecting a gigantic column to him, which they then worshipped. A correspondence to "Irmin" can also be seen in Old Norse *jörmun*, a word that is also used in reference to the Midgard Serpent (*Jörmun-gandr*). One of Odin's names is Jörmunr ("Powerful One"), and the Old High German poem the *Hildebrandslied* (Lay of Hildebrand), written down in the ninth century, also mentions a "people of Irmin" (*irmindeot*).

📖 Norbert Wagner, "Irmin in der Sachsen-Origo: Zur Arbeitsweise des Widukind von Corvey," *Germanisch-Romanische Monatsschrift* 59 (1978): 385–97.

IRMINSÛL ("Irmin's Column"): During his war against the Saxons, Charlemagne captured Eresburg (in 772) and destroyed such a column, a tree trunk that had been erected outside. The Latin glosses indicate that the location of the Irminsûl was sacred and constituted a holy site. The Irminsûl has been recognized as a depiction of the cosmic tree, the world pillar called Yggdrasill in Scandinavian mythology.

IRON FOREST: ✦ JÁRNVIÐR

IRON GLOVES: Among the wondrous objects owned by Thor, such as the hammer Mjöllnir and his belt of power, there is also a pair of gloves made of iron. "He cannot do without them when he picks up Mjöllnir," Snorri Sturluson tells us. The giantess Gríðr also has a pair of iron gloves and lends them to Thor when he goes to free Loki, who has been imprisoned by the giant Geirröðr.

IRPA: A goddess worshipped in the tenth century in Hålogaland (Norway) at the same time as Þorgerðr Hölgabrúðr. The *Njáls saga* (Saga of Burnt Njál) describes a temple containing images of Irpa, Þorgerðr, and Thor.

ÍVALDI: Father of the dwarves who built the marvelous boat Skíðblaðnir, which belongs to Freyr (and sometimes Odin), and who crafted Sif's golden hair and Odin's spear, Gungnir.

JAFNHÁRR ("Equally High"): One of the names of Odin and perhaps that of another god cited in the triad of Hárr, Jafnhárr, and Þriði.

JARÐARMEN: ✦ NECKLACE OF EARTH

JÁRNGREIPR: ✦ IRON GLOVES

JÁRNSAXA ("The One with Stone Knife [or Iron Knife]"): A giantess with whom Thor fathers a son, Magni. She is described as one of the nine mothers of Heimdallr. Her name is clearly that of a giantess and refers to the mineral domain with which these beings exist in close relation.

JÁRNVIÐR: The place where giants who take the form of wolves and witches live. This forest separates the world of men (Miðgarðr) from that of the giants (Jötunheimr).

JAZIE: The *Jazie* of the Galicia region of eastern Europe are akin to the *Didken* and always depicted as hostile and malevolent creatures. It is said they live in wooded regions. Surrounded by beautiful young women abducted from men, they lure young men, kill them, and plant their heads on spikes that stand in front of their homes. They feed on human flesh—especially that of young children—and drink warm blood. It is thought they might be a mythical vision of the wild animals that haunt the Carpathian forests.

 📖 Vernaleken, *Mythen und Bräuche des Volkes in Österreich*, 238–40.

JEROME: In the romance *Friedrich von Schwaben*, written in late Middle High German in the fourteenth century, Jerome is the queen of the dwarves. Friedrich meets her in the forest, where she becomes infatuated with him, lures him into the hollow mountain, and keeps him there. He becomes her lover, and they have a daughter, Zipproner, who is not a dwarf. Friedrich marries Jerome after the death of her first husband. Jerome seems to possess magical powers: with a wave of her hand she can cause darkness to fall in her apartments.

JÓL: Winter solstice festival of Yule; today it is the name for Christmas in the Scandinavian countries. Sacrifices were made at this time to the gods and to the dead to obtain a fruitful and peaceful year. Odin is associated with this celebration, as is Freyr (the animal regularly sacrificed on this occasion is a male boar) and the elves. In fact, another name for Jól is "Sacrifice to the Elves" (*álfablót*).

📖 Bø, *Vår norske jul;* Ronald Grambo, "Julen i Middelalderen: Hedenskap og Kristendom," *Mittelalter-Forum* I (1996): 24–35; Jorma Koivulehto, "Fest und Zyklus des Jahres: Jul und Kekri," *Neuphilologische Mitteilungen* 101 (2000), 235–52.

JÓLNIR ("Master of Jól"): One of Odin's names. There is no doubt whatsoever concerning this god's association with Jól (the pagan celebration that was later conflated with Christmas), but it is almost certainly because this feast was also that of the dead. A long-surviving folk belief in Norway maintained that during this time of the year the dead traveled in bands through the air stealing food and drink, much as Odin was reputed to have done to the detriment of King Halfdan the Black. These troops of the dead are one of the representations of the Wild Hunt, which is often called Odin's Hunt.

✦ *OSKOREIA, WILD HUNT*

📖 Falk, *Odensheiti.*

JORDBARN ("Children of the Earth"): A Norwegian name given to dwarves that stresses their chthonic nature and habitat (stones and caverns).

JÖRÐ ("Earth"): An Ásynja that is sometimes called a "giantess." She is the wife or lover of Odin and the mother of Thor. She is supposed to be the daughter of Nótt ("Night") and Anarr, her second husband. This is an interesting detail that reflects an aspect of the older worldview: night precedes day and everything comes from her. We should recall that the ancient Germanic peoples measured time in nights and not days, as was pointed out by Tacitus.

Worship of the Earth Mother was widespread, and she appears in various forms such as in the figures of Nerthus, Jörð, Hlóðyn, and Fjörgyn.

✦ *MOTHER GODDESSES*

📖 Grambo, *Svart katt over veien*, 78.

JÖRMUNGANDR ("Powerful Monster"): Another name for the Midgard Serpent. It can also be translated as "powerful spell" since *gandr* can also mean "magic wand."

JÖTUNHEIMR ("World of the Giants"): This mythical region is located somewhere to the east of Miðgarðr, the world of men, and separated from it by rivers and the Iron Forest. This is the home of the giants. Jötunheimr may be another name for Útgarðr ("Outer Enclosure"), the customary territory for these beings.

JÖTUNN (Old Norse, pl. *jötnar;* Norwegian *jutul*): Primitive giants who were constitutive elements of the material world. We know nothing of them save for the fact their name is related to the Old Norse verb *eta*, "to eat," which would make them ogres. In Old English they are called *eotenas* (sg. *eoten*). At the time of the written accounts, *Jötunn* had become simply a synonym for "giant." There are around forty Norwegian place-names that preserve the memory of these creatures; for example, Jotunheimen ("World of the Giants"), Jutulbrui ("Bridge of the Giant"), and Jutulhaugen, ("Mound of the Giant"). These names are explained by legends: it is said that beneath the mound a giant with copper boots lies buried; a giant allegedly took a large mass of stones to construct what resembles a bridge; and so forth.

✦ *GRÝLA, RISE, TROLL*

📖 Carl von Sydow, "Jätterna i mytologi och folktro," *Folkeminnen och Folktankar* 6 (1919): 52–96.

JURAN: In Der Stricker's thirteenth-century Arthurian romance *Daniel von dem blühenden Tal* (Daniel of the Flowering Valley), this is the name of a dwarf that forces his attentions on the daughter of a duke whose kith and kin he has murdered. He wants to marry her so that he can later repudiate her after atrociously mutilating her.

This could well be the echo of a poorly grasped legend. In any case, the theme is reminiscent of Chrétien de Troyes's *Yvain*. Juran can only be slain by his own sword. Daniel takes it and kills the dwarf with it.

📖 Resler, ed., *Der Stricker: Daniel von dem blühenden Tal.*

K

KÁRA: Reincarnation of the valkyrie Sigrún and protector of Helgi Haddingjaskaði, who is himself the reincarnation of Helgi Hundingsbani, the murderer of King Hundingr.

✦ *VALKYRIE*

KARI ("Gust"): A giant; the son of Fornjótr.

KASERMAN(N)DL, ALMBUTZ: The name of a spirit that takes possession of the Alpine pastures once animals and men have returned to the valleys. They are often cowherds or shepherds who return because they committed a transgression involving livestock, food, or tools. This is a widespread belief throughout the Alps.

    📖 Alpenburg, *Deutsche Alpensagen*, no. 74; Vernaleken, *Alpensagen*, 85.

KASERTÖRGGELEN (pl.): A collective term in the Tyrol that refers to child revenants that are generally harmless although they cannot tolerate curiosity. They will blind anyone who spies on them. They come down from the summer pastures in the Alps on Saint Martin's Day. Their name means "the Wobblers of the Chalet(s)." They are close relatives to the *Kaserman(n)dl.*

    📖 Alpenburg, *Mythen und Sagen Tirols*, 162–62, 169–70, 180; Heyl, *Volkssagen, Meinungen und Bräuche aus Tirol,* 73.

KENNING: Extended metaphors that were quite popular with the Norse skalds (poets) and to which we are indebted for much information on mythology. For example, gold is called "Fróði's flour," which refers to the mythical mill owned by Fróði and worked by the two giantesses Fenja and Menja. The sea is called "Ymir's blood," an allusion to the role of this giant in the creation of the world.

    Snorri Sturluson's *Skáldskaparmál* (Treatise on the Skaldic Art) is a collection of kennings with explanations, and of *heiti.*

✦ *HEITI*

KERAN: God whose name appeared in 848 and who is represented by a spear. It is thought that this weapon represents lightning, and Keran is commonly compared to Wodan.

KERLAUGAR: The name of the two mythical rivers that the god Thor crosses on a daily basis. It is possible that Kerlaugar refers to a myth that has not been preserved for us.

◆ *KÖRMT*

KLAUBAUF: In Tyrolean Christmas processions the *Klaubauf* is a type of wild man who most often appears in groups. He wears a fur mantle, large bells on his belt, and a terrifying mask. He accompanies Saint Nicholas on his travels through towns and villages, and when the saint enters a house he creates a huge racket outside. Once Saint Nicholas has finished his rounds, the *Klaubauf* still has full run of the land and behaves very aggressively.

◆ *KNECHT RUPRECHT, KRAMPUS, PERCHT, STAMPA*

KLABAUTERMANN, KLABOTERMAN, KALFATER, KLADER: A local land spirit of northern Germany, the *Klabautermann* is bound to a sailboat over which he keeps watch. If he leaves the ship it will sink. Most of the time he is invisible; on those occasions when he is seen, he appears as a homunculus the size of a bottle with red hair and a white beard. He has light-colored eyes, green teeth, and the face of an old man. He smokes a pipe, is dressed as a sailor, and carries a boatswain's hammer. He is said to be the spirit of a child who died unbaptized and was buried beneath a tree. His soul thus entered the tree, and when wood from it was used to build a ship, he entered the vessel.

📖 Gerndt, *Fliegender Holländer und Klabautermann;* Temme, *Die Volkssagen von Pommern und Rügen,* no. 253; Karin Lichtblau, "Klabautermann," in Müller and Wunderlich, eds., *Mittelalter Mythen,* vol. II, 343–52.

KLUDDE, KLEUDDE: A figure that takes many forms who was most likely a water spirit originally. It can be found in Holland, Flanders, and Belgium in a human shape—man, woman, wizard, revenant—or as a devil or nightmare. Its most frequent animal shapes are, in descending order, dog (black and rearing on its hind legs), calf, bear, and cat. *Kludde*

Fig. 40.
Klabautermann

Fig. 41. Kludde

is sometimes a were-creature, a bogeyman, or a perching spirit that makes its victim carry it for a certain distance, or a water spirit.

📖 Van den Berg, *De volkssage in de provincie Antwerpen in de 19de en 20ste eeuw,* vol. III, 1539ff.

KNECHT RUPRECHT ("Servant Ruprecht"): A bogeyman who accompanies Saint Nicholas and carries disobedient children away in his basket. In fact, this figure originally represented a water demon that was Christianized and attached to Saint Nicholas.

He is customarily masked and clad in animal hides, but he can change into a nice old man with white whiskers. He carries a staff that he uses to hit those whom he comes across. He promises to reward good children and to carry away in his sack those who hit their little sisters, or else to eat the bad children. In 1663, Knecht Ruprecht sang:

> *Ich bin der alte böse Mann*
> *Der alle Kinder fressen kann.*
> *("I am the old evil man who can eat all the children.")*

Fig. 42. Knecht Ruprecht and Saint Nicholas.
Drawing by F. Kollarz, after M. Rumpf, *Perchten*.

Etymologically, his name means "Radiant Fame," but because of his appearance and behavior, a folk etymology sees Ruprecht as deriving from *Rupel,* "hayseed."

✦ *KLAUBAUF, KRAMPUS, PERCHT, STAMPA*

📖 Lecouteux, "Nicchus—Nix," *Euphorion* 78 (1984): 280–88.

KOBOLD: The name of a local land spirit that is attached to various places and has a multitude of names depending on the country and region. He corresponds to the goblin and the gnome. As a household spirit he provides services but also plays all kinds of tricks. He can appear in a variety of guises such as that of a cat, a three-legged pig, or a ball of fire. People pay him for his help with an offering of gruel. If he is given red clothing in compensation for his services, he will disappear forever.

📖 Arrowsmith and Moorse, *A Field Guide to the Little People,* 135–39; Grimm, *Deutsche Sagen,* nos. 71–73; Keightley, *The World Guide to Gnomes, Fairies, Elves, and Other Little People,* 239–58; Lecouteux, *The Tradition of Household Spirits;* Hans F. Feilberg, "Der Kobold in nordischer Überlieferung," *Zeitschrift des Vereins für Volkskunde* 8 (1898): 1–20, 130–46, 264–77.

KÖR ("Illness"): The name of Hel's bed. Hel is the Norse goddess of the underworld.

✦ *HEL*

KÖRMT: One of the rivers Thor must cross when traveling to the assembly of the Æsir, which takes place beneath the cosmic tree. The other rivers are Örmt and the two Kerlaugar. It is thought that they form the border between our world and that of the giants.

KRAKEN: A gigantic sea serpent that haunted the coasts of Norway. The first narrative, dating from 1555 and written by the Swedish archbishop Olaus Magnus, informs us that it was decimating livestock and wreaking havoc among the creatures of the sea. At least 190 feet long, with a mane and burning eyes, it never hesitated to attack ships and pluck sailors from their decks.

It would seem that this monster is a form taken by the *hafstrambi,* first mentioned in the Old Norwegian *Konungs skuggsjá* (King's

Fig. 43. The Kraken as depicted in Olaus Magnus,
Historia de gentibus septentrionalibus, Rome, 1555

Mirror), which was written down around 1270. This beast is said to live in the waters off the coast of Greenland; it is both large and tall and able to stand upright above the waves. It is described as having human shoulders and throat, a head, eyes, mouth, and chin of a man, but no arms, and it becomes increasingly slender from the shoulders down. Its body resembles "an icicle." If it looks at the boat and dives in its direction, this is a sign that loss of life is imminent, but if it flees away from the ship, there will be no reason to fear storms.

📖 Heuvelmans, *Le Grand Serpent de mer;* Larson, trans., *The King's Mirror,*
135–36.

KRAMPUS, GRAMPUS: Name of a devil that accompanies Saint Nicholas in Upper Austria. He forms part of a winter procession of masked men and is accompanied by his peers (pl. *Krampusse*). All yell and ring the large bells that they wear on their belts. Their masks are black with white teeth, white pupils, and red lips, with rams' horns on each side and several goat horns on top. The tips of the goat horns are sometimes painted red. They wear sheepskins and hold a whip with which they strike anyone they meet—an action that is interpreted as a fertility rite—and they drag chains.

✦ *KLAUBAUF, KNECHT RUPRECHT, PERCHT, STAMPA*

KUDRUN: Title of a long poem in Middle High German written around 1240. It contains an echo of the myth of the Eternal Battle. The core plot element is the quest by King Hetel of Hegelingen for the hand of Hilde.

📖 Bartsch, ed., *Kudrun;* Carles, *Le Poème de Kûdrûn, étude de sa matière.*

✦ *HJAÐNINGAVÍG*

KUNAL-TROWS: On the Shetland Islands, these are gloomy and hopeless beings that are compelled to marry human women who die in childbirth; afterward, they never remarry.

✦ *TROW*

📖 Jean Renaud, "Le peuple surnaturel des Shetland," *Artus* 21–22 (1986): 28–32.

KUPERAN, KUPRAN, KUPRIAN: When seeking to free Kriemhild after she is abducted by a flying dragon, Seyfrid (Siegfried) has to fight a giant named Kuperan who holds the key to the cavern in

Fig. 44. The giant Kuperan battling Seyfrid. *Das Lied vom hürnen Seyfrid,* a sixteenth-century chapbook.

which she is imprisoned. Kuperan has one thousand other giants under his command, as well as a race of dwarves that he conquered and who now dwell beneath the mountain.

Kuperan fights without armor, and when he tries to strike Seyfrid with an iron bar, he misses and buries his weapon six feet in the ground. The hero wounds him just as he stoops down to recover his weapon. Kuperan then retreats to his cave to put on a suit of armor toughened with dragons' blood and takes up a sword and a square iron club with sharpened corners. During this second battle he receives sixteen wounds. Seyfrid spares him on the condition that he will help him to free Kriemhild. The giant agrees but treacherously strikes Seyfrid, and the hero is only saved by the intervention of the dwarf Eugel (✦ EUGEL), who makes him invisible. After the giant's treacherous action, the hero slays Kuperan.

📖 Lecouteux, "Seyfrid, Kuperan et le dragon," *Études Germaniques* 49 (1994): 257–66.

KVASIR: The principal character in the Norse myth of the origin of poetry. When the Æsir and the Vanir conclude a peace treaty they all spit into a cauldron, and this spittle gives birth to Kvasir, the wisest of all men. The dwarves Fjalarr and Galarr murder him and collect his blood in two vats called Boðn and Són and a pot called Óðrœrir. They blend the blood with honey and make a mead that has the property of transforming any man who drinks it into a poet. The dwarves then tell the Æsir that Kvasir had suffocated from an excess of intelligence because there was no one with enough skill to exhaust his knowledge with questions.

This story is closely analogous to that of the Asura demon Mada ("Intoxicator") in the Sanskrit epic *Mahabharata,* although Mada was crafted to be a weapon to compel the gods to make peace, whereas in the Germanic myth Kvasir is crafted as a symbol of the peace itself.

The second part of the myth tells how Odin stole the wondrous mead. The dwarves invite the giant Gillingr and his wife to visit and then slay both of them. Suttungr, Gillingr's father, learns of this foul deed and obtains the mead as compensation for this double murder. He stores it inside Hnitbjörg Mountain and entrusts his daughter Gunnlöð with the task of guarding it.

Odin tries in vain to obtain a mouthful of mead from Baugi, the brother of Suttungr, as payment for work performed (✦ BÖLVERKR). In response to his request, Baugi drills a hole into the mountain with an auger called Rati, after which Odin transforms into a snake and slides through the hole and into the chamber where Gunnlöð is guarding the mead. He sleeps with her for three nights in a row, and, in return, she lets him drink a mouthful from each of the containers. Odin's three mouthfuls, however, completely empty the two vats and the pot. Odin then changes into an eagle and flies away. Seeing this, Suttungr changes himself into an eagle to pursue him but is unable to catch him. When Odin reaches Ásgarðr, he spits the mead back out into vessels that are brought forth by the Æsir.

Fig. 45. The theft of the mead. Illustration by Ólafur Brynjúlfsson, *Snorra Edda*, 1760.

LÆRAÐR: The tree that grows on the roof of Valhalla; the goat Heiðrún and the stag Eikþyrnir feed on its leaves. A miniature manuscript of the *Snorra Edda,* created by Ólafur Brynjúlfsson in the eighteenth century, depicts this scene. This tree is presumably identical to Yggdrasill.

LAND SPIRITS (Old Norse *landvættir,* sg. *landvættr*): According to ancient beliefs, the world belongs to the spirits. If someone wishes to colonize land and settle on it, the land spirits must be driven off it. This can be done, for example, by shooting a flaming arrow over the desired piece of land or by offering these spirits propitiatory sacrifices. The purpose of the grimacing figureheads on Viking ships was to disperse the spirits of the land being attacked so that victory would be won more easily. The laws of the time required that these detachable figures be removed from the prows of the ships when returning home. Land spirits gradually became conflated with elves and dwarves and were subsequently demonized by Christianity, but in folk traditions they continue to live in remote areas, cliffs, forests, and mountains. The Germanic view is hardly dissimilar from that of the ancient Romans, who said that the world was inhabited by beings called fauns, satyrs, woodland spirits, and so forth.

📖 Hultkrantz, ed., *The Supernatural Owners of Nature;* Lecouteux, *Demons and Spirits of the Land.*

LANDVÆTTR (pl. *landvættir*): ✦ LAND SPIRITS

LANGBARÐR ("Long-beard"): A nickname for Odin that probably refers to the following legend. When the Winnili were forced to wage war with the Vandals, Gambara, mother of the chieftains Ibor and Agio, went before Frea (Frigg), the wife of Godan (Odin), and begged her to grant victory to her sons. Frea advised her as follows: the Winnili women should let their hair fall in front of their faces like beards, then accompany their husbands at dawn in a place where Godan could not help but see them when looking out his window. When he saw them, he shouted out, "Who are these long-beards?" Frea suggested he grant victory to those whom he had just given a name. The Winnili were victorious and henceforth called themselves Langobards, meaning "Long-beards."

📖 Falk, *Odensheiti*.

LANGE WAPPER: This was a water spirit of the sixteenth century. Using trickery it would transform into a baby so it could nurse on women's milk. It can be found in Dutch and Belgian traditions. It can appear in the form of a human being (apprentice, sailor, priest, watchman, porter, egg or chicken merchant, or old woman), an animal (cat or dog), or even an object (napkin or garment). It haunts cemeteries, churches, and houses. It plays cards and punishes thieves. It can travel from Antwerp to Mechelen in a single step; it is also said that it can fly through the air, is a magician, and only comes out at night.

Fig. 46. Lange Wapper

Lange Wapper is also a bogeyman that parents describe to dissuade their children from going too close to the water. It has become a figure of folklore and entered into the retinue of processional giants.

   📖 Hageland and Lamend, *Lange Wapper en Kludde;* E. Willekens, "Lange Wapper, een Antwerpe legendarische figuur," *Antwerpen* I (1955): 119–22.

LANGTÜTTIN ("Long Breasts"): In the Passeier Valley (Val Passiria, Italy) of the southern Tyrol, this is the name of a hideous woman who runs after children offering her breast, but milk flows only from one and pus flows from the other. She is sometimes associated with a wild man.

   📖 Zingerle, *Sagen aus Tirol,* 110–11.

LAUFEY: Loki's mother.

LAURIN: King of the dwarves. He lives in the Tyrol Mountains, where he owns a wonderful rose garden that is vandalized by Dietrich von Bern (the epic and legendary transposition of Theodoric the Great)

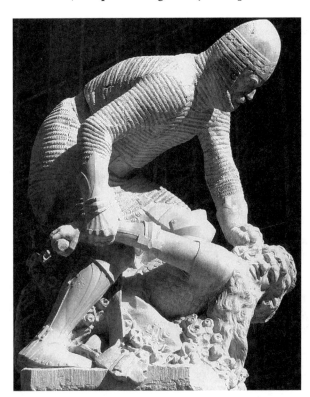

Fig. 47. Dietrich von Bern's battle with the dwarf king Laurin

and his companions Dietleib and Witege. Defeated by Dietrich, Laurin is only spared due to the intervention of Dietlieb—whose sister (named Kunhilt or Sinhilt) he had abducted—and he invites the knights to visit his hollow mountain. He then gives them a sleeping potion to drink and imprisons them in a dungeon. With the help of Kunhilt they are able to overturn their situation, and they go to Ravenna with Laurin, where he is then instructed in the Christian faith.

Laurin measures three spans (just over two feet), and his horse is the size of a roebuck. The dwarf owns a magic ring and belt, both of which give the wearer the strength of twelve men; he also possesses the cloak of invisibility (*Tarnkappe*). He is the nephew of Walberan, who rules over the dwarves that live between Judea and the Caucasus.

In another text, the *Wartburgkrieg* (Wartburg Contest), it is said that Laurin is the father of Sinnels, another dwarf king. Dietrich allegedly followed Sinnels and was never to be seen again, which is reminiscent of the legend of King Herla.

📖 Lecouteux, *Les Nains et les Elfes au Moyen Âge*.

LAUTERFRESSER: A Tyrolean spirit capable of assuming many shapes. It could take on the appearance of a fly, a mosquito, and sometimes that of a bear. In the form of a vagabond it caused rain to fall by throwing into the water the needles used to sew a shroud, hairs from a woman's head, sweepings, and stones. It owned a magic tube made from the shaft of a white goose feather in which were placed seeds from a fern harvested beneath the light of a comet, a mortuary needle, and the tongue of a white worm. When the spirit blew inside it, it would snow. The Lauterfresser knew how to make itself invisible and invulnerable, possessed superhuman strength, which it drew from Satan, and could provoke rats, mice, and horses as it knew their language. It cannot tolerate children and will make them disappear.

Originally this spirit was a historical figure, Mathias Perger (ca. 1587–1645), who was executed after being accused of witchcraft. He allegedly took part in a Sabbat where the devil, Belial, gave him a bearskin that allowed him to change his shape, and so forth. Aspects of his trial provided the basis for his legend and for his transformation into a mythical figure.

📖 Heyl, *Volkssagen, Meinungen und Bräuche aus Tirol*, 229.

LECKFRÄULEIN (pl.): Name given to the good fairies of the Italian Tyrol (✦ SALINGEN). They live in caves. When they visit a farm they bring good fortune, but when a farmwife refused them food one day, the prosperity of the place vanished.

📖 Heyl, *Volkssagen, Meinungen und Bräuche aus Tirol,* 276.

LENORE: The title and heroine of a famous ballad by Gottfried August Bürger (1747–1794), published in 1774. In despair at the death of her fiancé, a young woman commits blasphemy. At midnight the one whom she believes to be dead comes for her. He carries her off on a mad ride on horseback to the cemetery where the earth opens to swallow both of them up.

Bürger was inspired by an anonymous German poem that borrowed a theme common throughout Europe, namely in the Danish ballad *Aage og Else,* of "the return of the deceased fiancé." The most beautiful examples of this theme can be found in the Greek *Acritic Songs* and in a book titled *Kytice* by the Czech writer Karel Erben.

Bürger's text enjoyed great success. Walter Scott translated it into English as *William and Helen* in 1796, Johann Rudolf Zumsteg set it

Fig. 48. The Ballad of *Lenore.*
Illustration from a German textbook (1930).

to music in 1798, Henri Duparc made a symphonic poem based on it in 1875, and it was the inspiration for Vasily Zhukovsky's *Ludmila*. In 1839 the painter Horace Vernet depicted the dead man's ride with his fiancée mounted behind him in a painting that is now housed in the Museum of Fine Arts in Nantes, France.

✦ *AAGE and ELSE*

LÍF ("Life"): One of the two survivors of Ragnarök, the other being Lífþrasir. Both are fathers to a new generation of humanity.

LÍFÞRASIR ("Striving for Life"): He and Líf survive the destruction of the Earth during Ragnarök because they find refuge in the grove called Hoddmímir ("Treasure-Mímir"), in other words, Yggdrasill, at the foot of which lies the Well of Wisdom, "Mímir's treasure." They feed on morning dew and engender the next race of men.

LIGHT ELVES (Old Norse *ljósálfar,* sg. *ljósálfr*): The name Snorri Sturluson gave to elves to distinguish them from dwarves, which he seems to confuse with dark elves. They inhabit the hall called Gimlé ("Shelter from the Flames").

LIGO: God of spring and joy for the ancient Prussians. Virgins kept a fire of oaken logs permanently burning for him. He was worshipped on the summit of the Rinau (Galtgarbenberg).

📖 Rhesa, *Prutena,* 147–49.

LINDWURM: One of the names for a dragon in the Middle Ages. The word translated the Latin term *iaculus,* which designates a serpent that hurls itself on its prey from the treetops; hence it should be considered to be a flying serpent. It is also a hydra.

LITR ("The Colored One"): The name of a dwarf who abruptly shows up at Baldr's funeral. Thor dispatches him with a kick into the funeral pyre. The meaning of this odd passage is clarified when one knows that dwarves maintained close relations with the dead. Litr could be a psychopomp charged with guiding the dead man to the home of Hel, the goddess of the underworld.

LITTLE GRAY MAN (GRAUMÄNNCHEN): In central and northern Germany this is a ghost that announces a death but also a bogeyman and a guardian of treasures. He has become conflated with kobolds and dwarves.

LJÓSÁLFAR: ✦ LIGHT ELVES

LÓÐURR: God mentioned in a triad together with Hœnir and Odin. Nothing is known of him except that Odin was his companion.

LŒÐING: The first of the three fetters that the gods used to bind the wolf Fenrir. He breaks it, along with the second one, Drómi. Only the third fetter, Gleipnir, holds him fast.

LOFN ("The Sweet One"): A kind Ásynja who asked Odin and Frigg for the power to bring together men and women whose marriages had been forbidden until that time.

LOGAÞORE: A sixth- or seventh-century fibula discovered in Nordendorf bears a runic inscription that has yielded the names of three gods: Logaþore, Wodan, and Wigiþonar. Attempts have been made to equate Logaþore with Lóðurr and with Loki, but none of the solutions has proved satisfactory, and this deity remains a mystery.

LOGI ("Fire"): Name of a giant who is one of the three sons of Fornjótr and, perhaps, a personification of the all-devouring fire. He is Loki's adversary in the following tale. Thor has gone to the home of the giant Útgarðaloki in Jötunheimr, accompanied by Loki, Þjalfi, and Röskva. Útgarðaloki asks them what test they would like to take, and Loki boasts that he can eat faster than anyone. The giant named Logi devours the meat that is provided them including the bones and the bowl it was served in, while Loki can only manage to eat the meat surrounding the bone. Loki is therefore defeated, but Útgarðaloki explains that it was through magic because Logi is nothing other than "wildfire."

LOHENGRIN: ✦ SWAN KNIGHT

LOKI: This is probably the most complex god in the entire Germanic pantheon. He is the father of all the enemies of the gods, causes the death of Baldr and prevents his return to the Æsir, and offers a wealth of harmful advice, but he also helps the gods to extricate themselves from difficult situations that he personally caused. He is the son of Laufey or Nal and the giant Farbauti. His brothers are Byleistr and Helblindi. His wife's name is Sigyn, and they have one son, Nari (or Narfi). Loki slept with the giantess Angrboða, who gave him three children: the wolf Fenrir, the Midgard Serpent, and Hel, the goddess of the underworld. He has the gift of transforming himself into an animal and into an old woman. Among other things he becomes a mare, a falcon, a fly, and a seal. He is evil by nature, very fickle in his behavior, and the skaldic metaphors (*kenningar*) call him "slanderer of the gods" and "instigator of Baldr's murder." Loki is small in size.

Loki is an unabashed thief, a trait that likens him to the dwarves. He steals, for example, the apples of youth from Iðunn, Sif's hair,

Fig. 49. Loki

Freyja's necklace, Thor's iron gloves, and Andvari's ring. He is also a craftsman and fashioned the "Harmful Twig" (Lævateinn) with which the bird Viðofnir can be killed. He is also the inventor of the fishing net. The ancient mythographers made him Odin's blood brother. During Rägnarok, Loki is the enemy of the gods. He pilots the boat out of the north that carries the troops of Hel, the evil dead who will join in the assault on Ásgarðr.

It is Loki who kills Heimdallr. Scholars believe that Loki developed out of folk beliefs and was originally an evil spirit, goblin, or demon. In any case, he is a well-known character of Indo-European mythologies—the trickster—and Georges Dumézil has demonstrated that he has a counterpart in the Ossetian trickster figure Syrdon.

Many of Loki's traits are simply epiphenomena: he is, first and foremost, the embodiment of evil; the wicked spirit that prevents the world from enjoying happiness; the troublemaker and the sower of strife. It is easy to see why neither place-names nor personal names show any trace of him.

For bringing about Baldr's death, Loki receives a punishment that befits his malignant nature. The Æsir capture him and imprison him in a cave where they stand three flat stones on end and make a hole in each of them. They then fetch Loki's sons Vali and Narfi and transform Vali into a wolf, who proceeds to tear his brother Narfi to pieces. The Æsir use Narfi's guts to bind Loki to the three stones, set up in a way to cause as much pain as possible; these fetters then change to iron. Skaði sets a viper above Loki so that its venom will drip onto his face, but Loki's wife, Sigyn, collects the poison in a cup. When the cup becomes full she empties it, and the venom that falls on Loki's face at these moments causes him to writhe so terribly the world shakes. This goes on until Ragnarök.

📖 Dumézil, *Loki;* Jerold C. Frakes, "Loki's Mythological Function in the Tripartite System," *Journal of English and Germanic Philology* 86:4 (1987): 473–86; Tomoaki Mizuno, "Loki as a Terrible Stranger and a Sacred Visitor," *Studies in Humanities: Culture and Communication* 30 (1996): 69–90.

LOPTR: One of Loki's names, which—like the Old Norse word *lopt*— means "air." This name can be seen as reflective of Loki's ungraspable and inconstant nature.

LORANDIN: In *Seyfrid von Ardemont,* a romance attributed to Albrecht von Scharfenberg (thirteenth century), this dwarf is one of the hero's advisers. He warns Seyfrid about the strength of the dragon the hero must fight and offers him counsel. After the battle he loosens the knight's helmet, brings him drink, and gives him roots with certain virtues to eat. When Seyfrid must contend with the giant Amphigulor, Lorandin gives him weapons and roots that increase his strength. After this battle he offers Seyfrid a magic ring set with gems that puts an end to the sufferings endured by five young women imprisoned by Amphigulor on behalf of a wizard. Lorandin finally provides the small band with five horses, alerts his people to the giant's death, and henceforth regards himself as Seyfrid's vassal.

LORELEI, LORELEY, LORE LEI, LURLEI: This nixie lives on a large rock, the Lurlenberg (mentioned as early as the thirteenth century), on the bank of the Rhine. She owes her existence to the 1802

Fig. 50. Lorelei

novel by Clemens Brentano, *Godwi oder Das steinerne Bild der Mutter* (Godwi, or The Stone Statue of the Mother), but her popularity is due to the poem Heinrich Heine wrote about her in 1824. The Lorelei is sometimes a water fairy (*Meerfei*) with golden hair and sometimes a seductive demon, a magician who beguiles the minds of men. She was banished by a bishop and cast into the Rhine from atop the large rock that bears her name.

📖 Holbek and Piø, *Fabeldyr og sagnfolk,* 70; Petzold, *Kleines Lexikon der Dämonen und Elementargeister,* 124–25; Willy Krogmann, "Lorelei, Geburt einer Sage," *Rheinisch-westfälische Zeischrift für Volkskunde* 3 (1956): 170–96.

LORG, ORG (masc.): A fantasy creature in Tyrolean legends that is described in various ways. It is sometimes a shapeless mass resembling a haystack, and it behaves like a perching spirit; sometimes it is a cubit in size and looks like a cat skin that moves by rolling. It could also be a large black man carrying his head under his arm, a one-eyed giant who comes out for the Twelve Days, or, lastly, a horseman dressed in a white mantle, who assumes gigantic size and terrifies all whom he meets.

📖 Alpenburg, *Mythen und Sagen Tirols,* 119–20; Zingerle, *Sagen aus Tirol,* 2–3, 124, 208–10.

LUTCHEN (pl., "The Little Folk," "The Wee Folk"): The *Lutchen* or *Ludki* were pagans and the first inhabitants of Lusatia. They are little individuals of both sexes, barely any taller than a foot, who wear red caps and jackets. They dwell in the dunes of the arid plateau, especially in the woods at the foot of the Koschenberg (Lower Lusatia). They maintain friendly relations with men, take part in their celebrations, and love to dance. They sometimes help people while they work and, in return, borrow their tools. When one of their race dies they incinerate his body and bury the ashes and remains in urns and weep copiously during the funeral. Together, the closest relatives hold small cups beneath their eyes to collect their tears, which are then placed around the urns.

📖 Lohre, *Märkische Sagen,* nos. 71–72.

LYFJABERG ("Healing Mountain"): A mountain guarded by a giant where Menglöð lives. Any woman who climbs it will be cured, even if she suffers from disabilities or old age. The ill and wounded will find comfort there.

LYNGVI: A small island in Lake Amsvartnir. The Æsir lure the wolf Fenrir there and bind him. Fenrir will not break his chains until Ragnarök.

M

MÆLKEHARE ("Hare-milker" or "Suckler"): A demonic animal, working in the service of a sorcerer, that steals milk from cows. Evidence for this belief has existed since 1750 in Norway (Gudbrandsdal) and can also be found in Scandinavian charms. A similar albeit more monstrous milk-stealing entity is the *tilberi* ("Fetcher") of Icelandic folk belief.

✦ *TILBERI*

MAGNI ("The Strong One"): Son of Thor and the giantess Járnsaxa. When Thor kills the giant Hrungnir his body falls to the ground with one of his feet on top of the god, who is unable to get himself out from beneath it. Magni, aged three, is the only one able to free his father, who as a reward offers him Hrungnir's steed, Gullfaxi.

MAHR (masc. and fem. German *Mahr, Mahrd, Mahrt, Mor* [island of Rügen dialect]; Old English *mare;* Old Norse *mara*): The name of a demon of folk mythology that is also evident in the second part of the English word "nightmare" (likewise in French *cauchemar,* and German *Nachtmahr*). The *mar* was replaced by the elf in those Germanic regions where a nightmare is today referred to as an *Alptraum,* "elven dream," and *Alpdruck,* "elf-pressure." In the Roman world this entity sits on the sleeper's chest and causes respiratory distress. This sense is evident in various Romance words for "nightmare" such as Spanish *pesadilla,* Portuguese *pesadela,* and the Italian *perurole,* which are all nouns coined from a Latin verb that means "to weigh." In southern Germany the name of this being is *Trud;* in Frisia it is *Walriderske,* and in Switzerland, *Doggeli.*

The *Mahr* and *Trud* are complex figures: they can be a dead individual who is unhappy with his or her fate and seeks vengeance (✦ DRAUGR), or the Double (alter ego) of a living person, especially a magician or sorcerer.

In folk traditions the *Mahr* designates a woman whose spirit leaves her body during sleep to go and torment the person she loves. Care must be taken not to move the woman's body while she sleeps or else her spirit will not be able to reenter it, and she will die.

✦ *ALP*

📖 Bridier, *Le Cauchemar: étude d'une figure mythique;* Holbek and Piø, *Fabeldyr og sagnfolk,* 186–98; Terramorsi, ed., *Le Cauchemar;* Van den Berg, *De volkssage in de provincie Antwerpen in de 19de en 20ste eeuw,* 1573–83. Lecouteux, "Mara—Ephialtes—Incubus: le cauchemar chez les peuples germaniques," *Études Germaniques* 42 (1987): 1–24.

MANDRAKE: This marvelous, mythical plant is called the "Little Gallows Man" (*Galgenmännchen*) in folk traditions, at least since the sixteenth century. This is primarily due to the fact that its root vaguely resembles a human body, and secondly because it is allegedly engendered by the urine or semen of hanged men and grows beneath the shadow of the gallows.

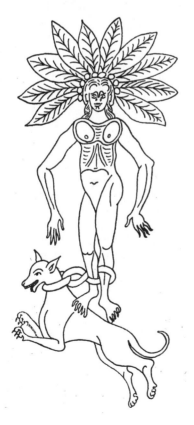

Fig. 51. Depiction of mandrake in a thirteenth-century English manuscript

Fig. 52. The Gold-shitter

Our "Little Gallows Man" is also called the "Wee Moneyman," the "Little Man of the Hedge" (*Heckmännchen*), and the "Gold-shitter" (*Geldschißer*) or "Gold-hatcher" (*Geldbrüter*). The names vary, as always, according to region: the *Heckmännchen* is found more often in Saxony or Thuringia, the *Geldschißer* in Bavaria, the *Alraunel* in Lower Austria, and so forth. The Gold-shitter has become a popular figure that has been anthropomorphized and depicted as seen in the illustration above.

It should be pointed out that the money he provides is not stolen from another individual. In fact, the increase of this fortune is entirely magical and is a result of the very nature of this creature.

MÁNI ("Moon"): Máni is the god who rules the moon. The word is a masculine noun. It is possible that this god was a giant. He is the son of Mundilfari, and his sister is Sól (the sun). When he crosses through the sky he is pursued by the wolf Hati, who is also called "Moon-devourer."

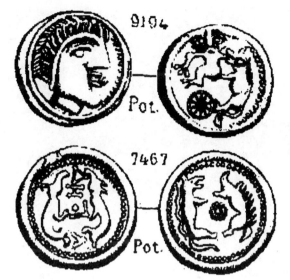

Fig. 53. Gaulish coins representing (top) the wolf trying to eat the sun and (bottom) the wolf and the moon

According to one tradition the Æsir placed Máni in the sky to count the years (✦ MAN IN THE MOON). According to another account, when Mundilfari gave Sól's hand in marriage to a man by the name of Glenr, the Æsir were angered and placed her in the sky with Máni. Since that time, Máni had guided the course of this heavenly body and rules the new moon and the last quarter (✦ BIL, HJÚKI).

MAN IN THE MOON: The dark patches on the moon have always intrigued human beings, who developed a myth-turned-legend that can be found throughout Germanic literature. Máni, the god who rules the new moon and the last quarter, abducts a young girl, Bil, and a young man, Hjúki, from the Earth as they were leaving the spring called Byrgir, carrying over their shoulders the pole Simul, on which the pail Sægr was hung. They were the children of Viðfinnr. Henceforth they followed the moon, as could be seen from the Earth.

Bil and Hjúki are personifications of moon phases. In more recent Basque, Belgian, English, and German traditions, the man in the moon is carrying a bundle of sticks. In the Limousin region of France it is said that it is Saint Gerard who was sent up there because he spent his Sundays repairing hedges. Starting in the twelfth century the belief arose that this same individual was being punished for

Fig. 54. Portal of the Evangelical Church of Großen-Linden (tenth century), near Gießen (Hesse, Germany), with depictions of mythological scenes, including the wolf Hati trying to devour the moon

breaking an ecclesiastical law, an idea that underpins the bulk of the later legends.

📖 Robert J. Menner, "The Man in the Moon and Hedging," *Journal of English and Germanic Philology* 48 (1949): 1–14.

MANNUS: According to Tacitus, this is the son of Tuisto, the mythical ancestor of the Germanic peoples. He corresponds to Manu in the Vedic cosmogony. Mannus has three sons, from whom descend the Ingvaeones, the Herminones, and the Istvaeones. We can infer from these names that his sons were named Ing(vi) (which corresponds to the god Freyr), Hermin/Irmin, and Istvi. This family tree is parallel to that of the ancient Scandinavians: Búri, who sprang out of the ice, became the father of Odin, Vili, and Vé.

MARDÖLL: One of the names of the goddess Freyja. The name implies a possible connection between the goddess and the sea (*mar*) and might mean "She Who Illuminates the Sea."

✦ *FREYJA*

MARGYGR ("Giantess of the Sea"): Monster of the waters off Greenland that the Old Norwegian text *The King's Mirror* (ca. 1270) describes as follows:

> This appears to have the form of a woman from the waist upward, for it has large nipples on its breast like a woman, long hands and heavy hair, and its neck and head are formed in every respect like those of a human being. The monster is said to have large hands and its fingers are not parted but bound together by a web like that which joins the toes of water fowls. Below the waist line it has the shape of a fish with scales and tail and fins. It is said to have this in common with the one mentioned before, that it rarely appears except before violent storms. Its behavior is often somewhat like this: it will plunge into the waves and will always reappear with fish in its hands; if it then turns toward the ship, playing with the fishes or throwing them at the ship, the men have fears that they will suffer great loss of life. The monster is described as having a large and terrifying face, a sloping forehead and wide brows, a large mouth and wrinkled cheeks. But if it eats the fishes or throws them into the sea away from the ship, the crews have good hopes that their lives will be spared, even though they should meet severe storms. (trans. Larson)

📖 Larson, trans., *The King's Mirror*, 136–37.

MAROOL ("Sea-wolf"): A monstrous fish of the Shetland waters. It appears during storms and can be heard howling with joy when a vessel capsizes.

📖 Briggs, *Dictionary of Fairies*, 281; Jean Renaud, "Le peuple surnaturel des Shetland," *Artus* 21–22 (1986): 28–32.

MARS: In the *interpretatio romana* of the Germanic deities, Mars designates *Tiwaz (the deity that became Old Norse Týr, Old High German Ziu, Old English Tiw). The name Mars can be found in the French weekday name *mardi* (from *martis dies,* "Day of Mars"), which in English is Tuesday, "Tiw's Day." However, several Germano-Roman votive inscriptions have been discovered that call the association between Mars and *Tiwaz somewhat into question. While the connection is valid, for example, in the case of Mars Thingsus, it is dubious in that of Mars Halamardus.

MARS HALAMARDUS: Name that appears on a Germano-Roman votive inscription dating from the first century CE, found near Roermond, Holland. The etymology does not permit it to be associated with any of the known gods of the Germanic pantheon.

MARS THINGSUS: Name that appears on a Germano-Roman votive inscription, dating from the third century CE, found along Hadrian's Wall in northern England. Some believe it refers to the god *Tiwaz (the deity that became Old Norse Týr, Old High German Ziu, Old English Tiw); others have argued that it would correspond to the Germanic thunder god (Donar, Thor).

   📖 Shaw, *Pagan Goddesses in the Early Germanic World,* 38–39.

MÄUSETURM: ✦ MOUSE TOWER

MENGLÖÐ ("She Who Loves Necklaces," or "Adorned by a Necklace"): A hypostasis of the goddess Freyja or perhaps another name for the goddess herself. Menglöð lives in the hall called Hýr, which is located on the "Healing Mountain" (Lyfjaberg) and surrounded by flames. The giant Fjölsvinn defends the entrance to her dwelling; sometimes the guardians are two dogs. Menglöð has nine maidens in her service: Hlíf ("Protection") and Hlífþrasa ("Eager to Protect"), Þjóðvarta ("Guardian of the People"), Björt ("The Bright One"), Bleik ("The Pale One"), Blíð ("The Blithe One"), Fríð ("The Fair One"), Eir ("Peace/Mercy"), and Aurboða ("Gravel"). The young Svipdagr seeks to marry Menglöð and wins the riddle contest that Fjölsvinn (Fjölsviðr in another tradition) imposes on him. Svipdagr may be equivalent to the mysterious Óðr, whom Freyja has long awaited and who was promised to her by fate.

MENJA: Giantess and slave of Fróði, the mythical Danish king. He is the owner of the marvelous mill called Grotti that has the power to grind whatever the miller says. Menja and Fenja are responsible for working the mill.

MERCURY: This is the designation the Romans gave to the supreme god of the German and Norse pantheon: Wodan/Odin. Numerous Germano-Roman votive inscriptions dating from the first centuries of the Common Era are dedicated to Mercury, but only a portion of them concern Odin (examples being Mercurius Chann[i]us and Mercurius Cimbrianus); the remainder refer to underlying Celtic deities (such as Mercurius Dumidus [Mercury of Puy-de-Dôme], Mercury Arvernus, and so on). In Norse skaldic poetry Odin is hailed as the "God of Cargoes" (Farmatýr), thus of merchants, and votive inscriptions confirm the antiquity of this aspect of the god's character as they yield the names of Mercurius Negotiator, Mercurius Mercator, and Mercurius Nundinator.

MERMAID/MERMAN: ✦ NYKR, WASSERMANN

📖 Petzold, *Kleines Lexikon der Dämonen und Elementargeister,* 173–75 *(Wassergeister).*

Fig. 55. Merman musician

MERMEUT: A demon of the atmosphere. We know of his existence due to a eleventh-century charm that reads: "I bless you, air, in the name of the Lord / I implore you, devil and your angels / I implore you to not kindle / The tempest or anything else. / And you have nothing to say / Because no one contradicts you. / God and the Son of God forbid you, / He who is the source of all creatures. / Saint Mary forbids you. / I implore you, Mermeut, you and your companions / Who rule over the tempest, / I implore you in the name of he who was at the origin / Heaven and Earth. / I implore you, Mermeut, by this right hand / That shaped Adam, the first man, in His image. / I implore you, Mermeut, by Jesus Christ / Son of the one God, / I conjure you, demon and Satan, / I conjure you to have no power / to do harm in this place or this village, / to bring the tempest there, / To cause violent rain," and so on.

 📖 Lecouteux, *Dictionary of Ancient Magic Words and Spells,* 218–19 (Mermeut).

MERMINNE: One of the Germanic names for fairies in the Middle Ages and a synonym for *merwîp.* It also sometimes applies to water nymphs.

MERSEBURG CHARMS: These are two charms dating from the tenth century; they were inscribed on the flyleaf of a Latin sacramentary that was probably written down at the abbey of Fulda. The texts were discovered in the cathedral library of Merseburg (Saxony-Anhalt, Germany). They are important for the names they contain as well as for their content. Here is a translation of the first charm: "Once upon a time, *Idisi* (divine women) sat here and there. Some fastened bonds, some hemmed in armies, some released fetters. Escape the bonds! Flee the enemy!" (✦ DISES, HERFJÖTURR). The second charm recounts the healing by Wodan (Odin) of Balder's horse: "Phol and Wodan went into the woods. Balder's horse dislocated his ankle. First Sinthgunt incanted, then her sister Sunna; then Frija incanted followed by her sister Volla; then Wodan spoke the incantations, as he well knew how. . . ." The names of Sinthgunt, Sunna, and Phol have given rise to all kinds of speculation, but a good deal of mystery still surrounds them.

 ✦ *PHOL, SINTHGUNT, SUNNA, VOLLA, WODAN*

 📖 Beck, *Die Merseburger Zaubersprüche;* Jean-Paul Allard, "Du second Charme de Mersebourg au Viatique de Weingarten," *Études Indo-Européennes* 14 (1985): 33–53, with an additional note by Jean Haudry at 54–59.

MERWUNDER ("Sea-wonder"): In Middle High German this word designates not only a sea monster but also hybrid creatures like centaurs, minotaurs, sirens, mermaids, and the man-fish, or supernatural entities like fairies and lamia. It also designates the hydra, the whale, and the dragon. Several rare testimonies from the early Middle Ages indicate that *merwunder* can also be translated as "dwarf," "nymph," and *"penates."*

> 📖 Lecouteux, "Le *merwunder:* contribution à l'étude d'un concept ambigu," *Études Germaniques* 32 (1977): 1–11; Lecouteaux, *Études Germaniques* 45 (1990): 1–9.

MIÐGARÐR ("Middle Enclosure"): This term designates the world inhabited by human beings. In the more or less concentric depiction of the various worlds—those of the gods, giants, and men—Miðgarðr is the central realm. Miðgarðr is separated from the lands of the giants by rivers and forests. It is said to have been created from the eyebrows of the primordial giant Ymir, but this should only apply to its frontier marker, most likely the forest, which is an image that corresponds fairly well to eyebrows. The name "Middle Enclosure" reveals that man organized the universe starting from himself, from his home, which, by extrapolation, became the world of human beings. The name is ancient; in Gothic, *midjungards* translates the Greek word *oikoméne,* meaning "inhabited world" (similar to Latin *orbis terrae*), and the Old English *middangeard* translates as "cosmos." In the Middle English period we find a corresponding term, *middylle erthe,* "middle earth."

MIÐGARÐSORM ("Midgard Serpent"): A large serpent living in the ocean that surrounds the world and thus ensures its horizontal cohesion. The tenth-century skaldic poet Úlfr Uggason calls it the "stiff rope of the Earth." It corresponds to the serpent Ananta of Vedic tradition, which carries the world and guarantees its stability. It is also called Jörmungandr, meaning "Gigantic Magic Ring," and kennings refer to it as the "twisted shining ring of the Earth" and the "coal-fish that bounds all lands." The Midgard Serpent frequently plays a role in the myths. Thor tries to catch it in vain. Loki is its father and the giantess Angrboða its mother. When Ragnarök occurs this serpent will stir up the sea over the land causing a huge flood. The Midgard Serpent is depicted in various forms, from Bronze Age petroglyphs to

Fig. 56. The god Thor goes fishing for the Midgard Serpent.
Illustration by Ólafur Brynjúlfsson, *Snorra Edda*, 1760.

the carved stones of the Viking era. In England this sea serpent can be seen depicted on the Gosforth Cross.

MILAURO (masc.): Name of a small worm that only lucky children can find; when someone possesses one, it is put in a purse and the money there will multiply over night. However, this only lasts as long as the owner of the purse behaves well. It corresponds to the *brekkusnígall,* a slug and demon found in Icelandic beliefs.

📖 Maurer, *Isländische Volkssagen der Gegenwart vorwiegend nach mündlicher Überlieferung,* 174; Zingerle, *Sagen aus Tirol,* 326.

MÍMAMEIÐR ("Mímir's Tree" or "Mímir's Beam"): One of the names for the cosmic tree, Yggdrasill.

MIMIR/MIME: The smith who rescues Sigurðr (Siegfried) according the *Vilkina saga* (Saga of the Vilces; a section of the *Þiðreks saga*). He is the brother of Reginn who, changed into a dragon, took their father's treasure. Mimir sends Sigurðr to make charcoal in the forest. The hero meets the dragon in the forest and kills it, and then returns to the forge to take his vengeance on Mimir. In fact, the nuthatches had told him that the smith hopes that the monster would get rid of him. Sigurðr received the sword Gramr and a suit of armor from Mimir, who sought to thereby appease him.

In other accounts of Sigurðr's childhood Mimir is named Reginn. In medieval German epics Mimir is called Mime.

    📖 Haymes, trans. *The Saga of Thidrek of Bern;* Lecouteux, trans., *La Saga de Théodoric de Vérone,* 171ff, 201; Lecouteux, "Siegfried's Jugend: Überlungungen zum mythischen Hintergrund," *Euphorion* 89 (1995): 221–27.

MIST: A valkyrie. Her name may mean "Cloud, Mist."

✦ *VALKYRIE*

MISTLETOE: Heeding the deceitful advice given him by Loki, Höðr slew his brother Baldr with a branch of mistletoe.

    📖 Arild Hvidtfeldt, "Mistilteinn og Balders Død," *Aarbøger for nordisk oldkyndighed og historie* (1941): 169–75.

MITHOTHYN: In the work of Saxo Grammaticus this is the name of a magician who seized power among the gods at one point when Othinus (Odin) was absent. When the god returned, Mithothyn fled to Fyn, where the inhabitants killed him. His corpse caused a pestilence that only came to an end when a stake was planted in the dead man's chest, a measure that can be found in stories of revenants (✦ DRAUGR, STAKE) and, more recently, in those of vampires.

MJÖÐVITNIR ("Mead-thief" or "Mead-wolf"): The name of a dwarf. The implications of the name, however, seem more fitting for Odin (✦ KVASIR), unless the term *mead* does not metonymically refer to the blood of Kvasir used by the dwarves Fjalarr and Galarr to brew the wondrous beverage.

MJÖLLNIR ("Crusher"): Hammer of the god Thor.

Mjöllnir was forged by the dwarves Sindri and Brokkr, but Loki, having shapeshifted into a fly, pestered Sindri while he was working on it, and as a result the handle he forged for the hammer was too short. Mjöllnir is the god's weapon: when he throws it, it causes thunder and lightning, and the hammer returns to Thor's hand of its own accord. To handle Mjöllnir, Thor must put on iron gloves. The list of giants slain by Mjöllnir is a long one. This hammer is also a religious instrument that can be used to bless or consecrate, and clear depictions of it can be seen on Bronze Age rock carvings. Mjöllnir is in many ways reminiscent of Indra's *vajra* ("lightning bolt") and the *vazra* of the Iranian Mithra.

The giant Þrymr stole Mjöllnir one day and said he would not return it unless he would be given Freyja to have as his wife. Thor disguised himself as Freyja, killed Þrymr, and recovered his favorite weapon. Another myth tells of how Thor can eat his goats and then resurrect them afterward by blessing their bones, arranged in proper order on their hides, with his hammer. When Thor is killed during Ragnarök, his sons Móði and Magni will inherit Mjöllnir.

It should be noted that in ancient Germanic law a ritual for taking possession of a piece of land involved the throwing of a hammer, and laying a hammer in the lap of a young woman consecrated her marriage. The great medieval German poet Heinrich von Meissen (known as Frauenlob; died 1318) seems to echo this custom in his poem known as *Marienleich* (The Song of Mary; I, 11).

📖 John Lindow, "Thor's 'hamarr,'" *Journal of English and Germanic Philology* 93:4 (1994): 485–503.

Fig. 57. Mjöllnir, Thor's hammer. Amulet found in Skåne, Sweden, and dated to around the year 1000.

MOÐGUÐR ("Ferocious Battle"): A maiden assigned to guard Gjallarbrú, the bridge that spans the Gjöll, one of the rivers of Hel.

✦ *GJALLARBRÚ*

MÓÐI ("Courage"): The name of one of Thor's sons. He is, in fact, the incarnation of one of this god's qualities.

MODRANIHT ("Night of the Mothers"): The Anglo-Saxon monk and scholar the Venerable Bede (673–735) mentions a pagan festival called *modraniht* (or *modraneht*) that was celebrated around the time of Christmas Eve. The sacrifices made were certainly directed at fertility goddesses equivalent to the Germano-Roman *Matronae*. This festival is akin to the Nordic *dísablót* ("Sacrifice to the Dises") and also to the feast of the fairies, which is referred to in various places throughout medieval literature. It was also believed that dead women of influence traveled about the land on that night.

✦ *DISES, MOTHER GODDESSES*

📖 Shaw, *Pagan Goddesses in the Early Germanic World;* Lecouteux, "Romanisch-germanische Kulturberührungen am Beispiel des Mahls der Feen," *Mediaevistik,* vol. 1 (1988): 87–99.

MÖGÞRASIR: In an obscure passage of the *Vafþrúðnismál* (Lay of Vafþrúðnir), this figure seems to be a giant that would be the father of the goddesses of destiny (*hamingjur*).

MÖKKURKÁLFI: To aid Hrungnir in his battle against Thor, the giants craft a clay giant to which they gave a mare's heart. Thor's servant Þjálfi has no difficulty dispatching it. Georges Dumézil has shown that this episode is a myth of warrior initiation in which the hero is actually Þjálfi. It has its Indo-Eurpoean counterpart in Vritahan's duel against Trisiras and Vritra. Similarities are also apparent between Mökkurkálfi and the Jewish legend of the Golem, although a genetic link between these two myths has yet to be demonstrated.

📖 Dumézil, *Gods of the Ancient Northmen,* 68–71.

MÖRNIR: The *Völsa þáttr* (Tale of the Völsi), which is preserved in the Icelandic *Flayteyjarbók* (fourteenth century), describes a pagan ritual in which the sex organ of a horse is offered to Mörnir after being passed from hand to hand by the other members of his household. Listed are the head of the household and his wife, son, and daughter, as well as his slave and his maidservant, each of whom speaks a verse that ends with "May Mörnir accept this offering." Several hypotheses have been advanced with regard to Mörnir's identity, and it is thought this figure may be a hypostasis of the god Freyr (representing the Dumézilian third function of fertility and fecundity). Folke Ström has suggested it may refer to the giantess Skaði, the erstwhile wife of Njörðr. More recently, Gro Steinsland has shown that *mörn*, the singular form of *mörnir*, means "giantess" (*jotunkvinne*) and that the worship reflects a sacred marriage (*hieros gamos*) between Freyr, represented by the *völsi* (the horse's penis), and the feminine powers of the world of the giants.

📖 Steinsland, *Norrøn Religion*, 350–52.

MOTHER GODDESSES: The greatest evidence of their worship is supplied by the votive inscriptions found in the parts of Germania occupied by the Romans, with a heavy concentration in the Rhineland provinces, as well as others found in England near Hadrian's Wall. All of these inscriptions date from the period between the first and fifth centuries of the Common Era. Along the lower course of the Rhine the epigraphy reads *Matronae*, whereas in Britain the inscriptions refer to *Matres*. It is difficult to say what differences, if any, may underlie the two names. The sculptures almost always depict three women sitting or standing, one of whom is holding a basket of fruit. Their names vary depending on location; the most frequently occurring are the Aufaniae, the Suleviae, the Vacallinehae, the Austriahenae, and Nehalennia. They were presumably the protectors of the clan, the people, and places as is indicated by inscriptions such as "To the Suevian Mothers" or "To My Paternal Frisian Mothers." Connections have also been established between the Albiaheniae with the town of Elvenich, the Mahlinehae with Malines, and the Nersihenae with the river Niers. The etymological interpretations of the 108 names attested in these votive inscriptions show that the mother goddesses had the role of guardians and providers of goods and that some of them are clearly spring or river goddesses. Their worship appears to have survived into the Middle Ages in the form of the *dísir*.

📖 Boyer, *La Grande Déesse du Nord;* Gutenbrunner, *Die germanischen Götternamen der antiken Inschriften;* Shaw, *Pagan Goddesses in the Early Germanic World;* Edgar C. Polomé, "Some Aspects of the Cult of the Mother Goddess in Western Europe," in *Vistas and Vectors: Essays Honoring the Memory of Helmut Rehder,* ed. Lee B. Jennings and George Schulz-Behrend (Austin, Tx.: Dept. of Germanic Languages, 1979), 193–208.

✦ *DISES, MODRANIHT*

MOUSE TOWER (Mäuseturm): In 914, 968, or 974 (depending on the source), a huge famine raged in Germany. Hatto I, the archbishop of Mainz from 891–913, had the starving poor imprisoned in a barn, which was then set on fire. As the wretched victims wailed, he said, "Listen to them, they sound like mice!" But God punished him. By both day and night mice ate everything he owned. He had a tower built in the middle of the Rhine near Bingen, but this did not stop the mice, which devoured him alive.

Fig. 58. The Mouse Tower

This folk legend is known to have first appeared in a chronicle dating from 1599, but a similar story can be found earlier in the work of Thietmar of Merseburg (975–1018). In it, a knight who had forcibly seized the property of Saint Clement was attacked by mice in large numbers. He had himself sealed within a chest to wait for this plague to run its course, but when the chest was opened it was seen that he had been eaten alive by other mice.

📖 Liebrecht, *Zur Volkskunde: Alte und neue Aufsätze*, 1–16 (der Mäusethurm); Rolf-Dieter Kluge, "Die Sage von Bischof Hattos Mäusetod im alten Russland," *Mainzer Almanach* (1968): 142–54.

MUNDILFARI: Father of Máni and Sól (the moon and the sun).

MUNINN ("Memory"): One of Odin's two ravens. Along with Huginn ("Thought"), he travels out over the world and reports back to the god about what he has seen and heard. In light of Odin's shamanistic traits, Muninn could be seen as one of his Doubles. In chapter 7 of the *Ynglinga saga,* Snorri Sturluson informs us:

> Odin could shift his appearance. When he did so his body would lie there as if he were asleep or dead, but he himself, in an instant, in the shape of a bird . . . went to distant countries on his or other men's errands. (trans. Hollander)

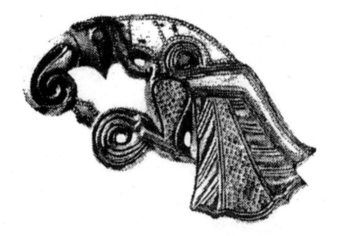

Fig. 59. Muninn, one of Odin's ravens. Bronze harness clasp found in Vadstena on the island of Gotland, Sweden.

MUSPELL (Old High German *muspilli*): This word designates the destruction of the world by fire. In northern Scandinavia a giant bears this name. He is the owner of Naglfar, the ship made from the fingernails of the dead, upon which his sons (or vassals) will embark to attack Valhalla during Ragnarök.

MUSPELLSHEIMR ("World of Muspell"): Name of a fiery land located in the south that is the polar opposite of Niflheimr, the land of shadows and ice. Muspell's fire makes the ice of Niflheimr melt, bringing about the appearance of Ymir, the primordial giant.

MYRKVIÐR ("Dark Forest"): A mythical forest located at the border of the world of the gods, separating it from the world of the giants. Originally this was very likely the forest that formed the frontier between the Goths and the Huns. In the tenth century Thietmar of Merseburg mentions the equivalent name *Miriquidui* in reference to a forest that may be that of the Erzgebirge (Ore Mountains) on the border area between Saxony and Bohemia. J. R. R. Tolkien used this name in the form of Mirkwood in his novel *The Hobbit* (1937).

MYTHICAL RIVERS: The poem *Grímnismál* (The Lay of Grímnir) in the *Poetic Edda* gives us a list of the rivers that gird the homes of the gods. Here are their names: Síð ("Late"), Víð ("Wide"), Sœkin ("Gushing"), Eikin ("Savage"), Svöl ("Chilly"), Gunnþrá ("Arrogant"), Fjörm ("Fast One"), Fimbulþul ("Great Murmurer"), Rín ("Rhine"), Rennandi ("The Running One"), Gipul ("Chatterer"), Gömul ("Old"), Geirvimul ("Spear-teeming"), Þýn ("The Raging One"), Vín ("Woman-friend"?), Þöll ("Young Fir Tree"), Höll ("Sloping"), Gráð ("Greedy"), Gunnþorinn ("Battle-bold"), Vína (= "Dvina"?), Vegsvinn ("Swift Way"), Nyt ("Benefit"), Nöt ("The Burning One"), Nönn ("The Quickly Flowing One"), Hrönn ("Wave"), Slíðr ("Perilous"), Hríð ("Gust"), Sylgr ("Gulf"), Ylgr ("She-Wolf"), Ván ("Hope"), Vönd ("Difficult"), Strönd ("Shore"), Gjöll ("Tumult"), and Leiptr ("Lightning "). Some of these names are not attested in any other texts, but we can recognize those of the rivers that surround Hel, the world of the dead: Geirvimull, Slíðr, and Gjöll.

📖 Christopher Hale, "The River Names in Grímnismál 27–29," in *Edda: A Collection of Essays*, ed. Robert J. Glendinning and Haraldur Bessason (Winnipeg: University of Manitoba Press, 1983), 165–86.

NACHZEHRER: A particular kind of Germanic revenant. The name means "He Who Continues to Devour (after his death)" or "He Who Lures While Devouring." The first account of a *Nachzehrer* comes from Heinrich Kramer and Jacob Sprenger, who were responsible for the suppression of witchcraft in the Rhineland during the last quarter of the fifteenth century.

> An example was brought to our notice as Inquisitors. A town was once rendered almost destitute by the death of its citizens; and there was a rumor that a certain buried woman was gradually eating the shroud in which she had been buried, and that the plague could not cease until she had eaten the whole shroud and absorbed it into her stomach. A council was held, and the Podesta with the Governor of the city dug up the grave, and found half the shroud absorbed through the mouth and throat into the stomach and consumed. In horror at this sight, the Podesta drew his sword and cut off her head and threw it out of the grave, and at once the plague ceased. (*Malleus Maleficarum,* I, 15)

Martin Luther himself faced the problem posed by the belief in these wicked dead. A pastor named Georg Rörer wrote to him from Wittenberg that a woman living in a village had died and, after being buried, began eating herself in her grave; this caused all the inhabitants of this village to suddenly die (*Table Talk,* no. 6823). The *Nachzehrer* corresponds to the eighteenth-century French *Mâcheur* (from Latin *manducator*), the "Chewer."

✦ *DRAUGR*

📖 Lecouteux, *The Secret History of Vampires,* 70–75, 89, 91, 124, 131; Gerda Grober-Glück, "Der Verstorbene als Nachzehrer," in *Atlas der deutschen Volkskunde* (Erläuterungen zu den Karten 43–48), 427–56; Günter Wiegelmann, "Der 'lebende Leichnam' im Volksbrauch," *Zeitschrift für Volkskunde* 62 (1966): 161–83.

NAGLFAR ("Nail-ship"): This is the ship of the dead. It is made from the fingernails and toenails of the dead. This is why it is always necessary to trim the nails of the deceased before burying them, for if this is not done the nails will provide building material for the construction of Naglfar. The completion of the ship-building will be the sign that the end of the world has begun. The sons of Muspell will then travel on Naglfar to join the assault on Ásgarðr.

📖 Hallvard Lie, "Naglfar og Naglfari," *Maal og Minne* (1954): 152–61.

NÁGRINDR ("Corpse-fence"): Name of the metal gate that seals Hel, the underworld, and is also called Helgrindr ("Hel's Fence") and Valgrindr ("Fence of the Fallen"; the first element of the latter name is from *valr,* "the slain").

NAL: The name of Loki's mother according to Snorri Sturluson, whereas the *Poetic Edda* mentions only Laufey. The etymology of the name is uncertain: it could be related to Old Norse *nál,* which means "needle," or it might possibly refer to death (*nár* means "corpse").

NANNA: Wife of Baldr and daughter of Nepr, who is sometimes presented as Odin's son. She is the mother of Forseti. She perishes from grief at Baldr's death and is cremated with her husband. According to Snorri Sturluson, she is an Ásynja. Saxo Grammaticus calls Nanna the daughter of Gevarus, the king of Norway. She marries Hötherus (Höðr) but is loved by Balderus (Baldr), whom her husband kills.

NÁR ("Corpse"): The name of a dwarf; its meaning shows how closely these beings are connected to the dead.

NARFI: The son of Loki. In skaldic poetry Hel is referred to as "sister of the Wolf (Fenrir) and Narfi." Narfi therefore appears to have a certain relationship with the realm of the dead, but we do not know what it is.

NÁSTRÖND ("Corpse-shore"): A place far from the sun where stands a hall whose door opens to the north. This hall is "woven with the spines of serpents," with "poison drops falling through its roof," says the *Völuspá* (The Prophecy of the Seeress) in the *Poetic Edda*. It is most likely one of the dwellings of Hel, the underworld, and its description was perhaps influenced by the Christian literature of revelations.

NECKLACE OF EARTH (Old Norse *jarðarmen*): When two people swear an oath of blood brotherhood (*fóstbrœðralag*) the ceremony, which is magical in nature, is accompanied by walking under a "necklace" (in fact, a strip) made of turf. According to the *Fóstbrœðra saga* (Saga of the Sworn Brothers), "It is necessary to cut three strips of sod with grass upon them and with both ends remaining set in the ground, which are then raised up in the form of arches so it is possible to pass beneath them." Furthermore, the blood brothers must cut themselves so their blood can flow into and mix with the dirt. While doing this they swear their oath. It is possible that a magical relationship was thus established through an archaic form of worship of the Earth Mother and that this act was the equivalent of a journey into the maternal womb.

NEHALENNIA: A goddess whose name is known from third-century votive inscriptions. Temples to her existed at Domburg on the island of Walcheren and at Colijnsplaat (both in Zeeland, Netherlands). She is often depicted with a basket of fruit and is sometimes leaning on the prow or oar of a ship. In some cases she is accompanied by a dog. Nehalennia may correspond to the "Suebian Isis" mentioned by Tacitus and whose cultic image is in the form a ship. The dog's presence in some images of Nehalennia could represent a connection with the otherworld, although the basket of fruit suggests that she is a guardian of fertility. We do know, however, that the dead can also play an important role in the latter domain.

  📖 Gutenbrunner, *Die germanischen Götternamen der antiken Inschriften*, 75–78.

NERTHUS: What we know about this goddess comes essentially from Tacitus, who reports of the Germanic peoples:

> Collectively they worship Nerthus, or Mother Earth, and believe that she takes part in human affairs and rides among the peoples. On an island in the Ocean is a holy grove, and in it a consecrated wagon covered with hangings; to one priest alone is it permitted so much as to touch it. He perceives when the goddess is present in her innermost

recess, and with great reverence escorts her as she is drawn along by heifers. Then there are days of rejoicing, and holidays are held whenever she deigns to go and be entertained. They do not begin wars, they do not take up arms; everything iron is shut away; peace and tranquility are only then known and only then loved, until again the priest restores to her temple the goddess, sated with the company of mortals. Then the wagon and hangings and, if you will, the goddess herself are washed clean in a hidden lake. Slaves perform this service, and the lake at once engulfs them. (*Germania,* chap. 40, trans. Rives)

The name of this mother goddess corresponds linguistically to that of the male Norse god Njörðr, and both names can be assumed to derive from an earlier proto-Germanic form, *Nerthuz. The shift that seems to have occurred here from a goddess to a god has been explained as either a division of a Freyr-Freyja kind, or as a result of the deity's original hermaphroditic nature. In Zealand, Denmark, where the worship of Nerthus would have taken place, there is a place named Niartharum (present-day Nærum), in which the name of Nerthus/Njörðr can be recognized. The son of Nerthus is Tuisto, which means "double, twofold," in other words, a hermaphrodite like the giant Ymir. It should be recalled that the ancient Germanic deities were often androgynous, a feature for which we can find substantial traces. The most striking examples of this tendency are the numerous pairs of corresponding male and female deities such as the one described here (Nerthus-Njörðr), or the various female deities with male names.

NEUNTÖTER ("Nonicide"): Dead who are predestined to come back because, at birth, they have teeth or a double row of teeth. They die young and cause the death of nine of their close relatives (hence the name, which literally means "Nine-killer"). It was believed that the *Neuntöter* attracted those to itself whom it had liked most, or else that some unfortunate circumstance had occurred at his or her death: a cat had been allowed to walk over the corpse; the eyes of the deceased had refused to close; the scarf of a woman laying out the body had brushed the lips of the corpse; and so forth. The *Neuntöter* was also said to spread plague. The preferred method for getting rid of a *Neuntöter* was decapitation.

📖 Lecouteux, *The Secret History of Vampires,* 64–66, 89.

NEUTRAL ANGELS: The clerics of the Middle Ages often explained the origins of demons and spirits, under whatever name (giants, dwarves, elves, and so on), by the legend of the neutral angels. When Lucifer rebelled against God, some timorous or hesitant angels did not choose to stand with either side. God therefore cast them down to Earth, while Lucifer was consigned to live in hell. Some of these angels fell into the forests, some into the water, and others remained in the air; it is from them that elves, fairies, and similar beings originate. In Ireland it is believed that fairies were members of this group of angels condemned to remain on Earth.

📖 Marcel Dando, "The Neutral Angels," *Archiv für das Studium der neueren Sprachen und Literaturen* 217 (1980): 259–76; Bruno Nardi, "Gli angeli che non furon ribelli né fur fedeli a Dio," in Nardi, *Dal 'Convivio' alla 'Commedia': Sei Saggi Danteschi* (Rome: Instituto Storico Italiano per il Medio Evo, 1960), 331–50.

NIBELUNGENLIED (**Lay of the Nibelungs**): Written at the start of the thirteenth century but drawing on older sources, the *Nibelungenlied* consists of two parts: the legend of Siegfried and the story of Kriemhild's vengeance. An outline of the *Nibelungenlied* goes as follows: Siegfried is the son of King Sigemund and Sigelinde, who live in Xanten. He goes to the Burgundian court in Worms because he wishes to wed King Gunther's sister Kriemhild. When Siegfried introduces himself, the anonymous author of the saga gives a brief overview of his mythic exploits: he slew a dragon and bathed in its blood, which made him invulnerable except between his shoulders, where the leaf of a linden tree had fallen; he slew the kings Schilbung and Nibelung and took their treasure after defeating their vassal, the dwarf Alberich (from whom he took the *Tarnkappe,* the "cloak of invisibility") and their allies, twelve strong giants. Siegfried helps Gunther win Brünhild's hand in return for his promise to let him wed Kriemhild. Using the cloak of invisibility, he procures Gunther's victory over Brünhild in the contests that the lady imposes on all her suitors. (If the suitor is defeated, he must surrender his life!) After returning to Worms, Gunther weds Brünhild and Siegfried weds Kriemhild. When Gunther is unable to subdue his bride in their nuptial bed, he turns to his brother-in-law, who, invisible and unrecognizable, takes his place in bed, subdues Brünhild, and takes her belt and ring, which he then gives to his own wife. In the course of a quar-

Fig. 60. Hagen kills Siegfried.
Illustration from a German
textbook, Paris, 1926.

rel between the two women over status, Kriemhild reveals to Brünhild
what happened on her wedding night and shows her the stolen objects.
This triggers an act of vengeance from Brünhild. The deed is carried
out by Hagen, who stabs Siegfried with his spear near a spring in the
Odenwald. Hagen seizes Siegfried's treasure and casts it into the Rhine
to prevent Kriemhild from having the necessary means to get revenge.

King Etzel (Attila) requests and obtains the hand of the Burgundian
king's widowed sister in marriage. Kriemhild moves to Etzelburg, where
she lives at his side and has two sons. She invites her brothers to visit, and
they accept despite the warnings of Hagen, who has guessed Kriemhild's
true motive. Traveling to Etzelburg, they meet sirens on the banks of
the Danube, and Hagen sees his intuition confirmed: the Burgundians
will die during this journey. At Etzelburg they are all slaughtered, except
for Gunther and Hagen, who are taken prisoner. Kriemhild has her
brother decapitated because Hagen refuses to tell her where he sank

the treasure for as long as Gunther lives. Taking Gunther's head by the hair, Kriemhild presents it to Hagen, who says, "No one shall know now where the treasure is, outside of God and me!" Kriemhild then draws Siegfried's sword, Balmung, from its scabbard and lops off Hagen's head, but she perishes immediately afterward when she is cut down by Hildebrand, the armorer of Dietrich von Bern.

✦ *SIEGFRIED*

📖 Colleville and Tonnelat, trans., *La Chanson des Nibelungen;* Hatto, trans., *The Nibelungenlied;* Lecouteux, *La Légende de Siegfried d'après le Seyfrid à la peau de corne et la Thidrekssaga;* Lecouteux, "Stratigraphische Untersuchungen zur Siegfriedsage," in *Sagen- und Märchenmotive im Nibelungenlied,* ed. Gerald Bönnen and Volker Gallé (Worms: Stadtarchiv Worms, 2002), 45–69; Lecouteux, "Der Nibelungenhort: Überlegungen zum mythischen Hintergrund," *Euphorion* 87 (1993): 172–86; Lecouteux, "Seyfrid, Kuperan et le dragon," *Études Germaniques* 49 (1994): 257–66.

NIÐAFJÖLL ("Mountain of Darkness"): The mountain in the underworld that is the native home of the dragon Niðhöggr. According to Snorri Sturluson, this is the location of Sindri, a hall made of pure gold where the good and virtuous live after Ragnarök.

NIÐAVELLIR ("Dark Plains"): A site located in the north, where stands the hall of the dwarves of Sindri's race. Ordinarily dwarves live underground, in the stones and mountains.

NÍÐHÖGGR ("He Who Delivers Hateful Blows" or possibly "He Who Strikes from Darkness"): A dragon native to Niðafjöll who lives in the kingdom of the dead. On Náströnd he sucks on the corpses of the dead. He too will live on in the renewed world following Ragnarök. One tradition says that he dwells beneath the cosmic ash, Yggdrasill, and gnaws at its roots.

NIFLHEIMR ("World of Darkness"): A northern area that existed long before the creation of the world. This is the location of the spring Hvergelmir, which is the source of ten rivers. It is possible that Niflheimr is identical to Nifhel and would thus be one of the names of Hel.

NIFLHEL ("The Dark Hel"): This is one part of Hel; it is the ninth domain and the deepest of them all. This notion, most likely related to shamanic perceptions of the beyond, may also have been influenced by visionary literature: in the Christian descriptions of hell there is always an abyss, such as in *The Visions of the Knight Tondal.*

NIGHTMARE: ✦ MAHR

NISS: A place spirit similar to a dwarf that is often malicious and even sometimes malevolent. When it is friendly it is called a *Goaniss* (Sweden). One legend claims it is a fallen angel. In Norway it is the size of a five- or six-year-old child and has only four fingers on each hand (it has no thumbs). Its hands are also hairy.

Fig. 61. Niss, from a Norwegian Christmas card

In Sweden it is an old bearded man wearing a red cap and gray clothing. Offerings of food are given to it and placed in the farmyard beneath a stone that is assumed to be its dwelling or at the foot of a tree. It is sometimes confused for another household spirit, the *Puk* or *Puge.*

📖 Arrowsmith and Moorse, *A Field Guide to the Little People,* 165–69; Holbek and Piø, *Fabeldyr og sagnfolk,* 155–62; Keightley, *The World Guide to Gnomes, Fairies, Elves, and Other Little People,* 139–47; Hans F. Feilberg, "Der Kobold in nordischer Überlieferung," *Zeitschrift des Vereins für Volkskunde* 8 (1898): 1–20, 130–46, 264–77; Ottar Grønvik, "Nissen," *Maal og Minne* (1997): 129–48; Oddrun Grønvik, "Ordet *nisse* o.a. i dei nynorske ordsamlingane," *Maal og Minne* (1997): 149–56.

NISSPUCK: The name for the *Niss* in Schleswig-Holstein.

📖 Erika Lindig, *Hausgeister,* 78ff.

NIX(E): ✦ FOSSEGRIM, NYKR, WASSERMANN

NJÖRÐR: Vanir god, the father of Freyr and Freyja and a medieval reflex of the goddess Nerthus. He married the giantess Skaði, the eponymous goddess of the Scandinavian lands. Snorri Sturluson tells us: "Njörðr lives in Noatún ["Ship-enclosure"]. He rules over the motion of wind and moderates sea and fire. It is to him one must pray for voyages and fishing. He is so rich and wealthy that he can grant wealth of lands or possessions to those that pray to him for this" (*Gylfaginning,* trans. Faulkes). He was raised among the Vanir, who later traded him as a hostage to the Æsir in exchange for Hœnir.

The union of a maritime god with an Earth-based goddess resulted in a famous myth. Njörðr could not tolerate the mountains and their snow, while Skaði could not sleep by the sea because of the noise of the waves and the cries of the gulls. They then decided to divide their time between both residences, alternating nine days on the coast followed by nine days in the mountains, but this was not enough to prevent their separation.

Njörðr is regularly invoked in oaths along with Freyr and the "*allmáttki áss*" (the "almighty god," Odin). Sacrifices should be made to him at the same time as Odin and Freyr to ensure a peaceful and fruitful year. Njörðr has left substantial traces in Scandinavian place-names, for example that of Narvik, Norway, which can be assumed to derive from an earlier form, *Njarðarvík,* meaning "Njörðr's Bay."

📖 Dumézil, *From Myth to Fiction: The Saga of Hadingus,* 20–22, 225–27.

NOATÚN ("Ship-enclosure"): Njörðr's place of residence.

NORÐRI ("North"): One of the four dwarves that hold up the heavenly vault at the four cardinal points; this vault was created from the skull of the giant Ymir. One kenning calls the sky the "burden of Norðri's relatives," and this dwarf's name appears in *Óláfsdrápa* (strophe 26).

    📖 Lecouteux, "Trois hypothèses sur nos voisins invisibles," in *Hugur: mélanges d'histoire, de littérature et de mythologie offerts à Régis Boyer pour son 65e anniversaire,* ed. Lecouteux and Gouchet, 289–92.

    ✦ *AUSTRI, COSMOGONY, SUÐRI, VESTRI*

NORGEN, NÖRGL, NÖRGLEIN, NÖRGGELEN (neut., sg. and pl., "grumpy one[s]"): In Tyrolean belief, these are fallen angels that became place spirits. When they were driven out of heaven not all of them reached hell. During their fall, many of those who had gone along with the rebels, but who did not share their wicked nature, remained clinging to the trees and mountains. They still live in trees and in hollows, and they must remain on Earth until the day of Final Judgment. Many people claim that the *Nörglein* are sneaky because they made common cause with Lucifer and envied humanity's good fortune.

    📖 Zingerle, *Sagen, Märchen und Gebräuche aus Tirol,* no. 83.

NÖRGL (masc.), NÖRGIN (fem.): A merman and mermaid of the Tyrolean lakes.

    📖 Alpenburg, *Mythen und Sagen Tirols,* 54; Zingerle, *Sagen, Märchen und Gebräuche aus Tirol,* nos. 81–84, 98, 105, 127.

NORNS: The goddesses of fate who almost always appear as a group of three figures. About them, Snorri Sturluson writes: "A beautiful hall stands under the ash by the well [i.e., beneath Yggdrasill], and out of this hall come three maidens whose names are Urðr ["Past"], Verðandi ["Present"], and Skuld ["Future"]. They shape the lives of men. We call them Norns" (*Gylfaginning*).

These maidens are giantesses who sprinkle clear water and white clay on the tree every day. They are depicted as wicked and ugly; their verdict is irrevocable. It is said they come from the sea. Snorri goes on to remark: "There are also other Norns who visit everyone when they are born to shape their lives, and these are of divine origin, though others

Fig. 62. The three Norns at the foot of Yggdrasill.
Drawing by Arthur Rackham (1867–1939).

are of the race of elves, and a third group are of the race of dwarves"
(*Gylfaginning,* trans. Faulkes).

The Norns correspond to the Fates—the Greek Moirai and the
Roman Parcae—as well as to the fairies of Celtic and Roman legends.
In fact, several texts in Old French depict three fairies around a cradle
who endow a child with beneficial or harmful aspects, a theme also
found in the fairy tale *Sleeping Beauty.* Only the Norn Urðr appears
to be ancient and authentic (the Old Norse name is cognate to *wurt*
in Old High German and *wurd* in Old Saxon); Skuld and Verðandi
appear to be later additions to form a triad modeled on the Parcae.
Furthermore, the spring at the foot of Yggdrasill is named the "Well of
Urðr" (Urðarbrunnr).

📖 Bek-Pedersen, *The Norns in Old Norse Mythology.*

NÖRR ("Narrow"): Name of the father of Nótt ("Night").

NÓTT ("Night"): The personification of night. This is how the texts describe her:

> Nörfi or Narfi was the name of a giant who lived in Jötunheimr. He had a daughter called Night [Nótt]. She was black and dark in accordance with her ancestry. She was married to a person called Naglfari with whom she had a son, Auðr. Next she was married to someone called Annar. Their daughter was called Jörð [Earth]. Her last husband was Delling, he was of the race of the Æsir. Their son was Day [Dagr]. He was bright and beautiful in accordance with his father's nature. Then All-father [Alföðr = Odin] took Night and her son Day and gave them two horses and two chariots and set them up in the sky so that they have to ride around the earth every twenty-four hours. Night rides in front with a horse named Hrímfaxi, and every morning he bedews the earth with the drips from his bit. Day's horse is called Skinfaxi, and light is shed all over the sky and sea from his mane. (Snorri Sturluson, *Gylfaginning*, trans. based on Faulkes)

NYBLINC: In a fifteenth-century poem, *Das Lied vom hürnen Seyfrid* (The Lay of Horn-skinned Siegfried), Nyblinc is a dwarf introduced as the owner of a treasure stolen by Seyfrid. He therefore corresponds to Nibelung of the *Nibelungenlied*.

📖 Lecouteux, *La Légende de Siegfried d'après le Seyfrid à la peau de corne et la Thidrekssaga.*

NYKR (Old Norse, pl. *nykar;* Old English *nicor*): Mythical animal and water spirit that has an etymological connection to the German *Nix(e)*. It was originally capable of assuming a thousand different forms (in Old High German *nihhus* even means "crocodile"). In Scandinavia a *nykr* can sometimes take the shape of a dapple-gray horse, a color indicative of its supernatural origin. It is called a "horse of the lakes" (*vatnahestur*) in Icelandic folklore. It is also said to be able to take a human form. In Norway it is called *nøkk;* in Denmark, *nøkke;* and in Sweden, *näck*. In Norway we also find the names *fossekall* and *fossegrim* ("waterfall-spirit") and *kvernknurre* ("watermill-spirit"). In the Shetlands the nykr becomes the *njuggel;* it is depicted as a horse with a wheel for a tail. It lurks near lochs and waterways. It hides its tail and adopts a tame disposition when it invites the weary traveler to climb on its back. But once the unfortunate victim is in the saddle, it flies away like lightning, with its tail in the air and its mane streaming, to the nearest loch to drown him. The only way the poor rider can save himself is to speak its name, for it will then lose its power. The *njuggel* also stops the wheel of watermills if no one offers it grain or flour. To chase it away, people then light a fire.

✦ *FOSSEGRIM, MERMAID/MERMAN, UNDINE, WASSERMANN*

📖 Arrowsmith and Moorse, *A Field Guide to the Little People*, 101–4; Grambo, *Svart katt over veien*, 117 (*nøkken*); Keightley, *The World Guide to Gnomes, Fairies, Elves, and Other Little People*, 147–55, 258–63; Van den Berg, *De volkssage in de provincie Antwerpen in de 19de en 20ste eeuw*, 1425–36; Brita Egardt, "De svenska vattenhästsägnerna och deras ursprung," *Folkkultur* 4 (1944), 119–66; Hans F. Feilberg, "Der Kobold in nordischer Überlieferung," *Zeitschrift des Vereins für Volkskunde* 8 (1898): 1–20, 130–46, 264–77; Lecouteux, "Nicchus–Nix," *Euphorion* 78 (1984): 280–88.

OAK: Oak trees were particularly worshipped in Prussia, where they were believed to house the gods Perkunos (Thunder), Pikollos (Death), and Potrimps (War and Fertility). The Romove Oak in Nadruvia was six ells in thickness and remained green in winter and summer. Gilded curtains that were eight ells high surrounded it. They were only opened on feast days or when a Prussian noble visited to make a rich sacrifice. Another renowned sacred oak was that of Heiligenbeil; it shared the same characteristics as the Romove tree but housed Gorcho, the god of food and drink. Bishop Anselm cut it down. There was also the oak of Geismar, chopped down by Saint Boniface.

📖 Schütz, *Historia rerum Prussicarum,* 4; Simon Grunau, *Preussische Chronik,* vol. II, 5.

ÓDÁINSAKR ("Deathless Field"): A paradisiacal place mentioned in the later genre of legendary sagas known as *fornaldarsögur* (sagas of ancient times). It can be compared with various names for the Celtic afterlife that reflect the same notion of the survival of heroes in the otherworld.

ODIN (Old Norse *Óðinn;* Old English *Woden;* Old Saxon *Wodan;* Old High German *Wuotan*): The principal deity of the Norse and Germanic pantheon is a cruel and spiteful god, a cynical and misogynistic double-dealer whom the Romans interpreted as being similar to Mercury. He is one-eyed because he offered one of his eyes as a pledge to the giant Mímir in return for access to knowledge. He is old and graying, with a long beard, and has a hat pulled low over his brow. He wears a blue cloak. Etymologically his name means "Fury," as was noted by Adam of Bremen (*"Wodan id est furor"*) in his eleventh-century chronicle, *History of the Archbishops of Hamburg-Bremen.*

Odin is the son of the giant Burr (who is the son of Búri and Bestla, Bölþorn's daughter), and he has two brothers, Vili and Vé. Together

Fig. 63. Odin in all his majesty. Illustration by
Ólafur Brynjúlfsson, *Snorra Edda*, 1760.

Odin and his brothers slay the primordial giant Ymir, whose body
becomes the world. Odin's wife is Frigg, with whom he had a son, Baldr.
Thor was born as a result of Odin's relations with the giantess Jörð,
and another son, Váli, came from his liason with the giantess Rindr.
In Ásgarðr, Odin lives in Valhöll (Valhalla), seated on his throne,
Hliðskjálf, from which he can see the entire world. His attributes are
the spear Gungnir, which he casts over the combatants before a battle
begins in order to determine who will be victorious; his ring, Draupnir,
from which drip eight other similar rings every ninth night; and his
horse, Sleipnir, which has eight legs. According to Snorri Sturluson, he
also owns the wondrous boat Skíðblaðnir, although this object is usu-
ally attributed to Freyr.

Odin is a psychopomp like Mercury as well as a necromancer. He
is called "Lord of the Revenants" and "God of the Hanged Men." He
enchanted the severed head of the giant Mímir and regularly consults
with it. He is master of the "Hall of the Slain" (Valhöll), where he lives

Fig. 64. Odin devoured
by the wolf Fenrir.
Thorwald's Cross
(tenth to eleventh
century), Kirk Andreas,
Isle of Man.

exclusively on wine and gives all his food to the wolves Geri and Freki. The dead men he has selected through his intermediaries, the valkyries, are his fellow inhabitants of Valhalla and are called *einherjar*, the "elite, single warriors." He owns two ravens, Huginn and Muninn ("Thought" and "Memory"), who fly out each day and return to report all the news of the world to him, for he has given them the power of speech.

Odin is omniscient and knows runes, magic, and poetry. He likes to test his learning against that of the giants (✦ VAFÞRÚDNIR) and has the power of rendering his foes blind, deaf, and paralyzed (✦ HERFJÖTURR). He can stop arrows in flight, and he can make his supporters invulnerable.

He resuscitates the hanged and other dead men and is the leader of the Wild Hunt (*Wodans Jagd, Wuotes her*) in all Germanic countries.

Odin is adept in the magical technique known as *seiðr* (✦ SEIÐR), and he is the master of poetry because he drank the magical mead brewed from the blood of Kvasir. He is also a kind of god-shaman, and his entire character is evidence of the survival of a substantial substratum of shamanistic beliefs. He acquired his powers through a nine-night initiation during which he hung upside down from a wind-battered tree. As as result of this he is both a seer and a sorcerer. He can become cataleptic or enter into trance to allow his Double (alter ego) to fare forth and travel the world in the guise of an animal while his body remains lifeless.

In the euhemeristic interpretation of Snorri Sturluson's *Ynglinga saga,* Odin is an Asiatic king ruling over Ásgarðr, which is located east of the Don River. One time while Odin was away traveling, his two brothers shared his inheritance between them, including his wife, but he took everything back when he returned. He warred against the Vanir. Due to his gift of prophecy, he knew that his descendants would settle in the north. He therefore gave Ásgarðr back to his brothers, Vili and Vé, and set off northward, eventually reaching the sea where he settled first on the island of Odinsey (Odense) and then on the shores of lake Løgrinn (today called Mälaren) in Sigtuna (Signhildsborg, Sweden).

A vast number of theophoric place-names provide evidence for both

Fig. 65. Odin mounted on Sleipnir. Illustration by Ólafur Brynjúlfsson, *Snorra Edda,* 1760.

Odin's importance and his antiquity. The literary texts have also preserved more than 170 names and titles of Odin that are reflective of his deeds and his personality (✦ GÖNDLIR). His name is also evident in the weekday name Wednesday (which derives from Old English *wodnesdæg,* "Woden's Day").

In terms of his structural function in the mythology, Odin corresponds to the Mithra-Varuna pair of the Indo-Aryans and to the Roman Jupiter.

✦ *WODAN, WODEN*

📖 Kershaw, *The One-eyed God;* Régis Boyer, "Óðinn d'après Saxo Grammaticus et les sources norroises: étude comparative," *Beiträge zur nordischen Philologie* 15 (1986): 143–57; Peter Buchholz, "Odin: Celtic and Siberian Affinities of a Germanic Deity," *Mankind Quarterly* 24:4 (1984): 427–37; Lotte Motz, "Óðinn's Vision," *Maal og Minne* 1 (1998): 11–19; Clive Tolley, "Sources for Snorri's Depiction of Óðinn in *Ynglinga Saga:* Lappish Shamanism and the *Historia Norvegiae,*" *Maal og Minne* 1 (1996): 67–79.

ÓÐR ("Fury," "Magical Inspiration"): Husband of Freyja, with whom he had a daughter, Hnoss ("Jewel"), also called Gersimi ("Treasure"). He went away on long journeys, and Freyja wept tears of red gold. The close kinship of the names Óðr and Óðinn, along with the parallel nature of the Óðr-Freyja and Óðinn-Frigg couples and also the fact that Freyja and Odin share the dead warriors between them, shows that a very close bond exists between these four figures.

OÐRŒRIR: One of the containers used by the dwarves Fjalarr and Galarr to collect the blood of Kvasir.

ÖLNIR: Name of a dwarf presented as Odin's son.

ÖLRUN: The name of a valkyrie and the daughter of King Kiarr of Valland. She is described as a swan maiden and is the sister of Hervör *alvitr* and Hlaðguðr *svanhvít.* These three sisters marry Völundr (Wayland) and his brothers. Her name is interesting: *öl* could mean "ale," in which case Ölrun would mean "Ale-secret," and this in turn may refer to Freyr's sphere of activity (✦ BYGGVIR). But *öl* might also derive from the root **alb-,* meaning "elf" (with the etymological sense of a "white, ghostly being"); in this case, the name Ölrun would be identical to that of Albruna, the name of a Germanic seeress mentioned by Tacitus, and both would have the meaning of "Elf-secret" or "Secret of the White Being."

✦ *HERVÖR ALVITR, HLAÐGUÐR SVANHVÍT, SWAN MAIDEN, VALKYRIE, WAYLAND THE SMITH*

ÖLVALDI ("Beer Master"): A giant who was father to Þjazi, Iði, and Gangr. When he divided up his property among them, each of them was allowed to take only a mouthful of gold, which is why gold is called "Þjazi's (or Iði's or Gangr's) mouthful" in skaldic poetry.

ÖNDVEGISSÚLUR: The "support posts of the high seat," meaning the seat of honor for the head of the household. These were sculpted, carved, or painted, most likely with the image of a god or goddess. When the early Norse settlers left Norway and sailed to Iceland to colonize the island, they brought their high-seat posts with them. As they came within sight of land they threw the posts overboard with the stated intention of seeing where the guardian spirit would take them. They would settle in the place where the post washed ashore.

ORDEAL (Norwegian *ordal;* German *Urteil,* "Judgment"): In northern Germanic legal custom, the most common form of the ordeal is that of "iron-bearing" (*járnburðr*). In this procedure the defendant had to bear a piece of red-hot iron for some nine paces, namely to carry it up to a cauldron. In a variant version the defendant had to walk across twelve red-hot plowshares. Another ordeal consisted of retrieving an object the size of an egg with one's bare hands from a cauldron of boiling water. If the ordeal was successfully accomplished before the official witnesses, this was taken as evidentiary proof of the defendant's innocence or truthfulness.

ORG (pl. *Orgen*): The *Orgen* are woodland dwarves of the Tyrol who only go out at night. They are the size of a cat. If one is touched it feels like a sack of flour. They will slip into solitary houses but only those close to the forest. Their favorite activity is chopping wood. In the Val Passiria (South Tyrol), an *Org* measures one span and resembles a cat. It leaps on passersby and forces them to carry him.

📖 Zingerle, *Sagen aus Tirol,* 84–86, 209.

ÖRHHELER: ✦ NORGEN

ORK, ORG, NORG, LORKO, ORCO: A demon of the Tyrolean Alps whose name means "ogre." The traditions are highly varied: sometimes it is solitary and sometimes it lives in a group; in can be gigantic or it can be a dwarf. It is the Master of Animals. Starting around 1250 it turns up in adventure tales where it is named "Orkise" or "Wunderer."

✦ *WUNDERER*

📖 Alpenburg, *Mythen und Sagen Tirols,* 72–75; Insam, *Der Ork;* Petzold, *Kleines Lexikon der Dämonen und Elementargeister,* 138–39.

ÓSKMEY, ÓSKMÆR: Synonymous term for a valkyrie. The word is a combination of *ósk,* "wish," and *maer,* "maiden." These individuals would therefore be "the maidens who grant the wishes" of Odin and/ or of warriors.

✦ *VALKYRIE*

OSKOREIA ("The Terrifying Ride"): One of the names in Norway for the Wild Hunt. It either involves a troop of masked men or else spirits traveling by horseback (*ridende julevetter,* "riding Yule-wights") between Christmas and Epiphany or on the feast of Santa Lucia (whose name also underlies another designation for the Wild Hunt: Lussiferdi) on December 13. In Scandinavia the cycle of the Twelve Days (also known in German as the *Rauhnächte* or *Rauchnächte,* a cycle of twelve nights) can run from December 13 to Christmas, or from Christmas to January 6.

Other names for the Wild Hunt in Norway include the *Julereia, Trettenreia, Fossareia,* and *Imridn,* all of which contain the word *rei, reid,* "to ride as a company on horseback," sometimes grafted to the determiner *Jul/Jol* ("Christmas") or *Imbre/Imbredagene,* terms designating the four days of Lent of the liturgical year (*ieiunia quatuor*), or *Fosse* (the name of a spirit). *Trettenreia* or *Trettandreia* refers to "the troop of riders of the thirteenth day [of winter]."

The troop travels through the sky or parades in a file over land and is characterized by two essential motifs: a bond with horses and a connection to food and drink. The first motif recalls the comments by thirteenth-century authors that, during the period of Twelve Days, spirits slip into the stables and make off with the horses, returning them later covered with sweat as if they had been galloping great distances. It was said by the common people that the members of the Oskoreia or Lucia had ridden them (*at merri var Lussi-ridi*). The second motif is the theft of food and drink—especially drink. The "Oskoreians" sneak into the houses and cellars, steal the food, and empty the casks of their beer and replace it with water.

📖 Edvardsen, *Gammelt nytt i våre tidligste ukeblader*, 79–124 (texts); Lecouteux, *Phantom Armies of the Night*; Walter, ed., *Le Mythe de la Chasse sauvage dans l'Europe médiévale*; Christine N. F. Eike, "Oskoreia og ekstaseriter," *Norveg* 23 (1980): 227–309, maps at 242 and 247.

OSTARA (Old English *Eastre*): This may be the name of an ancient goddess of spring. The Venerable Bede (673–735) designates the month of April as *Eastermonaþ*. Eastre can be seen underlying the name of the festival of Easter.

📖 Shaw, *Pagan Goddesses in the Early Germanic World*, 49–71.

OURK: Name of the Wild Huntsman in Floruz, in the Gadler parish of the Tyrol. There is an odd twist to the hunting motif in this local legend; it features the strange atonement of the man who demanded—and received—the hand of a dead man. The guilty party has to wear a copper kettle on his head, take a cat under his arm, hold a rosary in his hand, and then utter this appeal: "Wild Huntsman, come back quick and take this prey, it is of no use to me!"

📖 Zingerle, *Sagen aus Tirol*, 2–3.

P

PERCHT(A): A female figure as well as a complex of German folk beliefs. In the Middle Ages she was said to have either an iron nose or a long nose. She was conflated with the Parcae and with Diana. She leads a troop of her peers who enter houses at night to eat.

Berthold of Regensberg (ca. 1210–1272) violently condemned the beliefs of the Bavarians, admonishing in a Latin sermon:

> You should in no way believe in folk who travel by night (*nahtvaren*) nor in their fellows, no more than in the Good Folk (*hulden*) and in the Evil Ones (*unhulden*), in sprites (*pilwiz*), in nightmares (*maren*) of both sexes, in the ladies of the night (*nahtvrouwen*), nor in the nocturnal spirits or in those that travel about riding this or that; they are all demons. Nor should you set the table for the Blessed Ladies (*felices dominae*).

In another sermon Berthold explains: "The foolish peasants really believe that the ladies of the night and the night-walking spirits visit

Fig. 66. Long-nosed Percht. Hans Vintler, Die *Pluemen der Tugent,* 1486.

them, and they set their tables for them." Around 1350 we learn that offerings were made to them: "Sinners also are those who on Epiphany night leave food and drink upon the table so that everything smiles upon them during the year and they are lucky in all things. . . . Thus they also are sinners who offer food to Percht and red snails [or shoes] to the Howler (*scrat*) or to the nightmare."

The *Thesaurus pauperum* of 1486 says this:

> The second type of superstition, a kind of idolatry, is that of those who leave out open containers filled with food and drink at night intended for the ladies expected to come then, Lady Abundia and Satia, whom the vulgar commonly and collectively give the name of Frau Percht or Perchtum; this lady arrives with a troop. They do this, for if they find all objects holding food and drink open, they will subsequently refill them and grant their hosts prosperity and greater abundance. Many believe that it is during the holy nights, between the birth of Jesus and the Epiphany, that these ladies, at whose head is Lady Perchta, visit their homes. Many are those who, during the course of these nights, leave out on their tables bread, cheese, milk, meats, eggs, wine, water, and foodstuffs of this kind, as well as spoons, plates, cups, knives, and other similar objects with an eye to the visit of Lady Perchta and her troop, so they will find it pleasant and that, consequently, they will look kindly in turn on the prosperity of the home and the conduct of temporal matters.

In the German-speaking lands Percht is the equivalent of Abundia and Satia, who are fairies in the Romance-language countries. In Germany there are also other nocturnal visitors: Phinzen, Sack semper, and Sacia. Phinzen is the personification of Thursday, and Sack semper is a bogeyman, a member of the Christmas processions as well as the personification of Sempertac, which falls eight days after Three Kings Day.

In Styria milk is left out on the table on the night of Three Kings Day so that Percht can quench her thirst; in Carinthia it is pasta and bread; and in the Tyrol it is noodles and eggs, but dairy products are predominant everywhere. Percht has become the leader of a troop of

Die Butzen-Bercht.

Fig. 67.
Butzenbercht
carrying off
children (1764)

dead children who pass through during the Twelve Days; sometimes these children take the form of puppies. In the Poitou region of France the Galopine Hunt is made up of dead children.

✦ *STAMPA, ZODAWASCHERL, ZUSERBEUTLEIN*

📖 Grimm, *Teutonic Mythology,* vol. II, 272–82; Rumpf, *Perchten.*

PERKEO: Dwarf and court jester of Charles III Philip, Elector Palatine (1661–1742). Born in the southern Tyrol, Perkeo entered into legend for his capacity to drink and his gift for repartee. While still alive he was memorialized with a wooden statue that can still be seen today in a cellar of Heidelberg Castle. Countless stories are told about him, and he is the hero of many student songs, the most famous of which is the one composed by Joseph Victor von Scheffel in 1849: "There Was Once a Dwarf Named Perkeo."

📖 Jürgen Fröhlich, "Perkeo," in Müller and Wunderlich, eds., *Mittelalter Mythen,* vol. II, 461–66.

PFINZDA-WEIBL (neut., "Friday Woman"): In Lower Austria all work comes to a halt for Carnival, especially spinning. The Pfinzda-Weibl exercises her authority from Fat Thursday to Ash Wednesday, as well as on all the evenings of the year. Whatever she commands is carried out. If she tells the poker to open the door for her, it will.

   📖 Vernaleken, *Mythen und Bräuche des Volkes in Österreich*, 293.

PHOL ("Force"): A deity mentioned in the *Second Merseburg Charm*. A link has been sought between him and Volla with the idea that there could be a pair of gods, the masculine Phol/Fol and the feminine Folla/Volla, which would thus correspond to Freyr/Freyja. In Thuringia, not far from the Saale River, there is a place called Pfuhlsborn, "Phol's Spring." This has given rise to the legend that a temple was built for this god near the spring. Other place-names, one dating from 744 (Pholesouwa, "Phol's Meadow," which is Flasau, near present-day Passau) and another from 788, refer to this god, as does a site attested in 1138, Pholespunkt ("Phol's Point"), near Melk, Austria.

   ✦ *MERSEBURG CHARMS*

   📖 Beck, *Die Merseburger Zaubersprüche;* Jean-Paul Allard, "Du second Charme de Mersebourg au Viatique de Weingarten," *Études Indo-Européennes* 14 (1985): 33–53.

POLTERGEIST ("Knocking Spirit"): Also still called a *Rumpelgeist* ("rumbling spirit"), the poltergeist is essentially a devil, a specter, or a revenant in the sixteenth-century texts. In later sources the poltergeist becomes an imp. In 1666, Johannes Prätorius wrote an essay on knocking spirits in which he states: "The ancients could only believe that poltergeists had to be veritable human beings who looked like small children and wore little robes or multicolored garb. . . . Superstitious folk think they are the souls of people murdered in their houses earlier." In the Thompson *Motif-Index of Folk-Literature*, "(Motif F473) *Poltergeist*" serves as a synonym for an "invisible spirit (sometimes identified as ghost or witch) responsible for all sorts of mischief in or around a household"— in other words, it is employed as a rather imprecise and generic term for designating an entity that is responsible for all kinds of disruptions in the house, such as mistreating people, making noises, and throwing objects or making them act in ways contrary to their nature.

In psychical research the "poltergeist" has been classified as a phenomenon of psychokinesis, a term that describes the effect of mind over matter. However, this usage stems from speaking of a poltergeist every time manifestations like noises and the movement of objects occur in a "wild" (i.e., spontaneous and uncontrolled) manner, whereas the term *psychokinesis* is used for all other cases.

📖 Lecouteux, *The Secret History of Poltergeists and Haunted Houses.*

PORENUT: Thunder god of the ancient Rugians. His statue had four heads and a face on his chest. His left hand was touching his brow, and his right rested on his hip. He was a foe of lust and adultery.

📖 Krantz, *Wandalia*, 164; Saxo Grammaticus, *Gesta Danorum*, XIV, 39, 41; Schwarz, *Diplomatische Geschichte der Pommersch-Rügischen Städte Schwedischer Hoheit*, 601–2.

POREVEIT, BOREVEIT: The god of weather (which he made) or god of the forest for the ancient Rugians. His statue was in Carenza (Garz, Rügen). He was an enemy of lust and adultery.

📖 Saxo Grammaticus, *Gesta Danorum*, XIV, 39, 41; Krantz, *Wandalia*, 164.

PÖSCHI (masc.): The *Pöschi* is a gigantic fire spirit that possesses colossal strength. He has only one eye and bears horns. He does not speak but bellows like a bull.

📖 Heyl, *Volkssagen, Meinungen und Bräuche aus Tirol*, 19–20.

PUKI (Danish *Puge*, Norwegian, and Swedish *Puke*): Small demon of folk belief. He is sometimes a dwarf, sometimes a revenant, and sometimes a devil that haunts the latrines. He can be found in all the Germanic lands, and Shakespeare featured him as Puck at Oberon's side in *A Midsummer's Night Dream*. He has been conflated with the *Niss*, a place spirit, as is evident in the name *Nisspuck*, and he has also been conflated with dwarves. In 1598 a spirit called Pück lived in the Franciscan monastery in Schwerin (Germany) and rendered all kinds of services. For his wages he asked for a multicolored frock coat with small bells before disappearing.

✦ *DWARVES, HOUSEHOLD/PLACE SPIRITS, NISS, RÅ*

📖 Lindig, *Hausgeister*, 80ff.

PUTZ, ALMPUTZ: A generic name given to all kinds of fantastic beings in the Tyrol. It can designate a perching spirit similar to the *Aufhocker;* a poltergeist; a fire spirit; a white man who is sometimes gray and has no head, and is sometimes accompanied by a dog; an undead surveyor; or an elderly homunculus that cannot tolerate jokes. The *Putz* sometimes wears wooden clogs, and his arrival is a herald of snow. He can also appear in the form of a pig. According to one legend he rewards peasants by giving them a loaf of bread that never grows smaller.

R

RÅ: This word designates a supernatural being in Sweden that lives in certain places and rules over them (as in the verb *råda,* "to rule"). In the water there is the *sjörå;* in the mountains, the *bergrå;* in the forest, the *skogsrå;* in the house, the *husrå* or *gardsrå;* in the stable, the *stallrå;* in the church, the *kirkrå,* who is often the first person buried on this site; and in the mines, the *gruvrå.* When building on a site, a human being or sow would be sacrificed to the *rå.* The *rå* is also the Master of Animals, and sometimes he has buried treasure in his keeping. He occasionally assumes the appearance of a seductive woman with a fox-tail and a back that is hollow like a kneading trough. This final detail is found in German charms against elves.

The Swedish also use the term *rådande,* the male or neuter present participle of *råda,* to designate the *rå.*

📖 Granberg, *Skogsrået i yngre nordisk folktradition,* 205–9; Hultkrantz, ed., *The Supernatural Owners of Nature.*

RAGNARÖK ("Judgment of the Ruling Powers [= Gods]"): The name for the Norse apocalypse, the end of the world, which was later popularized by Wagner as the *Götterdämmerung,* "Twilight of the Gods." The catastrophic scenario takes place as follows. Three dreadful winters follow each other in succession. Hel's three roosters—Fjalarr, Gullinkambi, and the "soot-red rooster"—crow in a dire manner as Fenrir (or Garmr) shakes his chains. He breaks them, swallowing the sun and moon. Yggdrasill trembles, the Earth convulses, the Midgard Serpent writhes up out of the sea and causes widespread flooding. The giants leave their land on the boat Naglfar, and one of them, Surtr, throws himself into the assault of Valhalla by way of the rainbow bridge. Odin is slain by Fenrir, who is then slain by Víðarr. Freyr falls to Surtr, and Thor and the Midgard Serpent slay each other. The same is true for Týr and Garmr, and Loki and Heimdallr. Surtr then sets the entire world ablaze.

The Earth then emerges from the waves, beautiful and green. Víðarr and Váli live in Iðavöllr, on the site where Ásgarðr once stood. They are joined there by Thor's sons, Móði and Magni, who bring Mjöllnir with them. Baldr and Höðr return from Hel's domain. Two humans survive named Líf and Lífþrasir; they remained hidden and were spared by Surtr's fire. They will repopulate the Earth. The sun reappears because Sól had given birth to a daughter just as beautiful as she was before she perished.

📖 Martin, *Ragnarök*.

RÁN ("Robbery"): Goddess of the sea, the wife of Ægir, and mother of the waves. She owns a net that she uses to capture all the men who fall into the sea. In the realm of the dead beneath the sea, she rules over all of the sailors who died on the waters.

RATATOSKR ("Rat-tooth"): Name of the squirrel who nests in the branches of the cosmic tree, Yggdrasill. He climbs up and down constantly, bringing the words of the eagle perched in its highest branches down to Níðhöggr at its base, and vice versa.

RATI ("Borer"): Name of the drill used by the giant Baugi to pierce a hole in the side of Hnitbjörg Mountain where Gunnlöð keeps watch over the wondrous mead made from Kvasir's blood.

Fig. 68. Baugi bores into the mountain with Rati to gain possession of the wondrous mead. Illustration by Ólafur Brynjúlfsson, *Snorra Edda*, 1760.

RAUE ELSE ("Wild Else"): Wild woman and water nymph in the legends surrounding Wolfdietrich. A first version tells how the hero was sleeping beneath a tree one day when a nymph came out of the sea and hid his sword. She stands behind the tree and waits for him to wake up. She wears a scaly hat and is covered with aquatic plants and hair that falls from her chin to her feet. Her entire body is muddy and dank; her eye sockets are two fingers deep, and her feet are the size of spades; her forehead measures an ell in length. Although repulsive, she asks Wolfdietrich to marry her. If he consents, she will give him three kingdoms, for she rules over all that is covered by the sea. The knight objects, saying that if he were to wed her the devil would attend the ceremony. She then slips out of her scales and reveals herself to be a great beauty. Wolfdietrich, who was starving, asks her for something to eat and tells her he cannot get married until he frees his family. She then asks him to grant his brother to be her husband and gives him roots that will provide him with the courage of a lion and prevent him from

Fig. 72. Wild Woman. Hartmann Schedel,
Liber Chronicarum, Nürnberg, 1493.

Fig. 69. Rome carrying Wolfdietrich. *Das Heldenbuch*
(Strasbourg: Johann Prüss, circa 1483).

Fig. 71. Battle between a knight and a wild woman.
Das Heldenbuch (Strasbourg: Johann Prüss, circa 1483).

suffering from hunger or thirst. She then tells him how to get back to Lombardy.

In a second version the lady is named Else the Hairy, and she is in love with Wolfdietrich, who refuses to reciprocate because he believes her to be a devil. Furious, she casts a curse on him that causes him to lose his mind, and she takes his horse and his sword. When the hero regains his senses and sets off to find his weapons and companions, she creates a magic path that Wolfdietrich follows for twelve leagues before he sees her perched in a tree. She repeats her request, and he again rejects her. She bewitches the valiant knight a second time and cuts off a lock of his hair and his nails. He goes mad and wanders the forest like an animal for six months. His loyal vassal Berchtung, who had set out to find him, eventually runs into Else, and she relates to him all that has happened. However, God sends an angel to the woman, who orders her to break the evil spell. She obeys and asks Wolfdietrich if he would truly marry her. He agrees on the condition that she will consent to be baptized. She agrees and leads him to a ship. They cross the sea to Else's kingdom, where there is a fountain of youth on a high mountain. She dives into it and reemerges as a ravishing beauty; all the hair that had covered her body remains in the fountain. Once baptized, she takes the name Sigeminne ("Victorious Love").

RAVEN: The sacred bird of Odin. His ravens Huginn ("Thought") and Muninn ("Memory") travel across the world and then return to perch on his shoulders and tell him what they have seen and heard. The cries of a raven were believed to be oracular, and sacrifices were made to ravens when the petitioners sought to address Odin. The image of a raven was used as a battle emblem, and the Bayeux Tapestry shows William the Conqueror followed by a soldier carrying a raven banner. It was believed that victory would be assured if the banner spread out properly, but its bearer was doomed to die. Numerous personal names attest to the raven's popularity. A Gallo-Roman statue from Compiègne depicts a male figure who has two ravens on his shoulders speaking into his ears, an image that is strongly reminiscent of Odin.

Grambo, *Svart katt over veien*, 124–25; Sylvia Huntley Horowitz, "The Ravens in Beowulf," *Journal of English and Germanic Philology* 80 (1981): 502–11.

RED: This color had a very pejorative connotation in ancient times. The first medieval German romance, *Ruodlieb* (eleventh century; written in Latin by a German poet), offers the advice to never make friends with a red-haired man: *Non tibi sit rufus umquam specialis amico* (V, 451). In the legend of Pope Gerbert there appears the phrase "*Rufus est, tunc perfidus*" (He is a red head, therefore perfidious). This has remained proverbial wisdom in the Tyrol, where it is said, "A red beard rarely hides a good nature," and, similarly, in the Upper Palatinate with the proverb "Red hair and firewood don't grow in good soil." In *Daniel von dem blühenden Tal* (Daniel of the Flowering Valley), a thirteenth-century romance by Der Stricker, a malevolent red-haired man appears who hypnotizes all who hear him with his voice. He slits the people's throats above a tub, for he takes a bath in blood once a week.

📖 Resler, ed., *Der Stricker: Daniel von dem blühenden Tal.*

REGINN ("The Powerful One"): Smith and foster father of Sigurðr (Siegfried). He is the brother of Fáfnir, Otr, Lyngheiðr, and Lofnheiðr and the son of Hreiðmar. He forges the sword Gramr for Sigurðr, which the hero then uses to slay Fáfnir, who has changed into a dragon. After the hero is warned by the nuthatches that his foster father seeks to get rid of him, Sigurðr slays Reginn.

REVENANT: ✦ DRAUGR

RÍGR ("King," the Old Norse word is a borrowing from Old Irish *rí*): Name given to the god Heimdallr in the *Rígsþula,* a gnomic Eddic poem of the fourteenth century. It is Rígr who establishes the three ancestral lineages of the slaves, peasants, and nobles.

RINDR ("Bark"?): Mother of Váli, Odin's son who will avenge the death of Baldr. She is an Ásynja. In *The History of the Danes,* Saxo Grammaticus tells us that a Finn (Sámi) magician predicted to Othinus (Odin) one day that only Rinda could give him the son who would avenge Balderus (Baldr). Othinus tried to seduce the beautiful woman in various guises but finally made her ill and took advantage of her: "Imediately he touched her with a piece of bark inscribed with spells and made her like one demented, a moderate sort of punishment for the continual insults he had received" (III, 71, trans. Fisher). She gives birth to Bous, while Othinus is banished for his crime.

RISE, BERGRISE (German *Riese*, "giant"): A Scandinavian name for giants that live in the mountains. The *rise* is large and ugly and leads a life similar to that of humans with families, farms, and animals. In Norway place-names like Risabbakken (Rogaland), Risareva (Hordaland), and Risarøysa keep their memory alive.

ROCHELMORE: A mystical being of Switzerland who travels through the air making a noise that sounds like the grunting of a sow (*Färlimore*); in Grindelwald it is a portent of bad weather.

RÖKSTÓLAR ("Thrones of Judgment"): The thrones on which the Æsir sit when exercising their duties as judges and sovereigns.

ROME: The name of a wild woman in the legends surrounding the hero Wolfdietrich. She has black skin, and her hair is the color of a donkey's coat. Wolfdietrich meets her when he is lost on the mountain. She gives him lodging in the castle where she lives with seven of her fellows. These women are most likely fairies, because they possess uncommon knowledge. The knight stays with them three days, after which Rome carries him under her arm, together with his horse, for a distance of twenty-two leagues and sets him down on the right path on the other side of the mountain.

RÖSKVA: Sister of Þjálfi and, like him, a servant of the god Thor. She was forced to enter into Thor's service as reparation for the mutilation of his goats.

ROSSTRAPPE ("Print of the Horseshoe"): Name of a steep crag in the Harz Mountains of Germany. A gigantic shape of a horseshoe print can be seen on the edge of the Rosstrappe, which has given birth to a legend about its cause. Pursued by a giant named Bodo, Princess Emma leaped over the Bodotal (Bode Gorge) to land on this rock, and her horse left the print of his hoof in the stone. The giant failed to make

Fig. 70. Rosstrappe. Illustration from a German textbook.

the leap, however, and fell into the valley, thus giving his name to the river that flows there, the Bode.

Similar legends exist in France (le Saut de la Pucelle) and in Spain (Lo Salt de la donzella), with both names meaning "the Maiden's Leap."

RÜBEZAHL: A type of legendary mountain spirit who was originally confined to the Krkonoše Mountains (in German they are called the Riesengebirge, "Mountains of Giants") of Bohemia and Silesia in the sixteenth century but has since spread into other regions. Rübezahl ("Turnip-counter") is also called Riesezahl, Rübenzagel, and Rubinzalius. He is a solitary and multifarious demon who can appear alternately as a person, a thing, or an animal. He is sometimes friendly and will help lost travelers find their way, but if they mock him, he will either slap them or send them astray. The features of several different demons have become merged together in his form. Originally he was a spirit of the mines.

📖 Peuckert, *Deutscher Volksglaube des späten Mittelalters*.

RUEL THE STRONG: Giantess or wild woman who appears in Wirnt von Grafenberg's *Wigalois* (ca. 1204–1215). Her head is enormous, with long gray eyebrows, a large mouth, and huge teeth. She is as hairy as a bear and hunchbacked. Her breasts hang down like sacks, her feet are twisted, and her fingers are griffon claws. Seeking to avenge her husband, the giant Feroz, she attacks Wigalois and carries him off under her arm. She binds him and has the intention of killing him. However, the neighing of the hero's horse scares her off, because she believes it to be the cry of a dragon. The author notes in passing: "A short night would age any man that shared her bed because she was so skilled at making love."

RUGIVIT: War god of the Rugians. His statue, which was carved from the trunk of an enormous oak tree, stood in the city of Carenz (Garz, Rügen). It had seven heads, each topped by a hat, and seven swords. The god held an eighth sword in his hand in a threatening gesture.

📖 Krantz, *Wandalia*, 164; Schwarz, *Diplomatische Geschichte der Pommersch-Rügischen Städte Schwedischer Hoheit*, 601–2.

RUNES: The letters of the ancient Germanic script. Consisting of twenty-four signs, the runic alphabet appeared toward the end of the second century. The symbols themselves were probably modeled on an ancient Italic script. Because of the inherent difficulty in carving them, runes were used mainly for brief inscriptions, the bulk of which dealt with propitiation, protection, spells, and so forth. In later periods, notably during the Viking Age, they were often used for large and elaborate memorial stones.

The runic alphabet is called the Fuþark, so named after its first six letters in their traditional order. Each rune has a name, and the rune phonologically represents the first letter of that name. The rune names have been reconstructed based on linguistic evidence.

The original rune row of twenty-four letters is known as the Elder Fuþark. Over time, significant regional linguistic variations developed that affected not only the number of the runes but also their names and their phonological values. In the Viking Age a shorter sixteen-rune alphabet, known as the Younger Fuþark, was in use in Scandinavia. By

ᚠᚢᚦᚨᚱᚲᚷᚹ·ᚺᚾᛁᛃᛈᛉᛊ·ᛏᛒᛖᛗᛚᛜᛞᛟ
f u þ a r k g w , h n i j ę p ẓ s , t b e m l ŋ̃ d o

Fig. 73. Elder Fuþark

ᚠᚢᚦᚨᚱᚲ · ᚺᚾᛁᛆᛋ · ᛏᛒᛘᛚᛦ
f u þ o r k , h n í a s , t b m l R

Fig. 74. Younger Fuþark

ᚠᚢᚦᛟᚱᚲᚷᚹ · ᚺᚾᛁᛃᛖᛈᛉᛋ · ᛏᛒᛖᛗᛚᛝᛞ · ᚩᚪᚫᚣ
fuþorkgw, hnijẹp x s, t b e m l ŋ̃ d œ a ä æ y

Fig. 75. Anglo-Saxon Fuþorc

contrast, in Frisia and England, a longer rune row developed; this is known as the Anglo-Saxon (or Anglo-Frisian) Fuþorc.

The referents for the original rune names fall into five different categories or domains: the animal world (aurochs, horse, elk); weather (hail, ice, sun, water, day); plant life (good fruitful year, birch, yew, thorn); the human world (property/wealth, riding, boil[?], gift, joy, need, man, and estate); and, finally, the divine world (thurse/giant, Æsir god, Týr, Ingvarr/Freyr). The *Old English Rune Poem,* written during the first half of the ninth century, gives us insight into the meaning of the runes. Each of the poem's twenty-nine verses begins with the name of a rune and then describes some of its qualities.

Runes have been found on carved stones, weapons, pieces of wood, in manuscripts, and quite frequently in charms. Here are examples of two sorts of common uses. On the Gallehus Horn, an ornate golden metal horn discovered near Tönder (Denmark) and dated to the fifth century CE, the runic inscription reads: "I, Hlewagast, son of Holt, made this horn." The commemorative stone of Hällestad in Scania, erected to the memory of Toki, the son of King Gorm of Denmark, reads: "He did not flee at Uppsala. The young men erected a stone, strengthened by runes, in memory of their brother, on the mountain."

They were your closest kin, Toki, son of Gorm." An inscription that is magical in nature appears on the Stentoften Stone from Blekinge, Sweden: "To the new dwellers, to the new guests . . . Haþuwulf gave [a] fruitful year . . . powerful runes I hide here, a row of bright runes. Consumed by rage and [doomed to a] woeful death [will be] he who breaks this."

📖 Barnes, *Runes;* Düwel, *Runenkunde;* Elliott, *Runes;* Looijenga, *Texts and Contexts of the Oldest Runic Inscriptions;* McKinnell, Simek, and Düwel, *Runes, Magic, and Religion;* Musset, *Introduction à la runologie;* Page, *Runes;* Stoklund et al., eds., *Runes and Their Secrets.* A fine study of the matter can be read in the special issue devoted to runes of the journal *Études Germaniques* 52 (1997): 507–92, which includes an extensive bibliography.

RÜTTELWEIB, RITTELWEIB: One of the many names for a wood woman or bush woman; they are also called *Buschweiblen* in Westphalia or *Fenngen* in the Tyrol. She can be seen in the procession of the Wild Hunt. It is said that she steals children who are six weeks old or younger, or substitutes changelings for them.

◆ *CHANGELING*

RYLLA: The name given to an illness demon in some Norwegian charms.

RYMR ("Roar"): One of the bynames of the god Thor.

SACRIFICIAL BOG (Old Norse *blótkelda*): Men would be tossed into the bog during sacrificial feasts, which almost precisely mirrors what Tacitus tells us about the worship of the goddess Nerthus by the early Germanic peoples: after the slaves have bathed the goddess in the waters of the lake, they are drowned. Archaeologists have discovered such sacrifices in the peat bogs of Scandinavia and northern Germany. Many of these bodies have been perfectly preserved due to the particular chemical composition of the bogs.

    📖 Glob, *The Bog People*.

SAÐ/SANN ("True, Sooth"): One of Odin's bynames.

    📖 Falk, *Odensheiti*.

SÆHRÍMNIR ("Sea-soot," "Sooty Sea Beast"?): The boar cooked by Andhrímnir at Valhalla; this is the customary food for the *einherjar,* Odin's warriors. The boar's flesh grows back on its bones each night, which is reminiscent of a shamanic theme more clearly depicted in the story of Thor's goats.

SÁGA ("She Who Sees"): A secondary goddess or a hypostasis of Frigg. All we know is that she drinks with Odin in the hall in Ásgarðr called Sökkvabekkr ("Sunken Bank").

SALINGEN (pl.): Tyrolean fairies that are kind to good folk and hostile to wicked ones. They are always referred to in the plural since they consistently appear in groups of three. They love to sing and dance and take care of livestock but are prone to jealousy. Wild men are their enemies. The oldest mention of them can be found in the *Eckenlied* (ca. 1250), where they appear in the form of three "queens" living in a remote castle in the mountains. The name most likely comes from the Middle High German *sælig,* "blessed," and one of the fairies is named

Frau Sælde. In the modern era the *Salingen* have become *tempestarii;* in other words, witches that create bad weather.

📖 Alpenburg, *Mythen und Sagen Tirols,* 3–9, 18–23, 27–30; Heyl, *Volkssagen, Meinungen und Bräuche aus Tirol,* 273, 401–6, 520–21; Zingerle, *Sagen aus Tirol,* 32–39; 42–43.

SALVANEL: A mythical being of Valsugana (the Sugana Valley, southeast of Trentino in the Italian Tyrol). It is depicted as a red-skinned man who lives in caves in the middle of the woods, where he keeps large flocks of fat, wooly sheep. At night he is in the habit of going out to drink the milk the cowherds milked that day. He likes little girls one to three years in age, whom he kidnaps and carries off to his cavern. He feeds them and keeps them nearby.

📖 Schneller, *Märchen und Sagen aus Wälschtirol,* 213–15.

SALVANG: The name of a Tyrolean woodland spirit. The name most likely derives from Sylvanus. He is small in size, bearded, very old, and naive despite his magical powers. His wife's name is Ganna or Gannes. He stays in remote forests and inaccessible caverns near woodland springs and is regarded as a protector of peasants and their flocks. His benevolence ends if someone makes fun of him, at which point he will try to get even. He rewards serving maids by giving them a ball of yarn that never ends unless someone says, "Is that ball of yarn endless?" At this point the fortunes of the household will begin to decline. Sometimes mention is made of Salvangs in the plural, but this is actually a reference to dwarves. In the French Alps the Salvang corresponds to the spirit called Servant.

📖 Heyl, *Volkssagen, Meinungen und Bräuche aus Tirol,* 613–15; Zingerle, *Sagen aus Tirol,* 123.

SANNGETALL ("The One Who Guesses True"): One of Odin's names. It refers to the fact that this god always wins riddle contests.

📖 Falk, *Odensheiti.*

SAXIE AND HERMAN: The names of two giants who inhabit, respectively, the heights of Saxa Vord and Hermaness of the Shetland Islands, which are separated by a branch of the sea—the fjord Burra Firth. These giants quarreled constantly, and a common story concerns how, after he caught a whale in the fjord, Herman wanted to borrow Saxie's cauldron to cook it in but refused to share any of the animal with him. In a rage, he threw an enormous rock at Saxie, who dodged it. The stone fell into the sea, and it became the reef that is known today as Herman's Stack. The two giants fell in love with a mermaid who was combing her hair sitting on a rock in the open sea, the Out Stack, the northernmost point of all the British Isles. She told them that she would wed the one who could swim all the way to the North Pole without touching land. The giants undertook that journey and were never seen again.

📖 Jean Renaud, "Le peuple surnaturel des Shetland," *Artus* 21–22 (1986): 28–32.

SAXNÔT (Old English *Seaxnet, Saxneat, Saxnat*): God mentioned in the Saxon Baptismal Vow and in the royal genealogy of the East Saxons. The name could mean "Sword-companion."

SAXON BAPTISMAL VOW: Ninth-century text that contains the phrase the catechumen had to recite: "I renounce Thunær, Uuôden, and Saxnôt, and all the demons that are their companions." While it is easy to recognize Thunær as corresponding to Donar/Thor and Uuôden as corresponding to Odin/Woden/Wotan, the identity of Saxnôt remains a mystery.

SCEAF ("Sheaf of Wheat"): Mythical ancestor of Odin in the Anglo-Saxon royal genealogies. It is said that Sceaf came to an island in the ocean named Scani in a small boat. He was a very young child and surrounded by weapons. The region's inhabitants raised him and made him their king. The most recent account, written by William of Malmesbury (1095/6–1143), is more detailed. Sceaf landed at the Germanic island called Scanzda (Scandinavia). He was sleeping with a sheaf of wheat for his pillow in a boat without oars. The inhabitants welcomed him, and he became king of the town formerly called Slaswic (Schleswig) and later called Haitebi (Hedeby, Holstein). A character named Scyld Scefing (in other words, "Scyld, son of Sceaf") appears in the Anglo-Saxon epic *Beowulf* (written before the year 1000).

📖 Grimm, *Teutonic Mythology*, vol. I, 369–70; vol. IV, 1719–20, 1724–29.

SCHIMMELREITER ("The Rider on the White Horse"): *Der Schimmelreiter* is the title of a famous novella by Theodor Storm (1888), which is based on an old belief: for a dike to hold together, it was necessary that someone be walled up inside it alive, a feature common to numerous building legends in Europe. The Rider on the White Horse is a ghostly apparition that appears on the coasts of Schleswig-Holstein; it can be seen on days when the weather is stormy.

Fig. 76. Illustration by Jens Rusch for *Der Schimmelreiter*

SCHLEMIHL, PETER ("Unlucky Peter"): Adelbert von Chamisso's tale *Peter Schlemihls wundersame Geschichte* (The Wonderful History of Peter Schlemihl), written in 1813 by and published in 1814, tells how one day Peter met a man in a gray coat who gave him a purse that would never become empty in exchange for his shadow. Peter manages to hide its absence and is on the verge of marrying his beloved when a lackey spills the beans. The man in gray reappears and offers to return Peter's shadow in exchange for his soul after he dies. Peter refuses, throws away the purse, gains possession of some seven-league boots, and travels the world satisfying his passion for the natural sciences.

According to the Talmud the real Schlemihl would have been a Jew who had an affair with a rabbi's wife and was caught and condemned to death.

The theme has been the subject of other adaptations, such as by E. T. A. Hoffmann in "The Story of the Lost Reflection," included as part of *Die Abenteuer der Sylvester Nacht* (A New Year's Eve Adventure), published in 1815.

✦ *FYLGJA, HAMR*

📖 Chamisso, *Peter Schlemihl,* trans. John Bowring; Lecouteux, *Witches, Werewolves, and Fairies,* 138–46; Julius von Negelein, "Bild, Spiegel und Schatten im Volksglauben," *Archiv für Religionsgesellschaft* 5/1 (1902): 1–37; Fritz W. Pradel, "Der Schatten im Volksglauben," *Mittheilungen der schlesischen Gesellschaft für Volkskunde* 12 (1904): 1–36; E. L. Rochholz, "Ohne Schatten, ohne Seele: der Mythus vom Körperschatten und vom Schattengeist," *Germania* 5 (1860): 69–94.

SCHLETTO: Giant founder of Sélestat (Schlettstadt in German). According to legend he lived during the time the Sea of Alsace was retreating. His bones were those of a sea animal. His rib measured twenty feet. A variety of constructions are attributed to him.

SCHRAT ("Howler"): A figure of Germanic folk belief whose character incorporates features of varied origin. He is a wicked dead man and revenant, a household spirit with a connection to horses reminiscent of the Romanian spirit *catabali,* and a dwarf. In medieval German glosses the word *scrat* is defined as "evil spirit" (Latin *larva*) and "enchanter" (Latin *incarminator, incantator*), and today Old Scratch is a name for the devil. In German folk traditions the *Schrat* becomes conflated with dwarves.

📖 Lecouteux, "Vom Schrat zum Schrättel: Dämonisierungs-, Mythologisierungs- und Euphemisierungsprozeß einer volkstümlichen Vorstellung," *Euphorion* 79 (1985): 95–108.

SCHRECKMÄNNLEIN ("Terrifying Little Man"): An entity who causes children to awaken suddenly and start crying, which is called night cries or night terrors (*Nachtgeschrei, Nuochtkräsch, Nachtweinen*). It is said in Styria that this happens when the moon enters the child's room, or when its bed has been exposed to moonlight. In Transylvania these cries are produced for seven nights in a row.

SEIÐR ("Magic"): Very elaborate ritual of auspicious or harmful magic that also can have divinatory properties. Odin is the high master of *seiðr,* about which Snorri Sturluson remarks: "Thanks to it, Odin had the power to know the destiny of people and things that had yet to occur, as well as the power to cause death or ill health; in addition it gave him the power to steal the good sense or strength of one person and give it to another." The Vanir introduced *seiðr* to the Æsir, and Freyja was its practitioner. Men were advised to avoid the practice of *seiðr* because it would make them more effeminate.

Seiðr required certain accessories; these included a staff and a kind of scaffold construction in which the magic worker needed to place herself. A *seiðr* session was accompanied by songs intended to attract the spirits.

✦ *VARÐLOKUR*

📖 Boyer, *Le Monde du double;* Strömbäck, *Sejd.*

SELKIES: The large gray seals called selkies in the Shetland Islands were in fact transformed men and women. The islanders were reluctant to kill seals, which they did for their hides and fat, because they felt it could bring misfortune. Selkies would resume their human forms on certain occasions. A story tells how an Unst fisherman saw an entire group dancing on the rocks after removing their skins. He hid one of these skins, which proved to be that of a beautiful young woman. Completely nude, she searched vainly for it on the beach so she could leave with her companions. The fisherman married her, and they had children. Years went by, but one day one of the children discovered the sealskin that their father had hidden and showed it to his mother. She recognized it at once and put it on and left to rejoin her faithful seal companions. She was never seen again.

By spilling seven tears into the sea at high tide, a woman can win the love of a selkie. In Yell a maiden collecting shells on the Sands of Breckon met one and found herself pregnant. She gave birth to a son with a seal head. People are found in some families with webbed feet or hands; they are said to be the descendants of a selkie.

✦ *UNDINE, WASSERMANN*

📖 Jean Renaud, "Le peuple surnaturel des Shetland," *Artus* 21–22 (1986): 28–32.

SELKIE WIVES: The name for mermaids in the Shetlands. It is said how one caught on a hook begged some fishermen to free her in exchange for which she would grant all their wishes. They freed her, and she dove back into the sea while singing. Now only one fisherman believed her promise. He found a magnificent pearl inside a fish, and the wish he made was granted. A story is also told about a mermaid who tried to take back the hide of a poor seal that a fisherman had skinned and who perished in the attempt.

✦ *UNDINE, WASSERMANN*

📖 Jean Renaud, "Le peuple surnaturel des Shetland," *Artus* 21–22 (1986): 28–32.

SELKOLLA ("Seal-head"): The following can be read in the *Selkolluvísur* (Seal-head Verses) by the skald Einar Gilsson, who is documented to have lived between 1339 and 1369. A couple was traveling to have their child baptized. While on their way the couple felt a desire for carnal union. They placed the child on a rock and went to a secluded spot. When they returned, their child was dead and cold and a "horrible woman" appeared to them. Everything seemed to indicate that their child had assumed this monstrous shape. The woman had a seal's head, and the local inhabitants called her Selkolla. From this time on the monster haunted Steingrímsfjörðr. She could be seen both day and night, sometimes as a beautiful maiden and sometimes hideous. In the form of a woman she paid visits to a certain Dálkr, who began to wither away. His friend Þorgísl came to keep watch over him, but Selkolla attacked him and put his eyes out. The bishop Guðmundr was called in. After suffering one of her attacks, Guðmundr succeeded in putting an end to Selkolla's schemes. Einar describes Selkolla as a demon using such terms as *óhreinn andi* ("unclean spirit"), *fjándi* ("foe"), *djöfull* ("devil"), *gýgr* and *troll* (both meaning "giantess"), *meinvaettr* ("hurtful wight"), as well as *mörn* and *flagð* (both meaning "ogress").

Einar's poem served as the source for a passage in the version of the *Guðmundar saga Arasonar* (Saga of Guðmundr Arason) written around 1345 by Arngrímr Brandsson (possibly in Latin and then translated into Icelandic). Furthermore, the saga storyteller alters the passage relating to Selkolla's "birth" and has the child living on in a monstrous form.

The last account of Selkolla is provided by the *Jarnteinabók Guðmundar byskups* (Book of Miracles of Bishop Guðmundr;

chap. 20–21), which must have been written around 1400 but is likewise based on Einar's poem. The vocabulary is the same as that found in the saga, but Selkolla's birth is explained this way: the child's parents and the local inhabitants believed that an unclean spirit had slipped into the corpse.

📖 *Guðmundar saga Arasonar eftir Arngrím ábóta,* in Jónsson, ed., *Byskupa sögur,* III, 145–474; story of Selkolla, 294–302; verses, 302–13; *Jarteinabók Guðmundar byskups* in Jónsson, ed., *Byskupa sögur,* II, 437–93; Lecouteux, *Au-delà du merveilleux,* 92–95; Wolf von Unwerth, "Eine isländische Mahrensage," *Wörter und Sachen* 2 (1910): 161–82.

SERPENT WORSHIP: Snakes were sacred to the ancient Prussians, as they represented the household spirit. They were worshipped in several places; this could be behind the oven or in a secret part of the house. Prayers were used to attract them to a table covered with a white linen cloth on which the head of the house had set all kinds of foods. If the snake ate them, it was a sign of good fortune. If the reptile did not come out of its hiding place, or did not touch anything on the table, then misfortune would strike the home. In a treatise on the gods of the Lithuanians, Jan Lasicki (Latinized as Johannis Lasicius, 1534–1620) informs us:

> Furthermore, the Lithuanians and the Samogitians keep serpents in their houses, beneath the stove or in the corner of the steam room, where the table is. At certain times of the year, they honor them like gods, inviting them to their tables with sacrificial prayers. Leaving their lairs, these reptiles climb upon the table with the help of a clean sheet and settle in. After having tasted a little of each dish, they then go back down into their holes. After they leave, the people gaily eat the dishes they tasted, hoping that the year will be a fortunate one. If, however, despite the prayers of those willing to make this sacrifice, the snakes do not appear and refuse to taste the dishes served there, they then believe that great misfortune will strike that year. (*Die diis Samagitarum libellus,* 48)

The German writer Ernst Jünger describes exactly the same thing in his 1939 novel *Auf den Markorklippen* (On the Marble Cliffs).

In Sweden a snake would be buried near the doorsill or in a hole that had been bored into it, and this snake was sometimes called "spirit-serpent of the house" (*tomtorm*). Around 1400, *Siælinna tröst* (The Consolation of the Soul), a Swedish treatise of moral edification, forbid belief in domestic serpents, and, in 1555, Olaus Magnus informs us that they were considered like *Penates,* playing with children in their cradles and even sleeping with them. In Ödåkra, in Skåne (Sweden), serpents had nests in the barns, and the milkmaid gave them milk so that the cows would be nice and fat. In Asarum, in Blekinge (Sweden), the milkmaid killed a snake and her best cow died, which clearly shows that said reptile was a household spirit assigned to the well-being of animals. In Austria people feel a respectful fear toward the domestic viper; it is sometimes said that this snake wears a crown.

📖 *Acta Borussica ecclesiastica, civilia, literaria,* vol. II, 407; Olaus Magnus, *Historia de gentibus septentrionalibus,* XXI, 48 (776).

SGÖNAUNKEN (pl.): The name for dwarves in Westphalia. These dwarves live inside a hill that is two hours by road away from Osnabrück. They captured a woman to nurse their watchdogs. This stretched out her breasts so much that she could sling them over her shoulders.

📖 Kuhn, *Sagen, Gebräuche und Märchen aus Westfalen,* vol. I, no. 292; Zingerle, *Sagen, Märchen und Gebräuche aus Tirol,* no. 64.

SHADOW: ✦ SCHLEMIHL

SHAMANISM: The contact between the Scandinavian peoples and the Lapplanders (Sámi) resulted in Norse mythology becoming marked with some typically shamanic features. Odin, for example, obtained his extraordinary knowledge and magical powers following an initiation that is suggestive of this worldview; his journeyings to remote regions and his ability to shapeshift are shamanistic traits. There is also the unique concept of a plural soul that can still be found today among the Uralic peoples on the shores of the Baltic Sea. Medieval texts in Old Saxon and Old English show that shamanic influence did not leave its stamp only on the northern Germanic peoples.

✦ *HAMR*

Fig. 77. A shaman in trance while his Double leaves him. Olaus
Magnus, *Historia de gentibus septentrionalibus*, Rome, 1555.

📖 Boyer, *Le Monde du double*; Buchholz, *Schamanistische Züge in der
altisländischen Überlieferung*; Dubois, *Nordic Religions in the Viking Age*; Eliade,
Shamanism; Glosecki, *Shamanism and Old English Poetry*; Hoppál and Sadovsky,
Shamanism; Tolley, *Shamanism in Norse Myth and Magic*; Ronald Grambo,
"Sjamanisme i norske sagn fra middelalderen," *Forum Medievale* 4–5 (1983): 5–13.

SÍÐHÖTTR ("Long Hat"): One of Odin's bynames. It alludes to the
fact that this god was known for concealing his facial features beneath
his hat.

📖 Falk, *Odensheiti.*

SÍÐSKEGGR ("Long beard"): A byname of Odin, who is described
as wearing a long, gray beard.

📖 Falk, *Odensheiti.*

SIEGFRIED (Old Norse *Sigurðr*): The legend of Siegfried is Frankish
in origin and its historical backdrop is the period of the great invasions
when the Germanic tribes were in the midst of settling in all parts of
Europe. Recollections of the Merovingian period can also be detected
in it, and behind Siegfried's marriage with Kriemhild we can detect
that of the historical Merovingian king Sigebert I with the Visigothic
princess Brunhilda.

Only three versions of the Siegfried legend remain in the southern Germanic lands: the *Nibelungenlied,* set down in Bavaria during the first years of the thirteenth century; *Diu Klage* (The Lament), a long poem on the death of the Nibelungen heroes; and *Das Lied vom hürnen Seyfrid* (The Lay of Horn-skinned Siegfried), a later, less literary work that is very interesting as its information matches that of the Scandinavian texts.

The elements that allow us to reconstruct the life and death of Siegfried are to be found in the Scandinavian sources: the thirteenth-century Icelandic collection *The Poetic Edda,* which includes poems dating back to the ninth and tenth centuries; the *Völsunga saga* (Saga of the Volsungs); the *Skáldskaparmál* (Treatise on the Skaldic Art) by the great scholar Snorri Sturluson (1179–1241); and, finally, the *Þiðreks saga af Bern* (Saga of Dietrich von Bern). There are about a dozen Eddic poems that are particularly striking in this regard; the most notable of them are the *Grípisspá* (Grípir's Prophecy), a summary of the hero's life; the *Reginsmál* (Lay of Regin); the *Fáfnismál* (Lay of Fáfnir); the *Sigrdrífumál* (Lay of Sigrdrífa); and the *Brot af Sigurðarkviðu* (Fragment of a Lay of Sigurðr).

As is true for the majority of heroes of ancient times, opinions differ on the youth of Siegfried, for myth and heroic legend have merged together to create a fascinating whole that is rich in themes and motifs from a wide variety of sources.

The *Þiðreks saga af Bern* is all the more interesting because it is a Norse translation of heroic continental Germanic material that has not otherwise survived the passage of time. In it, Sigurðr is the son of the King Sigmund and Sisibe; betrayed by the two noblemen Artvin and Hermann, the queen is taken to the Swabian forest to be executed, but, overtaken by remorse, Hermann turns his sword against his accomplice. At that moment the queen gives birth to a very handsome child. From the chest she carried, she pulls out a glass vessel, swaddles her newborn child, and places him inside it. She then closes it and sets it down next to her. The two knights continue dueling valiantly, but Artvin eventually falls to the ground next to the queen. His foot strikes the glass vessel holding the child and it rolls into the river. When the queen sees what has befallen her child, she loses consciousness and dies. This leaves us with the infant Sigurðr heading into an unknown future.

The glass vessel is carried down the river into the sea, where the tide deposits it on the shore. During this time the child had grown visibly larger. When the glass vessel strikes the beach it breaks, and the child begins crying. A doe approaches and picks up the child with her mouth. She brings him back to her resting place, where she has two fawns, and nurses him along with her own young. He stays with her for twelve months and is soon as strong and large as a four-year-old child.

This detail represents a fundamental part of the Indo-European mythic pattern for royal childhoods: every hero predestined to become a king must spend the beginning of his life in the wilds and form a bond with nature, because later he will have a symbiotic existence with it; for example, when the hero becomes sick, nature will likewise wither away. Here, through the doe's intervention, nature acknowledges his status as a future sovereign, and the supernatural character of this brief childhood is evident from Sigurðr's extremely rapid growth. He undergoes his first initiation in the natural world but now must return to the world of men. In the *Þiðreks saga* this is the point where the smith named Mimir becomes part of the story. (In the *Poetic Edda* version the smith is Reginn.) He gives the boy a name and calls him Sigurðr.

The boy grows up at Mimir's home until he is nine years old, at which point he is so large and strong that no one can equal him. His difficult nature and bullying of Mimir's apprentices at the forge make it so that none can tolerate him. Frightened, Mimir goes to see his brother Reginn, and they both plot to kill our hero. Mimir asks Sigurðr to go into the forest to make charcoal, and Sigurðr agrees. There, a large dragon approaches the hero; Sigurðr strikes it down and kills it.

In other sources there are variations regarding what happens to Mimir's dragon brother. In the *Poetic Edda,* Sigurðr follows the monster's trail, digs a ditch, and lies inside it with his sword extended. When the beast slithers over the ditch, the hero stabs him. The *Fáfnismál* reports the dialogue between Fáfnir and Sigurðr, in which Fáfnir says, "But I will tell you something true: the ringing gold, the glowing-red treasure, those rings will lead you to your death." And the poem closes with these words: "Sigurðr found a huge quantity of gold there, and he filled two chests with it. He took the helm of terror, the gold mail-coat, the sword Hrotti, and many other treasures."

After this Sigurðr cooks the dragon. When he thinks it is done, he dips his finger into the boiling cauldron, burns it, and sticks it into his mouth to cool it. Once the broth has touched his tongue and throat he hears two birds chatting in a tree and can understand all they are saying: "It would be better if this man knew what we know. He should go back and slay Mimir, his foster father, because he would be dead if everything had gone as Mimir had envisioned it. This dragon was Mimir's brother, and if he does not strike down Mimir, then Mimir will avenge his brother and slay him." Sigurðr then takes the dragon's blood and rubs it on his hands and then all over his body. Everywhere he touches, his skin becomes as hard as horn. He takes off his clothes and covers his whole body with the blood wherever he can reach, but it is impossible for him to touch between his shoulders. He puts his clothes back on and takes the road back home, carrying the dragon's head in his hand. The German texts explain that Siegfried's vulnerability is due to the fact that a linden leaf fell on the spot between his shoulders and prevented the hero from covering that spot with the blood. The Old Swedish *Didrikskrönikan* (The Chronicle of Dietrich) contains a version of the story that may be more faithful to the original than the German version with regard to the type of tree: "A maple leaf fell between his shoulders, and the blood did not cover his skin at this spot" (chap. 158).

Sigurðr returns to the forge, and all the apprentices flee at the sight of his arrival. Mimir alone stays to welcome Sigurðr back and gives him a helmet, a hauberk, and a shield. He also tells him of a splendid steed named Grani on Brynhildr's stud farm. He then gives Sigurðr the sword Gram ("Wrath"), which Sigurðr takes and uses to slay Mimir. He then goes to Brynhildr's castle, knocks down the gate, and kills its seven guards. Brynhildr learns of this and goes down to question Sigurðr. She reveals his true identity to him and gives him Grani.

In the *Völsunga saga* version Sigurðr spends a longer period of time with Brynhildr, who teaches him the secrets of the runes, which is a form of magic. In short, he goes through another initiation.

At this point in the story it would be appropriate to take a longer look at the treasure that will lead Siegfried to his death. Beyond what the *Völsunga saga* and certain lays from the *Poetic Edda* tell us, we know little about this treasure. In the *Nibelungenlied,* Siegfried stole it from the kings Schilbung and Nibelung. The *Völsunga saga* is much more detailed and basically relates the following (chap. 14).

The treasure belonged to the dwarf Andvari, who, in the form of a pike, lived in a waterfall that bore his name. One day when the gods Odin, Hœnir, and Loki were traveling, they came to the edge of this cascade, and Loki killed an otter. It so happens that this was Otr, the son of King Hreiðmar, a member of the race of giants. The gods stop at Hreiðmar's home for the night, and the king, when informed of the murder, demands compensation. Loki returns to the falls, captures Andvari, and demands that he give him the treasure he has in his keeping. Andvari does so but keeps one ring; Loki spots this and wrests it away from him. The dwarf then curses the treasure with these words: "This gold shall lead to the deaths of two brothers and to that of eight princes in war. No one shall enjoy my gold." The "two brothers" turn out to be Hreiðmar's other sons, Fáfnir and Mimir, and the "eight princes" are the family of the Burgundian kings and Sigurðr, along with the two children that Sigurðr's widow will bear for her second husband, Atli (Etzel in the continental German versions). Hreiðmar receives the treasure and refuses to share it with his sons, who then slay him while he sleeps. Fáfnir steals the treasure and changes into a dragon to guard over it. The despoiled Mimir takes up the trade of blacksmith.

Once Siegfried/Sigurðr gains possession of this gold, its destructive nature is made manifest: naively, the hero is ensnared into committing certain misdeeds, which ultimately lead to his death at the hands of the treacherous Hagen.

✦ *ANDVARI, ALBERICH, ATLI, BRYNHILDR, FÁFNIR, GRANI, GUÐRÚN, GURO RYSSEROVA, HAGEN, KUPERAN, MIMIR (MIME), NIBELUNGENLIED, NYBLING, REGINN*

📖 Batts, ed., *Das Nibelungenlied;* Boyer, *La Saga de Sigurdr ou la Parole donnée;* King, ed., *Das Lied vom Hürnen Seyfrid;* Lecouteux, *La Légende de Siegfried d'après le Seyfrid à la peau de corne et la Thidrekssaga;* Neckel, ed., *Edda;* Olsen, ed., *Völsunga saga ok Ragnars saga loðbrókar;* Lecouteux, "Der Nibelungenhort: Überlegungen zum mythischen Hintergrund," *Euphorion* 87 (1993): 172–86; Lecouteux, "Siegfrieds Jugend: Überlegungen zum mythischen Hintergrund," *Euphorion* 89 (1995): 221–26.

SIF: She is an Ásynja, mother of the god Ullr, and wife of Thor. Only one story speaks of her: "Loki . . . had done this out of mischief: he had cut off all Sif's hair. And when Thor found out, he caught Loki and was going to break every one of his bones in until he swore that he would get black-elves [dwarves] to make Sif a head of hair out of gold that would grow like any other hair" (Snorri, *Skáldskaparmál*, trans. Faulkes). Loki went to the dwarves Brokkr and Sindri, the sons of Ívaldi, who crafted the requested object. This is why "Sif's hair" is a kenning for gold.

✦ *ÆSIR*

SIGENOT: This giant is the uncle of Grim (✦ GRIM) and seeks to avenge the latter's death. He meets Dietrich von Bern, overcomes him, and carries him off under his arm. Hildebrand frees his master and kills Sigenot during a battle in which he cuts off his left hand and wounds his leg. The giant's weapon is an iron bar, twelve rods long.

SIGFAÐIR/SIGFÖÐR ("Father of Victory"): A byname of Odin that refers to his role as the master of battles. Other similarly compounded names given to him include Siggautr ("Victory-Goth") and Sigþrór ("Victory-Þrór").

📖 Falk, *Odensheiti.*

SIGRDRÍFA: Another name for the valkyrie Brynhildr.

✦ *VALKYRIE*

SIGRÚN ("Victory-rune"): Valkyrie, daughter of Högni and lover of Helgi Hundingsbani. She is reborn as Kára.

✦ *VALKYRIE*

SIGYN: Ásynja, wife of Loki.

✦ *ÆSIR*

SINDRI ("Smith"?): A dwarf, son of Ívaldi and brother of Brokkr. He is the one who forges the treasures of the gods.

✦ *DRAUPNIR, GULLINBORSTI, GUNGNIR, MJÖLLNIR*

SINTHGUNT: An unknown deity mentioned in the *Second Merseberg Charm*, which presents her as a sister of Sunna (who is most likely the sun; cf. German *Sonne*, fem.). Her name is formed from *sint*, "way, road, journey" and *gund*, "combat." This name is rather that of a valkyrie, a celestial and martial goddess summoned to travel across the sky in the company of Sunna. In the manuscript the name appears as Sinhtgunt.

✦ *VALKYRIE, MERSEBURG CHARMS*

📖 Beck, *Die Merseburger Zaubersprüche;* Jean-Paul Allard, "Du second Charme de Mersebourg au Viatique de Weingarten," *Études Indo-Européennes* 14 (1985): 33–53.

SJÖFN: Goddess who turns men's minds to love, therefore most likely a guardian deity of marriage or kinship.

SKAÐI: Eponymous goddess of Scandinavia, daughter of Þjazi, wife of Njörðr, and mother of Freyr. When Thor slew her father she took up arms and demanded reparation from the Æsir, who proposed that she choose a husband from among their number. Skaði, who secretly desired Baldr, had to choose by contemplating the feet of the gods sticking out from beneath a curtain, but it was Njörðr who had the most beautiful feet, and she married him. The marriage did not last, because Skaði yearned for the mountains and Njörðr loved the sea, and they separated. Skaði then wed Odin, with whom she had many children.

In skaldic poetry Skaði is called the "bright bride of the gods," the "ski-goddess" and the "ski-Dise." Although she is a goddess of the Dumézilian third function (fertility, fecundity), her name is declined as a masculine noun, which may be an indication of an ancient androgynous figure. Skaði embodies the frozen land of winter.

📖 Boyer, *La Grande Déesse du Nord,* 184–95; Schröder, *Skadi und die Götter Skandinaviens;* Margaret Clunies Ross, "Why Skaði Laughed: Comic Seriousness in an Old Norse Mythic Narrative," *Maal og Minne* (1989): 1–14.

SKÍÐBLAÐNIR: A wonderful ship owned by Freyr. It can be folded up after use to a size so small that the god can carry it in his pocket, and it will always have a favorable wind when the sail is raised. It is large enough to hold all the Æsir.

This ship is strangely reminiscent of the processional ship that can

254 SKILFINGR • SKRÝMIR

be taken apart and folded up and which the Finns still paraded during the summer solstice even into the nineteenth century. A passage from the *Chronicle of the Abbey of Saint Trond* (Limburg, Flanders) notes that in 1133 a processional boat was paraded from town to town. This also brings to mind the circumambulation of the goddess Nerthus mentioned by Tacitus, and it will be recalled that a ship is also the emblem of Nehalennia.

SKILFINGR: One of Odin's names. It connects this god to the line of the Scylfingas, the Anglo-Saxon name for the royal house of Sweden, the Ynglingar. According to Scandinavian traditions, however, this family is supposed to have descended from Yngvi-Freyr.

SKINFAXI ("Shining Horse"): The horse that carries in the day and belongs to Dagr ("Day," cf. German *Tag*).

SKÍRNIR ("Shining One"): A servant of Freyr who may also be a hypostasis of the god. He is known for carrying the god's marriage request to the giantess Gerðr.

SKOGSNUFVA, SKOGSJUNGFRU ("Lady/Maiden of the Forest"): A name that in Sweden designates a land spirit similar to the Roman fairy.

SKÖLL ("Mockery"): The name of the wolf that pursues the sun and will eventually devour it. It may be identical to Fenrir.

SKRATI ("Giant"): This Old Norse word can designate sorcerers as well as revenants and giants.
♦ *SCHRAT*

SKRÝMIR: Another name for the giant Útgarðaloki, who plays a role in the following story.
　　Thor and Loki are on the way to Jötunheimr. They find lodging in a large hall but are awoken in the middle of the night by an earthquake. They then find another room in which they spend the rest of the night. When leaving the next morning, they see Skrýmir, who tells them that they spent the night in his glove. He offers to accompany them and also carries all their provisions in a sack. That night they find

a place to stop, and Skrýmir goes to sleep. Thor is unable to undo the sack cord, becomes irate, and gives the giant a smack with his hammer. Skrýmir wakes up thinking that a leaf from a tree had landed on him. Thor strikes him two more times, but to no effect. That morning Skrýmir leaves Thor and Loki. When they reach Jötunheimr, they are told they must undergo some tests. Thor does not manage to empty Útgarðaloki's drinking horn in three swallows, cannot lift the giant's cat off the ground, and cannot defeat the wet nurse Elli. The next day Útgarðaloki informs Thor that he was the giant Skrýmir and then explains why the god failed the various tests: the sack cord was an iron string; the three hammer blows struck three hills and made deep valleys; one end of the drinking horn was placed in the ocean; the cat was the Midgard Serpent; and the wet nurse was age, which defeats all men. Having been deceived by the giant's enchantments, Thor seeks vengeance but Útgarðaloki and his dwelling suddenly vanish.

SKULD ("Future"): One of the three Norns, the Germanic Fates.

✦ *NORNS*

SLEIPNIR: Odin's horse. It is gray and has eight legs. It is the son of Loki, who had shapeshifted into a mare, and Svaðilfari, the stallion of the giant who built Ásgarðr. Sleipnir's descendant is Grani, Sigurðr's (Siegfried's) horse.

Fig. 78. A picture stone depicting (on top) a dead warrior arriving at Valhalla riding Sleipnir, Odin's steed. A valkyrie is welcoming him and offering him drink. Historiated stone of Tjängvide on the island of Gotland, Sweden, eighth century.

Fig. 79. Sleipnir. Illustration by Ólafur Brynjúlfsson, *Snorra Edda*, 1760.

Sleipnir is frequently mentioned in the myths. Hermóðr rides him when he goes to Hel in his attempt to bring Baldr back from the underworld; this is a reference to Sleipnir's role as a psychopomp and its connections with the dead. Sleipnir is depicted on eighth-century Gotlandic picture stones (Tjängvide and Ardre), where he is easily recognizable by his eight legs.

📖 Dumézil, *Loki*, 27–30.

SLÍÐR ("Dangerous"): One of the rivers of the underworld; its waters carry weapons. An image of a similar river can be found in a twelfth-century Christian visionary text, the *Visio Godeschalci*.

SLÍÐRUGTANNI: ✦ GULLINBORSTI

SMITHS: The Norse and Germanic lands have known three great mythical smiths: Mime (Mimir), Hertrich, and Wayland (Wieland, Völundr, Velent). Here is how they are depicted in lines 125–78 of *Biterolf und Dietleib,* an anonymous Middle High German epic poem written between 1254 and 1260.

In a book I heard it said
that three swords were forged
by a fine master smith
who avidly applied
both thought and craft
that their like was not to be found in other lands
for he was quite clever
more than any other [smith] during this time.
He lived in Azzaria
twenty miles from Toledo.
His name I'll tell to you,
he is called Myme the Old.
His art cut down more than one [warrior],
who otherwise would likely have lived much longer
and instead found his death
because of the sword's power.
I can name no other man
in all the princes' realms
whose mastery compares to his
except for one whose name I shall give you
so that his worth in this matter be known:
he was named Hertrich
and lived in Gascony.
By their great wisdom
they joined company in their work and in all things

so that they could truly achieve
what had eluded them singly.
What powerful knowledge has been attributed
to Wieland.
He forged a sword that Witege
the intrepid warrior carried
and a very fine helmet
called Lymme;
he also forged all the armor
that went with the sword.
Witege carried it shamelessly
he, the honorable companion.
He [Wieland] had it forged for his child, the best that
        he could—
and he did not feel at all
that he had been praised as highly
in this matter
as Myme and Hertrich;
their art was very different,
as I am about to teach you:
There were twelve swords
forged by these two men
as I have made known to you;
Wieland forged the thirteenth
which was called Mimung.

✦ MIMIR/MIME, REGINN, WAYLAND, WITEGE

📖 Schnyder, ed., *Biterolf und Dietleib.*

SNÆR/SNJÓR ("Snow"): Legendary king of Norway, son of Frosti ("Ice"), son of Kari ("Wind," "Gust"), and the last descendant of Fornjótr ("Old Giant"?). What we have here is most likely a genealogy of frost giants (*hrímþursar*).

SNAKKUR: ✦ TILBERI

SÖKKVABEKKR ("Sunken Bank" or "Hall"): This is Sága's dwelling in Ásgarðr.

SÓL ("Sun"): This goddess, presented as an Ásynja, is the personification of the sun.

According to Snorri Sturluson:

There was a person whose name was Mundilfari who had two children. They were so fair and beautiful that he called the one Máni [Moon] and his daughter Sól [Sun], and gave her in marriage to a person called Glenr. But the gods got angry at this arrogance and took the brother and sister and set them up in the sky; they made Sól drive the horses that drew the chariot of the sun which the gods had created, to illuminate the worlds, out of the molten particle that had flown out of the world of Muspell. The names of these horses are Arvakr ["Early Riser"] and Alsviðr ["Most Rapid"]. Under the shoulders of the horses the gods placed two bellows to cool them. (*Gylfaginning*, trans. Faulkes)

Sól is pursued by the wolf Sköll, who wants to devour her, which will happen during Ragnarök.

A solar chariot has been discovered in Trundholm, Denmark, that dates from 1200 BCE and is evidence of sun worship. The weekday name Sunday (cf. Old Norse *sunnudagr* and German *Sonntag*) refers to

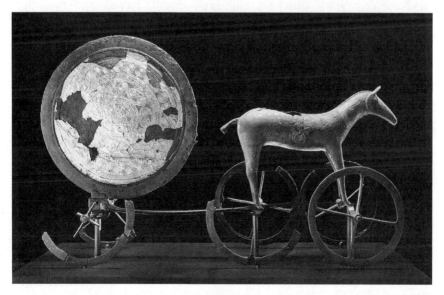

Fig. 80. Sól

a deity called Sunna (Sun), mentioned in the *Second Merseburg Charm*. Furthermore, there are numerous place-names coined from Sól. Sól appears fairly briefly in the myth of the building of Ásgarðr: the giant builder demands Freyja, Sól, and Máni as payment for his work but does not get them.

SÓLBLINDI ("Blinded by Sunlight"): Dwarf whose three sons forged Þrymgjöll, the iron gate that seals the hall of Menglöð. His name is an allusion to the fact that dwarves cannot tolerate sunlight because it turns them to stone.

SÓN: One of three containers holding the wondrous mead made from the blood of Kvasir.

SONNTAGSKIND ("Sunday's Child"): A child is given this designation when it is born before or during Sunday mass, or between the two ringings of the bells that announce it, or during the consecration, or between eleven o'clock and noon, or between noon and one o'clock, or the night of Saturday into Sunday, or on Sunday into Monday, between midnight and one o'clock. It is also a child born on Sunday and baptized on a Friday, or a holy day (Nativity, the Twelve Days, First Day of the New Year, Saint John's Day). This child will succeed in every undertaking, and all of his or her dreams will come true. A *Sonntagskind* will be beautiful and will become rich because he or she can see hidden treasures and find them. Such a child is a seer who foresees death, sees spirits, and sees dwarves even when these latter are wearing cloaks of invisibility; he or she can recognize witches, cannot be bewitched, and possesses magical power. This child can banish spirits, free tormented souls, stop hemorrhages, calm the wind, and halt fire. He or she will die of old age. In France such a child is said to be born lucky.

📖 Pohl, *Die Volkssagen Ostpreussens,* 209.

SOUL: ✦ FYLGJA, HAMR

SPRINGS: Throughout the medieval West, worship of springs was highly developed both among the Celts and the Germans. Evidence for this is provided by archaeology as well as by the ecclesiastical literature that anathematized it and replaced the deities of the springs with saints. The Norse mythology tells us of various springs and wells: the Well of Urðr; the Well of Mímir; and the spring called Hvergelmir, which gives birth to the rivers. Perhaps springs should be compared to the sacrificial bogs (*blótkelda*) in which human victims were drowned. A huge number of texts speak of the worship given to springs and the offerings made to them. Such offerings were intended to obtain the protection or neutrality of the numinous being that was believed to reside at or within the spring.

SPRENGWURZEL ("Spring Root"): A plant with the virtue of being able to open everything that is shut. It is first mentioned in classical antiquity. Humans discovered it through observation of the behavior of a bird, the woodpecker (whose other name is "locksmith") or the hoopoe. In German folk belief the same properties were ascribed to the fern and primrose (*Schlüsselblume:* "Key-flower"). The *Sprengwurzel* removes the hobbles from horses, opens rocks hiding a treasure, and also confers invulnerability. Several writers make reference to these beliefs, such as Hans Jakob Christoffel von Grimmelshausen in *Das wunderbarlich Volgelnest* (The Enchanted Bird's Nest, 1672) and Clemens Brentano in his drama *Die Gründung Prags* (The Founding of Prague, 1815).

   📖 Rosinus Lentilius, "De radice effractoria vel apertoria, vulgo Spreng-Wurzel," *Miscellanea Acad. Nat. Curiosa* VII–VIII (1699–1700): 144–52.

STAKE: A protective measure against suspect dead individuals (✦ DRAUGR). In his *Decretum,* written between 1012 and 1023, Bishop Burchard of Worms makes an allusion to impalement: "If a very young infant dies before being baptized, these women take its corpse to a secret place and stab its body through with a staff, saying that if they did not do this, the child would return and cause people great harm." The same would be done to a woman who died in childbirth. A superimposition of Christian and pagan elements is evident in the *Eiríks saga rauða* (Saga of Erik the Red) with regard to impalement. A woman has just died, and the anonymous saga author notes (chap. 6): "It was customary in Greenland, since the introduction of Christianity, to bury the people of the farm where they died in unconsecrated earth. A stake was then stabbed through the dead individual's chest, and when the clergy arrived, it would be removed, holy water thrown into the grave, and a large funeral service would be held there." This custom clearly reflects the fear of revenants and the undead. Holy water replaces the stake, and consecrated earth is supposed to form an obstacle to the demons that slip into the corpses and animate them. Until 1824 it was still common in England for a stake to be planted in the chest of a suicide whose grave would be dug at a crossroads.

STALLO ("He Who Is Clad in Steel"): A cruel, cannibalistic giant of Lappland (Sámi) belief, often depicted as naive and stupid. He travels about during Christmas in a sleigh drawn by lemmings or mice, wearing elegant garments or an iron cloak, and he can make himself invisible. A reserve of water is prepared for him near campsites; otherwise he will suck the blood of children to quench his thirst. Whoever can defeat Stallo will become rich by taking possession of his remains.

In southern Norway he leads the Christmas processions that bear his name (*Ståleferdi*). Numerous place-names attest to the distribution of this belief.

Stallo owns a dog named Rakkas ("Doggy"), or Shieka, who guards his money. Whoever kills Stallo must also kill his dog; otherwise he will lick his master's blood and restore him to life.

Stallo's wife is named Luttak ("Stink Bug"); she has an iron tube she uses to suck the blood out of living creatures. She can be killed by forcing her to swallow live coals.

📖 Bø, Grambo & Hodne, *Norske Segner,* no. 65; Mériot, *Les Lapons et leur société;* Rolf Kjellström, "Ven var egentligen Stallo?" *Rig* 58 (1975): 113–15; G. Sandberg, "Om lappernes tro paa 'Stallo' i vore dage," *Folkevennen* (1879): 345–70; Rolf Kjellström, "Är traditionerna om Stalo historiskt grundade?" in *Nordisk Folktro: Studier tillägnade Carl-Herman Tillhagen,* ed. Bengt af Klintberg, Reimund Kvideland, and Magne Velure (Stockholm: Nordiska museet, 1976), 155–78.

STAMPA, GSTAMPA, STAMPE: The Stampa is a bogeyman of the Tyrol and southern Bavaria, a close relative to the Percht. She appears on the night of Epiphany and leads a troop of dead children. She carries a chain that can be heard clanking from a great distance away. Sometimes she is invisible, and her terrible whistles and moans can be heard during the Twelve Nights. She abducts children and women in labor. She sometimes has a horse's head, or else she has a human face with a very long nose. Holy water will neutralize her. Food offerings are left for her on windows on the night of Epiphany to ensure that she remains in a good mood. According to her name, which derives from a verb meaning "to stamp, trample" (*stampfen*), the Stampa is one of the oppressively heavy spirits (*appesarts*).

📖 Heyl, *Volkssagen, Meinungen und Bräuche aus Tirol,* 165, 429; Zingerle, *Sagen aus Tirol,* 26–28.

STARKAÐR: A monstrous giant equipped with four pairs of arms. He abducted a maiden, whose father turned to Thor for assistance. The god slew the abductor and brought the young woman back home. Pregnant, she gave birth to a handsome boy with black hair and extraordinary strength. He was named Stórvikr. He married a princess of Hålogaland, and together they had a son that they named, in accordance with custom, after his grandfather, Starkaðr.

STARKAÐR (Latin *Starcatherus*): Son of Stórvikr. King Haraldr of Agðir killed his father and reared him at the same time as his son Víkarr. Herþjófr, king of Hördaland, killed Haraldr and took the children as booty. He entrusted them to a certain Grani (in fact, Odin in disguise), who raised them on the island of Fenhring. Starkaðr grew large and strong and helped Víkarr win back his kingdom, but Odin had decided that Víkarr should be sacrificed and that Starkaðr should be the one to do it. One night Grani brought the hero to a clearing where eleven people were sitting on high seats, and one seat remained empty.

Grani, who revealed his identity as Odin, took the remaining high seat and opened the meeting. Its subject was to settle Starkaðr's fate. Thor and Odin took opposite sides. For every harmful fate bestowed by Thor, Odin responded with a beneficial one. Starkaðr would have no children, but he would have three lives. He would commit a crime in each of them, but he would own the best weapons and clothes. He would own no land or estate, but he would have movable goods. He would never feel that he had enough, but he would enjoy success and victory in all battles. He would be gravely wounded in each battle, but he would have the gift of poetry and improvisation. He would forget everything he composed, but he would enjoy the favor of the nobles

Fig. 81. Starkaðr. Olaus
Magnus, *Historia de gentibus
septentrionalibus*, Rome, 1555.

and the great. Thor had the last word: Starkaðr would be despised by
the common folk. The hero's fate followed its ordained course: Starkaðr
commits three crimes, and so forth.

Underlying this myth Georges Dumézil found an Indo-European
archetype that is very visible in the *Mahabharata* where Śiśupāla is also
the stakes in a contest of the gods.

📖 Dumézil, *The Stakes of the Warrior*.

STONES, WORSHIP AND USE: Evidence for the worship of
stones can be found throughout Europe and many details about these
practices are supplied by ecclesiastical writs, texts, canons, decrees, and
penitentials. Between 443 and 452 the Council of Arles (cap. 23) condemned those who worshipped stones; in 506 the Council of Agde forbade the swearing of oaths on stones; and in 567 the Council of Tours
(cap. 23) condemned those who performed actions near stones that
were incompatible with the laws of the church. The Synod of Toledo
(cap. 11) mentioned stone worshippers in 681, and Charlemagne's
Admonitio Generalis (cap. 65) of 789 informs us that fires were lit and
certain practices took place around stones. In tenth-century England

the *Law of the Northumbrian Priests* (cap. 54) condemned those who gathered around stones. The acts of the Council of Agde indicate that a stone (or stones) was being used as an altar, "as if some deity resided within it." During the Middle Ages these deities became dwarves, elves, and spirits. Clear evidence for this is supplied by the *Kristni saga* (Saga of Icelandic Christianity; chap. 2): "In Gilja stood a stone to which Kodran's parents had made their sacrifices and in which, they claimed, their guardian spirit dwelt." And in the *Þorvalds þáttr víðförla* (Tale of Thorvald the Far-traveled), which gives us a variation on the same theme, the spirit is called "seer" (*spámaðr*), undoubtedly because it can predict the future.

Stones played a role in ancient law that is often overlooked. Charters from the year 1225 tell us that judges sat near a stone or sat on stones, as did the accused. In medieval Sweden there would be three, seven, or twelve such stones. In the Eddic poem *Helgakviða Hundingsbana* II (Second Lay of Helgi Hundingsbane, str. 31), we have the "stone of Unn," by which Dag swore the oaths he later betrayed. The *Hænsna-Þóris saga* (Saga of Hen-Thorir) includes a scene in which Hersteinn swears an oath in the following way: "He made his way to where stood a certain stone, set his foot upon the stone, and spoke: 'I solemnly swear that before the Althing is over I shall have had Arngrim the priest (*goði*) banished utterly.'" We should probably view this custom as similar to that of royal coronation: when a new king was being crowned, he climbed atop a stone to be consecrated and acclaimed. A stone of this sort was called Mora in Sweden and Danaerygh in Denmark, and strophe 10 of the Eddic poem *Hlöðskviða* (Lay of Hlöðr) also seems to allude to the custom. In an ordeal by water a stone had to be plucked from a cauldron of boiling water, as the *Grágás* (chap. 55), a collection of early Icelandic laws, informs us, and the *Poetic Edda* tells how Guðrún exonerated herself of an unjust accusation this way: "She plunged her white hand to the bottom [of the cauldron] / and took hold there of the precious stones." In Old Norse this was called *taka í ketil*, "to take from the cauldron." Adulterers carried stones, Olaus Magnus informs us, and medieval Scandinavian common law included a provision that is worth citing, if only for its burlesque nature: "If a married woman commits a lustful act with a married man, they should pay a fine. . . . If the man does not pay, a string shall be tied to his penis and the woman will tie it to the communal stone, and then lead her lover throughout the town."

One form of execution involved dropping a huge stone, typically a millstone, on a person's head. The Swedes executed the Icelander Ref in this way. Saxo Grammaticus tells us: "They resorted to villainy and got rid of him while he slept by crushing him with a rock; what they did was suspend a millstone high up and later cut the ropes so that it fell on his neck as he lay beneath" (*The History of the Danes*, VIII, 16, trans. Fisher). In his *Skáldskaparmál* (Treatise on the Skaldic Art, chap. 2), Snorri Sturluson relates that when the wife of the giant Gilling was mourning the death of her husband, whom they had slain, the dwarves Fjalarr and Galarr killed her: "Fjalarr then told his brother to climb above the doorway when she was going out, and to drop a millstone on her head, because he was tired of her wailing." The execution of sorcerers seems to have been handled in a particular way: according to the *Saga of King Olaf Tryggvason* (chap. 63), which Snorri Sturluson wrote around 1230 as part of his Norwegian royal history *Heimskringla,* they were transported to a large rock that would be submerged under water at high tide. This is what happened to a certain Eyvindr, and from that point on the rock was known as Skrattasker, "Sorcerers' Skerry." The same author provides us with another interesting bit of information at the conclusion of the aforementioned story of Gilling: Suttung, the son of Gilling, captured the dwarves Fjalarr and Galarr and placed them on a skerry that would be covered at high tide; he spared their lives, however, in exchange for the wondrous mead made from the blood of Kvasir.

A stone also played a role in suicides. The *Gautreks saga* features a huge rock called *Ætternisstapi,* which means "Family Rock," located at the top of Gilling Cliff (*Gillingshamarr*): "It is so high that no one who ever falls from it can survive. It is called 'Family Rock' because we use it to reduce the size of our family . . . All our parents die there and go back to Odin." The saga states explicitly that those who choose this death go to Valhalla. A later version of the *Landnámabók* (Book of the Settlement of Iceland), the *Skarðsárbók,* indicates that during a famine the elderly and indigent would be slain by hurling them from the tops of giant boulders.

There are also magical stones. In *Kormáks saga* (chap. 12), Bersi owns a "life-stone" (*lífsteinn*) that he wears in a pouch around his neck; it allows him to win a swimming contest. The *Þiðreks saga af Bern* (Saga of Dietrich von Bern) mentions a "victory stone" (*sigrsteinn*).

We may conclude by mentioning the number of personal names that have been coined in the Norse and Germanic countries from the word *stein* ("stone") since the Frankish period. In Iceland there are sixteen men's names and two women's names of this sort; examples include Steinbjörn, Steinþór, and Steinhildr. In Germany we can find seven names before the year 1000.

📖 Lecouteux, "La face cachée des pierres," in *La pierre dans le monde médiéval,* eds. Claude Thomasset & Danièle James-Raoul (Paris: P.U.P.S., 2010), 133–61.

STRÄGELE, STRÄGGELE: A mythical creature of the Swiss Alps. The *Strägele* is an ugly woman who abducts and devours spinners who have worked on the third Saturday of Advent or during the Ember Days, or who have otherwise neglected their work. This being is also called *Strunze.*

📖 Grimm, *Deutsche Sagen,* no. 269; Vernaleken, *Alpensagen,* 56–58.

STRZYGON (masc.; pl. *Strzygonie*): Evil spirits or half-demons, the *Strzygonie* appear most often near churches. They hold their heads under their arms or else in its place and wear white shirts. It is believed that they turn into pitch when the bells are rung. In the town of Oświęcim (Auschwitz) their origin is explained in the following way. When God banished the rebel angels from heaven some fell into the water and others landed on solid ground. The first group became mer-creatures, the second became the Strzygonie, or headless men; those who fell down to hell became devils.

📖 Vernaleken, *Mythen und Bräuche des Volkes in Österreich,* 358–59.

SUÐRI ("South"): One of the four dwarves at the four cardinal points who hold up the vault of the sky created from the primordial giant Ymir's skull. It should be noted that in Old Norse the word *dvergr,* "dwarf," can also mean "pillar, beam."

✦ *AUSTRI, COSMOGONY, NORÐRI, VESTRI*

SUNNA: Deity mentioned in the *Second Merseberg Charm.* She is certainly a personification of the sun. Her name can be found in the Germanic names for Sunday such as the Old Norse *sunnudagr* and the German *Sonntag.*

SURTR ("The Dark One"): He is one of the three giants that orchestrate the end of the world. He is the guardian of Muspell. Surtr and Freyr kill each other in the eschatological battle. "Surtr's Fire" designates the conflagration that ravages the world during Ragnarök.

As an anecdote we may note the name the Icelandic people gave to the new islet that was created off their southern coast as a result of a volcanic eruption in 1963: Surtsey, "Surtr's Island."

📖 Bertha Phillpotts, "Surt," *Arkiv för nordisk filologi* 21 (1905): 14–30.

SUTTUNGR: A giant who obtained the mead made from Kvasir's blood as compensation for the murder of his father, Gillingr. He entrusted it to the keeping of his daughter Gunnlöð inside the mountain Hnitbjörg. When Odin snuck in, stole the brew, and made off with it in the shape of an eagle, Suttungr likewise transformed himself into an eagle and flew off in pursuit, but he was unable to catch the god.

SVAÐILFARI: The stallion that belonged to the giant who built Ásgarðr. It mated with Loki when the latter had transformed himself into a mare, and thus became the father of Sleipnir, Odin's horse.

SVÁFNIR: One of the serpents that lives beneath Yggdrasill, the cosmic tree.

SVANHILDR (Latin *Suanilda*): Sister of Guðrún, Hamðir (Ammius), and Sörli (Sarus) in the *Hamðismál* (Lay of Hamðir), one of the oldest poems in the *Edda*. Guðrún incites her brothers to avenge the death of Svanhildr, whom King Jörmunrekkr (Ermanaric) had killed by having her trampled by horses. Her brothers died in their attempt. Jordanes, the Gothic historian, was the first author to relate this legend (*Getica,* chapter XXIV).

> Now although Ermanaric, king of the Goths, was the conqueror of many tribes . . . while he was deliberating on this invasion of the Huns, the treacherous tribe of the Rosomoni, who at that time were among those who owed him their homage, took this chance to catch him unawares. For when the king had given orders that a certain woman of the tribe I have mentioned, Sunhilda by name, should be bound to wild horses and torn apart by driving them at full speed in

opposite directions (for he was roused to fury by her husband's treachery to him), her brothers Sarus and Ammius came to avenge their sister's death and plunged a sword into Ermanaric's side. Enfeebled by this blow, he dragged out a miserable existence in bodily weakness. Balamber, king of the Huns, took advantage of his ill health, to move an army into the country of the Ostrogoths . . . (trans. Mierow)

The *Guðrúnarhvöt* (Guðrún's Incitement), a poem from the *Poetic Edda,* spells out the beginning of the story. King Jörmunrekkr has wed Svanhildr, the daughter of Guðrún and Sigurðr. The counsellor Bikki suggests to the king's son, Randvér, that he take Svanhildr as his mistress, and then Bikki denounces the lovers to the king. Jörmunrekkr has Randvér hung and Svanhildr crushed beneath a horse's hooves. A shield decorated with several legendary scenes is mentioned in the poem *Ragnarsdrápa* by the skald Bragi Boddason. One of these scenes was the story of Jörmunrekkr. According to Bragi, the attack took place at night.

Snorri Sturluson's *Prose Edda* echoes the tradition of the surprise attack, but adds several further details. Jörmunrekkr sends Randvér as his envoy to ask Svanhildr's father, Jónakr, for the hand of his daughter in marriage, and it is during the journey that Bikki offers his ill counsel to the young man. Later, before he dies, Randvér plucks the feathers from his falcon and has the bird delivered to his father, thereby signifying that the king, by executing his own son and only heir, is dooming his kingdom to impotence. In the grip of rage King Jörmunrekkr slays his wife: returning from the hunt following the death of his son, he finds her washing her hair in the river and charges at her with his entire retinue. She is trampled to death by the hooves of their horses.

The *Völsunga saga* (Saga of the Völsungs) tells a similar story: after the incident with the plucked falcon, the king wishes to pardon Randvér but Bikki has already carried out his sentence. As for Svanhildr, she is legally convicted before being executed. The armor of the brothers seems as if it is almost endowed with magical powers. Finally, it is Odin and not the king who demands that Svanhildr's two brothers be stoned to death.

In Saxo Grammaticus's version the young prince (Broderus) is spared, and the hatred of the courtier has a motivation: the king had put his brothers to death earlier. Suanhilda has four brothers. Saxo leaves the figure of Erpr out of the story entirely. Finally, the invulnerability of the brothers is explicitly the result of the use of magic and spells, because a witch named Guthruna gives them assistance. The name of Suanhilda's mother has become that of the sorceress.

Several accounts attest to the existence of this legend not only in Scandinavia but also in Germany, where it was scarcely developed. The *Annals of Quedlinburg* report the attack of Hernido, Serilo, and Adaocaro against Ermanaric, who had killed their father. Ekkehard of Aura's version of the *Chronicon universale* places the reign of Ermanaric during the era of the Emperors Valentinian and Valens and tells of the mortal wound that the brothers Sarus and Ammius inflicted on the king.

✦ *HARLUNGEN*

📖 Zink, *Les Légendes héroïques de Dietrich et d'Ermrich dans les littératures germaniques,* 169–89.

SVANHVÍT: ✦ HLAÐGUÐR SVANHVÍT

SVARTHÖFÐI ("Black-head"): Giant described as the ancestor of all sorcerers who practice *seiðr.*

SVÁVA: Valkyrie, daughter of King Eylimi. She is the one who gave a name to Helgi, the son of Hjörvarðr, and later married him. It is said that both of them were reincarnated.

✦ *VALKYRIE*

SVÖL: Name of the shield placed in front of the sun that prevents its rays from burning the Earth.

SWAN KNIGHT: Wagner popularized this figure under the name of Lohengrin, and his legend is well known. There are several different versions in France, Germany, and the Netherlands. Wolfram von Eschenbach was the first to recount the Loherangrin (Lohengrin) legend at the end of his *Parzival,* written around 1210, as follows. The Duchess of Brabant is the target of the attacks of an unwanted suitor. One day an unknown knight arrives in a gondola drawn by a swan. He becomes her champion, then marries her after having her swear an oath to never ask where he came from. They have children. The duchess

Fig. 82. The Swan Knight arrives in Nijmegen. Editions Copland, 1509.

breaks her oath; the swan returns for the knight, who vanishes, leaving a sword, a horn, and a ring to his sons.

In all likelihood the swan knight is the hypostasis of a Germanic god of the Dumézilian third function, probably Freyr, an agrarian deity, although the swan also connects him to Njörðr (to whom this bird is sacred) and and to Freyja (who also has an association with birds due to her magical feather-cloak). The swan knight also seems to be linked in some way to the Anglo-Saxon figure of Sceaf.

📖 Lecouteux, *Mélusine et le Chevalier au Cygne*. Lecouteux, "Zur Entstehung der Schwanrittersage," *Zeitschrift für deutsches Altertum* 107 (1978): 18–34.

SWAN MAIDEN: They almost always appear in threes, as in the legend of Völundr (Wayland the Smith). Commonly confused for valkyries, they are actually members of Freyja's domain and seem to act as her emissaries. They take off their swan plumage when they want to bathe, and if someone manages to steal it, he can force them to remain among humankind and marry him. They make a brief appearance in the *Nibelungenlied* when Hagen steals their plumage and forces them to reveal the future to him. The romance *Friedrich von Schwaben* (fourteenth century) exploits this motif, but in this case the otherworldly beings take the form of pigeons. The Celts and the Germans share this myth, and clearly legible traces of it can be found in the Old French lays of the twelfth and thirteenth centuries. It appears, for example, in *Graelent* and *Désiré*, as well as in a Celtic legend of the birth of Conchobar, which recounts the deeds of the legendary king of Ulster.

📖 Holmström, *Studier over svanjungfrumotivet i Volundarkvida och annorstädes;* Ann C. Burson, "Swan Maidens and Smiths: A Structural Study of the *Völundarkviða,*" *Scandinavian Studies* 55 (1983): 1–19; Arthur Thomas Hatto, "The Swan Maiden: A Folk Tale of North Eurasian Origin?" *Bulletin of the School of Oriental and African Studies* 24 (1961): 326–52.

SWANTOWIT ("Powerful Lord"): God of war and fertility for the Rugians. The worship of this god took place at the northernmost point of the island of Rügen, at Arkona in a wooden temple with a carved exterior. Two walls surrounded the building, and there was only a single entrance. Inside stood an enormous statue with four heads: two looked ahead, and two looked back; one turned to the left and the other to the right. In his right hand the god held a drinking horn made of precious metals, which the priest filled each year with mead in order to predict the harvest of the coming year. His left hand rested on his hip. The god wore a robe that fell to his calves. Beside the statue were the bit, saddle, sword of the god, and a pile of slaughtered wild beasts. The statue was destroyed in 1168, and the worship of Swantowit was abolished by the Christians.

Swantowit owned three hundred horses, of which one was particularly sacred: no one could mount it or touch its mane or tail, because the god was supposed to ride it at night against the enemies of the country. This horse was also used to predict the outcome of military campaigns.

📖 Kantzow, *Pomerania*, I, 161–73; Micraelius, *Antiquitates Pomeraniae*, I, 163; II, 30; Saxo Grammaticus, *Gesta Danorum* XIV, 39, 1–10.

SYN ("Protest"): Guardian goddess of doors. We know nothing about her. Among the Romans, several deities were assigned to the protection of doors, such as Forculus and Forcula, and Limentius and Limentina.

SÝR ("Sow"): A byname of Freyja. It may be an allusion to the worship that was given to her: because a boar was sacrificed to the god Freyr, it seems likely that a sow would be sacrificed to Freyja.

TANGIE: The name of a horselike monster in the Shetlands that lives in the depths of the ocean. Tides or storms inspire it to haunt the rocky coasts or sandy beaches in search of a maiden to abduct and wed.

📖 Jean Renaud, "Le peuple surnaturel des Shetland," *Artus* 21–22 (1986): 28–32.

TANNHÄUSER: The name of a troubadour who was active between 1228 and 1265. The legend that grew around him says the following. Tannhäuser was a German knight who after many long journeys came to the home of Lady Venus in Hörselberg. He stayed there awhile, surrounded by beautiful women, but his conscience began gnawing at him and he asked to take his leave. Lady Venus did all she could to keep him there, even offering him one of her companions as a wife. Tannhäuser responded that he did not wish to be damned for all eternity and left. He went to Rome to ask the pope for forgiveness. The pope gave him a staff and told him, "When this turns green again, your sins will be forgiven." In despair, Tannhauser returned to the company of Lady Venus. The staff eventually flowered, but it was too late, and the knight will remain in the mountain until Final Judgment.

The first attestation of this legend is in 1515. Ludwig Tieck made an adaptation of it in 1800, and many other writers followed his example, including Heinrich Heine in 1836. In 1845, Richard Wagner wrote an opera that combined this legend with that of the minstrel singing contest of Wartburg.

📖 Grimm, *Deutsche Sagen,* no. 170; J. M. Clifton-Everest, *The Tragedy of Knighthood. Origins of the Tannhäuser-legend.*

TATZELWURM: Still called *Beißwurm* ("biting dragon") and *Stollenwurm* ("dragon of the mine tunnels"), the *Tatzelwurm* is a dragon with two feet, a large head that is around eighteen inches, and a lizard's body. It can stand up on its feet, and it has poisonous breath. It has a piercing gaze and makes earsplitting shrieks. It chiefly resides in the Alps, and the descriptions of it vary from one region to the next.

📖 Joseph Freiherr von Doblhoff, "Altes und Neues vom 'Tatzelwurm,'" *Zeitschrift für österreichische Volkskunde* 1, 5–6 (1895): 142–66; Doblhoff, "Zur Sage vom Tatzelwurm," *Zeitschrift für österreichische Volkskunde* 1, 8–9 (1895): 261–65.

TELL, WILLIAM: The name of William Tell first appears around 1470 in a chronicle relating the birth of the alliance of the people of the mountainous Waldstätten region (Uri, Schwyz, Obwald, and Nidwald). The historical elements of this period became blended with legend. One day Tell refused to doff his hat to Gessler, a bailiff working for the Hapsburgs, beneath the Altdorf linden tree. The magistrate

Fig. 83. William Tell. Illustration by Heinrich Vogeler.

ordered him to shoot an apple off his son's head with a crossbow arrow. This episode has been attached to Tell's story and is reflective of a very ancient motif, that of the master shot, which appears earlier in the thirteenth-century work of Saxo Grammaticus, in the *Þiðreks saga af Bern* (Saga of Dietrich von Bern), and in the legend of Wayland the Smith. It can be seen in Friedrich Schiller's 1804 play *Wilhelm Tell* (Act III, 3; IV, 1 and 3).

📖 Helmut de Boor, "Die nordischen, englischen und deutschen Darstellungen des Apfelschußmotivs: Texte und Übersetzungen mit einer Abhandlung," in *Quellenwerk zur Entstehung der schweizerischen Eidgenossenschaft* 3/1, ed. Hans Georg Wirz (Aarau: Sauerländer, 1947), appendix, 1–53; Hans-Peter Naumann, "Tell und die nordische Überlieferung: Zur Frage nach dem Archetypus vom Meisterschützen," *Schweizerisches Archiv für Volkskunde* 71 (1975): 108–28; variants originating in Bavaria and in Schleswig-Holstein can be found in Petzold, *Historische Sagen*, vol. I, 442ff.

THEUTANUS: Eponymous ancestor of the Teutons. Around 1240, Thomas of Cantimpré (*De Natura rerum*, III, 5, 40) recounts how his body was discovered on the banks of the Danube near Vienna. He measured ninety-five cubits (around 144 feet!), and his teeth were huge, larger than a palm leaf.

ÞJÁLFI: Companion and manservant of Thor. He entered into the god's service to make up for some harm he caused: he had maimed one of the god's goats out of ignorance and gluttony. He helped Thor in his battle against Hrungnir and slew Mökkurkálfi, the clay giant.

ÞJAZI: This giant is the father of Skaði, Njörðr's wife. He is involved in the following story.

Odin, Loki, and Hœnir were traveling and had run short of food. They saw a herd of oxen in a valley and killed one. They tried to cook it to no avail, and they were wondering why.

They then heard a voice from the oak tree above them saying that he was the reason the meat would not cook. They looked up and saw an eagle, which continued, "If you will let me eat my fill of that ox, I will make it so that the oven will cook."

The three Æsir accepted, but the eagle took both hams and both

Fig. 84. Þjazi. Illustration by Ólafur Brynjúlfsson, *Snorra Edda,* 1760.

shoulders of the ox. Loki grew angry and struck a violent blow with
a long pole at the eagle, and it began to fly off. But the pole remained
stuck to the eagle's back, and Loki's hands were stuck to his end of it.
Loki begged the eagle for a truce; the eagle accepted on the condition
that Loki promise to bring Iðunn and her apples of rejunvenation out
of Ásgarðr. Loki accepted, and a little later he lured Iðunn into a forest. Þjazi, still in the form of an eagle, carried her off and took her to
Thrymheimr.

Deprived of Iðunn's apples, the Æsir began to age, and when they
discovered Loki's misdeed they threatened to kill him. With the help of
Freyja's falcon cloak, Loki then flew to Jötunheimr and arrived at the
home of Þjazi, who was away. He changed Iðunn into a walnut, picked
her up in his claws, and flew back to Ásgarðr as fast as he could. On
his return the giant discovered the absence of his prisoner, assumed his
eagle form, and launched himself in pursuit of her abductor. Seeing Loki
arrive with Þjazi right at his heels, the Æsir built a fire that burned the
eagle's feathers. The giant fell to the ground, and the Æsir killed him.

The rest of the story tells how Skaði obtained compensation for this killing. Odin, among other things, cast Þjazi's eyes into the sky where they became stars.

📖 Eugen Mogk, "Þjazi," in *Reallexikon der germanischen Altertumskunde,* ed. Johannes Hoops, 1st ed. (Straßburg: Trübner, 1918–1919), vol. IV, 321.

THOR ("Thunder"; Old Norse *Þórr;* Old High German *Donar;* Old English *Þunœr;* Old Saxon *Thunœr*): Son of Odin and Jörð, his wife is Sif, with whom he has two sons, Magni ("Strength") and Móði ("Courage"), and a daughter, Þrúðr ("Power"). He lives in Þrúðvangr or Þrúðheimr, and his hall is called Bilskírnir; it has five hundred doors. His servants are Þjálfi and his sister Röskva. Thor owns two goats, Tanngnjóstr ("Teeth-gnasher") and Tanngrísnir ("Teeth-barer"), who pull his chariot when he travels. Thor has a red beard and is endowed with a fabled appetite; he is truculent and quick to anger. He is also called Ásaþórr ("Thor of the Æsir" or "Æsir-Thor") and Ökuþórr, which roughly translates as "Thor the Traveler" or "Thor the Driver."

He is the strongest of gods and men. He owns three precious objects: the hammer Mjöllnir, with which he massacres the giants; a pair of iron gloves, necessary to wield the hammer; and a belt that doubles his strength. He represents a military function (the second function, according to Dumézil's classification) and corresponds to the Roman Mars and Hercules, as well as the Indian Indra. In Gaulish

Fig. 85. Thor

Fig. 86. Thor
and the Midgard
Serpent. Runestone
carving from
Altuna, Sweden.

(Celtic) mythology his counterpart is Taranis. Thor is the champion of the Æsir, whom he defends against the giants (✦ GEIRRÖDR, HRUNGNIR, HYMIR, SKRÝMIR, ÞRYMR, ÚTGARÐALOKI).

He is also the initiator of young warriors (✦ MÖKKURKÁLFI). In certain respects he is akin to the proto-Germanic *Tiwaz (the deity that evolved into the Norse Týr), several whose of attributes Thor seems to have assimilated over time.

Thor is also connected to the Dumézilian third function (fertility, fecundity). He rules over thunder and lightning and wind and rain (fertilizing), a feature that strongly survived in the beliefs of certain Lapplanders who had assimilated Thor into their native worldview. He shares the dead with Freyja and Odin but receives only the thralls ("slaves," although here this perjorative term is most likely just a reference to peasants as opposed to nobles).

Thor is famous for a number of exploits: his fishing expedition to try to catch the Midgard Serpent (whose venom will later kill him at Ragnarök), his resuscitation of his goats, and his journeys to the land of the giants. He is the preeminent Viking god, one of the rare deities to have survived in the medieval Danish ballads (*folkeviser*). His name is still evident in that of the weekday Thursday, "Thor's day" (cf. Old Norse *þórsdagr* and modern German *Donnerstag*). The frequent appearance of Thor in place-names as well as in personal names attests to his popularity. In France, Thor survives in the Norman name "Turquetil" (from Old Norse *Þórketill*, "Thor's Cauldron").

Etymologically, Thor is the "thunder," which can be found in lightning and the noise that accompanies the flight of his hammer.

✦ *MJÖLLNIR, VIMUR*

📖 Arnold, *Thor;* John Lindow, "Thor's Visit to Útgarðaloki," *Oral Tradition* 15/1 (2000): 170–86; Riti Kroesen, "Thor and the Giant's Bride," *Amsterdamer Beiträge zur älteren Germanistik* 17 (1982): 60–67; Carl von Sydow, "Tors färd till utgård," *Danske Studier,* 1910: 65–105, 145–82.

Fig. 87. Thor. Illustration by Ólafur Brynjúlfsson, *Snorra Edda*, 1760.

ÞORGERÐR HÖLGABRÚÐR, HÖRÐABRÚÐR: Goddess to whom a temple in Norway was dedicated in the tenth century; her sister is Irpa. She may be a local deity and patron of Hördaland. The best source of information on her is the *Jómsvíkinga saga* (Saga of the Jómsvíkings), written down around 1200. Þorgerðr granted victory to the *jarl* (earl) Hakon when he sacrificed his son to her. A dark, black cloud arrived at top speed to the battlefield, followed by a hailstorm, thunder, and lightning. The men gifted with second sight saw Þorgerðr there, and it seemed to them that an arrow flew from each of her shining fingers, killing a man each time.

Þorgerðr Hölgabrúðr is most likely a protective goddess of fertility, as the denomination *-brúðr* is associated in other texts exclusively with the Vanir—therefore agrarian—deities. In her temple at Hlaðir (present-day Lade, Norway) an image of her stood beside one of Thor in his chariot and one of Irpa. She wore a gold bracelet and a hood.

According to Snorri Sturluson, Þorgerðr was the daughter of Hölgi, or Helgi; according to Saxo Grammaticus, she was the daughter of Gusi, King of the Finns, and she wed King Helgi of Hálogaland.

📖 Boyer, *La Grande Déesse du Nord,* 84.

ÞORRI: Name of the winter month going from mid-January to mid-February. It is also that of a giant in the family of Fornjótr. Þorri is the son of King Snaer ("Snow"), and he had two sons, Norr and Gorr ("Wind?"), and a daughter, Gói ("Powder Snow?").

ÞRÍVALDI ("Triply Powerful"): Nine-headed giant killed by Thor in a myth that has not come down to the present.

ÞRÚÐR ("Power," "Strength"): Name of a valkyrie as well as the daughter of Thor. It can be found in the name Gertrude (Old Norse Geirþrúðr). The German cognate *Drude* means both "witch" and "nightmare."

✦ *VALKYRIE*

ÞRÚÐGELMIR ("The Powerful Shouter"): Six-headed giant, son of Aurgelmir and father of Bergelmir, all frost giants.

ÞRÚÐHEIMR ("World of Strength/Force"): Thor's domain in Ásgarðr.

ÞRÚÐVANGR ("Force Field"): Thor's domain in Ásgarðr. This name alternates with Þrúðheimr.

ÞRYMGJÖLL ("The Resounding One"): An iron gate sealing the home of Menglöð, the guardian of the Gjallarbrú bridge, on the road that leads to the underworld. The sons of Sólblindi, the dwarves, forged it. Anyone who lifts it off its hinges is paralyzed immediately.

ÞRYMHEIMR ("World of Noise"): The home of the giant Þjazi and his daughter, Skaði.

ÞRYMR ("Noise"): The giant who once steals Thor's hammer. Having borrowed Freyja's feather cloak, Loki makes his way to Jötunheimr, where Þrymr tells him: "I hid the hammer eight leagues beneath the sea. No man can recover it unless I am given Freyja for my wife." Taking Heimdallr's advice, Thor disguises himself as the giant's would-be bride and, accompanied by Loki, recovers his hammer and slays Þrymr and his entire family.

ÞUNOR: Anglo-Saxon name of Thor/Donar. In Old Saxon it is Thunær.

THURSE: The designation for a race of giants whose existence is attested in all the Germanic countries (Old Norse *þurs;* Old English *þyrs;* Old High German *Turs/Durs*). It is also the name of the rune **þurisaz* (in Old Norse the rune name becomes *þurs*), which is transliterated as /th/. The *thurses* are harmful by nature; the best known of them are the frost giants (*hrímþursar*), who are all descendants of Bergelmir and his wife. Attestations of the thurses are rare in Germany, but the ones we do find show that these giants were known there too. For example, in the legend of the founding of a monastery in Wilten near Innsbruck, the giant that opposed the civilizing hero (✦ HAYMON) was named Thyrsus.

✦ *TUSS*

TILBERI ("Fetcher"): In Icelandic folk tradition the *tilberi* (also known in some areas as the *snakkur,* the "snakelike imp") is a being that steals milk from the livestock of neighbors and then transforms its booty into gold. Only women who are competent in sorcery can create a *tilberi*. This is done in the following manner: The woman must dig up a human rib bone from a grave on Whitsunday (Pentecost), swaddle it in gray wool, and carry it between her breasts. During communion on each of the next three Sundays she spits sacramental wine on the bundle, which will bring it to life. The woman then has to carve a nipple on the inside of her thigh; the *tilberi* will attach itself to the nipple and feed, growing in size and strength.

📖 Árnason, *Icelandic Legends,* vol. II, xcii–xcv; Heurgren, *Husdjuren i nordisk folktro;* Kvideland and Sehmsdorf, eds., *Scandinavian Folk Belief and Legend,* 179; Þorvarðardóttir, *Brennuöldin,* 175–84; Wall, *Tjuvmjölkande väsen i äldre nordisk tradition.* See also the information on the *tilberi* that can be found at the website of Strandagaldur, the Museum of Icelandic Sorcery and Witchcraft: www.galdrasyning.is.

*TIWAZ: Proto-Germanic name of the god that evolved into the Old Norse Týr (Old English Tiw, Tig, or Ti; Old High German Ziu).

TOGGELI, DOGGELI ("Little Oppressor"): The name of the entity in Switzerland known as the nightmare (*Alp, Mahr, Trude*). It is also the name of a night butterfly and a name used to designate dwarves.

TOMPTA GUDHANE ("The Gods of the Building Terrain"): Swedish place spirits. They were granted one-tenth of the livestock, bread, and drink, which is the tacit contract negotiated with them so that they will not obstruct the smooth operation of the farm.

📖 Lecouteux, *The Tradition of Household Spirits;* Lecouteux, *Demons and Spirits of the Land;* Hultkrantz, ed., *The Supernatural Owners of Nature.*

TOMTE: ✦ HOUSEHOLD/PLACE SPIRITS, NISS

📖 Holbek and Piø, *Fabeldyr og sagnfolk,* 51–54.

TOMTEBISSENS STUGA ("Tomte's Room"): Name of a large stone located on a hill of Västmanland (Sweden), under which a place spirit lived.

Fig. 88. Tomte.
Olaus Magnus,
*Historia de gentibus
septentrionalibus*,
Rome, 1555.

TOMTETRÄD ("Tomte Tree"): This is the Swedish designation of the tutelary tree that grows in the farmyard or garden on which the prosperity of the household or farm depends. No harm should be done to it. On Thursday evening, to stave off misfortune or illness affecting men or animals, milk or beer would be poured on its roots, which is a form of propitiatory sacrifice to the spirit that has made its home there. This tree is also called *tuntré* in Iceland, and *vårträd* and *bosträd* in Sweden.

📖 Martti Haavio, "Heilige Bäume," *Studia Fennica* 8 (1959): 35–48.

TREES: There is evidence for tree worship throughout the medieval West. The species most often mentioned in the Germanic countries are the ash (Yggdrasill, the cosmic tree, is an ash, and the first man was created from the trunk of an ash), the aspen, and the linden tree, which is extremely popular east of the Rhine. One Norse myth fragment says that a rowan branch saved Thor. The sacred space inside of which a duel took place was marked off by hazel posts. The most famous tree is the Geismar oak (Hesse) that was cut down by Saint Boniface and which was most likely a representation of the Irminsûl, the name for the cosmic tree in medieval Germany. Less well known but equally important is the sacred yew that grew by the temple in Uppsala, Sweden, where sacrifices were performed. In his *History of the Archbishops of Hamburg-Bremen*, Adam of Bremen (eleventh century) says this about the temple:

The sacrifice is of this nature: of every living thing that is male, they offer nine heads. . . . The bodies they hang in the sacred grove that adjoins the temple. Now this grove is so sacred in the eyes of the heathen that each and every tree in it is believed divine because of the death or putrefaction of the victims. Even dogs and horses hang there with men. (trans. Tschan)

A more recent scholium adds: "Feasts and sacrifices of this kind are solemnized for nine days. . . . This sacrifice takes place about the time of the vernal equinox."

TRIGLAF ("Three-headed One"): God of the Pomeranians worshipped in Julin and Stettin. His three heads (Slavic *tri* + *glava*) indicate that he ruled over heaven, Earth, and the underworld. His statue had a gold cover over its face so he would not see the evil deeds of men. Triglaf owned a fat, black, sacred horse that was forbidden for anyone to ride; its saddle was made of gold and silver, and a priest was assigned to its service. This horse served as an oracle. The monk Idung of Prüfening says this in his *Life of Othon, Bishop of Bamberg* (II, 11), written before 1144: "Having planted a number of spears here and there, they then walked Triglaf's horse through them. If he did not touch any of them, the omen was considered favorable to leave on horseback for a pillaging expedition, but if he trounced even one of them, they took that as a sign that the god forbade them to mount their horses." Herbord (died 1168), a monk of Michelberg, states more explicitly that there were nine spears, and the horse went back and forth between them three times (*Dialogus de Vita S. Ottonis,* II, 26 and 31). According to the author of the *Knýtlinga saga* (Saga of Cnut's Descendants, chap. 125), a history of the Danes from 950 to 1190, written around 1256, Triglaf was a god of the Rugians. The inhabitants of Stettin worshipped a walnut tree, from which a spring seeped, because they believed Triglaf lived there.

📖 Kantzow, *Pomerania,* vol. I, 107–11; Micraelius, *Antiquitates Pomeraniae,* vol. I, 150.

TROLDHVAL: A monstrous cetacean of the northern seas that sinks ships. This beast appears to be a variant of the Kraken.

✦ *KRAKEN*

TROLL: Name of a race of ugly and malevolent giants that are always associated with water. The word is also used with the sense of "monster," "demon," and "revenant." Today trolls have become dwarves, and, in the Shetland archipelago, they are called *trows*. They are malicious spirits who are often deformed and generally live in forests.

Fig. 89. Trolls. Drawing by Johann Eckersberg for
the fairy tale *The Gold Bird*, 1850.

In folktales the troll possesses several heads that are able to grow back unless they are severed with a single blow. They have long noses and have either long hair or are hairy all over. It is also an ogre and creature of the night. It is turned to stone by sunlight. Its death can also take the following form: it explodes with anger when it realizes that it has been tricked.

In Norway its memory lives on in numerous proverbs; for example: "When one speaks of trolls, they are not far away" (which corresponds to "Speak of the Devil [and he will appear]") and "A fine face can hide a troll" (i.e., "Don't judge a book by its cover"). Another saying is "When the sun rises, the trolls die."

In Norway there are one hundred place-names coined from "troll" and five hundred others that contain the word. It should be noted that the word never appears in village names or personal names.

✦ *GRÝLA, JÖTUNN, RISE*

📖 Amilien, *Le troll et autres créatures surnaturelles dans les contes populaires norvégiens;* Arrowsmith and Moorse, *A Field Guide to the Little People,* 94–139; Lindow, *Trolls.*

TROW: The name given to trolls in the Shetlands, the archipelago where the Norwegians began settling in the ninth century. Small in size, gray clad, and very ugly, the *trows* resemble humans. They like music and to eat and drink inordinately. They live in caves in cliffs or near the lochs, and time passes more slowly in their world than it does for humans.

Trows only come out after sunset and appear most frequently during winter when the nights are long. It is said that they will turn to stone if sunlight catches them by surprise. This is how a stone circle in Fetlar, which has two other standing stones in its center, got its name of Haltadans. These stones would be *trows* that were changed into rock while dancing, with the fiddle player and his wife in the middle. It is said that to overhear a *trow* conversation is a good omen but that to see a *trow,* share his meal, or accept a reward from him can bring misfortune. On the other hand, when a *trow* has forgotten some personal possession by accident, it is a guaranteed good-luck charm for its new owner.

They have a tendency to steal babies at times, especially little girls, and to replace them with a sickly, stupid infant (✦ CHANGELING), and the explanation for this is that they can only procreate boys. To rescue the child one must obtain a pail of seawater and three pebbles, pass the child through the flames of a peat fire, burn its effigy, and then feed it during its convalescence with three kinds of food offered by nine women, each of whom has given birth to a son.

They will also steal milk cows, and a popular story tells of the steps that an old woman named Maron took to wrest her cow from the *trows'* power. With a torch in hand, she walked around the cow three times, poking it each time with a blade; then she waved a page of the Bible over the animal while speaking incomprehensible spells in the Old Norse tongue. Stuck in a bucket of tar tied around the animal's neck, the torch gave off a thick smoke. Maron then pulled the tail of a cat three times, which had been placed on the animal's back, and afterward fed it three crabs of a very specific kind. As a result, the animal was freed of the *trows*.

Trows sometimes need the services of humans. It is told how a midwife, whose skills were well known, had just put her fish on to cook for dinner when the *trows* abducted her to assist at a birth. When she returned home two weeks later she simply asked her husband if the fish was cooked yet.

To avoid attracting the vengeful anger of the *trows,* people take pains not to lock the entrance door to the house, or that of a closet, and the house is tidied up before going to bed, to ensure their displeasure is not aroused. Young children and animals can be protected from them with the sign of the cross and by leaving an open Bible near the child; animals can be protected by placing two sheafs of straw in the form of a cross nearby. A knife also renders *trows* powerless. A black rooster, the only one capable of detecting an invisible presence, was also very useful, especially at the approach of Christmas.

During the winter of 1803, Gibbie Laurenson of Gruting went to grind grain at the water mill of Fir Vaa. Dozing near a small peat fire, he suddenly heard a group of *trows* who entered and sat around the fire, thinking him to be asleep. A woman changed her baby's diaper and hung it to dry on Gibbie's thumb. One of the *trows* then said, "What are we going to do to this sleeper?" "Leave him alone," responded the woman, "he is not wicked! Tell Shanko to play him a tune!" And Shanko played a tune on his fiddle, after which the entire group left. Gibbie whistled this tune to his son, who was a fiddle player. His son named it *"Fader's ton"* (Papa's Tune), but it was later given the name of a loch near the Fir Vaa water mill: *"Winyadepla."* Here is the music:

Fig. 90. Papa's Tune

📖 Arrowsmith and Moorse, *A Field Guide to the Little People,* 164–67; Briggs, *Dictionary of Fairies,* 413–15.

TRUTE: ✦ DRUDE

TUISTO ("Double"): The information we have about this god comes from Tacitus. Tuisto is born of the earth, which makes him a son of Nerthus. Apparently by himself he engendered the first human being, who was named Mannus, which corresponds to Manu, son of Vivasant in Vedic cosmogony, and to the Phrygian Manès. Tuisto is certainly an androgynous deity; he shows a clear kinship with Yama from the *Rig Veda* and with the Norse Ymir.

TÜRSCHT/DÜRST: The name of the Infernal Hunstman in Switzerland. The Türscht is accompanied by a large sow and her piglets. He arrives from the east with bad weather. His retinue is called "Dürst's Hunt" (*Dürstengejäg*).

📖 Vernaleken, *Alpensagen,* 59; Grimm, *Deutsche Sagen,* no. 269; Elsbeth Liebl, "Geisterheere und ähnliche Erscheinungen," in *Atlas der schweizerischen Volkskunde,* commentary, 2nd part (Basel: Schweizerische Gesellschaft für Volkskunde, 1971), 768–84.

TUSS(E)/TASS(E): In the folklore that surrounds the underground dwellers, this name, a derivative of *thurse,* designates spirits and land spirits that are the inhabitants of mounds and mountains. In Sweden (Uppland, Värmland) and in eastern Norway (Austlandet), this term means "wolf." In Vestragothia this name was applied to a man suspected of being a werewolf. *Tussen* is also the name given in Norway to the black cat of the sorcerer or witch, when it is not called a *trollkatten,* "troll-cat."

✦ *THURSE, UNDERGROUND DWELLERS*

TWILIGHT OF THE GODS: Popular and Wagnerian name for the eschatological battle—it is based on an erroneous translation of the word *ragnarök,* which can be properly understood as meaning the "judgment (or destiny) of the ruling powers (gods)."

✦ *RAGNARÖK*

TÝR ("God"; Proto-Germanic *Tiwaz; Old English Tiw, Tig, Ti; Old High German Ziu): This Æsir god is either the son of Odin or of

Fig. 91. Týr

Fig. 92. The god Týr confronts the wolf Fenrir during Ragnarök.
Illustration by Ólafur Brynjúlfsson, *Snorra Edda*, 1760.

the giant Hymir. Structurally, he alternates with Odin like Mithra does
with Varuna in Sanskrit mythology. He represents war as well as the
exercise of law: he is the jurist god representing the forces that protect
the order of the world. He is the patron of the Thing, the assembly of
free men where legal cases are settled. In a Germano-Roman dedicatory

inscription found near Hadrian's Wall in Britain, a reflex of Tiwaz is certainly the god that underlies the name Mars Thingsus.

The sole myth we have about Týr relates the following: Seeing that the wolf Fenrir was growing larger, the Æsir grew alarmed and decided to shackle him. When they slipped the fetter called Gleipnir on him after two fruitless attempts, the now suspicious Fenrir demanded that a god place his hand in his mouth as a pledge of their good intentions. Týr agreed to this condition, and his hand was bitten off when Fenrir realized he could not break his bonds. Týr is the prototype for the hero whose sacrifice saves the world from chaos; in Rome his counterpart would be the one-armed Mutius Scaevola, and in Celtic epics it would be Nuada of the Silver Hand.

Etymologically, the name Týr is cognate to the Sanskrit *dyaus,* the Greek *Zeus,* the Latin *deus,* and the Old Irish *día.* The god's name is evident in the weekday name "Tuesday" (from Old English *tiwesdæg,* "Tiw's day"; cf. Old Norse *týsdagr*), and the rune corresponding to the letter /t/ is also named after him. Numerous place-names attest to his worship.

📖 Régis Boyer, "La dextre de Týr," in *Mythe et Politique,* ed. François Jouan and André Motte (Paris: Les Belles Lettres, 1990), 33–43; Kaarle Krohn, "Tyrs högra hand, Freys svärd," in *Festskrift til H. F. Feilberg* (Stockholm: Norstedt & Söner, 1911), 541–47.

U

ÜBERZÄHLIGER ("Supernumerary"): Name given to the devil that slipped into a group of dancers or card players in order to abduct one and bear him or her off to Hell. This legend comes from the clerical literature (such as various *exempla,* meaning "sermons"), which forbids these kinds of pleasures, hence the adage *Ubi saltatio, ibi diabolus* ("Where there is dancing, you'll find the devil").

📖 Bø, Grambo & Hodne, *Norske Segner,* no. 76; Ronald Grambo, "Guilt and Punishment in Norwegian Legends," *Fabula* 11 (1970): 254–56; Leopold Kretzenbacher, "Tanzverbot und Warnlegende: Ein mittelalterliches Predigtexempel in der steirischen Barockpassiologie," *Rheinisches Jahrbuch für Volkskunde* 12 (1961): 16–22.

UÐR ("Wave"): One of the nine daughters of Ægir and Rán, deities of the sea.

ULFHEÐNAR (pl.; "Wolf-coats"): Another name for berserkers, Odin's wild warriors.

ULFRÚN ("Wolf-rune"): Name of one of the giant mothers of the god Heimdallr.

ULLERKENS: Name for dwarves in Pomerania. They allegedly live in the hills, visit humans, and sometimes borrow a kneading bowl. They go down into the cellars and play music but can only tolerate their own light, so they vanish when someone, drawn by the noise, comes down with a candle.

📖 Temme, *Die Volkssagen von Pommern und Rügen,* no. 217.

ULLR: A very ancient deity also referred to as the "god of the bow," "god of snowshoes" or "god of skis," and the "hunting god." He is the

Fig. 93. Ullr. Illustration by Ólafur Brynjúlfsson, *Snorra Edda,* 1760.

son of Sif and lives in Ýdalir ("Yew Dales"). The oath ring placed in temples was dedicated to him.

According to Saxo Grammaticus, who calls him Ollerus, he can sail on a bone. During the time when Othinus (Odin) was banished, Ollerus is supposed to have ruled over the gods. This is revealing of how important he must have been, a fact that is confirmed by Swedish and Norwegian place-names.

The name Ullr may derive from the same root as the Gothic word *wulþus,* "splendor." Ullr would therefore be the god of the sunny skies of spring or summer, in any case a solar god.

UNDERGROUND DWELLERS: Name given to dwarves in northern Germany and in Denmark. They are called *Önnerbänkissen* on the islands of Föhr and Amrum, *Unnereske* and *Dwarge* in Schleswig-Holstein, *Önnererske* on the island of Sylt, and *Ellefolk, Biergfolk,* and *Unnervoetstöi* in the Danish-speaking part of Schleswig.

📖 Grambo, *Svart katt over veien,* 174–76 (*underjordiske*); Müllenhoff, *Sagen, Märchen und Lieder der Herzogthümer Schleswig, Holstein und Lauenburg,* nos. 380, 381, 383, 421, 428.

UNDINE: A mermaid that has no soul but can acquire one through marriage with a mortal. Her fame comes from the 1811 novel of the same name by Friedrich de la Motte-Fouqué, who drew his conception from the theory of elemental spirits of Paracelsus. The latter offers a precise description of mermaids (*Undenen*) and mentions the precedents of Peter von Staufenberg (ca. 1300) and Melusine. Undine's marriage with the knight Huldbrand is subject to two implicit taboos (of the Melusinian type): do not marry another woman, and never lose your temper with her while on the water. After the second taboo is broken, Undine vanishes and Huldbrand contemplates remarrying. His mermaid wife comes to him in a dream and demands that he abstain from doing so, but he disregards her request and she is obligated to follow the law of the elemental spirits and bring about his death. The theme appealed to many authors and dramatists (see, for example, Jean Giraudoux's drama *Ondine*). In the German story Undine kills her unfaithful husband, but in Han Christian Andersen's tale of *The Little Mermaid* the siren refuses to do the same and dissolves into the water but with the promise that she will acquire a soul three hundred years later.

Fig. 94. Undine

📖 Lecouteux, *Mélusine et le Chevalier au Cygne*; Lecouteux, "Quelques remarques sur la préhistoire de Undine," *Mythes, Symboles, Littératures* 3 (2002): 183–91.

UNG'SCHICHT (neut.): The name of a household spirit in the Tyrol (Lower Inn) that lives in the outbuildings of the farm and in the chalets adjacent to the summer pastures in the mountains. In Stubai it is called the *Litzenmannl*.

📖 Heyl, *Volkssagen, Meinungen und Bräuche aus Tirol*, 84–85.

UNKATL (neut.): In the Tyrol, where it is still called *Ung'heu*, "monster, revenant," this is the name of a spirit that is sometimes a mischievous, teasing kobold, sometimes a revenant with eyes like burning coals, and sometimes a household spirit that looks like a minuscule woman. The *Unkatl* appears during the Ember Days and on the eves of all major religious holidays.

📖 Heyl, *Volkssagen, Meinungen und Bräuche aus Tirol*, 222–25.

UPPER SEA: A belief once existed regarding ships that sailed through the air; this gave birth to a legend, the first traces of which can be found at the beginning of the thirteenth century in book I, chap. 13 of the *Otia Imperialia* (Recreation for an Emperor) by Gervase of Tilbury (ca. 1152–1218):

> A strange event in our own time, which is widely known but nonetheless a cause for wonder, provides proof of the existence of an upper sea overhead. It occurred on a feast day in Great Britain, while the people were straggling out of their parish church, after hearing high mass. The day was very overcast and quite dark on account of the thick clouds. To the people's amazement, a ship's anchor was seen caught on a tombstone within the churchyard wall, with its rope stretching up and hanging in the air. They were advancing various opinions on the matter to each other, when after a time they saw the rope move as if it were being worked to pull up the anchor. Since, being caught fast, it would not give way; a sound was heard in the humid air as of sailors struggling to recover the anchor they had cast down. Soon, when their efforts proved vain, the sailors sent one of their members down, using the same technique as our sailors here

below; he gripped the anchor rope and climbed down it, swinging one hand over the other. He had already pulled the anchor free, when he was seized by the bystanders. He then expired in the hands of his captors, suffocated by the humidity of our dense air as if he were drowning in the sea. The sailors up above waited an hour, but then concluding that their companion had drowned; they cut the rope and sailed away, leaving the anchor behind. And so in memory of this event it was fittingly decided that the anchor should be used to make ironwork for the church door, and it is still there for all to see.

Gervase of Tilbury reports another extraordinary event that took place in Bristol.

A native of that place once went on a voyage, leaving his wife and children at home. After covering a great distance in the course of a long voyage, when the ship was sailing in a remote part of the ocean, the citizen in question sat down to eat with the sailors at about nine o'clock one morning. After the meal he was washing his knife at the ship's rail when it suddenly slipped from his hand. That very hour it fell through an open window in the roof of the citizen's own home—the kind of window the English call a skylight—and stuck fast in a table which stood beneath it, before the eyes of his wife. The woman stared at it in amazement, struck by the strangeness of the occurrence. She kept the knife, which she recognized from former days, and when, a long time afterward, her husband returned, she learned from him that the day on which the accident occurred during his voyage coincided with the day on which she had acquired the knife. Who then will doubt, given the manifest proof of the event, that there is a sea situated above the world we live in, in the air or above the air? (trans. Banks and Binns)

📖 Gervase of Tilbury, *Otia Imperialia: Recreation for an Emperor*, ed. and trans. Banks and Binns.

URÐR ("Past," "Fate"): One of the three Norns (which are a Norse conception roughly corresponding to the Roman Parcae, the Fates) and likely the oldest of the three. She owns the well that bears her name

(Urðarbrunnr) and which is located next to the cosmic tree, Yggdrasil, or beneath its roots. This is the spot where the Æsir hold their deliberations. Urðr embodies all-powerful destiny (*wurt* in Old High German and *wyrd* in Old English). She and her sisters are said to have come from the sea.

✦ *NORNS*

UTBOREN (Norwegian, "Exposed Child"): The term in fact means a child killed by its unwed mother who did not want her "transgression" to be revealed.

In 1687, in Nordland, a certain Nille Jensdatter abandoned her baby like this, and the dead infant continued crying to her: "Mama Nille! Mama Nille!" Someone asked what the child wanted, and it responded: "I want to nurse!" The mother confessed that she had buried him in the yard.

The term also designates a child who has died unbaptized and comes back. To give it final rest the standard baptism phrase was used in 1320, but other means also existed such as reciting the Lord's Prayer either in the normal way or else backward. An *utboren* child can even transform into a demon as big as a horse. If it meets someone it will suck up his organs and sometimes his head or back as well. When a person is chased by the infant revenant he must cross over running water, because the dead child will be unable to cross it. There are also baptismal charms such as the following:

> Eg døype deg på ei von. Guri eller Jon.
> E du gut skal du heite Gubran, e du gjente, ska du heite Guri.
> Eg døyper dei på ei von, Johannes eller Jon.
>
> (I baptize you on a hope. Guri or Jon.
> If you are a boy your name will be Gubran, if a girl, your name will
>   be Guri.
> I baptize you on a hope, Johannes or Jon.)

or:

> Jeg døber dig i Navn, fra Gud og til Fa'n, enten Johannes eller
>   Johanna.
>
> (I baptize thee, from God and unto the Devil, either Johannes or
>   Johanna.)

PLEASE SEND US THIS CARD TO RECEIVE OUR LATEST CATALOG FREE OF CHARGE.

Book in which this card was found _____

☐ Check here to receive our catalog via e-mail.

	Company _____
	☐ Send me wholesale information

Name _____   Phone _____

Address _____

City _____ State _____ Zip _____ Country _____

E-mail address _____

Please check area(s) of interest to receive related announcements via e-mail:

☐ Health	☐ Self-help	☐ Science/Nature	☐ Shamanism
☐ Ancient Mysteries	☐ New Age/Spirituality	☐ Visionary Plants	☐ Martial Arts
☐ Spanish Language	☐ Sexuality/Tantra	☐ Family and Youth	☐ Religion/Philosophy

Please send a catalog to my friend:

Name _____   Company _____

Address _____

City _____ State _____ Zip _____ Country _____

Order at 1-800-246-8648 • Fax (802) 767-3726

E-mail: customerservice@InnerTraditions.com • Web site: www.InnerTraditions.com

INNER TRADITIONS
BEAR & COMPANY

Inner Traditions • Bear & Company

P.O. Box 388
Rochester, VT 05767-0388
U.S.A.

Affix
Postage
Stamp
Here

The important thing is to give the young dead thing a name—in other words, an identity.

📖 Grambo, *Svart katt over veien*, 176–77; Pentikäinen, *The Nordic Dead-Child Tradition;* O'Connor, *Child Murderess and Dead Child Traditions;* Martti Haavio, "A Running Stream They Dare Na' Cross," *Studia Fennica* 8 (1959): 125–42, 236–38.

ÚTGARÐALOKI ("Loki of the Outer Enclosure"): A giant who is an expert in magic. Under the name of Skrýmir, he takes advantage of Thor with his spells.

✦ *SKRÝMIR*

📖 Régis Boyer, "Le voyage chez Útgarða-Loki selon les sources norroises et Saxo Grammaticus," in *Diesseits- und Jenseitsreisen im Mittelalter,* ed. Wolf-Dieter Lange (Bonn: Bouvier, 1992), 25–40; Michael Jacoby, "Der Kampf gegen die Übermacht Leviathan-Satan: Strukturelle Analyse zur Parallele zwischen 'Sir Gawain and the Green Knight' und Þors Fahrt zu Útgarðaloki in der 'Gylfaginning,'" *Amsterdamer Beiträge zur älteren Germanistik* 23 (1985): 97–129.

ÚTGARÐR ("The Outer Enclosure"): Territory located to the east or to the north of Miðgarðr and Ásgarðr; it is inhabited by giants and monsters. This eastern region is also that of Jötunheimr ("World of the Giants") and Járnviðr ("Iron Forest"), home of the wolf-shaped giants. Later, Útgarðr was seen as located in the north, the territory of the frost giants (*hrímþursar*), and of Hel, the realm of the dead. Útgarðr is separated from the world of men and that of the gods by a perilous sea, by rivers that never freeze over, and by Myrkviðr (the "Dark Forest") in the south.

VAÐGELMIR ("Ford-shouter"): A river that had the property of punishing liars.

VAFRLOGI: ("Wavering Flame"): The name of the wall of flames surrounding the home of the giantess Gerðr. Freyr's servant Skírnir must cross through it when he brings Gerðr the god's request for her hand in marriage. This wall of flames reappears in the story of Brynhildr, the valkyrie punished by Odin. Curiously, a Latin version of the legend of the swan children mentions a Mountbrant; in other words, "Burning Mountain." It should be noted that in medieval Christian mythology a wall of flames is supposed to surround the earthly paradise.

VAFÞRÚÐNIR ("Strong at Entangling"): A giant of great learning whom Odin, while in disguise, challenges to a knowledge contest. Vafþrúðnir is able to answer all of the questions except for the last one: "What did Odin whisper in Baldr's ear before he was on his pyre?" At this point the giant realizes the identity of his adversary.

VAGNOPTHUS ("Seal Head"?; Old Norse *Vagnhöfði*): According to Saxo Grammaticus, Vagnopthus (variously spelled Vagnophtus, Wagnhofthus, etc.) is one of the two giants that reared Guthormus and Hadingus, the sons of Gram. His daughter is Harthgrepa; she was the wet nurse and teacher of Hadingus and later his lover.

VALASKJÁLF: Name of one of the dwellings of the Æsir. It is quite ancient and covered in silver, but the identity of the god residing there remains unknown. Its name suggests that it could be Váli, one of Odin's sons.

VALFÖÐR ("Father of the Slain"): One of Odin's names. It reflects his role collecting the warriors fallen in combat who will then dwell in Valhalla. Synonymous bynames that appear in skaldic poetry are Valgautr ("Gautr of the Slain"; we know that Gautr, "Goth," is also one of Odin's names) and Valtýr ("God of the Slain").

📖 Falk, *Odensheiti.*

VALHALLA ("Hall of the Slain"; Old Norse *Valhöll*): Odin's dwelling in Ásgarðr and the paradise of warriors. One cannot enter it if death came as a result of illness or old age. Armor lies strewn about on the benches. The roof is made of spears and shields. Atop it is where the goat Heiðrún stands; she chews on the leaves of Læraðr (Yggdrasill), and from her udders comes the mead that the valkyries serve to the *einherjar.* Near her is the stag Eikþyrnir ("Oak-thorny") who munches on the branches of the tree; moisture flows from his antlers. Valhalla has 540 doors. Each day the warriors emerge from them to fight each other in the courtyard for amusement, and they return to the hall when the signal for dinner has sounded. The cook, Andhrímnir, then serves them the meat of the boar Sæhrímnir. On the day of Ragnarök the warriors will leave Valhalla to confront the forces of chaos.

Fig. 95. Valhalla, manuscript of the *Poetic Edda*, circa 1680

VÁLI: Son of Odin and the giantess Rindr. According to Snorri he is also called Áli. He is essentially known for avenging his half-brother, Baldr. He was nine years old when he slew Höðr, the unintentional murderer of Baldr. Váli is bold and skilled with a bow. He will survive Ragnarök.

VALKYRIE ("Choosers of the Battle-slain"; Old Norse *valkyrja*, pl. *valkyrjar*): The valkyries are representative of the Dumézilian second function (warfare) but are also magicians, guardians, female lovers of heroes, bird-women, and keepers of knowledge. They are concerned with fertility and fecundity and have many points in common with the Dises (deities of the third function), the Norns (the Germanic Fates), and the *fylgjur* (personal tutelary spirits).

They are in Odin's service, and their names are most often of a warlike nature, formed from words like *battle, combat, sword, spear, fury, bravery,* and so forth. Régis Boyer has analyzed the thirty-eight valkyrie names that have been preserved in the texts; from his study it becomes apparent that they escape any strict Dumézilian classification as one-third of them are engaged in two different functions.

The valkyries select the slain warriors who will populate Valhalla. They attach themselves to the kings and princes who are worshippers of Odin, helping them, counseling them, bringing them luck, and even marrying them after their death. If they disobey Odin they are punished—as in the case of Brynhildr, who, pricked by the sleep-thorn, lies on Hindarfjall Mountain waiting for the one who will awaken her. In Valhalla the valkyries serve beer to the warriors.

✦ *HELGI, SIGRÚN, SVÁVA*

📖 Régis Boyer, "Les Valkyries et leurs noms," in *Mythe et Personification: Actes du colloque du Grand Palais (Paris), 7–8 mai 1977,* ed. Jacqueline Duchemin (Paris: Belles Lettres, 1980), 39–54.

VANADÍS ("Dise of the Vanir"): This byname for Freyja anchors the goddess in the Dumézilian third function (fertility/fecundity) by establishing a connection between her and the Dises.

✦ *DISES, FUNCTIONS*

VANAHEIMR ("World of the Vanir"): Place where the god Njörðr is supposed to have been raised.

VANIR: The second family of gods after the Æsir in the Germanic pantheon. Its representatives are Njörðr and his children, Freyr and Freyja. These are typical gods of the Dumézilian third function (✦ FUNCTIONS), representatives of an agrarian culture. They correspond to the Nāsatya or Ashvins of Indic mythology and to the Roman Quirinus. The Vanir are connected to the earth and to water (✦ NJÖRÐR, NERTHUS); they dispense the goods and pleasures of this world: wealth, fertility, peace, joy, and love. They are also seers and experts in magic—Freya is the master of *seiðr*, which she introduced to the Æsir—and they also have a connection with the dead, who, as we know, play an important role in everything relating to fertility. It should also be recalled that Freyja receives half of the warriors slain in battle and that the swan maidens are part of her sphere of influence.

The Æsir and Vanir were once at war with each other but then made peace (✦ KVASIR) and exchanged hostages: Njörðr and Freyr were sent to the Æsir, while Mímir and Hœnir went to the Vanir. This myth has been interpreted as the transposition of an actual historical confrontation that took place between two classes of archaic society, the warriors (equated with the Æsir) and the peasants (equated with the Vanir). Peace between them allowed for the birth of the religious and social structure of the Indo-Europeans.

VARÐLOKUR, VARÐLOKKUR: A song intended to conjure (if the second part of the compound derives from the Old Norse verb *lúka*) or, alternatively, to entice (if it derives from the verb *lokka*) guardian spirits (*verðir,* sg. *vörðr*). The interpretation depends on the spelling of the word, which appears in both forms in the texts. According to the *Eiríks saga rauða* (Saga of Erik the Red), the *varðlok(k)ur* was sung by a woman and the practice of *seiðr* was permitted.

VARTARI ("Strap"): Name of the string the Æsir used to sew shut the mouth of Loki when they punished him for causing the death of Baldr.

VÉ ("Sanctuary"): Brother of Odin, son of Burr (or Borr) and the giantess Bestla. According to the Ynglinga saga, Vé and his brother Vili ruled over Ásgarðr when Odin was exiled—and both shared Frigg. According to Snorri Sturluson, Odin, Vili, and Vé created the first humans, Askr and Embla, but other sources say it was Odin, Hœnir, and Loðurr.

VEGTAMR ("The One Accustomed to Journeys"): A byname of Odin when he travels to Hel, the realm of the dead, to awaken a deceased seeress through necromancy so that he can question her.

📖 Falk, *Odensheiti*.

VENEDIGER ("The Venetian"): In the Salzburg region this is the name for a small, gray-clad, mountain kobold barely any bigger than a hand. He lives in mountains where veins of metal ore or hidden treasures can be found. It is said that during the Middle Ages, Venetians exploited the Carinthian mines; another tradition maintains that this name comes from Italian treasure hunters.

📖 Vernaleken, *Alpensagen*, 313.

Fig. 96. Venediger

VERATÝR ("God of Men"): This byname of Odin alludes to his role in the creation of the first man and first woman.

✦ *ASKR*

📖 Falk, *Odensheiti*.

VERÐANDI ("Present"): One of the three Norns, the Germanic Fates.

✦ *NORNS*

VESTRI ("West"): Name of one of the four dwarves that stand at the four cardinal points to support the celestial vault formed from the skull of Ymir, the primordial giant.

✦ *AUSTRI, COSMOGONY, NORÐRI, SUÐRI*

VÍÐARR: Æsir god presented as the son of Odin and the giantess Griðr. He is called the "silent god" and possesses a shoe that has been in the making since the dawn of time. It is made from the leather strips that men cut from the fronts and backs of their own shoes.

During Ragnarök, after the wolf Fenrir has swallowed Odin, Víðarr will crush the wolf's lower jaw with his shoe-clad foot and then grab his upper jaw and tear it off, killing him.

Fig. 97. Columns from the crypt of Freising Cathedral (Bavaria), circa 1200

VÍÐBLÁINN ("Wide Blue"): Name of the third heaven where the most beautiful of all halls is located. It is called Gimlé "("Shelter from the Flames") and is more brilliant than the sun. The light elves live in Víðbláinn.

VIÐFINNR: Father of Bil and Hjuki.

◆ *MÁNI*

VIÐOFNIR: Name of the rooster that perches on the branches of Mímameiðr ("Mímir's Tree"), meaning Yggdrasill, and who argues constantly with the fire giant Surtr and with Sinmara, an unknown individual; perhaps it is Surtr's companion. Viðofnir can only be slain by the weapon called Lævateinn ("harmful twig"), crafted by Loptr (Loki).

VIÐÓLFR ("Wolf of the Woods"): Ancestor of all magicians and seers. The variant spelling of the name as Vittólfr is interesting, because *vitt* means "magic, witchcraft" (cf. *vita*, "to know"). This would be more fitting, although it may represent a more recent reconstruction.

◆ *VILMEIÐR*

VIEHSCHELM ("Cattle-imp"): This is a bull whose front half alone forms a body. From the waist down it is nothing but skin. When it appears, it causes a pestilence that kills livestock.

📖 Leoprechting, *Aus dem Lechrain*, 75–76.

VILI ("Will"): Brother of Odin and Vé, son or Burr (or Borr) and the giantess Bestla. During the creation of man (◆ ASKR), Vili endowed him with movement and consciousness.

VILMEIÐR: Figure presented as the ancestor of all magicians.

◆ *VIÐÓLFR*

VIMUR: River crossed by Thor when making his way to the home of the giant Geirröðr. Geirröðr's daughter urinates in the river, and the resulting current threatens to carry Thor away. He only manages to extricate himself out of a desperate situation by grabbing a rowan branch.

VINDR ("Wind"): Giant who is the son of Fornjótr and brother of Ægir and Eldr. In other frost-giant genealogies he is named Kari.

VITRA: Name of a nature spirit in the Västerbotten region of Sweden, adjacent to the Baltic Sea. He can be found wherever there are hunters, fishermen, and herdsmen.

VOLLA: Goddess of the Dumézilian third function (✦ FUNCTIONS) mentioned in the *Second Merseburg Charm,* where she is described as a sister of Freyja. She is most likely identical to Fulla, which suggests that Phol/Volla and Freyr/Freyja may represent parallel pairs of related male and female deities.

✦ *MERSEBURG CHARMS*

📖 Beck, *Die Merseburger Zaubersprüche;* Jean-Paul Allard, "Du second Charme de Mersebourg au Viatique de Weingarten," *Études Indo-Européennes* 14 (1985): 33–53.

WADE (Old English *Wada;* Old Norse *Vadi;* Middle High German *Wate*): Famous warrior of Ermanaric in German epics and legends. In the *Þiðreks saga af Bern* (Saga of Dietrich von Bern) he is a giant, the son of King Vilkinus and a mermaid. He is presented as the father of Velent (Wayland the Smith).

 📖 Haymes, trans. *The Saga of Thidrek of Bern;* Lecouteux, trans. and commentary, *La Saga de Théodoric de Vérone.*

WÆLCYRGE ("Chooser of the Slain"; pl. *wælcyrgean*): Name for valkyries in Old English. In an early-eleventh-century sermon by Bishop Wulfstan of Winchester, he uses the term as a designation for evil witches. Several Old English glosses of the ninth and tenth centuries explicitly equate *wælcyrgean* with the Greek Furies and Gorgons, as well as Bellona, the Roman war goddess.

WAGOLLT: Demon abductor in an Arthurian romance written by Ulrich Füetrer (died ca. 1500). This demon lived on an island and knew magic and spells. The hero of the tale, Persibein, slew him and freed many knights and ladies.

 ✦ *GARMANEYS*
 📖 Lecouteux, *Demons and Spirits of the Land,* 174–76.

WAIDELOTTE (masc.), WAIDELOTTIN (fem.): Name of the priests and priestesses of the pagan worship of the ancient Prussians.

WALBERAN: In the tale bearing his name, he is the king of the dwarves that inhabit the Armenian mountains, and he rules over Sinai and Mount Tabor. All the dwarves from Judea to the Caucasus are his vassals. He has subjugated the land of Canaan, inhabited by giants. A vassal of Laurin (✦ LAURIN) has requested his aid; his suzerain was captured by Dietrich von Bern and taken to Ravenna. Walberan assembles an army and arrives to lay siege to the city. He makes his troops invisible; only Dietrich and those close to him can see them, because Laurin—who has, in the meantime, converted to Christianity—has supplied them with magic rings. Thanks to Laurin the battle never takes place. The text lingers long over the wealth and the equipment of the dwarf king: his Arabian coat of mail made of gold and hardened in salamander blood; his breastplate fashioned in the Caucasus and bearing images of the sun, moon, and stars, and from which small bells are hanging; and more.

WALL OF FLAMES: ✦ VAFRLOGI

WALRIDERSKE ("The Hedge-rider"): Name of a female supernatural creature in Lower Saxony. This creature sometimes behaves like a nightmare and sometimes like a fairy or witch.

📖 Mackensen, *Niedersächsische Sagen*, vol. II, no. 67.

WASSERMANN (German, masc., "Merman"; Scandinavian *havmand, marmennil, åmand, havtrold, vandmand*; **fem.** *havfrue* **"Mermaid"):** Water has always been the dwelling place for a host of mythical beings, of which the mermen represent the anthropomorphic aspect. During the Middle Ages, Heinrich von Neustadt gave us a good portrait of one of them. He is as long as a lance, wide at the bottom and thin at the top, his body is green, his buttocks are covered with fish scales, and he also has a long fish tail. His feet are webbed, his face is a rod in length and framed by two wild boar snouts that come out of his mouth, his nose is hooked like a bird's, his nails are curled, his eyes sit deep in their sockets, and his ears are long. His breath "stinks as bad as a manure pit." Armed with a club, he is the guardian of a kind of earthly paradise called the Valley of Gold. In the legend of Saint Brendan the merman is a hybrid, half man and half fish, who is hairy; in one version of the legend he has horned skin.

In the thirteenth century Heinrich von dem Türlin suggested a different description of mermen. The sea king's envoy is the size of a six-year-old child with scaly skin, long eyebrows, hair that resembles flippers, large elongated ears, and eyes as big as those of an ostrich and iron gray

Fig. 98. The *Wassermann*. Illustration from the poem of the same name by Justinus Kerner (1786–1862).

Fig. 99. The *Wassermann*

in color. His nose is fat and short, wide at the end and flat in the middle. This figure rides a seahorse that is half horse and half dolphin.

Generally speaking, medieval mermen are hostile. They abduct people and attack knights that travel over or along the waterway, but some kidnap children to rear them at the bottom of a lake or the sea. In the more recent tales the *Wassermann* has retained this dangerous nature.

A story that is widespread in the Germanic lands tells how a handsome young man appeared at an evening ball and danced there with a young maiden before disappearing with her forever (he should have aroused suspicions because the lower portion of his clothing was wet!).

A number of Scandinavian ballads are centered on the encounter of a person with a merman. In *Agnete og Havmanden* (Agnete and the Merman) the heroine follows a merman to the bottom of the sea and has seven children with him in eight years. One day she hears bells ringing and asks permission to go to church. She is allowed to do so and meets her mother, whom she tells of her life beneath the waves. The merman comes and asks her to return; in some versions of the ballad Agnete refuses, but in other versions she goes back with him. In *Harpens kraft* (The Power of the Harp) a young bride-to-be is upset because she is doomed to fall into a river. Her promised husband has a solid bridge constructed, guarded by his men. But while they are crossing it her horse stumbles, and she falls into the water. Her fiancé sends for his harp and plays it so wonderfully that all nature is moved by it, and the merman is forced to relinquish his prey. However, a variant of this story says that the woman is dead when she comes back to the surface of the water. Another very popular ballad tells how a merman (*nekken*) dressed as a gentleman abducts a young woman and takes her into the depths, but she saves herself by speaking the merman's name. The texts also speak of mermaids seducing a young man and later dying of grief when he leaves them. *Herr Luno og Havfruen* (The Ballad of Mister Luno and the Mermaid) also tells us how to protect ourselves from these creatures with charms and runes. In Germany, Heinrich Heine (1786–1862) wrote one of his poems, *Der Wassermann,* about a merman abductor.

All waters have their demons. For example, there is also the *Högermann* ("the man with the fang") in the Alsace region and Ranscroufte ("John the Hunchback") in Wallonia (Belgium).

📖 Holbek and Piø, *Fabeldyr og sagnfolk*, 63–99; Nielsen, ed., *Danske Folkeviser,* vol. II, 110–117, 137ff; Lecouteux, *Les Monstres dans la littérature allemande du Moyen Âge*, vol. II, 140–45; Lecouteux, "Les génies des eaux: un aperçu," in *Dans l'eau, sous l'eau: le monde aquatique au Moyen Âge*, ed. Danièle James-Raoul and Claude Thomasset (Paris: P.U.P.S., 2002), 253–72.

WATER: The role of water in the beliefs of all the Germanic and Norse countries is as important as it is in the Celtic world. A good reflection of this can be seen in the large number of mythical rivers that surround Hel, the underworld of the dead, and likewise the halls of the gods. Sagas tell us of the worship that was given to waterfalls, and the clerical literature incessantly fulminated against pagans who made offerings to the waters. In the thirteenth century the Icelandic bishop Guðmundr Arason performed an exorcism, complete with sweeping arm gestures, of springs and fountains. During this era people believed that spirits dwelled in the waters. More recent traditions speak of "water-horses" (the *vatnahestur* in Iceland or the *kelpie* in Scotland). In the continental Germanic regions we have nymphs and nixies.

✦ *NYKR, WASSERMANN*

WAYLAND THE SMITH (Middle High German *Wieland;* Old Norse *Völundr* and *Velent*): Known as the Germanic Icarus, this figure enjoyed extraordinary renown during the Middle Ages, and the texts in Old French call him Galen. According to the legend, the three brothers Völundr, Egill, and Slagfiðr came across several swan maidens who were spinning flax near a lake. They stole their feather garments and hid them, and the wondrous creatures agreed to marry the brothers, as they were unable to fly away. After several years the swan maidens found their clothes and vanished forever. While Egill and Slagfiðr set off to find their respective wives, Völundr remained by himself in Úlfdalir ("Wolf-dales") and devoted himself to the smithing art. King Niðuðr stripped him of his wealth and, at the demand of his wife, had him crippled. Völundr got his revenge, however: he killed Niðuðr's two sons and raped his daughter before flying off on the wings he had crafted.

According to the *Þiðreks saga af Bern* (Saga of Dietrich von Bern), where he is called Velent, his grandfather is King Vilkinus and his grandmother is a mermaid. His father is Vadi (Wade), a giant, and his

Fig. 100. Wayland the Smith, the main scenes of the legend as carved on the
Franks Casket (Anglo-Saxon, eighth century), in the British Museum

son is named Viðga (Witege). In the *Poetic Edda,* Völundr is called
"prince of the elves," which establishes a connection to Álfheimr, the
world of Freyr.

It has been suggested that it is possible to see a kinship in Wayland
with the Etruscan Velchans, the Ossetian Wærgon, and the Cretan
Zeus Felchanos. In *The Gallic War* (VI, 21), Caesar mentions a triad
of gods—Sun, Vulcanus, Moon—which he says were worshipped by
the ancient Germanic peoples. In this context "Vulcanus" may well
correspond to Wayland, who is clearly an ancient deity that, over
time, became reduced to the rank of a hero. There are also some trou-
bling resemblances between the figure of Wayland and Hephaistos
(Vulcan): both are crippled and both commit a rape (Hephaistos
raped Minerva).

The legend inspired the carvings on the so-called Franks Casket, a
small chest made of whalebone discovered in Auzon, France, one side of
which depicts the key episodes of the story.

📖 Beckmann and Timm, *Wieland der Schmied in neuer Perspektive;* Motz, *The Wise One of the Mountain;* Nedoma, *Die bildlichen und schriftlichen Denkmäler der Wielandsage* (with a bibliography current up to 1988); Jean-Marie Maillefer, "Essai sur Völundr-Weland: la religion scandinave ancienne a-t-elle connu un dieu forgeron?" in *Hugur: mélanges d'histoire, de littérature et de mythologie offerts à Régis Boyer pour son 65e anniversaire,* ed. Lecouteux and Gouchet, 331–52.

WEEPER, THE (HAULEMUTTER, KLAGEMUTTER, KLAGEWEIR, WINSELMUTTER): In German-speaking regions, night noises, notably bird cries, are attributed to the weeping of a female being, and this belief has been in evidence since 1400. Hearing her is a herald of death. She remains invisible and soars around houses or else she appears as a shapeless black silhouette, a calf with red eyes, or a sheep. In Austria it is said that these lamentations are the sounds of a dead person grieving; in Saxony this is believed to be a woman whose son has drowned. In Allgäu (Bavaria) the Weeper forms part of a nightly troop of women or men carrying a coffin; she therefore falls into the category of what are called ghostly processions. In Switzerland she is called Huri ("Little Owl") and Tutursel or Tutosel ("Grand Duke") in the Brunswick region. This mythical creature closely corresponds to one that the French call the *Pleurant des Bois* ("Weeper of the Woods").

WEIDWIESENWEIBL ("The Little Woman of the Meadows"): A female Bavarian dwarf seen in the proximity of Reichenhall around 1782–1783. She was tiny, dressed in black, and carried a lit candle in her right hand. She was wearing an oversized hat that was so large it gave the impression she had no head. When people passed by the fields while returning home late at night, the little meadow woman would appear out of nowhere and guide them faithfully and true. However, once in a while she would mislead people, taking them to places they had no desire whatsoever to go and leaving them there. She never uttered a word, never caused anyone any harm, and no one feared her. Her services were happily accepted, but no one ever thanked her for them as they were taken for granted.

📖 Adrian, ed., *Alte Sagen aus dem Salzburger Land,* 83–84; Vernaleken, *Alpensagen,* 63.

Fig. 101. The
Little Woman of
the Meadows

WEREWOLF (Old Norse *vargúlfr*): Western traditions concerning the werewolf derive from three different sources. The first of these sources is classical antiquity; the second source is Germanic and relates to a particular belief regarding the soul, which can leave the body and take the form of any animal; and the third source is folkloric and turns up in countless tales and legends: one has to undress for the transformation to take place. Between 1160 and 1170, Marie de France echoed this third tradition in *Le Bisclavret,* The Werewolf, explicitly stating that if the wolf did not recover its clothes it could not change back into a man. Around 1209–1214, Gervase of Tilbury ventured an explanation for incidents of werewolfism: it is lunacy in the literal sense, brought on by the waxing phases of the moon.

"Rational" explanations for this phenomenon have also been offered: the metamorphosis is triggered by the stone set in a ring; by an ointment; by a branch or a glove; by a wolf pelt, with which you hit yourself while saying a certain spell; by a curse; by an evil spell; by possession; or, in folktales, by a belt or through atavism.

In northern Germany it was thought that the transformation was made possible by putting on a wolf skin. Among the medieval Slavs and Germans, the child born with a caul (meaning a piece of the amniotic

Fig. 102. Werewolves. Olaus Magnus, *Historia de gentibus septentrionalibus*, Rome, 1555.

membrane on his or her head) was predestined to be a werewolf. In German-speaking regions it was said that out of six girls born in a row to the same couple, one was sure to be a werewolf or a nightmare. There are several means by which a werewolf can return to human shape: by recovering its clothes; by being called a werewolf by someone who encounters it; or else by being wounded. Mutilation and flowing blood have a liberating effect. If the transformation was caused by a spell or curse one can also force the witch to utter the counterspell. The werewolf can be killed by virtue of a magic subterfuge: a silver bullet must be blessed in a chapel dedicated to Saint Hubert.

It was once believed that the human being had several animal Doubles and that they could be released during sleep, coma, or trance. This ability is a gift, often inherited from one's ancestors. Bishop Burchard of Worms (965–1025) writes: "Have you believed, as some have the custom of believing, that the women the common folk call Parcae exist or possess the powers attributed to them: to wit, at the birth of a man, they make of him what they will so that whenever that man chooses, he can be transformed into a wolf—called *Werewulff* in German—or into some other shape?" (*Decretum* XIX, 5, 151). The wolf is therefore only one of the possible animal forms; there are other kinds of were-creatures, as the ancient Scandinavian texts confirm.

In one Icelandic source, for example, we find a man who adopts the form of a bull to fight one of his enemies who has taken the form of a bear (*Landnámabók,* chap. 350). There is also the story of the warrior Bödvar Bjarki, whose Double, in the form of a bear, lends assistance to his men while they are fighting a battle. Behind all these transformations is the survival of shamanistic notions: when the shaman is in a trance his spirit leaves his body and, in human or animal form, goes into the otherworld to bring back the soul of a dead person or the means to heal someone. Because medieval Christians failed to grasp these elements, they thought it was a metamorphosis. Greatly influenced by the writings of classical authors, they saw the correctness of their explanation confirmed by the fact that wounds inflicted on the were-creature would be visible on the body of the human after he or she had returned to a normal state.

✦ *BERSERKR, HAMR*

📖 Grambo, *Svart katt over veien,* 100–101 (on the man-bear [*mannbjørn*]) and 182–84 (*varulv*); Grimm, *Deutsche Sagen,* nos. 213–14; Lecouteux, *Elle courait le garou: Lycanthropes, hommes-ours, hommes-tigres, une anthologie;* Lecouteux, *Witches, Werewolves, and Fairies;* Van den Berg, *De volkssage in de provincie Antwerpen in de 19de en 20ste eeuw,* 1854–1867; Grambo, "Fortrollet vilt: Varulv og mannbjørn," *Årbog for Norsk Skogbruks Museum* (1954–57): 75–81; Aðalheiðr Guðmundsdóttir, "The Werewolf in Medieval Icelandic Literature," *Journal of English and Germanic Philology* 106:3 (2007): 277–303.

WESTERKIND: This is the name given in regions of Germany to an infant who, without having taken in any food, dies shortly after baptism. Particular powers are attributed to it.

📖 *Schweizer Volkskunde, Korrespondenzblatt der Schweiz. Gesellschaft für Volkskunde* 37 (1947): 102–7.

WICHT (Archaic English *wight*): Name given in Germany to spirits of both the dead and of the land and to dwarves. It corresponds to the Norse *vættr* and the Norwegian *vätter.*

WIGGO: Demon whose misdeeds are recounted by Einhart of Fulda (ca. 770–840) in his *Translatio et miracula sancti Marcellini et Petri* (III, 14). While a young girl is being exorcised, Wiggo starts speaking and discloses that he and his eleven acolytes, disciples of Satan, have devastated the kingdom of the Franks, destroying grain, vines, and fruit and killing livestock with epidemics.

WILD HUNT: In all the Germanic countries this phenomenon bears the name of the "Army" or "Hunt" of Wodan/Odin (*Wuotes her, Odinsjagt,* and so on). In France it has close to forty different names (*Chasse Artus, Caïn, du Diable, Maligne, Mesnie Hellequin* [✦ HERLA], and so forth), depending on the region.

The Wild Hunt refers a retinue of the dead led by a one-eyed giant that appears during the Twelve Days of the Christmastide (also referred to in Germany as the Twelve Nights, or *Rauhnächte*). It has been interpreted as a personification of storms, but this is not the original meaning; it is more likely to be a reflex of a cult of the dead. The Twelve Days/Twelve Nights represent a key period when the deceased can return and the gateway to the otherworld is open. This notion is reminiscent of the Greek Anthesteria (in February) and the Roman Lemuria (May 9, 11, and 13) when the gods Forculus and Forcula (guardians of doors) and Limentinus and Limentina (guardians of the threshold) are powerless to halt the irruption of the dead into people's homes. The church interpreted these troops of the dead as those of the damned and integrated the Wild Hunt into the great cycle of the punishment of sin. The members of the band are then children who died unbaptized, suicides, murder victims, murderers, adulterers, those who disrupted a holy service, and those who broke their fast during Lent. Whoever finds himself in the path of the Wild Hunt risks being carried off, which just barely failed to happen to the sixteenth-century French poet Pierre de Ronsard, if we can believe his *Hymne des Démons* (Hymn of the Daimons). The first written account of the Wild Hunt dates from 1092 and is found in Orderic Vitalis's chronicle, *Historia Ecclesiastica.* Accounts began to multiply starting around 1170. This extremely popular mythic theme was gradually enriched with meaningful details: a cart became part of the troop, as did various animals.

The Bohemian composer Josef Triebensee wrote an opera titled *Divoká honba—Die wilde Jagd* (The Wild Hunt), which premiered in Prague in 1820.

✦ *ASGAARDSREIA, FASOLT, HACKELBERG, OSKOREIA*

📖 Lecouteux, *Phantom Armies of the Night;* Lecouteux, "Les chasses nocturnes dans les pays germaniques," *Iris* 18 (1999): 37–50; Lecouteux, "Chasse sauvage, Armée furieuse: Réflexions sur une légende germanique," in Walter, ed., *Le Mythe de la Chasse sauvage dans l'Europe médiévale,* 13–32; Various authors, "Autour de la chasse fantastique," *Cercle d'études mythologiques* VIII (1998): 7–140; and see the relevant articles in *Chasseurs & chamanes, Antaios* 12 (1977): 36–75.

Fig. 103. The Wild Hunt. Wood engraving by Haakon Adelsten Lunde, after a drawing by Maurice du Devant, 1852.

WILD HUNTSMAN (*Wilder Jäger*): Around 1250 the first accounts emerged in German regions about a demonic and often gigantic figure who hunted fairies or dwarves. In the *Eckenlied,* Dietrich von Bern (Theodoric the Great) meets a wild maiden in the Tyrolean forests named Babehilt who has a kingdom in the sea. The master of the forest was hunting her with his pack: "Fasolt is his name, and he rules over the wild lands." Fasolt is a giant that blows a horn, wears armor, and has his hair braided like a woman. When he sees Dietrich protecting Babehilt, he flies into a rage and yells, "You have taken my maiden from me. . . . I have been hunting her all day from that far away mountain. . . . Who gave you permission to take my game?" But because Dietrich was wounded, Fasolt did not wish to fight him. Fasolt and Babehilt are supernatural creatures, but the anonymous author of the story does not explain the reasons for this hunt.

Things become clearer when we turn to the *Virginal,* a late-thirteenth-century romance centered on the adventures of Dietrich von Bern and Virginal, the queen of a race of dwarves that inhabits the caverns of the Tyrol. Every year Virginal must surrender a young girl as tribute to a giant named Orkise (whose name reflects the notion of "ogre"). Once chosen, the victim must go out into the forest, where she will be hunted down by Orkise and eaten.

The theme of the Wild Huntsman inspired several operas titled *Der wilde Jäger*—such as by Hieronymous Payer (Vienna, 1806), Victor E. Nessler (Leipzig, 1881), and August Schultz (Braunschweig, 1887)—and the cantata of the same name by M. J. Beer (Olomouc, 1888).

📖 Lecouteux, *Phantom Armies of the Night.*

WILD RACE (*Die Wilde Fahrt*): This is the name of a night host akin to the Wild Hunt but consisting of spirits, which appears near Glurns in the Bolzano region of South Tyrol. This phenomenon has no equivalent in any other tradition. It travels on the night of Saint Martin and emerges as a crowd of black silhouettes that are extraordinary in appearance. It is led by a broom, which sweeps the way, followed by two empty shoes that have the properties of a pair of seven-league boots. Next there appears a twisted goose that used its beak to bite a woman who had witnessed this sight and laughed at it. The bite caused an intense pain that nothing could soothe. The injured woman was not rid of it until the following year, but the goose stated, "In return, there will always be someone twisted in your family."

Elsewhere in the Tyrol this troop is known as the *Wüthige Fahrt* (Lechtal) and *Wilde Fuhr* (Bolzano region).

📖 Zingerle, *Sagen aus Tirol,* 8–10.

WILLEWEIS (fem.): A mythical creature of Tyrolean legend. It appears in the form of a welcoming woman with knowledge of the future. Depending on the location, she is either alone or there are three women bearing this name. It is said this is an individual who has to

atone for a lack of thrift by using a new needle for sewing the shroud of
each dead person.

In Welschnofen (Völs Parish in the Brixen region of South Tyrol),
the *Willeweis* is a little old crone known for her silent and solitary
conduct and secrecy and for knowing the past and future. She likes
to stay beneath old spruce trees and has no other dwelling. No illness
or lightning bolt can strike her, nor can she suffer any harm from
fire and water. She cannot die. Her name can be interpreted to mean
"most learned."

According to Will-Erich Peuckert's theory, the name *Willeweis*
came into being at the end of the seventeenth century due to the confusion of *Wittfrauen* (*witten wiver*), the name for fairies, with the Sibyl.
In the Carinthia region of Austria the *Willeweis* is called *Billeweis;* in
Styria and the Upper Palatinate it is the *Sibylle Weiß.*

📖 Heyl, *Volkssagen, Meinungen und Bräuche aus Tirol*, 271, 411, 415; Zingerle,
Sagen aus Tirol, 53, 288–89; Will-Erich Peuckert, "Sibylle Weiß," in *"Volkskunde
ist Nachricht von jedem Teil des Volkes": Will-Erich Peuckert zum 100. Geburtstag,*
ed. Brigitte Bönisch-Brednich and Rolf Wilhelm Brednich (Göttingen: Schmerse,
1996), 45–70.

**WITEGE, WITTICH (Old Norse *Viðga;* Old English *Widia;*
Wudga):** Famous warrior of medieval German epics who was a traitor
and murderer of adolescents. In the legends surrounding Dietrich von
Bern (the epic transposition of Theodoric the Great), Witege killed the
sons of Frau Helche and Etzel (Attila). Pursued by Dietrich, Witege cast
himself into the sea where the mermaid Frau Wachilt, his ancestor, res-
cued him. His sword's name is Mimminc (Mimung) and was forged by
Wayland; his steed is Skemming. According to the *Þiðreks saga af Bern*
(Saga of Dietrich von Bern), which dates from the thirteenth century,
Viðga is the son of Velent (Wayland the Smith). Witege's inseparable
companion is Heime (Hama, Heimir).

In Old English texts he is called Widia or Wudga and is depicted as
an exile living at King Eormanric's court. A ninth-century poetic fragment, *Waldere,* also claims he is Wayland's son and tells us he helped
Dietrich/Theodric out of a fix when he was in the domain of monsters
(*fifela*), a deed for which Widia will be rewarded with weapons and
treasure. The anonymous poet recalls:

Ic wat ðæt hit ðohte Ðeodric Widian
selfum onsendon and eac sinc micel
maðma mid ði mece, monig oðres mid him
golde gegirwan; iulean genam,
þæs ðe hine of nearwum Nîðhades maeg
Welandes bearn. Widia ut forlet. (frag. B, 4–9)

("I know that Theodric thought of sending it [the
sword] to Widia himself, and much treasure with
the sword too, and adorning it with gold. Widia, the
kinsman of Nîðhad, son of Weland, received reward
for past deeds, because he had delivered him from
captivity.")

The figure of Witege certainly goes back to a Gothic warrior named Vidigoia, about whom Jordanes says in his Gothic history (*Getica*, XXXIV, 178) that, in the lands of Attila, "he perished, a victim of Sarmatian guile" around 330.

WITTFRAUEN: Although the name (which is always used in the plural) means the "white ladies," these figures have no connection to the ghosts of the same name. These are the evil fairies of Fehmarn island in the Baltic Sea who kidnap unbaptized children. To protect the newborn, lit candles are kept by the infants until they have been baptized.

WODAN: Name of Odin in the West Germanic branch of the Germanic languages. This is the form of the name in the *Second Merseburg Charm;* other continental West Germanic variants include Wuotan and Wotan. In German place-names this god's name is frequently combined with words for "mountain," "house," and "way."

📖 Beck, *Die Merseburger Zaubersprüche;* Jean-Paul Allard, "Du second Charme de Mersebourg au Viatique de Weingarten," *Études Indo-Européennes* 14 (1985): 33–53.

WODEN: Name of Odin in Old English. It is essentially known because of place-names, which attest to its importance. Woden appears in the *Nine Herbs Charm,* where he is depicted as a healer/magician: "A snake slithered up and bit a man. Then Woden took nine glory twigs [i.e., the nine herbs] and smote the snake, so that it flew apart into nine pieces." The Anglo-Saxon royal genealogies of Anglia, Kent, and Wessex made Woden the founding father of their lineages.

WOLTERKEN ("Little Walter"): The name of a household spirit in northern Germany. He washes the dishes, lights the fire, takes care of the horses, feeds the livestock, and so forth. He can be heard at night going up and down stairs or ladders, laughing when he yanks the covers off the beds of the servants, and throwing objects in all directions, which makes him akin to knocking spirits.

WOOD MAIDEN (*Holzfräulein*): An elfin spirit that appears in the form of an ugly old woman who is stooped over and covered with moss. She wears old-fashioned clothing and speaks a foreign language; she is, however, able to transform into a beautiful young woman. She loves to spend time in the company of men, is willing to entrust her children to the care of wet nurses, bakes cakes, and spins thread from an inexhaustible distaff. The last sheaf of the harvest is left to her as an offering. The maiden of the wood is kind and helpful; she gives gifts and knows remedies and the future, but she is also very touchy. She is the prey of the Wild Huntsman and escapes from him by making the sign of the cross and speaking the name of God. Depending on the region, she can also be dangerous; she leads travelers astray or jumps on their backs and also kidnaps and exchanges newborns. She is a syncretic figure that combines the features of the fairy, the wild woman, and demonic spirits.

◆ *CHANGELING*

WUNDERER: A giant that haunts the Tyrolean mountains where, with his dogs, he pursues a damsel. Because she turned down his proposal of marriage, he wants to devour her. He is equipped like a knight but is so strong that the iron gates barricading the entrance of Etzel's (Attila's) castle cannot resist his shove. Dietrich von Bern (the legendary and epic transposition of Theodoric the Great) kills him; when he falls, it shakes the castle walls. The damsel's name is Saelde, which means "chance" or "fortune," and God (*sic*) has given her supernatural powers in return for the vow of chastity that she took. She can, by granting her blessing to a warrior, prevent him from meeting his death in battle (a feature reminiscent of the valkyries), and she can instantly transport herself wherever she likes.

Behind these elements there is a mythic and legendary theme found in numerous other texts: that of the Wild Huntsman. In *Virginal* (thirteenth century) the hunted maiden is a handmaiden of the queen of dwarves, and the giant's name is Orkise (which is reminiscent of Orco, from which comes the word "ogre"). In the *Eckenlied* (ca. 1250) this giant is named Fasolt, which is also the name of a weather demon, and the damsel is a "wild maiden," meaning a fairy.

  ✦ *FASOLT, SALINGEN*

  📖 Georges Zink, *Le Wunderer*.

WUOTES HER: ✦ WILD HUNT

WURD ("Fate," Old Saxon): *Wurt* in Old High German and *wyrd* in Old English.

  ✦ *NORNS, URÐR*

  📖 Mittner, *Wurd*.

WYDEWIBLI: Name of a spirit that misdirects people in the Swiss canton of Glarus. The name means "wood woman."

  📖 Vernaleken, *Alpensagen*, 63.

ÝDALIR ("Yew-dales"): The place where the god Ullr lives.

YGGDRASILL ("Yggr's Steed," Yggr being Odin): This is the cosmic tree, the "ideogram of Scandinavian mythology" (Mircea Eliade). It corresponds to the Skambha, the cosmic pillar of the *Vedas,* to the Saxon Irminsûl, and to the World Tree of the Sámi people in Lappland. It is also called Læraðr and Mímameiðr ("Mímir's Tree"). It is an ash tree, the center and support of the world that it summarizes and symbolizes, the source of life and all knowledge, and all fate. Neither fire nor steel can scathe it, and its fruits heal the womb ailments of women.

Living beneath its three roots are men, frost giants, and the dead in Hel's realm. According to one tradition, one of its roots leads to the world of the Æsir in the sky. This is where the springs of Urðr (a Norn), Mímir (a giant), and Hvergelmir (the source of all rivers) are located. The dragon Niðhöggr also lives here. The second root goes to Jötunheimr, the world of the giants, and the third to Niflheimr, the world of the dead.

An eagle perches at its top. This is most likely Hræsvelgr ("Carrion Eater"), the flapping of whose wings gives birth to the winds—as well as the falcon Veðrfölnir ("Ash Covered by the Wind"?). The squirrel Ratatoskr climbs up and down the trunk. Five stags graze on its branches: Dáinn and Dvalinn ("Death" and "Torpid"; these are also dwarf names), Duneyrr ("Downy Ears"), and Duraþrór and Eikþyrnir ("Oak-thorny"), as well as the goat Heiðrún. Eight reptiles gnaw on its roots: Niðhöggr, Góinn, Móinn, Grafvitnir, Grafvölluðr, Grábakr, Ófnir, and Sváfnir (we may note in passing that alliterations are generally a sign of the antiquity of the elements). Each day the Norns sprinkle water and light clay over Yggdrasill. The Æsir customarily hold their deliberations beneath the cosmic tree near Urðr's fountain.

Yggdrasill ensures the vertical coherence of the world, while the Midgard Serpent guarantees its horizontal coherence.

📖 Régis Boyer, "Yggdrasill," *Pris-Ma* 5 (1989): 127–38; Hjalmar Lindroth, "Yggdrasils 'barr' och eviga grönska: En replik," *Arkiv för nordisk filologi* 30 (1914): 218–26.

YGGR ("Fearsome One"): One of Odin's bynames.

📖 Falk, *Odensheiti*.

YMIR ("Hybrid," "Hermaphrodite"; cf. Sanskrit *Yama*): Name of the primordial giant whose dismembered body formed the world. He was born from melting ice and is the ancestor of the frost giants, who also call him Aurgelmir. While he slept he began perspiring, and a man and woman were born from his left armpit; one of his feet engendered a son with the other one. Ymir fed on the milk of the cow Auðumla, who was also born from the melting ice.

Odin, Vili, and Vé killed him, and all the frost giants drowned in his blood except for Bergelmir and his wife. The three gods next took Ymir and placed him in the middle of Ginnungagap ("Gaping Void"); they created the Earth from him. From his blood they made the sea and lakes; from his flesh they made the land, and from his bones the mountains; stones and scree were made from his broken teeth and bones. They also took his skull and used it to form the sky above the Earth and placed it on four corners that were held up by four dwarves. To build Miðgarðr ("The World of Men"). They used Ymir's eyelashes; they created the clouds from his brains.

📖 Régis Boyer, "Le corps d'ymir," *Germanica* 4 (1988): 11–25; Olivier Gouchet, "Le sang d'Ymir," *Études Germaniques* 44 (1989): 385–95.

YNGVI: A byname of the god Freyr, from whom the royal family of Sweden (the Ynglingar of the ninth to fourteenth centuries) descends. It is thought that Yngvi corresponds to the eponymous god of the Ingaevones about which Tacitus speaks.

ZODAWASCHERL, HONAWASCHERL: The name of the thirteenth child in Percht's night host. He is a small child that died unbaptized and who drags along behind the procession holding a pitcher filled with his tears. When the peasants set a table on Three Kings' Night for Percht and her troop there are only twelve settings, so when Zodawascherl arrives there is nothing left for him.

The name is coined from words in regional dialect meaning "rags" and to "lag behind"; it can therefore be translated as "the raggedy straggler."

Fig. 104. Zodawascherl

ZUNDEL ("Firestarter," "Kindling"): Elemental spirit of fire according to Paracelsus. His appearance is the prelude to catastrophes like the end of a lineage or country.

ZUSERBEUTLEIN: Name of the child that lags behind at the end of Percht's host because he is constantly tripping over his shirttails.

Legend says that a female pilgrim saw him and exclaimed, "Hold on my *Zuserbeutlein!* I will fix your shirt," and the child answered, "God be praised! I now have a name." He had died unbaptized and could therefore find no rest. The name is coined from *Zuser,* a dialectal word designating the waxwing (a bird of the Passerine family), and a diminutive form of *Beutel,* "sack" or "purse."

📖 Lecouteux, *Phantom Armies of the Night,* 150–52.

ZWIESAUGER, DOPPELSAUGER ("One Who Twice Nurses"): This name designates children who, twenty-four hours after being weaned, go back on the breast one more time. They can be recognized by their red lips. After their death their bodies do not decompose in the grave. It is said that these folk eat their own flesh and suck the blood of their fellow family members, which makes them akin to vampires.

✦ *NACHZEHRER*

BIBLIOGRAPHY

Acta Borussica ecclesiastica, civilia, literaria oder sorgfältige Sammlung aller-hand zur Geschichte des Landes Preussen gehöriger Nachrichten, Uhrkunden, Schrifften und Documenten. 3 vols. Königsberg and Leipzig: Eckart, 1730–1732.

Adam of Bremen. *History of the Archbishops of Hamburg-Bremen.* Translated by Francis J. Tschan. New York: Columbia University Press, 2002.

Adrian, Karl, ed. *Alte Sagen aus dem Salzburger Land.* Vienna, Zell am See, and Sankt Gallen: Mirabell, 1948.

Alpenburg, Johann Nepomuk, Ritter von. *Deutsche Alpensagen.* Vienna: Braumüller, 1861.

———. *Mythen und Sagen Tirols.* Zurich: Meyer und Zeller, 1857.

Amilien, Virginie. *Le troll et autres créatures surnaturelles dans les contes populaires norvégiens.* Preface by Régis Boyer. Paris: Berg International, 1996.

Anonymous. *Das Heldenbuch.* Strasbourg: Johann Prüss, circa 1493.

Árnason, Jón. *Icelandic Legends.* Translated by George E. G. Powell and Eiríkur Magnússon. 2 vols. London: Bentley, 1864; London: Longmans, Green & Co., 1866.

Arnold, Martin. *Thor: From Myth to Marvel.* London and New York: Continuum, 2011.

Arrowsmith, Nancy, and George Moorse. *A Field Guide to the Little People.* London: MacMillan, 1977.

Atlas der deutschen Volkskunde. New Series. Edited by Matthias Zender. Marburg: Elwert, 1958–1985.

Bächtold-Stäubli, Hans, and Eduard Hoffmann-Krayer, eds. *Handwörterbuch des deutschen Aberglaubens.* 10 vols. Berlin and New York: De Gruyter, 1987 [1927–1942].

Baetke, Walther. *Das Heilige im Germanischen*. Tübingen: Mohr, 1942.

Barack, Karl August, ed. *Zimmerische Chronik*. 4 vols. Tübingen: Litterarischer Verein in Stuttgart, 1869.

Barnes, Michael. *Runes: A Handbook*. Woodbridge, U.K.: Boydell, 2012.

Bartsch, Karl, ed. *Kudrun*. Wiesbaden: Brockhaus, 1980.

Batts, Michael S., ed. *Das Nibelungenlied: Paralleldruck der hss. A, B und C nebst lesarten der übrigen Hss*. Tübingen: Niemeyer, 1971.

Beck, Wolfgang. *Die Merseburger Zaubersprüche*. Wiesbaden: Reichert, 2003.

Beckmann, Gustav Adolf, and Erika Timm. *Wieland der Schmied in neuer Perspektive*. Frankfurt and Bern: Lang, 2004.

Bek-Pedersen, Karen. *The Norns in Old Norse Mythology*. Edinburgh: Dunedin, 2011.

Blum, Ida. *Die Schutzgeister in der altnordischen Literatur*. Dissertation, Kaiser-Wilhelms-Universität, Strasbourg, 1912.

Bø, Olav. *Vår norske jul*. Oslo: Det Norske Samlaget, 1970.

Bø, Olav, Ronald Grambo, Bjarne Hodne, and Ørnulf Hodne. *Norske Segner*. Oslo: Det Norske Samlaget, 1995.

Boyer, Régis. *L'Edda poétique*. Paris: Fayard, 1992.

———. *La Grande Déesse du Nord*. Paris: Berg International, 1995.

———. *Héros et Dieux du Nord: Guide iconographique*. Paris: Flammarion, 1997.

———. *Le Monde du double: La magie chez les anciens Scandinaves*. Paris: Berg-International, 1986.

———. *La Mort chez les anciens Scandinaves*. Paris: Les Belles Lettres, 1994.

———. *Le Mythe Viking dans les lettres modernes*. Paris: Le-Porte-Glaive, 1986.

———. *La Poésie scaldique*. Paris: Le-Porte-Glaive, 1990.

———. *La Saga de Sigurdr ou la Parole donnée*. Paris: Cerf, 1989.

———. *Les Vikings*. Paris: Plon, 1992.

———. *Yggdrasill: La religion des anciens Scandinaves*. Paris: Payot, 1981.

Boyer, Régis, and Éveline Lot-Falck. *Les Religions de l'Europe du Nord: Eddas, sagas, hymnes chamaniques*. Paris: Fayard/Denoël, 1974.

Bridier, Sophie. *Le Cauchemar: Étude d'une figure mythique*. Paris: P.U.P.S., 2001.

Briggs, Katherine. *Dictionary of Fairies: Hobgoblins, Brownies, Bogies and Other Supernatural Creatures*. Harmondsworth, U.K.: Penguin, 1977.

Buchholz, Peter. *Bibliographie zur alteuropäischen Religionsgeschichte 1954–1964*. Berlin: De Gruyter, 1967.

———. *Schamanistische Züge in der altisländischen Überlieferung*. Dissertation, Münster, 1968.

Byock, Jesse L., trans. *The Saga of the Volsungs: The Norse Epic of Sigurd the Dragon Slayer*. Berkeley: University of California Press, 1990.

Caesar. *The Gallic War*. Translated by H. J. Edwards. Cambridge, Mass., and London: Harvard University Press, 2006.

Carles, Jean. *Le Poème de Kûdrûn, étude de sa matière*. Paris: P.U.F., 1963.

Chamisso, Adelbert von. *Peter Schlemihl*. Translated by John Bowring with illustrations by George Cruikshank. 3rd edition. London: Hardwicke, 1861.

Clemen, Carl. *Fontes historiae religionis Germanicae*. Berlin: De Gruyter, 1928.

Clifton-Everest, J. M. *The Tragedy of Knighthood: Origins of the Tannhäuser Legend*. Oxford: Society for the Study of Mediæval Languages and Literature, 1979.

Cöllen, Sebastian. *Heimdallr—der rätselhafte Gott: Eine philologische und religionsgeschichtliche Untersuchung*. Berlin: De Gruyter, 2015.

Colleville, Maurice, and Ernest Tonnelat, trans. *La Chanson des Nibelungen*. Paris: Aubier, 1945.

Crépin, André. *Beowulf: Édition diplomatique et texte critique, traduction française, commentaires et vocabulaire*. 2 vols. Göppingen: Kümmerle, 1991.

David, Lucas. *Preussische Chronik*. Edited by Ernst Hennig and Daniel Friedrich Schütz. 8 vols. Königsberg: Haberland, 1812–1817.

De Vries, Jan. *Altgermanische Religionsgeschichte*. 2nd edition. 2 vols. Berlin: De Gruyter, 1970.

Dillmann, F. X., trans. *Eddas, Récits de mythologie nordique*. Paris: Gallimard, 1991.

Doulet, Jean-Michel. *Quand les démons enlevaient les enfants. Les changelins: étude d'une figure mythique*. Paris: P.U.P.S., 2002.

Dubois, Thomas A. *Nordic Religions in the Viking Age*. Philadelphia: University of Pennsylvania Press, 1999.

Dumézil, Georges. *Les Dieux des Germains*. Paris: P.U.F., 1959.

———. *From Myth to Fiction: The Saga of Hadingus*. Translated by Derek Coltman. Chicago and London: University of Chicago Press, 1973.

———. *Gods of the Ancient Northmen*. Edited by Einar Haugen. Berkeley: University of California Press, 1973.

———. *Loki*. Paris: Flammarion, 1986.

———. *Mythe et Épopée I: L'idéologie des trois fonctions dans les épopées des peuples indo-européens*. Paris: Gallimard, 1968.

———. *Du mythe au roman: La Saga de Hadingus* (Saxo Grammaticus I, V–VIII) *et autres essais*. Paris: P.U.F., 1970.

———. *The Stakes of the Warrior*. Translated by David Weeks; edited and with an introduction by Jaan Puhvel. Berkeley and Los Angeles: University of California Press, 1983.

Düwel, Klaus. *Runenkunde*. 4th revised edition. Stuttgart: Metzler, 2008.

Edvardsen, Erik Henning. *Gammelt nytt i våre tidligste ukeblader: aktstykker om folketro og sagn i Illustreret Nyhedsblad og Norsk Folkeblad*. Oslo: Norsk Folkeminnelag/Aschehoug, 1997.

Eliade, Mircea. *Shamanism: Archaic Techniques of Ecstasy*. Translated by Willard R. Trask. Revised and enlarged edition. Princeton, N.J.: Princeton University Press, 1970.

Elliott, Ralph W. V. *Runes: An Introduction*. Manchester: Manchester University Press, 1989.

Enzyklopädie des Märchens: Handwörterbuch zur historischen und vergleichenden Erzählforschung. Berlin and New York: De Gruyter, 1977–2014.

Eskeröd, Albert. *Årets äring: Etnologiska studier i skördens och julens tro och sed*. Stockholm: Nordiska Museet, 1947.

Falk, Hjalmar. *Odensheiti*. Kristiania [Oslo]: Dybwad, 1924.

Feilberg, Henning Frederik. *Bjærgtagen: Studie over en gruppe træk fra nordisk alfetro*. Copenhagen: Schønberg, 1910.

Füetrer, Ulrich. *Das Buch der Abenteuer. Nach der Handschrift A (Cgm. 1 der Bayerischen Staatsbibliothek)*. Edited by Heinz Thoelen in collaboration with Bernd Bastert. Göppingen: Kümmerle, 1997.

Gerndt, Helge. *Fliegender Holländer und Klabautermann*. Göttingen: Schwartz, 1971.

Gervase of Tilbury. *Otia Imperialia: Recreation for an Emperor*. Edited and translated by S. E. Banks and J. W. Binns. Oxford and New York: Oxford University Press, 2002.

Glob, P. V. *The Bog People: Iron Age Man Preserved*. London: Faber and Faber, 1969.

Glosecki, Stephen O. *Shamanism and Old English Poetry*. New York and London: Garland, 1989.

Gouchet, Olivier. *Hagen von Tronje: Étude du personnage à l'aide des différents textes du Moyen Âge*. Göppingen: Kümmerle, 1981.

Grambo, Ronald. *Gjester fra Graven: Norske spøkelsers liv og virke*. Oslo: Ex Libris, 1991.

———. *Svart katt over veien: Om varsler, tegn og overtro*. Oslo: Ex Libris, 1993.

Granberg, Gunnar. *Skogsrået i yngre nordisk folktradition*. Uppsala: Lundequistska bokhandeln i distribution, 1935.

Grimm, Jacob. *Teutonic Mythology*. Translated by James Steven Stallybrass from the 4th edition. 4 vols. Gloucester, Mass.: Smith, 1976 [1882–1888].

Grimm, Jacob, and Wilhelm Grimm. *Deutsche Sagen*. Edited by Heinz Rölleke. Frankfurt: Deutscher Klassiker Verlag, 1994. English edition: *The German Legends of the Brothers Grimm*. Edited and translated by Donald Ward. 2 vols. Philadelphia: Institute for the Study of Human Issues, 1981.

———. *Kinder- und Hausmärchen*. Edited by Hans-Jörg Uther. 4 vols. Cologne: Diederichs, 1996 [1857].

Grunau, Simon. *Preussische Chronik*. 3 vols. Leipzig: Duncker & Humblot, 1875–1896.

Gutenbrunner, Siegfried. *Die germanischen Götternamen der antiken Inschriften*. Halle: Niemeyer, 1936.

Haavio, Martti. *Suomalaiset kodinhaltiat*. Porvoo and Helsingfors: WSOY, 1942.

Hageland, Albert van, and Margareta Lamend. *Lange Wapper en Kludde*. Antwerp: Beckers, 1981.

Hartlaub, G. F. *Der Gartenzwerg und seine Ahnen: Eine Ikonographische und Kulturgeschichtliche Betrachtung*. Heidelberg: Moos, 1962.

Hatto, A. T., trans. *The Nibelungenlied*. Harmondsworth, U.K.: Penguin, 1965.

Haymes, Edward, trans. *The Saga of Thidrek of Bern*. New York and London: Garland, 1988.

Heurgren, Paul Gerhard. *Husdjuren i nordisk folktro*. Örebro: Dagsblad, 1925.

Heuvelmans, Bernard. *Le Grand Serpent de Mer: Le problème zoologique et sa solution*. 2nd revised edition. Paris: Plon, 1975.

Heyl, Johann Adolf. *Volkssagen, Meinungen und Bräuche aus Tirol*. Brixen: Buchhandlung des Kath.-polit. Pressvereins, 1897.

Holbek, Bengt, and Iørn Piø. *Fabeldyr og sagnfolk*. Copenhagen: Politikens Forlag, 1967.

Hollander, Lee M., trans. *The Saga of the Jómsvíkings*. Austin: University of Texas Press, 1990.

Holmström, Helge. *Studier over svanjungfrumotivet i Volundarkvida och annorstädes*. Malmö: Maiander, 1919.

Hoppál, Mihály, and Otto von Sadovsky. *Shamanism: Past and Present*. Budapest: Ethnographic Institute, Hungarian Academy of Sciences; Los Angeles: International Society for Trans-Oceanic Research, 1989.

Hultkrantz, Åke, ed. *The Supernatural Owners of Nature: Nordic Symposium on the Religious Conception of Ruling Spirits (Genii Loci, Genii Speciei) and Allied Concepts*. Stockholm, Gothenburg, and Uppsala: Almqvist & Wiksell, 1961.

Insam, Bernd Dieter. *Der Ork: Studien zu einer alpinen Wort- und Erzählgestalt*. Munich: Fink, 1974.

Izzi, Massimo. *Il Dizionario illustrato dei mostri. angeli, diavoli, orchi, draghi, sirene e altre creature dell'imaginario*. Rome: Gremese, 1989.

Jónsson, Guðni, ed. *Byskupa sögur*. 3 vols. Reykjavík: Íslendingasagnaútgáfan, Haukadalsútgáfan, 1953.

Kalff, Jr., Gerrit. *De sage van den vliegenden Holländer naar behandeling, oorsprong en zin onderzocht*. Zutphen: Thieme & Cie, 1923.

Kantzow, Thomas. *Pomerania, oder Ursprung, Altheit und Geschichte der Völker und Lande Pommern, Caßuben, Wenden, Stettin, Rhügen*. 2 vols. Greifswald: Mauritius, 1816–1817.

Keightley, Thomas. *The World Guide to Gnomes, Fairies, Elves, and Other Little People*. New York: Avenel Books, 1978.

Kershaw, Kris. *The One-eyed God: Odin and the (Indo-) Germanic Männerbünde*. Washington, D.C.: Journal of Indo-European Studies, 2000.

King, K. C., ed. *Das Lied vom Hürnen Seyfrid*. Critical edition with introduction and notes. Manchester, U.K.: Manchester University Press, 1958.

Kramer [Institoris], Heinrich, and Jacob Sprenger. *Malleus Maleficarum*. Strasbourg: Prüss, 1486–1487.

Krantz, Albert. *Wandalia, Beschreibung wendischer Geschicht*. Lübeck: Albrecht, 1600.

Kuhn, Adalbert, and Wilhelm Schwartz. *Norddeutsche Sagen, Märchen und Gebräuche aus Meklenburg, Pommern, der Mark, Sachsen, Thüringen, Braunschweig, Hannover, Oldenburg und Westfalen*. Leipzig: Brockhaus, 1848.

———. *Sagen, Gebräuche und Märchen aus Westfalen und einigen andern, besonders den angrenzenden Gegenden Norddeutschlands*. 2 vols. Leipzig: Brockhaus, 1859.

Kuhn, Hans. *Kleine Schriften. Aufsätze und Rezensionen aus den Gebieten der germanischen und nordischen Sprach-, Literatur- und Kulturgeschichte*. Edited by Dietrich Hofmann in collaboration with Wolfgang Lange and Klaus von See. 3 vols. Berlin: De Gruyter, 1968–1972.

Kulturhistoriskt Lexikon för Nordisk Medeltid från vikingatid till reformationstid. 22 vols. Malmo: Alhem, 1956–1978.

Kvideland, Reimund, and Henning K. Sehmsdorf, eds. *Scandinavian Folk Belief and Legend*. Minneapolis: University of Minnesota Press, 1988.

Larrington, Carolyne, trans. *The Poetic Edda*. Oxford: Oxford University Press, 1999.

Larson, Laurence Marcellus, trans. *The King's Mirror (Speculum regale— Konungs skuggsjá)*. New York: American-Scandinavian Foundation, 1917.

Lasicius, Johannis [Jan Lasicki]. *Die diis Samagitarum libellus*. Vilnius: Vaga, 1969.

Lecouteux, Claude. *L'Allemand du Moyen Âge: I. le moyen-haut allemand.* Turnhout: Brepols, 1996.

———. *The Book of Grimoires.* Translated by Jon E. Graham. Rochester, Vt.: Inner Traditions, 2013.

———. *Charmes, Conjurations et Bénédictions: lexique et formules.* Paris: Champion, 1996.

———. *Chasses fantastiques et Cohortes de la nuit au Moyen Âge.* Paris: Imago, 1999. New edition: *Chasses infernales et Cohortes de la nuit.* Paris: Imago, 2013.

———, ed. *Elle courait le garou: Lycanthropes, hommes-ours, hommes-tigres, une anthologie.* Paris: Corti, 2008.

———. *Démons et Génies du terroir au Moyen Âge.* Preface by Régis Boyer. Paris: Imago, 1995.

———. *Demons and Spirits of the Land: Ancestral Lore and Practices.* Translated by Jon E. Graham. Rochester, Vt.: Inner Traditions, 2015.

———. "Le double, le cauchemar, la sorcière." *Études germaniques* 43 (1988): 395–405.

———. *Dictionary of Ancient Magic Words and Spells: From Abraxas to Zoar.* Translated by Jon E. Graham. Rochester, Vt.: Inner Traditions, 2015.

———. *Fantômes et Revenants au Moyen Âge.* Afterword by Régis Boyer. 3rd edition. Paris: Imago, 2009.

———. *Fées, Sorcières et Loups-Garous au Moyen Âge: histoire du double au Moyen Âge.* Preface by Régis Boyer. 3rd edition. Paris: Imago, 2005.

———. "Les génies des eaux: un aperçu." In *Dans l'eau, sous l'eau: le monde aquatique au Moyen Âge.* Edited by D. James-Raoul and C. Thomasset. Paris: P.U.P.S., 2002. Pp. 253–72.

———. *Histoire des vampires: Autopsie d'un mythe.* 3rd edition. Paris: Imago, 2009.

———, trans. *La Légende de Siegfried d'après le Seyfrid à la peau de corne et la Thidrekssaga.* Translated from Middle High German and Medieval Norwegian. Paris: Le Porte-Glaive, 1995. 2nd revised edition, Besançon: La Völva, 2015.

———. *Le Livre des grimoires: Aspects de la magie au Moyen Âge.* Paris: Imago, 2002.

———. *La Maison et ses Génies: croyances d'hier et d'aujourd'hui.* Paris: Imago, 2000.

———. *La Maison hantée: Histoire des poltergeists.* Paris: Imago, 2007.

———. *Mélusine et le Chevalier au Cygne.* Preface by Jacques Le Goff. 2nd revised edition. Paris: Imago, 1997.

———. *Mondes parallèles: L'univers des croyances au Moyen Âge.* Paris: Champion, 1994.

———. *Les Monstres dans la littérature allemande du Moyen Âge (1150–1350): Contribution à l'étude du merveilleux merveill.* 3 vols. Göppingen: Kümmerle, 1982. Second revised and enlarged edition, Besançon: La Völva, 2016.

———. *Les Monstres dans la pensée médiévale européenne.* 3rd revised and corrected edition. Paris: P.U.P.S., 1999.

———. "Les nains dans les traditions germaniques du moyen Âge." In *Du nain au nain de jardin.* Brussels: Fondation Marinus, 2000. Pp. 73–89.

———. *Les Nains et les Elfes au Moyen Âge.* Preface by Régis Boyer. 3rd edition. Paris: Imago, 2004.

———. "Der Nibelungenhort: Überlegungen zum mythischen hintergrund." *Euphorion* 87 (1993): 172–86.

———. "Les personnages surnaturels du Moyen Âge germanique." In *Fées, Elfes, Dragons & Autres créatures des royaumes de féerie.* Edited by Claudine Glot and Michel le Bris. Paris: Hoëbeke, 2002. Pp. 24–29.

———. *Phantom Armies of the Night: The Wild Hunt and the Ghostly Processions of the Undead.* Translated by Jon E. Graham. Rochester, Vt.: Inner Traditions, 2011.

———. "Ramsundsberget: L'arrière-plan mental de l'inscription runique." *Études germaniques* 53 (1997): 559–61.

———. *The Return of the Dead: Ghosts, Ancestors, and the Transparent Veil of the Pagan Mind.* Translated by Jon E. Graham. Rochester, Vt.: Inner Traditions, 2009.

———, trans. *La Saga de Théodoric de Vérone.* Presented with commentary by C. Lecouteux. Paris: Champion, 2001.

———. *The Secret History of Poltergeists and Haunted Houses: From Pagan Folklore to Modern Manifestations.* Translated by Jon E. Graham. Rochester, Vt.: Inner Traditions, 2012.

———. *The Secret History of Vampires: Their Multiple Forms and Hidden Purposes.* Translated by Jon E. Graham. Rochester, Vt.: Inner Traditions, 2010.

———. "Seyfrid, kuperan et le dragon." *Études Germaniques* 49 (1994): 257–66.

———. "Siegfrieds Jugend: Überlegungen zum mythischen Hintergrund." *Euphorion* 89 (1995): 221–27.

———. *The Tradition of Household Spirits: Ancestral Lore and Practices.* Translated by Jon E. Graham. Rochester, Vt.: Inner Traditions, 2013.

———. "Trois hypothèses sur nos voisins invisibles." *Hugur. Mélanges Régis Boyer.* Paris: P.U.P.S., 1997. Pp. 289–97.

———. *Eine Welt im Abseits: Studien zur niederen Mythologie und Glaubenswelt des Mittelalters.* Preface by Dieter Harmening. Dettelbach: Röll, 2001.

————. *Witches, Werewolves, and Fairies: Shapeshifters and Astral Doubles in the Middle Ages.* Translated by Clare Frock. Rochester, Vt.: Inner Traditions, 2003.

————. "Zwerge und Verwandte." *Euphorion* 75 (1981): 366–78.

Lecouteux, Claude, and Olivier Gouchet, eds. *Hugur: mélanges d'histoire, de littérature et de mythologie offerts à Régis Boyer pour son 65e anniversaire.* Paris: P.U.P.S., 1997.

Leoprechting, Baron Karl von. *Aus dem Lechrain: Zur deutschen Sitten- und Sagenkunde.* Munich: Literarisch-artistische Anstalt, 1855.

Lexikon des Mittelalters. 10 vols. Munich and Zurich: Artemis Verlag, 1977–1999.

Liebrecht, Felix, ed. *Des Gervasius von Tilbury. Otia imperialia.* Hanover: Rümpler, 1856.

————. *Zur Volkskunde: Alte und neue Aufsätze.* Heilbronn: Gebrüder Henninger, 1879.

Lindig, Erika. *Hausgeister: Die Vorstellungen übernatürlicher Schützer und Helfer in der deutschen Sagenüberlieferung.* Frankfurt and Bern: Peter Lang, 1987.

Lindow, John. *Murder and Vengeance among the Gods: Baldr in Scandinavian Mythology.* Helsinki: Suomalainen Tiedeakatemia, 1997.

————. *Trolls: An Unnatural History.* London: Reaktion, 2014.

Lindquist, Ivar. *Galdrar: De gamla germanska trollsångernas stil undersökt i samband med en runinskrift från folkvandringstiden.* Gothenburg: Wettergren & Kerber, 1923.

Linhart, Dagmar. *Hausgeister in Franken.* Dettelbach: Röll, 1995.

Lohre, Heinrich. *Märkische Sagen.* Leipzig-Gohlis: Eichblatt, 1921.

Looijenga, Tineke. *Texts and Contexts of the Oldest Runic Inscriptions.* Leiden: Brill, 2003.

Lorenz, Gottfried, ed. and trans. *Snorri Sturluson: Gylfaginning. Texte, Übersetzung, Kommentar.* Darmstadt: Wissenschaftliche Buchgesellschaft, 1984.

Luck, Georg. *Rhätische Alpensagen: Gestalten und Bilder aus der Sagenwelt Graubündens.* Davos: Verlag der Buchdruckerei, 1902.

Mackensen, Lutz. *Niedersächsische Sagen.* 2 vols. Leipzig-Gohlis: Eichblatt, 1923–1925.

Martin, John Stanley. *Ragnarök: An Investigation into Old Norse Concepts of the Fate of the Gods.* Assen: Van Gorcum, 1972.

Maurer, Konrad. *Isländische Volkssagen der Gegenwart vorwiegend nach mündlicher Überlieferung.* Leipzig: Hinrich, 1860.

McKinnell, John, with Rudolf Simek and Klaus Düwel. *Runes, Magic, and Religion: A Sourcebook.* Vienna: Fassbaender, 2004.

Mériot, Christian. *Les Lapons et leur société: étude d'ethnologie historique.* Toulouse: Privat, 1980.

Meyer, Elard Hugo. *Germanische Mythologie.* Berlin: Meyer & Müller, 1891.

Meyer-Matheis, Vera. *Die Vorstellung eines Alter Ego in Volkserzählungen.* Dissertation, University of Freiburg, 1974.

Micraelius, Johann. *Antiquitates Pomeraniae oder Sechs Bücher vom alten Pommerland.* Stettin & Leipzig: Kunckel, 1723.

Mittner, Ladislaus. *Wurd: Das Sakrale in der altgermanischen Epik.* Bern: Francke, 1955.

Monfort, Anne. *Les Jumeaux dans la littérature et les mythes germaniques.* Dissertation, University of Paris IV–Sorbonne, 2004.

Motz, Lotte. *The Wise One of the Mountain: Form, Function and Significance of the Subterranean Smith. A Study in Folklore.* Göppingen: Kümmerle, 1983.

Müllenhoff, Karl. *Sagen, Märchen und Lieder der Herzogthümer Schleswig, Holstein und Lauenburg.* Kiel: Schwers, 1845.

Müller, Ulrich, and Werner Wunderlich, eds. *Mittelalter Mythen.* 5 vols. St. Gallen: Fachverlag für Wissenschaft und Studium, 1999–2008.

Musset, Lucien. *Introduction à la runologie.* Paris: Aubier-Montaigne, 1965.

Neckel, Gustav, ed. *Edda: Die lieder des Codex Regius nebst verwandten Denkmälern.* Vol. I: Text. Heidelberg: Winter, 1983.

Näsström, Britt-Mari. *Freyja, the Great Goddess of the North.* Lund: University of Lund, 1995.

Nedoma, Robert. *Die bildlichen und schriftlichen Denkmäler der Wielandsage.* Göppingen: Kümmerle, 1988.

Nielsen, H. Grüner, ed. *Danske Folkeviser: Historiske viser fra Riddersal og Borgstue.* 2 vols. Copenhagen: Martins, 1925.

Nilssen, Kjell Tore. *Draugr: De norrøne forestillingene.* Dissertation, University of Oslo, 1993.

O'Connor, Anne. *Child Murderess and Dead Child Traditions.* Helsinki: Suomalainen Tiedeakatemia, 1991.

Olaus Magnus. *Historia de gentibus septentrionalibus.* Rome: n.p., 1555.

Olsen, Magnus, ed. *Völsunga saga ok Ragnars saga loðbrókar.* 2 vols. Copenhagen: Møller, 1906–1908.

Page, R. I. *Runes: An Introduction.* Revised edition: Woodbridge, U.K.: Boydell, 2006.

Pálsson, Hermann, and Paul Edwards, trans. *Gautrek's Saga and Other Medieval Tales.* New York: New York University Press, 1968.

Pentikäinen, Juha. *The Nordic Dead-Child Tradition. Nordic Dead-Child Beings:*

A Study in Comparative Religion. Helsinki: Suomalainen Tiedeakatemia, 1968.

Petry, Michael J. *Herne the Hunter: A Berkshire Legend.* Reading: Smith, 1972.

Petzold, Leander. *Historische Sagen.* 2 vols. Hohengehren: Schneider, 2001.

———. *Kleines Lexikon der Dämonen und Elementargeister.* Munich: Beck, 1990.

Peuckert, Will-Erich. *Deutscher Volksglaube des späten Mittelalters.* Stuttgart: Spemann, 1942.

Pohl, Erich. *Die Volkssagen Ostpreussens.* Königsberg: Gräfe und Unzer, 1943.

Puhvel, Jaan, ed. *Myth and Law among the Indo-Europeans: Studies in Indo-European Comparative Mythology.* Los Angeles: University of California Press, 1970.

Raudvere, Catharina. *Föreställningar om maran i nordisk folktro.* Lund: Lunds Universitet, 1993.

Reichert, Hermann. *Lexikon der altgermanischen Namen.* Vol. I: Text. Vienna: Verlag der österreichischen Akademie der Wissenschaften, 1987.

Renaud, Jean. *Les Dieux des Vikings.* Rennes: Ouest-France Université, 1996.

Resler, Michael, ed. *Der Stricker: Daniel von dem blühenden Tal.* Revised 2nd edition. Tübingen: Niemeyer, 1995.

Rhesa, Ludwig. *Prutena, oder preussische Volkslieder und andere vaterlandischen Dichtungen.* Königsberg: Degen, 1809.

Ridé, Jacques. *L'Image du Germain dans la pensée et la littérature allemandes, de la redécouverte de Tacite à la fin du XVIe siècle. Contribution à l'étude de la genèse d'un mythe.* 3 vols. Lille and Paris: Champion, 1977.

Rumpf, Marianne. *Perchten: Populäre Glaubensgestalten zwischen Mythos und Katechese.* Würzburg: Königshausen & Neumann, 1992.

Sansonetti, Paul-Georges. *Chevaliers et Dragons: Ésotérisme d'un combat.* Paris: Le Porte-Glaive, 1995.

Saxo Grammaticus. *The History of the Danes,* Books I–IX. Edited and translated by Hilda Ellis Davidson and Peter Fisher. Woodbridge, U.K.: Brewer, 1996.

———.Latin text and translation: Saxo Grammaticus. *Gesta Danorum: The History of the Danes.* Edited by Karsten Friis-Jensen and translated by Peter Fisher. 2 vols. Oxford: Oxford University Press, 2015.

Schmidt, Johann Peter. *Fastel-Abend oder Geschichtsmäßige Untersuchung der Fastel-Abends-Gebräuche in Teutschland.* Rostock: Martin Warningck, 1742.

Schneller, Christian. *Märchen und Sagen aus Wälschtirol: Ein Beitrag zur deutschen Sagenkunde.* Innsbruck: Verlag der Wagner'schen Universitäts-Buchhandlung, 1867.

Schnyder, André, ed. *Biterolf und Dietleib*. Bern and Stuttgart: Paul Haupt, 1980.

Schröder, Franz-Rolf. *Skadi und die Götter Skandinaviens*. Tübingen: Mohr, 1941.

Schulz, Katja. *Riesen: Von Wissenshütern und Wildnisbewohnern in Edda und Saga*. Heidelberg: Winter, 2004.

Schütz, Caspar. *Historia rerum Prussicarum: Warhaffte und eigentliche Beschreibung der Lande Preussen*. Leipzig: Grosse, 1599.

Schwarz, Albert Georg von. *Diplomatische Geschichte der Pommersch-Rügischen Städte Schwedischer Hoheit nach ihrem Ursprung und erster Verfassung*. Greifswald: Struck, 1755.

Shaw, Philip A. *Pagan Goddesses in the Early Germanic World: Eostre, Hreda and the Cult of Matrons*. London: Bristol Classical Press, 2011.

Simek, Rudolf. *Lexikon der germanischen Mythologie*. Stuttgart: Kröner, 1984. English edition: *Dictionary of Northern Mythology*. Translated by Angela Hall. Woodbridge, UK: Brewer, 1993.

Snorri Sturluson. *Edda: Prologue and Gylfaginning; Skáldskaparmál*. Edited by Anthony Faulkes. 3 vols. London: Viking Society for Northern Research, 1988–1998. English version: *Edda*. Translated by Anthony Faulkes. London, UK, and Rutland, Vt.: Everyman/Orion, 1995.

———. *Heimskringla: History of the Kings of Norway*. Translated by Lee M. Hollander. Austin: University of Texas Press, 1964.

———. *La Saga des Ynglingar*. Translated from Icelandic by Ingeborg Cavalié. Paris: Le Porte-Glaive, 1990.

Steinsland, Gro. *Norrøn Religion*. Oslo: Pax, 2005.

Stoklund, Marie, et al., eds. *Runes and Their Secrets: Studies in Runology*. Copenhagen: Museum Tusculanum Press, 2006.

Strömbäck, Dag. *Sejd: Textstudier i nordisk religionshistoria*. Stockholm: Geber, 1935. New edition: *Sejd och andra studier i nordisk själsuppfattning*. Reprint of the original book, with two additional studies by Strömbäck (including the English lecture, "The Concept of the Soul in Nordic Tradition") and contributions by Bo Almqvist, Hans Mebius, and Gertrud Gidlund; edited by Gertrude Gidlund. Hedemora: Gidlunds förlag, 2000.

Tacitus, Cornelius. *Germania*. Translated with introduction and commentary by J. B. Rives. Oxford: Oxford University Press, 2002.

Temme, Jodocus Deodatus Hubertus. *Die Volkssagen von Pommern und Rügen*. Berlin: Nicolai, 1840.

Terramorsi, Bernard, ed. *Le Cauchemar: Mythologie, folklore, arts et littérature*. Paris: S.E.D.E.S., Le Publieur, 2003.

Thiele, J. M. *Danmarks Folkesagn*. 3 vols. Copenhagen: Reitzel, 1843–1860.

Thompson, Stith. *Motif-Index of Folk-Literature: A Classification of Narrative*

Elements in Folktales, Ballads, Myths, Fables, Medieval Romances, Exempla, Fabliaux, Jest-books, and Local Legends. Revised and enlarged edition. Bloomington: Indiana University Press, 1955–1958.

Þorvarðardóttir, Ólina. *Brennuöldin: Galdur og galdratrú í málskjölum og munnmælum.* Reykjavík: Háskólaútgáfan, 2000.

Tolley, Clive. *Shamanism in Norse Myth and Magic.* 2 vols. Helsinki: Suomalainen Tiedeakatemia, 2009.

Tulinius, Torfi H. *La Matière du Nord: Sagas légendaires et fiction dans la littérature islandaise en prose du XIIIe siècle.* Paris: P.U.P.S., 1995.

Turville-Petre, E. O. G. *Myth and Religion of the North.* London: Weidenfeld and Nicolson, 1964.

Van Den Berg, Marcel. *De volkssage in de provincie Antwerpen in de 19de en 20ste eeuw.* Ghent: Koninklijke Academie voor Nederlandse taal- en Letterkunde, 1993.

Vernaleken, Theodor. *Alpensagen: Volksüberlieferungen aus der Schweiz, aus Vorarlberg, Kärnten, Steiermark, Salzburg, Ober- und Niederösterreich.* Edited by Hermann Burg. Salzburg and Leipzig: Anton Pustet, 1938 [Original edition published 1858].

———. *Mythen und Bräuche des Volkes in Österreich: Ein Beitrag zu Deutschen Mythologies, Volkskunde und Sittenkunde.* Vienna: Braumüller, 1859.

Wagner, Marc-André. *Le Cheval dans les croyances germaniques.* Paris: Champion, 2005.

Wall, Jan Inge. *Tjuvmjölkande väsen i äldre nordisk tradition.* Uppsala: University of Uppsala, 1977–1978.

Walter, Philippe, ed. *Le Mythe de la Chasse sauvage dans l'Europe médiévale.* Paris: Champion, 1997.

Ward, Donald. *The Divine Twins: An Indo-European Myth in Germanic Tradition.* Berkeley and Los Angeles: University of California Press, 1968.

Waschnitius, Viktor. *Perht, Holda und verwandte Gestalten: Ein Beitrag zur deutschen Religionsgeschichte.* Vienna: Hölder, 1913.

Weddingen, Otto, and Hermann Hartmann. *Der Sagenschatz Westfalens.* Minden: Bruns, 1884.

William of Auvergne. *Opera omnia.* 2 vols. Paris: Pralard, 1674.

Zingerle, Ignaz V. *Sagen aus Tirol.* Innsbruck: Wagner, 1891.

———. *Sagen, Märchen und Gebräuche aus Tirol.* Innsbruck: Verlag der Wagner'schen Buchhandlung, 1859.

Zink, Georges. *Les Légendes héroïques de Dietrich et d'Ermrich dans les littératures germaniques.* Lyon and Paris: IAC, 1950.

———. *Le Wunderer.* Paris: Aubier-Montaigne, 1949.